TELECOMMUNICATIONS NETWORK DESIGN AND MANAGEMENT

OPERATIONS RESEARCH/COMPUTER SCIENCE INTERFACES SERIES

Series Editors

Professor Ramesh Sharda
Oklahoma State University

Prof. Dr. Stefan Voß
Technische Universität Braunschweig

Other published titles in the series:

Greenberg, Harvey J. / *A Computer-Assisted Analysis System for Mathematical Programming Models and Solutions: A User's Guide for ANALYZE*

Greenberg, Harvey J. / *Modeling by Object-Driven Linear Elemental Relations: A Users Guide for MODLER*

Brown, Donald/Scherer, William T. / *Intelligent Scheduling Systems*

Nash, Stephen G./Sofer, Ariela / *The Impact of Emerging Technologies on Computer Science & Operations Research*

Barth, Peter / *Logic-Based 0-1 Constraint Programming*

Jones, Christopher V. / *Visualization and Optimization*

Barr, Richard S./ Helgason, Richard V./ Kennington, Jeffery L. / *Interfaces in Computer Science & Operations Research: Advances in Metaheuristics, Optimization, & Stochastic Modeling Technologies*

Ellacott, Stephen W./ Mason, John C./ Anderson, Iain J. / *Mathematics of Neural Networks: Models, Algorithms & Applications*

Woodruff, David L. / *Advances in Computational & Stochastic Optimization, Logic Programming, and Heuristic Search*

Klein, Robert / *Scheduling of Resource-Constrained Projects*

Bierwirth, Christian / *Adaptive Search and the Management of Logistics Systems*

Laguna, Manuel / González-Velarde, José Luis / *Computing Tools for Modeling, Optimization and Simulation*

Stilman, Boris / *Linguistic Geometry: From Search to Construction*

Sakawa, Masatoshi / *Genetic Algorithms and Fuzzy Multiobjective Optimization*

Ribeiro, Celso C./ Hansen, Pierre / *Essays and Surveys in Metaheuristics*

Holsapple, Clyde/ Jacob, Varghese / Rao, H. R. / *BUSINESS MODELLING: Multidisciplinary Approaches — Economics, Operational and Information Systems Perspectives*

Sleezer, Catherine M./ Wentling, Tim L./ Cude, Roger L. / *HUMAN RESOURCE DEVELOPMENT AND INFORMATION TECHNOLOGY: Making Global Connections*

Voß, Stefan, Woodruff, David / *Optimization Software Class Libraries*

Upadhyaya et al/ *MOBILE COMPUTING: Implementing Pervasive Information and Communications Technologies*

Reeves, Colin & Rowe, Jonathan/ *GENETIC ALGORITHMS—Principles and Perspectives: A Guide to GA Theory*

Bhargava, Hemant K. & Ye, Nong / *COMPUTATIONAL MODELING AND PROBLEM SOLVING IN THE NETWORKED WORLD: Interfaces in Computer Science & Operations Research*

Woodruff, David L./ *NETWORK INTERDICTION AND STOCHASTIC INTEGER PROGRAMMING*

TELECOMMUNICATIONS NETWORK DESIGN AND MANAGEMENT

Edited by

G. ANANDALINGAM
University of Maryland

S. RAGHAVAN
University of Maryland

Kluwer Academic Publishers
Boston/Dordrecht/London

Distributors for North, Central and South America:
Kluwer Academic Publishers
101 Philip Drive
Assinippi Park
Norwell, Massachusetts 02061 USA
Telephone (781) 871-6600
Fax (781) 871-9045
E-Mail: kluwer@wkap.com

Distributors for all other countries:
Kluwer Academic Publishers Group
Post Office Box 322
3300 AH Dordrecht, THE NETHERLANDS
Telephone 31 786 576 000
Fax 31 786 576 254
E-mail: services@wkap.nl

 Electronic Services <http://www.wkap.nl>

Library of Congress Cataloging-in-Publication Data

Telecommunications network design and management / edited by G. Anandalingam, S. Raghavan.
    p. cm. -- (Operations research/computer science interfaces series ; ORCS 23)
    "Sixth INFORMS telecommunications conference, Boca Raton, Fla. March 10-13, 2002"--Pref.
    Includes bibliographical references and index.
    ISBN 1-4020-7318-6 (alk. paper)
    1. Telecommunication systems--Management--Congresses. 2. Computer networks--Management--Congresses. 3. Telecommunication systems--Design and construction--Congresses. I. Anandalingam, G. II. Raghavan, S. III. Title. IV. Series.

TK5102.5 .T3953 2003
621.382'1--dc21
                                    2002035703

Printed on acid-free paper.
Printed in the United States of America.

Contents

Preface

This edited book contains selected papers presented at the Sixth INFORMS Telecommunications Conference held in Boca Raton, Florida, March 10-13, 2002. This book is an addition to the Computer Science/Operations Research Interface series edited by Ramesh Sharda (Oklahoma State University) and Stefan Voß (Technische Universität Braunschweig) and published by Kluwer Academic Publishers.

The 16 papers in this book were carefully selected after a thorough review process. They cover a wide range of topics in telecommunications network design and management, and reflect the spectrum of papers presented at the INFORMS conference. We thank the referees for reviewing the papers speedily, and the authors for the quick turnaround of the revised papers.

The first three chapters of the book deal with the design of wireless networks, including UMTS and Ad-Hoc networks. Chapters 4-6 deal with the optimal design of telecommunications networks. Techniques used for network design range from genetic algorithms to combinatorial optimization heuristics. Chapters 7-10 analyze traffic flow in telecommunications networks. The focus is on optimizing traffic load distribution and the scheduling of switches under multi-media streams and heavy traffic. In all papers, innovations in operations research and statistics techniques are used to analyze the problem. Chapters 11-14 deal with telecommunications network management. The papers examine bandwidth provisioning, admission control, queue management, dynamic routing, and feedback regulation in order to ensure that the network performance is optimized. Chapters 15-16 deal with the construction of topologies and allocation of bandwidth to ensure quality-of-service.

We believe the edited volume represents the state-of-art of applying operations research techniques to important problems in telecommunications network design and management. We expect both researchers and practitioners will benefit from this book. We hope that this book will fawn new research in the area.

G. (Anand) Anandalingam & S. (Raghu) Raghavan

Chapter 1

MODELLING
FEASIBLE NETWORK CONFIGURATIONS
FOR UMTS *

Andreas Eisenblätter, Roland Wessäly
Atesio GmbH, Rubensstr. 126, D-12157 Berlin, Germany
{eisenblaetter,wessaely}@atesio.de

Alexander Martin, Armin Fügenschuh, Oliver Wegel
TU Darmstadt, Schloßgartenstr. 7, D-64289 Darmstadt, Germany
{martin,fuegenschuh,wegel}@mathematik.tu-darmstadt.de

Thorsten Koch, Tobias Achterberg, Arie Koster
Konrad-Zuse-Zentrum für Informationstechnik Berlin, Takustr. 7, D-14195 Berlin, Germany
{koch,achterberg,koster}@zib.de

Abstract   Telecommunications operators worldwide are facing the challenge of deploying UMTS. These networks have to meet consumers' expectations, tight budget constraints and governmental regulations. The careful dimensioning of the radio access infrastructure plays an essential role in achieving these goals.

This paper presents an optimisation model for selecting well-tuned base station locations and configurations. The mixed integer programming model reflects the overall design problem fairly accurately. The interference limitations for successful up- and downlink transmissions, the need for sufficiently strong (cell) pilot signals, the limited downlink code capacity in each cell and the potential gain for mobiles from being in soft(er) hand-over are taken into account. This comprehensive model can be used as a core for refined UMTS planning tools.

Keywords: UMTS, radio interface, network planning, configuration, perfect power control, mixed integer programming, MOMENTUM, IST-2000-28088

*Supported by the European Community within the 5th Framework Programme, Information Society Technologies (IST), Key Action IV, Action Line IV.4.1 under the project title MOMENTUM, IST-2000-28088.

1.   Introduction

Dimensioning the radio interface between the users' mobile equipment and the network operator's fixed infrastructure is a key step during the initial deployment of an UMTS network and its subsequent expansions. The careful configuration of this interface is of vital importance to the network operator. The radio interface determines the coverage and capacity of the provided services, and it accounts for a major portion of the total network installation and maintenance costs. The layout decisions for the UMTS radio interface are driven by the capabilities of the mobile services that an operator intends to offer. The challenge of finding a suitable layout for the UMTS base stations can be phrased as follows: *select locations for the base stations from the set of possible sites and determine the configuration of the cells hosted at each location such that the desired services can be offered and the budget restrictions are met.*

The project "Models and Simulations for Network Planning and Control of UMTS" (MOMENTUM, cf. http://momentum.zib.de) addresses this challenge at several levels. MOMENTUM characterises new services UMTS is going to deliver, builds usage profiles and planning scenarios to model the future demands, develops flexible models, algorithms, and new simulation as well as evaluation approaches for the optimised configuration of the new wireless telecommunication infrastructure. The project is performed within the fifth European Framework Programme focusing on Information Society Technologies (IST). This article introduces a rather comprehensive mixed integer linear programming model for optimising the layout of an UMTS radio network.

The article is organised as follows. The next section introduces several of the challenges embodied in UMTS radio network planning and explains how the mathematical programming model can help to face them. This is followed by an extensive survey on (mostly) Operations Research literature dealing with UMTS radio network planning in a broad sense. Sections 4, 5 and 6 develop the model, starting from the input parameters over a comprehensive set of limiting constraints to the objective function. The concluding Section 7 contains a roadmap for further developments on the way to implementing this model in UMTS planning practice.

2.   Model Scope

We describe a mathematical programming model for the automatic planning and optimisation of the radio network interface. The focus is on the "static" installation of radio base stations. The following questions are addressed:

- which of the candidate sites shall be used to erect base stations

- what sectorisation shall be used at each selected site

- which antenna types shall serve the individual sectors
- what shall the heights and the tilts of the antennas be
- what shall the maximal transmission powers in each cell be
- how much power shall be allocated to the pilot signals
- how much hard capacity shall be provided for each cell

These decisions are to be taken for each site in a planning area. Other aspects of a base station installation are not considered here. Among these aspects are the planning of scrambling codes, multiple carrier frequencies and all settings related to radio resource management.

Optimisation presupposes an objective. A clear understanding of such an objective has not yet been established in the field—and may, in fact, never be. The ultimate decision on which of alternative radio network configurations is more appropriate has therefore to be taken by the radio network planners.

2.1   Blending Competing Planning Goals

We distinguish two major viewpoints on a network configuration. One perspective is performance centred, where a configuration is assessed according to how well it supports the expected traffic load. The other perspective is budget centred, where the focus is on the installation costs, running costs and the flexibility of the configuration to adopt changing demands and services. The performance centred view typically favours expensive over-dimensioned configurations due to their superior performance. The budget centred view typically favours comparably inexpensive configurations that can barely support the given traffic load.

Our objective function blends both aspects in the typical bi-criteria optimisation fashion. That is, scaling factors are used to balance the cost-oriented and the performance-oriented terms. Alternatively, one of the two terms could be taken as an additional restriction, whereas the other is optimised.

2.2   Performance Evaluation

The details of estimating the network costs are of course quite involved, but far more intricate is the estimation of the performance for the configuration under consideration.

By performance estimation we understand the estimation of the service coverage, capacity and quality of the network. It is well-known that resolving this question is much more complex for UMTS than it is for GSM due to the WCDMA technology employed. Simulations are typically used for this purpose. Such simulations should mimic the behaviour of the real system as closely as possible.

The state-of-the-art is to use so-called static system-level simulators, cf. Laiho et al., 2001, Chapter 3. The attribute "system-level" indicates that the radio transmission link is not simulated in full detail. Instead, its performance is estimated from link simulation and link measurement results for comparable radio signal propagation environments. The attribute "static" indicates that the dynamic system behaviour is mostly neglected, i. e., users are not moving, radio resource management algorithms are not executed, fast power control is not performed, etc. The impacts of these features are merely estimated from the statistics of "dynamic" simulations or live system observations.

A static system-level simulator generates traffic snapshots, assesses these snapshots and compiles statistics. A traffic snapshot is generated according to traffic estimates, which are given as input by locating users into the planning region. Each user is attributed with specific service demands. In total, the generated traffic snapshots have to comply with the prescribed traffic distributions, which is provided as input. The performance of the given network configuration with respect to each snapshot is assessed independently. The crucial part in this assessment is to determine which user is served by which base station at which power level. Both, the up- and the downlink direction have, to be analysed.

Once the power levels for the served users are determined and the rest of the users in the snapshot is put to outage, several figures are extracted, which describe how well this snapshot is handled by the network. The evaluation of many snapshots allows to conclude how well the network serves traffic that statistically conforms to the used traffic distribution.

In summary, the network simulator can be used to asses the given network's performance under one or several given traffic distributions (or profiles). The simulator is therefore used during the planning and optimisation of the UMTS radio network to compare alternative configurations.

2.3   Configuration Optimisation

As we turn to automatically planning and optimising the radio network configuration, the situation changes radically. The network configuration is no longer given, and the problem is to construct network configurations that perform well under a set of estimated future traffic profiles. The resulting network configurations are then analysed using an above mentioned simulator.

The planning objective is to select a network configuration that serves a number of alternative future demands well, that is, that optimises the expected value of users' satisfaction for these demands. In mathematical terms, we are faced with a nonlinear discrete optimisation problem with a lower semi-continuous objective function. The methods to solve such a problem strongly depend on the underlying probability distributions for the alternatives between the estimated demands. For the problem sizes we are faced with, such problems are in general far beyond tractability using the methods and the computer power available today, cf. Schultz, 2001.

The way to deal with this situation is the same as that for network performance evaluation. The network planning is performed on the basis of traffic snapshots, which are generated according to one or several traffic profiles. These traffic profiles capture the scenarios for which the network shall be tuned for. The resulting optimisation problem can be stated as follows: find network configurations that perform best with respect to all the given snapshots subject to the technical and financial side constraints. At the mathematical level, we deal with discrete probability distributions and the nonlinear discrete optimisation problem turns into in a huge mixed integer program.

We present such a mixed integer program. The model assigns a *network rating* to a configuration under a given set of traffic snapshots. The rating is used to compare network configurations during the optimisation. The rating may be assembled from various details on the network's performance and its cost.

3. Literature Survey

Many documents are concerned with the new UMTS standard and give definitions and descriptions related to UMTS, such as the SIR or CIR targets, power control, and code assignment. The book edited by Holma and Toskala, 2001, contains a comprehensive introduction to WCDMA, UMTS services and applications, radio interface protocols, and radio resource management, to name just a few. The contribution by Holma et al., 2001, provides a good survey about different aspects of the planning process such as coverage, capacity, and quality of service.

Just recently published, the book edited by Laiho et al., 2001, deals with planning and optimising UMTS radio networks. Among others, it sketches the network planning process, discusses the requirements of radio network planning tools, introduces a static system-level radio network simulator, addresses radio resource management, provides details concerning cell deployment, UMTS specific coverage and capacity enhancement methods as well as the technical management of radio network optimisation. This book does not, however, outdate this paper or renders it unnecessary. On the contrary, the book contains much of the information necessary to develop models and automated network planning/optimisation methods, which is otherwise hardly publicly available, but it does not itself contain such models and methods.

The literature focusing on methods and algorithms for automated UMTS radio network planning and optimisation is still rather limited.

Berruto et al., 1998, include a survey on research activities of the EU-founded ACTS (Advanced Communication Technologies and Services) projects

FRAMES (Future Radio Wideband Multiple Access Systems), RAINBOW (Radio Access Independent Broadband on Wireless) and STORMS (Software Tools for the Optimisation of Resource in Mobile Systems). The main areas of research are the development of a radio interface, the network subsystem, and network planning methodologies to provide a technology which fulfils the UMTS requirements.

Noblet et al., 2001, present the results of their simulation of a WCDMA network in terms of coverage, Quality of Service (QoS) and capacity. They point out the difference between WCDMA to TDMA and FDMA. The interference aspect as well as the different user profile (several services and data rates, circuit switched and packet data) are stated as the main differences. They discuss an example of a network using generated data of an UMTS static system simulator, which was based on an IS-95 Motorola simulator. As a result the authors state that GSM cells can be reused for planning a WCDMA network at the expense of adding new base stations.

Fallot-Josselin, 1998, describes a model for the base station location planning problem based on a combinatorial set covering model. WCDMA-typical constraints (like soft-capacity, power control mechanism) are not taken into account. The author suggests a genetic algorithm approach for the solution of the problem.

Ibbetson and Lopes, 1997, develop an algorithm for the automatic placement of cellular base stations. The authors concentrate on the traffic, i. e., the data rate, and do not take the CIR target into account. They also allow in their model that less than 100% of the mobiles are served. Two algorithms for finding the optimal base station configuration are developed. The first one uses a recursive search for the optimal configuration by taking the traffic into account and lowering the radius of the cells which have to serve a high demand. The second one uses a grid, where in each centre of the squares a base station is located. For squares carrying a high density, the square is divided into four quarters, and the whole procedure is iterated.

Tutschku et al., 1997, present a mobile radio network planning tool called ICEPT, which is based on an integrated design approach. The approach analyses the spatial distribution of the expected traffic located in a cellular system. They make use of the four major design areas of cellular networks: radio transmission, mobile subscriber, resource allocation, and system architecture. The authors concentrate on the traffic and do not take into account the interference of the base stations.

Molina et al., 1999, develop a meta-heuristic optimisation algorithm for the base station selection problem in microcellular scenarios. Computational experiments are reported in which the new heuristic compares favourably to other meta-heuristics, such as greedy and genetic algorithms. Concerning UMTS planning, the authors propose a rating criterion with three components, which is used to evaluate small selections of base stations within their heuristic. A number of control points reflect the (possibly inhomogeneous) traffic distribution. At these control points, the coverage in terms of reception power, the RMS delay spread and the capacity are assessed.

Amaldi et al., 2001a; Amaldi et al., 2001b; Amaldi et al., 2001c; Amaldi et al., 2001d, study integer programming models and discrete algorithms that aim at supporting the decisions in the process of planning where to locate new base stations. The authors consider the CIR as quality measure and two different power control mechanism: either keep the received signal power or the estimated CIR at a given target value. The authors argue that the uplink (mobile to base station) direction is more stringent (compared to the downlink) in the presence of full-duplex balanced connections as voice calls. This problem contains the uncapacitated facility location, an NP-hard problem, as a subproblem. General purpose MIP solvers fail in solving practical instances in reasonable time, hence Monte-Carlo greedy-type heuristics are developed. Computational results from small to large (realistic) instances are reported.

The model of Amaldi et al. is based on the well-known and well-studied classical uncapacitated facility-location problem. A set of candidate sites is given where a base station can be installed. The distribution of users is modelled by the use of test points (sometimes called demand nodes). Each test point can be considered as a centroid where a given amount of traffic (measured in Erlang) is requested and where a certain level of service (measured in terms of CIR) must be guaranteed. The propagation information is also assumed to be known. For each possible site and each test point one must compute the path loss beforehand.

The optimisation algorithm has two contradicting goals. On one hand it tries to minimise the overall installation cost of used sites. On the other hand it favours assignments of test points to base stations with smaller total power (and therefore tries to open many base stations). A trade-off parameter is used to weight between these two goals. Side constraints in this model guarantee coverage and QoS.

Mathar and Schmeink, 2000, address GSM and UMTS network planning. Concerning UMTS, they make use of a discrete mathematical programming approach in order to solve the cell site selection problem (considering the downlink). Their objective is to place base transmitter stations such that the network coverage/capacity is maximised subject to CIR constraints. The expected traffic is represented by spatially scattered weighted "demand nodes" that each carry a certain load of traffic. An integer linear program is set up to select an optimal set of base station locations from a given pool of configurations such that a) a maximum of users/demand nodes can be served and such that b) a given financial budget for the construction of the base stations is not exceeded. A branch-and-bound algorithm is devised for solving this problem. Optimal solutions are reported for an urban scenario (parts of the city of Munich) with up to 330 possible base station locations and up to 1,100 demand nodes.

Mathar, 2001, presents some MIP (mixed integer programming) models and computational studies for the cell site selection problem, which are more or less set covering based models with the budget as an additional knapsack constraint. Constraints due to the quality of service (such as CIR targets or power control mechanisms) are not included into the model but studied afterwards with stochastic methods.

Mathar and Niessen, 2000, model various aspects of the base station problem as integer linear programs. They start with an integer programming formulation for the problem of maximising the number of covered demand nodes by at most K base stations. This model is extended in several ways, for instance, by penalising multiple coverage, by minimising interference between base stations or by the number of blocked channels. For the solution of the problem the authors suggest simulated annealing. They exhaustively discuss their computational results for one real-world example.

Howitt and Seung-Yong, 1999, model the base station location problem as a nonlinear optimisation problem. For the solution of this problem they apply a global optimisation strategy based on modelling the objective function with a stochastic process. They compare their algorithm for an indoor scenario with one and two base stations with local optimisation techniques and derive an improvement of up to 90% for this instance.

Akl et al., 1999, discuss the problem of determining the maximal network capacity by optimising simultaneously the transmitted pilot-signal powers and the base station locations, whereas the locations can be moved continuously. This results in a constrained nonlinear optimisation problem, which is solved by gradient methods. They have tested their algorithms on an example with 36 base stations and conclude that for uniform user distribution a uniform network layout is best possible, whereas for non-uniform distributions the base stations need to be relocated inside the hot spots. The results also show that for congested base stations it is better to increase the pilot power than decreasing it in order to improve the network capacity.

Galota et al., 2000b, focus in on theoretical algorithmic aspects of the base station location problem. The authors prove that a simplified planning problem using rather weak constraints is $\mathcal{NP}$-hard. From this paper we conclude that our problem is also $\mathcal{NP}$-hard and is thus at least theoretically difficult.

Galota et al., 2000a, discuss a simplified model of the UMTS base station planning problem, where they assume the base stations and mobiles in the plane and where the fact whether a mobile is covered by some base station just depends on the distance. The authors give a profit function which depends linearly on the distances and model the hand-over by counting the number of base stations covering each mobile. For the solution of the problem the authors give a polynomial approximation scheme and show that in terms of complexity this is the best one can achieve (that is there exists no fully polynomial approximation scheme unless $\mathcal{P} = \mathcal{NP}$).

At first sight GSM is closely related to UMTS in terms of planning radio networks, that is, the same basic questions where to locate and how to configure base stations come up as well, see for instance the work by Aardal et al., 2001; Correia, 2001; Eisenblätter, 2001; Hurley, 2000; Koster, 1999; Tutschku et al., 1999; Konstantinopoulou et al., 2000; Mathar and Schmeink, 2000; Pasquale et al., 1998. Some of the basic constraints discussed there are contained in our models as well, but in GSM radio coverage and system capacity can basically be planned separately. Thus, the models for UMTS are far more complex and a comparison of the models and results for GSM and UMTS is hardly possible.

From the base station planning point of view, the commercial cdma-One system, formerly called IS-95, is much more alike UMTS than GSM. cdma-One uses code division multiple access just like UMTS, but in terms of service (essentially) only radio telephony is provided, see, for instance, the work by Ehrenberger and Leibnitz, 1999; Lee and Kang, 2000; Wong et al., 2001.

In summary, there is need for a comprehensive optimisation model for the UMTS radio network design, taking both up- and downlink into account. We develop such a model in the next three sections.

4. The Parameters

We assume that the reader is familiar with the basic properties of the UMTS radio interface. In-depth introductions to this topic are, for example, given in the books edited by Holma and Toskala, 2001 or Laiho et al., 2001.

This section introduces the notation for the input parameters to our model, see Figure 1.1 for an illustration. The unit of all noise and power parameters is Watt. (The appendix contains a compilation of all model parameters and variables, see page 21.)

4.1 Sites and Installations

Base stations can not be erected at arbitrary locations. We are therefore given a set of potential *sites*, denoted by S. If a site is selected from the set S, we have to configure the site with antennas (sectors, cells). Each antenna has settings to be specified. In particular, there are the geographic coordinates, height, direction, tilt and the type of the antenna.

Instead of dealing with all these aspects separately, we introduce the notion of an *installation*. Each installation corresponds to a specific antenna with fixed azimuth and tilt at a specific geographic location and height. It is often possible to select several installations per site. (These need not be co-located.) We assume, however, that all possible installations at a site are in principle

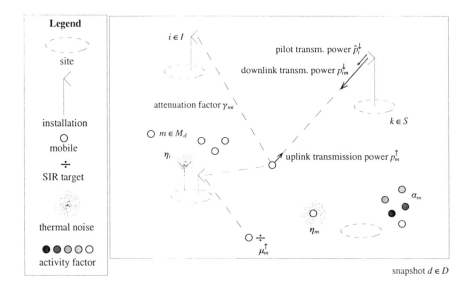

Figure 1.1.   Model parameters and variables

compatible. We denote by $\mathcal{I}(k)$ all potential installations of antennas that are allowed at site $k \in \mathcal{S}$ and by $\mathcal{I} = \bigcup_{k \in \mathcal{S}} \mathcal{I}(k)$ their disjoint union.

We denote by $\check{\Pi}_i^{\min\downarrow}$, $\check{\Pi}_i^{\max\downarrow}$ the minimal and maximal transmission power per link, by $\hat{\Pi}_i^{\min\downarrow}$, $\hat{\Pi}_i^{\max\downarrow}$ the minimal and maximal pilot transmission power, and by $\Pi_i^{\max\downarrow}$ the maximal total transmission power of an installation $i \in \mathcal{I}$.

The number of channel elements at a site limits the maximal transmission data rate. We do not model this restriction, since the air interface is expected to be the bottleneck and an operator can install sufficiently many channel elements at a site. Should this assumption turn out to be too optimistic, the channel element consumption can be modelled in a similar fashion as the code consumption, as shown below.

4.2   Mobiles

The radio network is designed to support some anticipated communications demand (or traffic). As mentioned in Section 2, this demand can be captured in terms of traffic *snapshots*. These snapshots are generated according to the anticipated demand distribution(s).

Effects due to mobility, varying traffic activity and bursty packet services are taken into account by dealing with a set of *snapshots* $\mathcal{D}$. We denote by $\mathcal{M}_d$ the set of mobiles within $d \in \mathcal{D}$ and by $\mathcal{M} = \bigcup_{d \in \mathcal{D}} \mathcal{M}_d$ their disjoint union. Note that not all mobiles in all snapshots necessarily have to get service. It is often sufficient that some (service specific) coverage criterion is met.

The minimal and maximal (uplink) transmission power for $m \in \mathcal{M}$ are denoted by $\Pi_m^{\min\uparrow}$ and $\Pi_m^{\max\uparrow}$.

4.3 Services

A service request is associated with each mobile in a snapshot. It suffices for our purposes to distinguish the services according to their received signal quality requirements, the up- and downlink activity factors, and their downlink code consumption.

The *carrier to interference ratio* (CIR) *target* for a radio link is the minimum required ratio for proper signal reception between the received carrier's signal strength and the sum over all interfering signal and noise powers. We denote the CIR targets for mobile $m \in \mathcal{M}$ by $\mu_m^{\uparrow}$ for the up- and by $\mu_m^{\downarrow}$ for the downlink. The CIR requirements for the (downlink) pilot channel are denoted by $\hat{\mu}_m^{\downarrow}$.

The CIR target C/I for a radio link depends on three factors. Let R denote the data rate of the carried service, W the UMTS specific chip rate of 3.84 Mcps, and E_b/N_0 the required ratio between signal bit energy and interference spectral density (including noise spectral density), then

$$\frac{C}{I} = \frac{E_b}{N_0} \cdot \frac{R}{W} \quad .$$

The quotient E_b/N_0 depends, among others, on the service type and on the speed of the mobile. E_b/N_0 values have so far been typically obtained from radio link simulations, see Laiho et al., 2001, Table 2.9. Life-system measurements are only gradually becoming available.

The *activity factor* indicates how active a mobile is engaged in a connection. We use service specific factors $\alpha_m^{\uparrow}$ and $\alpha_m^{\downarrow}$ for each mobile $m \in \mathcal{M}$ in the up- and downlink. The activity factor for speech service, for example, is often taken as 67%. If the mobile is using a service mix, the activity factor is a mixture of the corresponding factors. The factor may be different in up- and downlink. For more information related to service activity see Laiho et al., 2001, Chapter 3.

The amount of downlink *code consumption* for specific services is related to the spreading code(s) used for downlink transmission channel(s). These spreading codes are taken from a code tree. There is one primary code tree available in each cell. We model this consumption at the level of spreading factors. The sum over the inverse of the spreading factors associated with the downlink channels in a cell may not exceed 1. This can be generalised— although not in a straightforward way—once spreading codes from the upto fifteen secondary code trees shall be considered as well. We refer to the *code consumption* by mobile $m \in \mathcal{M}$ as λ_m. A large λ_m stands for a high data rate. The available resource budget at installation i is denoted by Λ_i. According to the above explanation Λ_i should always be equal to 1. Due to soft hand-over and code tree fragmentation, however, it might be set to lower values.

4.4   Radio Paths

A number of parameters concern the transmission, the radio path and the reception. For every pair of mobiles $m \in \mathcal{M}$ and installations $i \in \mathcal{I}$ the *attenuation* is defined as the ratio of energy received by the receiver to the energy emitted by the transmitter. This need not be symmetric, so there are attenuation $\gamma^{\uparrow}_{mi}$ for the uplink and $\gamma^{\downarrow}_{im}$ for the downlink. The values can be computed with data from a radio wave propagation prediction model together with the characteristics of the antennas.

Noise includes thermal noise and other noise sources, such as receiver noise, interference from distant antennas and all other kinds of man made noise. We use two sets of parameters, one for the installations' (uplink) η_i for $i \in \mathcal{I}$, the other for the mobiles' (downlink) η_m for $m \in \mathcal{M}$.

The *orthogonality* factor ω_{im} in the downlink between installation $i \in \mathcal{I}$ and mobile $m \in \mathcal{M}$ depends on the environment. Ideally, the CDMA signals for two distinct downlink connections in one cell are orthogonal, that is, they are not mutually interfering. Multi-path propagation and diffraction weaken this property. The orthogonality factor states how much of a signal may be considered orthogonal. The remainder is treated as interference at the receiving mobile. Perfect orthogonality is expressed by 1.0. We introduce $\bar{\omega}_{im} = 1 - \omega_{im}$ for notational convenience.

5.   Modelling Feasibility

In this section, we devise a mathematical model that describes what we consider a *feasible network configuration* with respect to the most dominant up- and downlink requirements. These requirements deal with the uplink and downlink CIR targets for dedicated channels, the pilot CIR requirements, and the downlink code resources in a cell.

Notice that we consider both, up- and downlink constraints. This extends the work of several other authors, e. g., Amaldi et al., 2001a; Amaldi et al., 2001b; Amaldi et al., 2001c; Amaldi et al., 2001d or Mathar, 2001. Indisputably, the uplink is the limiting direction if plain speech telephony is considered. This is because the up- and downlink activity are roughly equal, the up- and downlink CIR targets do not differ much, but the (downlink) transmission power per connection available at an installation is typically much larger than the total (uplink) transmission power at a mobile. Depending on whether few or many users try to get service per cell, the uplink transmission power is exhausted at mobiles distant from the base station because of the path loss being too large (coverage limitation) or because of the interference being too strong (capacity limitation).

The situation changes substantially for more asymmetric services such as high data rate video-streaming. An installation's downlink transmission power (per link, for the pilot channel or in total) may become exhausted much earlier than the uplink transmission power. In summary, it is not very hard to derive a set of traffic snapshots, where each of the snapshots cannot be properly served due to a different reason. In order to capture this fairly accurately, we include up- and downlink requirements.

The model presented here is a mixed integer linear program or MIP, for short. Each feasible solution for the MIP identifies a selection of sites to open, installations to use at each site, assignments of mobiles to installations and the power levels of each installation and mobile for each snapshot from $\mathcal{D}$. *Each mobile is connected to at most one installation.* A discussion on how to incorporate soft(er) hand-over follows at the end of this section.

5.1   Sites and Installations

Our first set of variables and constraints governs the selection of base station installations and the "assignment" of served mobiles to the selected installations. For the sites we introduce binary variables s_k, $k \in \mathcal{S}$ with the interpretation $s_k = 1$ if site k is used. Furthermore, we have binary variables z_i, $i \in \mathcal{I}$, where $z_i = 1$ if installation i is used.

For the assignment of the mobiles we have two types of binary variables, namely, w_m, where $w_m = 1$ if and only if mobile $m \in \mathcal{M}$ is served at all, and x_{mi}, where $x_{mi} = 1$ if and only if mobile $m \in \mathcal{M}$ is served by installation $i \in \mathcal{I}$.

The following constraints are associated with the selection of the sites. An installation i is only available if its site $\sigma(i)$ is selected:

$$z_i \leq s_{\sigma(i)} \qquad \forall i \in \mathcal{I} \tag{1.1}$$

An upper limit $\Upsilon_k^{\max}$ on the number of installations at site k can be specified:

$$\sum_{i \in \mathcal{I}(k)} z_i \leq \Upsilon_k^{\max} \qquad \forall k \in \mathcal{S} \tag{1.2}$$

Only a selected installation may serve mobiles:[†]

$$x_{mi} \leq z_i \qquad \forall m \in \mathcal{M}, i \in \mathcal{I} \tag{1.3}$$

[†]From a mathematical point of view, this constraint is redundant if inequality (1.5) is used.

Each mobile is served by exactly one installation if it is served at all:

$$\sum_{i \in \mathcal{I}} x_{mi} = w_m \qquad \forall m \in \mathcal{M} \qquad (1.4)$$

The serving of a mobile consumes code resources at the installation:

$$\sum_{m \in \mathcal{M}_d} \lambda_m x_{mi} \leq \Lambda_i z_i \qquad \forall i \in \mathcal{I}, d \in \mathcal{D} \qquad (1.5)$$

Notice: Since each mobile is served by at most one installation in our model, we cannot easily account for multiple code consumption of mobiles in soft(er) hand-over. We come back to this issue at the end of this section.

5.2   Uplink

The uplink transmission powers are under fast power control. The objective is to emit the necessary power to reach the base station with the appropriate CIR value. For the uplink power level of mobile m we use a continuous variable $p_m^{\uparrow}$. Each mobile has minimum and maximum transmission power level that have to be obeyed if the mobile is served.

$$\Pi_m^{\min\uparrow} w_m \leq p_m^{\uparrow} \leq \Pi_m^{\max\uparrow} w_m \qquad \forall m \in \mathcal{M} \qquad (1.6)$$

We assume in the model that the *power control* is *perfect*. This implies the transmission power is set to the minimum level necessary to fulfil the CIR target (see e. g. Bambos et al., 1995). It is currently not yet settled if and to which extent realistic power control mechanisms can be taken into account by systematically modifying the CIR targets. For each mobile the CIR-target in respect to the serving base station has to be met:

$$\frac{\gamma_{mi}^{\uparrow} p_m^{\uparrow}}{\sum_{\substack{n \in \mathcal{M}_d \\ n \neq m}} \gamma_{ni}^{\uparrow} \alpha_n^{\uparrow} p_n^{\uparrow} + \eta_i} \geq \mu_m^{\uparrow} x_{mi} \qquad \forall d \in \mathcal{D}, m \in \mathcal{M}_d, i \in \mathcal{I} \qquad (1.7)$$

Notice that while equations (1.7) as well as (1.13) and (1.14) below are not linear, they can be linearised to fit into the model, see Eisenblätter et al., 2002.

5.3   Downlink

Just like in the uplink case, the downlink transmission powers (for dedicated channels) are also under fast power control. We use continuous variables $p_{im}^{\downarrow}$ for the power level between installation i and mobile m. In addition, we have a continuous variable $\hat{p}_i^{\downarrow}$ for the pilot power of installation i. The following constraints describe the downlink case. The transmission power in the downlink is limited per link.

$$\dot{\Pi}_i^{\min\downarrow} x_{mi} \leq p_{im}^{\downarrow} \leq \dot{\Pi}_i^{\max\downarrow} x_{mi} \qquad \forall i \in \mathcal{I}, m \in \mathcal{M} \tag{1.8}$$

Also the pilot power and the total power per installation are limited:

$$\hat{\Pi}_i^{\min\downarrow} z_i \leq \hat{p}_i^{\downarrow} \leq \hat{\Pi}_i^{\max\downarrow} z_i \qquad \forall i \in \mathcal{I} \tag{1.9}$$

$$\hat{p}_i^{\downarrow} + \sum_{m \in \mathcal{M}_d} \alpha_m^{\downarrow} p_{im}^{\downarrow} \leq \Pi_i^{\max\downarrow} z_i \qquad \forall i \in \mathcal{I}, d \in \mathcal{D} \tag{1.10}$$

For notational convenience, let $\phi(m, i)$ denote the interference from other transmissions

$$\phi(m, i) = \sum_{\substack{n \in \mathcal{M}_d \\ n \neq m}} \left(\overbrace{\bar{\omega}_{im} \gamma_{im}^{\downarrow} \alpha_n^{\downarrow} p_{in}^{\downarrow}}^{\text{from same cell}} + \overbrace{\sum_{\substack{j \in \mathcal{I} \\ j \neq i}} \gamma_{jm}^{\downarrow} \alpha_n^{\downarrow} p_{jn}^{\downarrow}}^{\text{from other cells}} \right) \tag{1.11}$$

and let $\hat{\phi}(m, i)$ denote the interference from other pilot signals

$$\hat{\phi}(m, i) = \sum_{\substack{j \in \mathcal{I} \\ j \neq i}} \gamma_{jm}^{\downarrow} \hat{p}_j^{\downarrow} \tag{1.12}$$

Using this notation, the CIR formula for the downlink reads:

$$\frac{\gamma_{im}^{\downarrow} p_{im}^{\downarrow}}{\phi(m, i) + \underbrace{\bar{\omega}_{im} \gamma_{im}^{\downarrow} \hat{p}_i^{\downarrow}}_{\text{own pilot signal}} + \hat{\phi}(m, i) + \eta_m} \geq \mu_m^{\downarrow} x_{mi}$$

$$\forall d \in \mathcal{D}, m \in \mathcal{M}_d, i \in \mathcal{I} \tag{1.13}$$

We also have to meet a CIR requirement for the pilot signal, but the CIR is defined here using chip energy E_c/I_0 instead of bit energy E_b/N_0. Consequently, the own cell interference has to be fully accounted for:

$$\frac{\gamma_{im}^{\downarrow} \hat{p}_i^{\downarrow}}{\phi(m, i) + \underbrace{\gamma_{im}^{\downarrow} \alpha_m^{\downarrow} p_{im}^{\downarrow}}_{\text{own data signal}} + \hat{\phi}(m, i) + \eta_m} \geq \hat{\mu}_m^{\downarrow} x_{mi}$$

$$\forall d \in \mathcal{D}, m \in \mathcal{M}_d, i \in \mathcal{I} \tag{1.14}$$

The downlink requirements neglect the power consumed by and the interference caused by the common channels, which are not power controlled and whose power is typically set relative to the pilot channel's power. Both aspects can easily be incorporated into the constraints (1.10), (1.13), and (1.14) if the need arises.

Furthermore, the CIR requirements ensure that a sufficient carrier signal to interference ratio is achieved. It is not ensured, however, that the carrier signals are above the receiver sensitivity, i. e., that the received signal code power is high enough. In case this is not implicitly imposed by the CIR requirements, corresponding constraints can also be added easily.

5.4   Soft Hand-over Gain

The model as described above does not reflect the possibility that a mobile is in soft hand-over, that is, it is simultaneously linked to two installations. If the installations belong to the same site, this is called softer hand-over. Since more than two installations may serve a mobile, various combinations of soft and softer hand-over are possible.

We discuss next how to incorporate the effects of soft(er) hand-over into our model. An accurate modelling currently appears to be prohibitive, see Eisenblätter et al., 2002. Hence, we stick to the decision that each mobile is linked to at most one cell. Soft(er) hand-over can, thus, only be accounted for in a heuristic fashion in the inequalities (1.5), (1.7), and (1.13). We explain below how to do this for the uplink. The changes for the downlink are similar.

The gain that a mobile has from being in soft(er) hand-over depends on the size of the active set (AS) and the actual difference in attenuation. Figure 1.2 gives an idea of the relation.

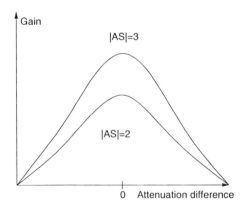

Figure 1.2.   Soft(er) hand-over gain depending on the attenuation difference

For a mobile to be in soft(er) hand-over with two or more cells, the attenuation between the mobile and each of the involved cells has to be approximately the same. A maximal difference between 3 and 6 dB is expected.

For every mobile m and every installation i we define the *candidate set* as

$$\mathcal{K}_{mi}(\delta) = \left\{ j \in \mathcal{I} \setminus \{i\} \mid \frac{1}{\delta} \leq \frac{\gamma_{mi}^{\uparrow}}{\gamma_{mj}^{\uparrow}} \leq \delta \right\} \qquad (1.15)$$

with maximum *soft(er) hand-over attenuation threshold* δ typically between 2 and 4. The installations contained in $\mathcal{K}_{mi}(\delta)$ are possible candidates for supporting installation i in serving mobile m, i. e., we do not yet know which of the installations in the set will be chosen to be used. Additional restrictions may apply and can be added to the definition in (1.15).

We describe the changes to inequalities (1.5) and (1.7) necessary in order to incorporate soft(er) hand-over gain based on the possible active/candidate-sets.

Site Selection. We change the resource consumption parameters to accommodate for the anticipated soft(er) hand-over rate. In inequality (1.5) the terms on both sides of the inequality sign can be changed.

From a global perspective, increasing λ_m indicates a generally higher resource consumption due to soft(er) hand-over connections. From a local perspective, decreasing Λ_i, possibly in dependence of the $\mathcal{K}_{mj}(\delta)$ sets containing i, reflects code resource reduction at installation i due to hand-over connections.

Phantom Powers in Up- and Downlink. The effect of soft(er) hand-over on a CIR target is modelled using what we call *phantom power*. Instead of explicitly lowering the required CIR target, a phantom power virtually increases the signal's transmission power, but not the interference.

The parameter $\rho_m^{\uparrow}$ describes the maximum possible (power) gain from being in soft(er) hand-over. The *phantom power* $v_m^{\uparrow}$ is a continuous variable controlling how much of this best possible gain is achieved. The actual gain depends on the actual conditions for mobile m, i. e., whether it is in soft(er) hand-over at all and, if so, which base station installations are processing its signal.

The benefit for mobile m from being in soft(er) hand-over between base station installations i and j is denoted by $\epsilon_{mij}^{\uparrow}$. We call the installation i with $x_{mi} = 1$ the *primary* server of m and all co-serving installations *secondary* servers. We allow multiple secondary servers, but assume that their combined gain can be approximated sufficiently well by adding up the gain of having each one of them as a secondary server alone (see inequality (1.17)).

Inequality (1.7) is replaced by

$$\frac{\gamma_{mi}^{\uparrow} \left(p_m^{\uparrow} + v_m^{\uparrow} \right)}{\displaystyle\sum_{\substack{n \in \mathcal{M}_d \\ n \neq m}} \gamma_{ni}^{\uparrow} \alpha_n^{\uparrow} p_n^{\uparrow} + \eta_i} \geq \mu_m^{\uparrow} x_{mi} \qquad \forall d \in \mathcal{D}, m \in \mathcal{M}_d, i \in \mathcal{I} \qquad (1.7')$$

and two new constraints governing the behaviour of $v_m^\uparrow$ are added:

$$0 \le v_m^\uparrow \le \rho_m^\uparrow \qquad\qquad \forall m \in \mathcal{M} \qquad\qquad (1.16)$$

$$v_m^\uparrow \le \rho_m^\uparrow - \rho_m^\uparrow x_{mi} + \sum_{j \in \mathcal{K}_{mi}(\delta)} \epsilon_{mij}^\uparrow z_j \quad \forall m \in \mathcal{M}, i \in \mathcal{I} \qquad (1.17)$$

6.   Objectives

We now come back to the point of rating configurations and introduce a linear objective function for our model. Without loss of generality, the objective function will be minimised. Since the word "cost" is used here also in the sense of capital expenditure, we use the word "merit" for the cost coefficients.

As mentioned before, the antipodal planning goals are minimising infrastructure cost and maximising network performance. These goals have to be balanced. Each of the following building blocks for the linear objective function will have its individual weighting factor.

6.1   Costs

There are two types of variables that naturally can be assigned costs to. The site decision variables s together with the site cost parameter c_k^s, $k \in \mathcal{S}$, reflect the cost for opening a new site, and the installation variables z are assigned the cost c_i^z, $i \in \mathcal{I}$ for deploying this particular installation.

Hence, within our model the expression

$$\sum_{k \in \mathcal{S}} c_k^s s_k \qquad\qquad (1.18)$$

captures the costs for opening the sites, and

$$\sum_{i \in \mathcal{I}} c_i^z z_i \qquad\qquad (1.19)$$

captures the costs for deploying the selected installations. The two expressions together represent the cost of a given network configuration.

6.2   Performance

For a fixed traffic snapshot $d \in \mathcal{D}$, the expression

$$\sum_{m \in \mathcal{M}_d} (1 - w_m) \qquad\qquad (1.20)$$

counts all unserved mobiles in this snapshot.

In addition to outage, one possibility to rate the performance of a network is to look at the *power headroom* available at each transmitter (mobiles and base stations). While it is questionable how accurately perfect power control resembles reality, the amount of headroom left is always an indication for the capacity left in the network. The expression

$$\sum_{m \in \mathcal{M}_d} (\Pi_m^{\max\uparrow} w_m - p_m^\uparrow) \tag{1.21}$$

sums the power headroom for all served mobiles from the snapshot in the uplink,

$$\sum_{i \in \mathcal{I}} (\hat{\Pi}_i^{\max\downarrow} z_i - \hat{p}_i^\downarrow) \tag{1.22}$$

sums the power headroom for the pilot signals, and

$$\sum_{i \in \mathcal{I}} \sum_{m \in \mathcal{M}_d} (\dot{\Pi}_i^{\max\downarrow} x_{mi} - p_{im}^\downarrow) \tag{1.23}$$

sums the headroom for the downlink—although this is usually considered less important. More important is the following term

$$\sum_{i \in \mathcal{I}} (\Pi_i^{\max\downarrow} z_i - \sum_{m \in \mathcal{M}_d} p_{im}^\downarrow), \tag{1.24}$$

which measures the downlink "power headroom" for each base station installation with respect to all served mobiles taken together. We make sure that always the least possible power level is selected.

Notice that we have not associated merits to serving certain mobiles. If we would like to express a preference for serving one mobile in comparison to serving some other, this could be added easily.

7. Conclusion and Outlook

A mixed integer programming model for planning and optimising the UMTS radio network has been developed. The primary goal in shaping the model was to capture all relevant practical side constraints. Accordingly, the focus has been on obtaining an appropriate rather than an easily accessible optimisation model. It reflects weeks of detailed discussions with UMTS and radio engineering experts within the MOMENTUM project. In contrast to a situation in which only a simplified model is available, it is now possible to assess much more precisely the compromises embodied in a simpler model.

The model has to allow to (roughly) assess a network's performance with respect to traffic snapshots. This presupposes that the model can be used as a surrogate for the core part of a static network simulator. Preliminary computational comparisons with a commercial static simulator indicate that this is indeed the case. The necessary, extensive testing of this property is ongoing within MOMENTUM.

An optimisation kernel is currently being built on the basis of the mathematical model described here. This kernel can be embedded into the regular planning process at the point, where the radio engineer would have to decide on which of the potential sites will receive a base station and on how to configure these base stations. The optimisation kernel has to compile the most favourable radio network configuration from the offered resources with respect to the traffic demand and cost constraints.

The input to the optimisation is received from two sources. One is the demand forecast, based on which traffic snapshots are generated. These snapshots capture the traffic mix, its spatial distribution, etc. (usually during the busy hour), the prospective network shall support. The other source is path loss prediction. The path loss from each potential site and each potential antenna installation at a site to all possible user locations has to be known. (Data for alternative configurations of one site can often be inferred from path loss predictions for an unmasked isotropic antenna at the site's location.) Some form of column-generation may, for example, be applied in order to start with a fairly small set of reasonable alternative site configurations. Furthermore, the kernel can be called repeatedly with augmented sets of traffic snapshots if the outcome of the external and thorough (static / semi-static) network performance analysis is not satisfactory—this may be seen as adding model cuts.

How the complex model can be handled with methods from Operations Research is currently being investigated. Among others, a reformulation of the model (including new variables) yields a much sparser constraint matrix; mixed integer rounding cuts based on the CIR constraints have been identified; and (heuristic) dominance criteria among mobile-to-installation assignments reduce the time needed to solve the model. Heuristic solution methods are also being devised. All these optimisation methods will be tested extensively on real-world instances available within the MOMENTUM project.

Acknowledgments

The authors thank the entire MOMENTUM team in general and Thomas Winter, Siemens AG, as well as Stefan Gustafsson, KPN Research, in particular for the stimulating discussions that shaped the model presented here.

Appendix: The Model Parameters and Variables

Parameters		
$\mathcal{S}$		set of (potential) sites
$\mathcal{I}(k)$		set of (potential) installations at site $k \in \mathcal{S}$
$\mathcal{I}$		$\bigcup_{k \in \mathcal{S}} \mathcal{I}(k)$ union of all possible installations
$\sigma(i)$		site of installation $i \in \mathcal{I}$, $\sigma(i) = k \Leftrightarrow i \in \mathcal{I}(k)$
$\mathcal{D}$		set of snapshots
$\mathcal{M}_d$		set of mobiles of snapshot d
$\mathcal{M}$		$\bigcup_{d \in \mathcal{D}} \mathcal{M}_d$ (disjoint) union of mobiles in all snapshots
k	$k \in \mathcal{S}$	site
i	$i \in \mathcal{I}$	installation
m	$m \in \mathcal{M}$	mobile
d	$d \in \mathcal{D}$	snapshot
$\Upsilon_k^{\max}$	≥ 1	maximum number of parallel installations at site k
$\gamma_{mi}^{\uparrow}$	$[0,1]$	uplink attenuation factor between mobile m and installation i.
$\gamma_{im}^{\downarrow}$	$[0,1]$	downlink attenuation factor between installation i and mobile m.
η_i	≥ 0	noise at installation i
η_m	≥ 0	noise at mobile m
$\Pi_m^{\min\uparrow}$	≥ 0	minimal uplink transmission power of mobile m
$\Pi_m^{\max\uparrow}$	≥ 0	maximal uplink transmission power of mobile m
$\Pi_i^{\max\downarrow}$	≥ 0	maximal total downlink transmission power at installation i
$\dot{\Pi}_i^{\min\downarrow}$	≥ 0	minimal downlink transmission power per link at installation i
$\dot{\Pi}_i^{\max\downarrow}$	≥ 0	maximal downlink transmission power per link at installation i
$\hat{\Pi}_i^{\min\downarrow}$	≥ 0	minimal (downlink) pilot transmission power at installation i
$\hat{\Pi}_i^{\max\downarrow}$	≥ 0	maximal (downlink) pilot transmission power at installation i
$\alpha_m^{\uparrow}$	$[0,1]$	uplink activity factor of mobile m
$\alpha_m^{\downarrow}$	$[0,1]$	downlink activity factor of mobile m
ω_{im}	$[0,1]$	orthogonality factor, $\bar{\omega}_{im} = 1 - \omega_{im}$
λ_m	≥ 0	code consumption for mobile m
Λ_i	≥ 0	code budget for installation i
$\mu_m^{\uparrow}$	≥ 0	uplink CIR target for mobile m
$\mu_m^{\downarrow}$	≥ 0	downlink CIR target for mobile m
$\hat{\mu}_m^{\downarrow}$	≥ 0	pilot CIR requirement for mobile m
δ	> 1	soft(er) hand-over attenuation threshold
$\mathcal{K}_{mi}(\delta)$		candidate-set for mobile m connected to installation i
$\rho_m^{\uparrow}$	≥ 0	maximal gain from being in soft(er) hand-over in uplink
$\epsilon_{mij}^{\uparrow}$	≥ 0	soft(er) hand-over gain in uplink
		if mobile m is served by i and supported by j

Variables		
s_k	$\in \{0,1\}$	is 1 if site k is used
z_i	$\in \{0,1\}$	is 1 if installation i is used
w_m	$\in \{0,1\}$	is 1 if mobile m is served at all
x_{mi}	$\in \{0,1\}$	is 1 if mobile m is served by installation i
$p_m^{\uparrow}$	$\in \mathbb{R}_+$	uplink transmission power from mobile m
$p_{im}^{\downarrow}$	$\in \mathbb{R}_+$	downlink transmission power from installation i to mobile m
$\hat{p}_i^{\downarrow}$	$\in \mathbb{R}_+$	(downlink) pilot transmission power from installation i
$v_m^{\uparrow}$	$\in \mathbb{R}_+$	uplink phantom power for mobile m

References

Aardal, K. I., van Hoesel, S. P. M., Koster, A. M. C. A., Mannino, C., and Sassano, A. (2001). Models and solution techniques for frequency assignment problems. Technical Report ZIB 01-40, Konrad-Zuse-Zentrum für Informationstechnik Berlin (ZIB), Germany.

Akl, R. G., Hegde, M. V., Naraghi-Pour, M., and Min, P. S. (1999). Cell placement in a CDMA network. *IEEE Wireless Communications and Networking Conference*, 2:903–907.

Amaldi, E., Capone, A., and Malucelli, F. (2001a). Base station configuration and location problems in UMTS networks. In *Proceedings of the 9th International Conference on Telecommunication Systems*, pages 341–348, Dallas, USA.

Amaldi, E., Capone, A., and Malucelli, F. (2001b). Discrete models and algorithms for the capacitated location problems arising in UMTS network planning. In *Proceedings of the 5th International Workshop on Discrete Algorithms and Methods for Mobile Computing and Communications ACM DIAL-M*, pages 1–8, Rome, Italy.

Amaldi, E., Capone, A., and Malucelli, F. (2001c). Improved models and algorithms for UMTS radio planning. *IEEE Vehicular Technology Conference*, 2(54):920–924.

Amaldi, E., Capone, A., and Malucelli, F. (2001d). Optimizing base station siting in UMTS networks. *IEEE Vehicular Technology Conference*, 4(53):2828–2832.

Bambos, N. D., Chen, S. C., and Pottie, G. J. (1995). Radio link admission algorithms for wireless networks with power control and active link quality protection. *IEEE*, pages 97–104.

Berruto, E., Gudmundson, M., Menolascino, R., Mohr, W., and Pizarroso, M. (1998). Research activities on UMTS radio interface, network architectures, and planning. *IEEE Communications Magazine*, 36(2):82–95.

Correia, L. M., editor (2001). *Wireless Flexible Personalised Communications – COST 259: European Co-operation in Mobile Radio Research*. John Wiley & Sons.

Ehrenberger, U. and Leibnitz, K. (1999). Impact of clustered traffic distributions in CDMA radio networks. Technical report, University of Würzburg, Germany.

Eisenblätter, A., Fügenschuh, A., Koch, T., Koster, A., Martin, A., Pfender, T., Wegel, O., and Wessäly, R. (2002). Mathematical model of feasible network configurations – Deliverable D 4.2. Technical report, IST-2000-28088 MOMENTUM.

Eisenblätter, A. (2001). *Frequency Assignment in GSM Networks: Models, Heuristics, and Lower Bounds*. Cuvillier Verlag, Göttingen, Germany.

Fallot-Josselin, S. (1998). Automatic radio network planning in the context of 3rd generation mobile systems. COST 259 (WG3) 98TD 102. Publication from AC016-STROMS.

Galota, M., Glaßer, C., Leibnitz, K., Reith, S., Tran-Gia, P., Vollmer, H., and Wagner, K. W. (2000a). Base station positioning in UMTS networks: an optimization framework. Technical report, University of Würzburg, Germany.

Galota, M., Glaßer, C., Reith, S., and Vollmer, H. (2000b). A polynomial-time approximation scheme for base station positioning in UMTS networks. Technical Report 264, University of Würzburg, Germany.

Holma, H., Honkasalo, Z., Haemaelaeinen, S., Laiho, J., Sipilä, K., and Wacker, A. (2001). *Radio Network Planning*, chapter 8, pages 149–182. In Holma and Toskala, 2001.

Holma, H. and Toskala, A. (2001). *WCDMA for UMTS*. John Wiley & Sons Ltd.

Howitt, I. and Seung-Yong, H. (1999). Base station location optimization. *IEEE Vehicular Technology Conference*, 4(50):2067–2071.

Hurley, S. (2000). Automatic base station selection and configuration in mobile networks. *IEEE Vehicular Technology Conference*, 6(52):2585–2592.

Ibbetson, L. J. and Lopes, L. B. (1997). An automatic base site placement algorithm. *IEEE Vehicular Technology Conference*, 2(47):760–764.

Konstantinopoulou, C. N., Koutsopoulos, K. A., Lyberopoulos, G. L., and Theologou, M. E. (2000). Core network planning, optimization and forecasting in GSM/GPRS networks. In *SCVT-200 Symposium on Communications and Vehicular Technology*, pages 55–61.

Koster, A. M. C. A. (1999). *Frequency Assignment - Models and Algorithms*. PhD thesis, Maastricht University, The Netherlands.

Laiho, J., Wacker, A., and Novosad, T., editors (2001). *Radio Network Planning and Optimization for UMTS*. John Wiley & Sons Ltd.

Lee, C. Y. and Kang, H. G. (2000). Cell planning with capacity expansions in mobile communications: A tabu search approach. *IEEE Vehicular Technology Conference*, 49(5):1678–1691.

Mathar, R. (2001). Mathematical modeling, design, and optimization of mobile communication networks. *DMV Jahresbericht*, 103(3):101–114.

Mathar, R. and Niessen, T. (2000). Optimum positioning of base stations for cellular radio networks. *Wireless Networks*, 6(6):421–428.

Mathar, R. and Schmeink, M. (2000). Optimal base station positioning and channel assignment for 3G mobile networks by integer programming. Technical report, RWTH Aachen, Germany.

Molina, A., Athanasiadou, G. E., and Nix, A. R. (1999). The automatic location of base-stations for optimised cellular coverage: a new combinatorial approach. *IEEE Vehicular Technology Conference*, 1(49):606–610.

Noblet, C. M. H., Owen, R. H., Saraiva, C., and Wahid, N. (2001). Assessing the effects of GSM cell location re-use for UMTS network. In *IEEE Second International Conference on 3G Mobile Communication Technologies*, pages 82–86.

Pasquale, A. D., Magnani, N. P., and Zanini, P. (1998). Optimizing frequency planning in the GSM system. In *IEEE 1998 International Conference on Universal Personal Communications*, volume 1, pages 293–297.

Schultz, R. (2001). Personal communication. Gerhard-Mercator Universität Duisburg, Germany.

Tutschku, K., Leibnitz, K., and Tran-Gia, P. (1997). ICEPT – An integrated cellular network planning tool. *IEEE Vehicular Technology Conference*, 2(47): 765–769.

Tutschku, K., Mathar, R., and Niessen, T. (1999). Interference minimization in wireless communication systems by optimal cell site selection. *3rd European Personal Mobile Communication Conference*.

Wong, J., Neve, M., and Sowerby, K. (2001). Optimisation strategy for wireless communications system planning using linear programming. *IEE Electronics Letters*, 37(17):1086–1087.

Chapter 2

OMNI-DIRECTIONAL CELL PLANNING

Roger M. Whitaker
Department of Computer Science
Cardiff University, UK
R.M.Whitaker@cs.cf.ac.uk

Steve Hurley
Department of Computer Science
Cardiff University, UK
S.Hurley@cs.cf.ac.uk

Abstract   The location and configuration of transmission infrastructure for cellular wire-less communication networks is a complex engineering task involving competing objectives. While minimising the number of locations used, adequate area coverage is required in addition to satisfying constraints concerning capacity and interference.

   We focus on the problem of commissioning omni-directional transmission equipment. This is particularly relevant to operators in the initial stages of network rollout. We address the problem of finding lower bounds on the minimum number of sites. An efficient technique for obtaining improved lower bounds on the minimum number of sites required for area coverage is presented. This approach also takes into account user defined interference and capacity constraints. Additionally, we present a unifying framework for cell planning when site selection and power configuration is required. Detailed computational results are presented and discussed.

Keywords: cell planning, network design, lower bounds

1.   Introduction

For cellular wireless network providers, the location and configuration of transmitters is a problem of fundamental importance. Fierce competition means that service providers are required to minimise the commitment to infrastructure while maintaining an adequate quality of service. Consequently, automated tools which can both assess the minimum number of sites needed and produce optimised cell plans are crucial.

Such software necessarily requires an estimate of radio wave propagation from potential sites. A prediction of potential radio traffic and its geographical distribution is also needed. Subsequently, procedures to select sites and configure infrastructure (e.g. allocate maximum radiated power for each transmitter) can be applied. Ideally, the transmitters should collectively provide a desired level of area coverage. This constitutes a region where the radiated signal power from antennae is received by listening equipment with sufficient power to be useful. At the same time, the total radio traffic serviced needs to be maximised, taking in to account capacity restrictions on transmitters.

Informally, a cell represents a region served by transmitter(s) at a single location. Cell planning is a necessary precursor to the allocation of radio spectrum to transmitters. Under the commonly used time division multiple access wireless protocols, this forms a separate and well studied optimisation problem called the channel assignment problem (Murphey et al., 1999). Geographically close transmitters require radio channels with adequate separation so that receiving equipment can filter out relatively strong unwanted signals. Despite being largely considered as an independent problem in the literature, frequency assignment considerations can be included in the cell planning process. Specifically, areas of multi-coverage can be restricted, as the associated transmitters are likely to require wide channel separation under such conditions. Avoiding multi-coverage will aid the re-use of channels within the network when channel assignment takes place.

1.1   Related Literature

Both the channel assignment and cell planning problems are NP-hard (Mathar and Niessen, 2000; Murphey et al., 1999) and consequently heuristic approaches are required for problem instances of a practical size. Meta-heuristics such as simulated annealing, genetic algorithms and tabu search have been applied to various specific cell planning scenarios. These include: indoor wireless systems (Fortune et al., 1995; Sherali et al., 1996), the placement of urban microcells (Tutschku, 1998; Molina et al., 2000), the GSM telephone service (Hurley, 2002; Ibbetson and Lopes, 1997), and broadband fixed wireless access systems (Allen et al., 2001). A more general model for the cell planning problem based on integer linear programming, has been given in Mathar and Niessen, 2000. A combination of exact methods, simulated annealing and greedy heuristics have been applied to these linear programming formulations. While the problem of area coverage receives much attention in the literature, fewer authors seek to resolve the issues of both area coverage and radio traffic simultaneously.

Despite cell planning being an *NP*-hard optimisation problem (Mathar and Niessen, 2000), it is often carried out as a manual task by frequency planners. Most commercial software packages aid this manual process, rather than performing cell planning. Algorithms may be designed to carry out cell planning in two different ways. The algorithm may focus on finding optimum cell plans for a given number of commissioned sites, as in Mathar and Niessen, 2000. This leaves the operator with the decision over how many sites to commission. Alternatively, cell planning algorithms may autonomously decide how many transmitter locations to commission, as in Ibbetson and Lopes, 1997. We call techniques with this property *automatic* cell planning algorithms.

In this paper we make a number of contributions. We concentrate on problems where location and power configuration of omni-directional equipment is required. Omni-directional transmitters radiate signals with equal power over 360°. This type of planning is particularly relevant in the initial stages of network roll out over a region, since increases in demand can be met by replacing omni-directional equipment with multiple directed beam antennae. However, omni-directional cell planning has received little explicit attention in the literature. We assume equipment operates using a frequency time division multiple access (FTDMA) protocol. FTDMA is widely used in mobile telephony (e.g. GSM Redl et al., 1995), private mobile radio networks (e.g. Macario, 1996) and broadband fixed wireless access systems (e.g. Allen et al., 2001).

In Section 2 we present a general cell planning model and explain the assumptions made. In Section 3, we introduce the problem of finding lower bounds on the number of sites required. In both automatic and non-automatic cell planning approaches, such estimates are very useful, but this problem has been over-shadowed by algorithms for the creation of cell plans. In Section 3, we formulate a graph based approach, and use a technique based on partial enumeration to obtain improved lower bounds on the minimum number of transmitter locations for large problem instances. Our approach incorporates both capacity and interference constraints as defined by the user.

In Section 4, we observe that all omni-directional cell plans may be interpreted using independent sets of vertices from a graph theoretic representation. This is useful in unifying and comparing cell planning algorithms presented in the literature. We extend the algorithm introduced in Section 3 to produce an effective automatic heuristic algorithm for cell planning, when site location and allocation of maximum radiated power is required. Detailed computational results are presented and discussed for simulated network planning scenarios of realistic size.

2.   A Model for Cell Plans

Candidate transmitter locations must be identified prior to selection and configuration. Service providers usually aspire to providing a service characterised by area coverage requirements, signal quality and an ability to handle peak capacity traffic requirements. These requirements can be formulated independently, through sampling at points within the region to be served. The set of points R, at which signal strength may be measured, are called *reception test points* (RTP). The set of points S at which a signal of usable strength is required are called *service test points* (STP). Additionally, teletraffic requirements are incorporated by estimating traffic demand at a set of locations, T, called *traffic test points* (TTP), and typically $T \subseteq S \subseteq R$. The subset of STP's adequately served by an individual transmitter is called a *cell*.

This model is based on that proposed in Reininger and Caminada, 1998a; Reininger and Caminada, 1998b for the European second generation GSM mobile telephone system, and is sufficiently general to subsume similar models proposed in the literature (e.g. Mathar and Niessen, 2000; Molina et al., 2000) for a variety of different systems where downlink planning is important (e.g. Allen et al., 2001).

2.1   Signal Propagation

Simulation of signal propagation is required to identify which test points can be serviced with an adequate strength signal. A variety of models have been proposed for this purpose such as Ikegami et al., 1984; Walfish and Bertoni, 1988. Each of these is based on the line-of-sight inverse square power law, with additional factors introduced to simulate propagation loss due to clutter, terrain and multi-path fading, for a variety of different transmission environments.

For purposes of experimentation, we have adopted the fundamental inverse square power law, although any of the other models could equally well be used in our approach. This means that the cells consist of STP's which are within a fixed radius r of the transmitter, where r is proportional to the power of the transmitter. Under this model, assigning power to transmitters is equivalent to assigning a maximum transmission radius, up to which the strength of a received signal is adequate.

2.2   Radio Traffic

The prospective level of radio traffic is an important factor for planning purposes. In all wireless systems, the level of traffic which can be carried through multiplexing is limited. This can prohibit cells from being large and therefore traffic distribution may increase the number of required antennae. Demand for calls can be measured in dimensionless units of Erlang, which characterise both the proportion of time and number of users requiring service at a particular location. Each TTP requires an estimate of demand in Erlangs, obtained in advance from traffic surveys. Clearly TTP's located at the most busy sites will be identifiable by higher associated traffic estimates.

The capacity of a transmitter is directly related to the number of channels it uses for communication. Table 2.1 shows the Erlang-B table, which predicts capacity assuming that blocked calls are dropped. The total traffic load carried in a cell is the sum of traffic from served TTPs. A cell is said to be *overloaded* if the traffic carried exceeds the permitted maximum.

Table 2.1. The amount of traffic carried with respect to number of channels.

Channels required	1	2	3	4	5	6	7	8
Erlang carried	2.9	8.2	15	22	28	35.5	43	58

2.3   Interference

STP's which can receive adequate strength signals from two or more antennae need to be carefully restricted. Not only should we consider restricting the total proportion of multi-covered STP's, but we need also consider the distribution of such points between cells. It is sensible to avoid pairs of cells which between them, cover too many common STP. To achieve this, we stipulate that for any pair of cells c_i, c_j, the number of STP's covered by both c_i and c_j should be less than some chosen proportion α of the STP covered in the smaller cell. We call proportion α the *interference threshold*. This parameter also affects the number of required transmitters.

3.   Estimating the Minimum Number of Sites Required

Lower bounds on the minimum number of sites required to service a region are very useful. This information can be used to estimate the required financial commitment and may also guide the cell planning process. Ideally, lower bounds need to be quick to obtain and reasonably accurate and informative. The only known published bounds are given in Allen et al., 2002 as follows. Throughout, for demonstration purposes, we assume that all cells can have the same maximum size and maximum capacity, although the lower bounds still apply if different maximum values are specified for individual cells.

Theorem 1 *Let max_{cov} denote the maximum size of a cell, in a region with n_{STP} service test points, where each STP is within the transmission range of at least one potential site. Then for 100% STP coverage the minimum number* *of transmitters, n_{trans}, satisfies:*

$$n_{trans} \geq \lceil \frac{n_{STP}}{max_{cov}} \rceil.$$

Proof: If the above inequality is not satisfied then there must be at least one transmitter covering more than max_{cov} STP, which is a contradiction.

Theorem 2 *Let max_{cap} be the maximum traffic capacity of each transmitter in a region with n_{TTP} traffic test points, where each TTP is within the transmission range of at least one potential site. Let e_i denote traffic from the ith TTP. Then if all traffic is to be carried, the minimum number of transmitters, n_{trans}, satisfies:*

$$n_{trans} \geq \lceil \frac{1}{max_{cap}} \sum_{i=1}^{n_{TTP}} e_i \rceil.$$

Proof: If the above inequality is not satisfied then there must be at least one transmitter serving more than max_{cap} Erlangs of traffic, which is a contradiction.

These lower bounds are potentially crude, since they do not take into account the topology of candidate sites. Note that all networks with the same number of both STP's and potential sites have the same lower bound by Theorem 1 and similarly for networks with the same number of both TTP's and potential sites by Theorem 2. It may not be possible to commission the predicted number of sites without violating constraints. This is shown in Figure 2.1 for Theorem 2. With a hypothetical max_{cap} value of 5 Erlangs, Theorem 2 infers that a minimum of two transmitters are required. However, commissioning both transmitters leads to a high level of multi-coverage, which is likely to violate a potential interference constraint.

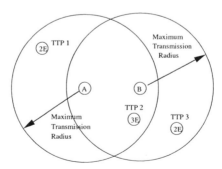

Figure 2.1. Two transmitters *A,B* in a capacitated network. Each TTP has a demand of 2,3,2 Erlangs respectively.

3.1   A Graph Based Approach

We derive an improved lower which takes into account interference, traffic demand and transmitter capacity given a maximum permitted transmission power p. Our approach is based on a labelled graph G_p whose vertices correspond to potential transmitter locations. This so-called *interference graph* can be regarded as a binary matrix $[\phi_{ij}]$ where $\phi_{i,j} = \phi_{j,i} = 1$ if commissioning transmitters i and j with power p leads to an interference constraint violation. Otherwise ϕ_{ij} is defined as zero. An example of such a graph is given in Figure 2.2.

$$\begin{pmatrix} 0 & 0 & 0 & 0 & 1 \\ 0 & 0 & 0 & 1 & 0 \\ 0 & 0 & 0 & 1 & 0 \\ 0 & 1 & 1 & 0 & 1 \\ 1 & 0 & 0 & 1 & 0 \end{pmatrix}$$

Figure 2.2.   A simple interference graph.

The use of graph based models for wireless networks dates back to at least the 1970's (Zoellner and Beall, 1977) where they were originally used for frequency assignment. More recently this approach has been explicitly used in cell planning (e.g. Chamaret and Condevaux-Lanloy, 1997; Chamaret et al., 1997). However, we extend this approach by labelling vertices to incorporate traffic capacity considerations. We assign a binary label, denoted *exclude*, to each vertex. This takes the value of 1 if the corresponding cell is above traffic capacity at power level p and takes the value zero otherwise. If *exclude* = 1, the corresponding vertex is said to be *excluded*.

An *independent set* of vertices in a graph is a subset of vertices such that no two members of the set are adjacent. Satisfying interference constraints corresponds to avoiding transmitters whose vertices in G_p are adjacent. Consequently independent sets are central to cell planning. Here we use independent sets to estimate lower bounds on the minimum required number of transmitters, as the following result states.

Theorem 3 *Let G_p denote an interference graph and let I be an independent set of vertices in G_p, with the property no $v \in I$ is excluded. Then, if the corresponding cellular network has no overloaded cells and no violated interference constraints, the minimum number of transmitters for maximum area coverage and maximum traffic capacity, n_{trans}, satisfies:*

$$n_{trans} \geq |I|.$$

Proof: We will show that the vertices in I correspond transmitters which once commissioned, form a cellular network with no overloaded cells or interference constraint violations. Since no $v \in I$ is excluded, commissioning the transmitter corresponding to v would not lead to an overloaded cell in the network. Also, every possible pair of distinct vertices in I are non-adjacent, since I is an independent set. Hence commissioning any pair of transmitters corresponding to vertices in I will not lead to an interference constraint violation. The minimum number of transmitters in the network is at least $|I|$ since I may not be a maximal set.

3.2   The Maximum Size of Independent Sets

Finding or estimating the size of a largest possible independent set of vertices I is an NP-complete problem which has been well-studied. It is equivalent to the well known *maximum clique problem* in graph theory which has received extensive attention in its own right. The reader is referred to a comprehensive survey given in Pardalos and Xue, 1994 for details of a wide range of algorithmic approaches to such problems. Problems concerning cliques, independent sets, set packing and covering (Borndorfer, 1998) frequently arise in telecommunication problems such as frequency assignment (e.g. Borndorfer et al., 1998; Murphey et al., 1999) and many ways of dealing with such problems have been proposed.

For our purposes, we are keen to adopt a computational approach which is suited to the needs of a typical end user who is likely to have available the use of a single processor on a laptop or PC. Ideally, the algorithm should find a guaranteed exact solution to small or medium size problems in a reasonable time frame. For larger problems, approximate solutions should be obtained rapidly. These needs have been reconciled by adopting a partial enumeration approach based on backtracking. Previously such enumeration has been considered intractable for problems of this nature (e.g. Molina et al., 1999) but progress has been made by using careful pruning. In Carraghan and Pardalos, 1990 such enumeration has been applied to the related maximum clique problem in graphs.

The algorithm uses the concept of *depth*. Each depth d, $d \geq 0$, is a list of transmitters denoted $t_{d,1}, \ldots, t_{d,i}, \ldots, t_{d,m_d}$. The notation $t_{d,i}$ identifies the ith transmitter in depth d. Depth 0 is a dummy list of transmitters only using to terminate the algorithm. Depth 1 is created by listing all the transmitters which are not excluded. A set of transmitters, $TRANS_{is}$, is maintained which form an independent set. The size of $TRANS_{is}$ is monitored as the algorithm progresses. The largest size attained up to the current iteration is recorded by the variable $CLIS$ (current largest independent set). Initially $TRANS_{is}$ contains only $t_{1,1}$. At each depth, the algorithm *expands* transmitters to create new depths where upon $TRANS_{is}$ and $CLIS$ are updated.

A transmitter $t_{d,i}$ is *expanded* by listing, in a new depth $d+1$, every transmitter $t_{d,i'}$, $(i' > i)$ which can be included with $t_{d,i}$ in the current $TRANS_{is}$. If no such transmitter exists then $t_{d,i}$ cannot be expanded, and $t_{d,i+1}$ is considered for expansion. If $t_{d,i}$ is expanded and a new depth $d + 1$ created, then $t_{d,i}$ is added to $TRANS_{is}$ and the next transmitter considered for expansion is $t_{d+1,1}$. The size of $TRANS_{is}$ is compared to $CLIS$, which is updated if required.

When all transmitters at a particular depth d have been considered for expansion we backtrack to the deepest previous depth d' ($d' < d$), such that d' contains a transmitter in position i' (i' minimal) which has not been considered for expansion. The set $TRANS_{is}$ is updated by removing any representatives belonging to depths $d', \ldots, d-1, d$, and depths $d'+1, \ldots, d-1, d$ are deleted.

The number of independent sets we consider is reduced by pruning. Note that when $d + (m_d - i) \leq CLIS$ the size of the largest independent set formed from expanding $t_{d,i}$ would be less than or equal to $CLIS$. Therefore we need only expand $t_{d,i}$ if $d + (m_d - i) > CLIS$. The algorithm terminates when we backtrack to the (dummy) depth 0 and the value $|I|$ is returned as $CLIS$. We give the pseudo-code for this algorithm in Figure 2.4. In Figure 2.3 we show the implementation of this algorithm for the interference graph in Figure 2.2.

		(boldface indicates the transmitter considered for expansion)
Depth 1:	t_a t_b t_c t_d t_e	$CLIS = 1$, $TRANS_{is} = \{t_a\}$
Depth 2:	t_b t_c t_d	$CLIS = 2$, $TRANS_{is} = \{t_a, t_b\}$
Depth 3:	t_c	$CLIS = 3$, not expandable
Depth 2:	t_b t_c t_d	$2 + (3 - 2) = CLIS$
Depth 2:	t_b t_c t_d	$2 + (3 - 3) < CLIS$
Depth 1:	t_a t_b t_c t_d t_e	$TRANS_{is} = \{t_b\}$
Depth 2:	t_c t_e	not expandable
Depth 2:	t_c t_e	not expandable
Depth 1:	t_a t_b t_c t_d t_e	$TRANS_{is} = \{t_c\}$, $1 + (5 - 3) = CLIS$
Depth 0:		Return $CLIS = 3$.

Figure 2.3. Determination of the largest independent set for the interference graph in Fig. 2.2 with 5 transmitters t_a, t_b, t_c, t_d, t_e (none are excluded).

3.3 Test Problems

The algorithm in Figure 2.4 has been implemented on a number of large scale test problems generated at random (see Table 2.2). In each case, the STP have been defined on a regular mesh with 100m intervals. Traffic test points have been chosen at a subset of STP locations. Call demand has been randomly allocated to TTP's. Traffic scenarios simulating light, moderate and heavy demand have been created (see Table 2.3). The number of TTP have been selected only for test purposes. Plots of numerous test cases are given in Figures 2.6, 2.8 and 2.10.

The difference between the bounds in Theorems 1,2 and 3 are shown in Figures 2.5 ,2.7 and 2.9 for particular network scenarios. The performance of these bounds over the possible range of interference thresholds ($0 \leq \alpha \leq 1$)

```
Create depth 1;
Set d = 1; Set i = 1;
Set CLIS = 1, TRANSᵢₛ = {};

while d > 0 do
    if (d + (mₐ − i) > CLIS) and (tₐ,ᵢ expandable) then
        Create depth d + 1;
        TRANSᵢₛ = TRANSᵢₛ + tₐ,ᵢ;
        if |TRANSᵢₛ| + 1 > CLIS then
            CLIS = d + 1;
        end if
        Set d = d + 1;
        Set i = 1;
    else
        if i < mₐ then
            i = i + 1;
        else
            Locate the deepest previous depth d', (d' < d) containing a transmitter in position i' (i' minimal)
            which has not been considered for expansion at that depth. Remove representative transmitters
            belonging to depths d', ... , d − 1, d from TRANSᵢₛ.
            Remove depths d' + 1, ... , d − 1, d.
            Set d = d';
            Set i = i';
        end if
    end if
    Return CLIS.
end while
```

Figure 2.4. A backtracking routine to calculate $|I|$, the size of the largest independent set.

Table 2.2. Summary of problem instances

Region	Size (km)	Number of Sites	Number of STP
A	15 × 15	15	22,801
B	15 × 15	25	22,801
C	30 × 30	60	90,601
D	30 × 30	90	90,601
E	45 × 45	120	203,401
F	45 × 45	180	203,401

is given. A transmitter capacity limit of 43 Erlangs has been used in all cases,
when is realistic for typical GSM networks.

The computation time taken for these examples are up to 600 seconds, using
a Pentium III 850 Mhz PC running C code. All test cases have been exhaustively
completed using the algorithm in Figure 2.4, except for the cases involving 120
or more potential sites. In these cases, only the instances with $\alpha = 1.0$ have

Table 2.3. Summary of different traffic profiles

Region	Identifier	Traffic Total (E)	No. of TTP	TTP Traffic (Erlangs)			Traffic per km^2
				Lowest	Highest	Average	
A, B	$T_{A,low}$	171.29	395	0.00001	1.68	0.43	0.76
	$T_{A,med}$	305.43	395	0.00001	3.08	0.77	1.35
	$T_{A,high}$	471.90	395	0.00001	4.86	1.19	2.09
C, D	$T_{B,low}$	571.81	699	0.00001	5.90	0.83	0.64
	$T_{B,med}$	1194.05	699	0.00002	9.79	1.71	1.33
	$T_{B,high}$	1836.75	699	0.00007	10.76	2.62	2.04
E, F	$T_{E,low}$	1406.35	1399	0.0001	3.18	1.01	0.69
	$T_{E,med}$	2734.31	1399	0.0001	7.35	2.71	1.35
	$T_{E,high}$	4176.83	1399	0.0001	12.21	2.98	2.06

been completed exactly. In the remaining instances, the backtracking algorithm was terminated after 40 million iterations.

Figures 2.5, 2.7 and 2.9 show that as the interference threshold increases, greater multi-coverage is permitted between cells, which increases the required number of sites. This factor, along with the particular location of candidate sites, is not taken into account by the bounds given in Theorems 1 and 2, which remain constant independent of potential site locations, location of traffic test points and interference constraints. Note that it may not be possible to realise the lower bounds given by Theorems 1 and 2 when these factors are considered. Consequently Theorems 1 and 2 may be open to mis-interpretation.

4. Cell Planning with Independent Sets

We observe that any omni-directional cell plan may be decomposed into independent sets of interference graphs in an obvious way. Let $p_1, p_2, \ldots, p_k$ represent the different maximum power values assigned to transmitters. If we assume that no interference constraints are violated and no transmitters are overloaded, then the transmitters assigned maximum power p_j form an independent set (denoted I_j) in the interference graph G_{p_j}. Algorithms proposed for automatic cell planning are unified by the common objective of finding independent sets $I_1, I_2, \ldots, I_k$ from the interference graphs $G_{p_1}, G_{p_2}, \ldots, G_{p_k}$. The objective is to find independent sets with the following properties:

- if $v_i \in I_i$, $v_j \in I_j$ then the transmitters corresponding to v_i, v_j do not violate an interference constraint.

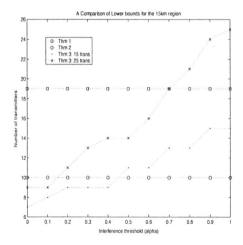

Figure 2.5.   Effects of varying the interference threshold for the lower bounds on regions A, B with traffic scenario $T_{A,med}$.

Figure 2.6.   Position of transmitters and traffic test points for region A with traffic scenario $T_{A,med}$. Large white locations represent candidate transmitter locations. Other locations are TTPs.

- each set $I_1, I_2, \ldots, I_k$ is *maximal*, that is the addition of a vertex to any of the independent sets would lead to an interference constraint violation.

- the number of vertices in $I_1 \cup I_2 \cup \cdots \cup I_k$ is as small as possible.

Based on these observations, we propose a heuristic approach to cell planning by extending the approach presented in Figure 2.4.

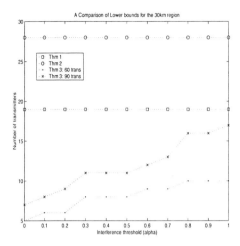

Figure 2.7. Effects of varying the interference threshold for the lower bounds on regions C, D with traffic scenario $T_{C,med}$.

Figure 2.8. Position of transmitters and traffic test points for region C with traffic scenario $C_{C,med}$. Large white locations represent candidate transmitter locations. Other locations are TTPs.

4.1 The Algorithm

We assume that a range of maximum power settings are available for assignment to potential transmitters, denoted $p_1, p_2, \ldots, p_k$, in decreasing order of magnitude. We also define a range of interference thresholds $\alpha_1, \alpha_2, \ldots, \alpha_k$, in correspondence with the maximum power settings. Independent sets of ver-

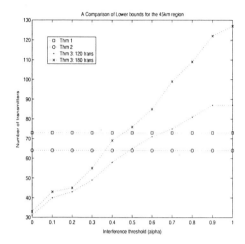

Figure 2.9.   Effects of varying the interference threshold for the lower bounds on regions E, F with traffic scenario $T_{E,med}$.

Figure 2.10.   Position of transmitters and traffic test points for region E with traffic scenario $C_{E,med}$. Large white locations represent candidate transmitter locations. Other locations are TTPs.

tices $I_1, I_2, \ldots, I_k$ are selected in sequence by repeatedly applying the approach presented in Figure 2.4. This means that we initially commission high powered transmitters, with maximum power setting p_1, followed by progressively lower power transmitters, down to a maximum power setting of p_k. Additionally we aim to chose independence sets which correspond to transmitters with desirable traffic characteristics.

At each iteration j, we need to generate the interference graph G_{p_j} taking into account the independent sets $I_1, I_2, \ldots, I_{j-1}$ which have been selected previously. In particular, if transmitter r is already commissioned, say with power p_i ($i < j$) then G_{p_j} is created using the threshold α_j with the following additional constraints:

- the vertex corresponding to r is labelled "exclude".

- $\phi_{r,s} = \phi_{s,r} = 1$ if operating transmitter r with power p_i and transmitter s with power p_j would lead to an interference constraint violation when using the threshold α_j.

Given G_{p_j}, we create I_j as a maximal independent set of non-excluded vertices whose transmitters can potentially serve the greatest total traffic. The procedure in Figure 2.4 for finding the size of I_j needs only slight modification. Specifically we search for an independent set of largest possible size and update the current set recorded if one is found which improves the total traffic carried. We order the transmitters in depth 1 by the amount of traffic that they serve, in a bid to include those with the greatest capacity in the largest independent set as soon as possible. This is particularly useful when the algorithm is terminated before completion. Note that defining a range of interference thresholds $\alpha_1, \alpha_2, \ldots, \alpha_k$ allows us to vary the maximum proportion of multi-coverage at different maximum power settings. The approach we use is summarised in Figure 2.11.

Define max. power settings $p_1, p_2, \ldots, p_k$
Define interference thresholds $\alpha_1, \alpha_2, \ldots, \alpha_k$

for $i = 1$ to k **do**
    Generate G_{p_i} using the threshold α_i, taking into account $I_1, I_2, \ldots, I_{i-1}$
    Find a maximal I_i with greatest traffic capacity using backtracking (Fig. 2.4)
end for

Figure 2.11. Finding independence sets for cell planning.

4.2 Results

Based on the test problems in Tables 2.2 and 2.3, cells plans have been obtained using the approach in Figure 2.11, using a range of input parameters relating to traffic scenario and setting of interference thresholds. Details of the input parameters used in each of the 18 test cases are shown in Table 2.4. Throughout, a largest maximum power setting (denoted p_1) provides a transmission range of 6km. Five possible maximum power settings have been defined ($p_1, \ldots, p_5$), with each additional setting providing a transmission range reduced by 1.2km. Throughout, the interference thresholds have been set low for high maximum power settings, and increased for the lower power settings. This has been adopted to avoid large regions of multi-coverage between cells served by high power transmitters.

In Table 2.5, statistics about the resultant cell plan are given, for each of the 18 test cases. These relate to number of transmitters commissioned, STP and TTP coverage and traffic carried. The proportion of STP's covered is recorded in column 8, and the proportion of those which are covered more than once is given in column 9. The proportion of TTP's covered is given in column 10 and the proportion of total traffic carried is in column 11. The average traffic load across commissioned transmitters in given in column 12. Details on the number of transmitters commissioned at each power setting is given in columns 2-7.

In Table 2.6, further information is given about the test cases. Information on lower bounds for each test case is given. Specifically, the results from applying Theorems 1 and 2 are presented. The results after applying Theorem 3 with each possible power setting are recorded. Those values indicated by an asterisk have been produced by terminating the algorithm in Figure 2.4 after 40 million iterations. Other values have been obtained by running the algorithm in Figure 2.4 to completion.

The effects of having more transmitters available in a region can be seen by comparing those scenarios involving A with those involving B, and similarly for $C, D,$ and E, F in Table 2.4. Generally, increasing the number of candidate transmitter locations increases the potential for coverage. However, this is also dependent on the specific distribution of candidate site locations. The effects of increased traffic can be clearly seen in the results for each region considered. As traffic increases, the number of transmitters commissioned at high maximum power settings decrease. Also, the total number of transmitters commissioned increases. Notice also that in test cases for regions E, F, the potential for interference (i.e. multicovered STPs) has increased. This is due to the higher levels of permitted interference defined by the interference thresholds $\alpha_1, \ldots, \alpha_5$.

Generally, omni-directional cell planning will be carried out under relatively light traffic conditions, at the initial stages of network roll-out. Under conditions of high traffic demand, omni-directional cell planning should take place with increased capacity at potential sites, representing the potential combined capacity of multiple directed antennae. Such equipment can be deployed and configured at individual sites where traffic demand is high. In Figures 2.12, 2.13, 2.14 we show pictures representing the cell plans produced for test cases F_l, F_m and F_h. These pictures show the effects of planning with insufficient capacity at potential sites. Areas which are covered and multi-covered are clearly shown. Uncovered traffic test points are indicated and the potential candidate locations are indicated in the cells in black.

Table 2.4. Specification of input parameters for cell planning test problems using 5 power settings and a maximum transmission range of 6km.

Test Case	Region	Traffic Scenario	Trans. Capacity (E)	Interference Threshold				
				α_1	α_2	α_3	α_4	α_5
A_l	A	$T_{A,low}$	43	0.1	0.1	0.2	0.2	0.2
A_m		$T_{A,med}$	43	0.1	0.1	0.2	0.2	0.2
A_h		$T_{A,high}$	43	0.1	0.1	0.2	0.2	0.2
B_l	B	$T_{A,low}$	43	0.1	0.1	0.2	0.2	0.2
B_m		$T_{A,med}$	43	0.1	0.1	0.2	0.2	0.2
B_h		$T_{A,high}$	43	0.1	0.1	0.2	0.2	0.2
C_l	C	$T_{C,low}$	43	0.1	0.1	0.2	0.2	0.2
C_m		$T_{C,med}$	43	0.1	0.1	0.2	0.2	0.2
C_h		$T_{C,high}$	43	0.1	0.1	0.2	0.2	0.2
D_l	D	$T_{C,low}$	43	0.1	0.1	0.2	0.2	0.2
D_m		$T_{C,med}$	43	0.1	0.1	0.2	0.2	0.2
D_h		$T_{C,high}$	43	0.1	0.1	0.2	0.2	0.2
E_l	E	$T_{E,low}$	58	0.2	0.2	0.2	0.3	0.3
E_m		$T_{E,med}$	58	0.2	0.2	0.2	0.3	0.3
E_h		$T_{E,high}$	58	0.2	0.2	0.2	0.3	0.3
F_l	F	$T_{E,low}$	58	0.2	0.2	0.2	0.3	0.3
F_m		$T_{E,med}$	58	0.2	0.2	0.2	0.3	0.3
F_h		$T_{E,high}$	58	0.2	0.2	0.2	0.3	0.3

Table 2.5. Number and power of transmitters commissioned, with coverage and capacity information for the networks produced.

Test Case	Number of Trans. Commissioned at:					STP Covered: once %	STP Covered: more %	TTP Cover %	Traffic Load %	Mean Load (E)	Time (secs)
	p_1	p_2	p_3	p_4	p_5						
A_l	2	2	0	0	0	86.7	2.4	85.1	87.5	37.5	10
A_m	0	1	3	2	2	65.3	2.7	65.5	67.3	25.7	9
A_h	0	0	1	6	2	53.5	1.8	52.1	53.9	28.3	7
B_l	3	0	1	0	0	83.9	0.5	83.0	84.5	36.2	9
B_m	0	1	4	2	0	73.9	4.0	72.9	74.5	32.6	9
B_h	0	0	1	8	1	65.2	3.1	65.0	66.2	31.2	8
C_l	5	4	3	2	3	78.1	0.5	79.1	78.7	26.5	64
C_m	0	1	9	9	6	57.3	2.1	55.5	53.5	25.6	62
C_h	0	0	3	19	8	46.3	2.6	43.9	41.3	25.3	62
D_l	5	4	5	1	1	82.3	6.1	82.9	81.7	29.2	114
D_m	0	1	13	13	9	73.6	6.3	75.9	73.5	24.4	112
D_h	0	0	3	27	8	59.4	4.2	58.5	55.7	26.9	131
E_l	11	12	3	8	0	87.7	9.4	86.9	86.1	35.6	277
E_m	1	8	22	15	4	69.4	6.8	68.9	65.4	35.7	265
E_h	0	4	9	45	7	57.9	5.5	56.2	52.4	33.7	339
F_l	13	15	1	4	5	91.9	14.9	91.9	90.7	33.6	476
F_m	1	9	23	21	7	76.8	9.4	77.9	76.6	34.3	532
F_h	0	4	12	52	13	67.8	8.0	66.8	65.0	33.5	740

Table 2.6. Performance of lower bounds on the number of transmitters required.

Test Case	Thm 1 (STP)	Thm 2 (TTP)	Thm 3 with power:				
			p_1	p_2	p_3	p_4	p_5
A_l	3	4	2	4	4	8	11
A_m	3	8	0	1	4	8	11
A_h	3	11	0	0	1	7	11
B_l	3	4	3	4	6	9	14
B_m	3	8	0	1	5	9	14
B_h	3	11	0	0	1	9	14
C_l	9	14	5	11	19^*	31^*	50^*
C_m	9	28	0	1	11	31^*	50^*
C_h	9	43	0	0	3	25	50^*
D_l	9	14	5	12	22	37^*	67^*
D_m	9	28	0	1	14	37^*	67^*
D_h	9	43	0	0	3	31^*	67^*
E_l	19	25	11	27^*	47^*	72^*	103^*
E_m	19	48	1	9	38^*	71^*	103^*
E_h	19	73	0	4	16	69^*	103^*
F_l	19	25	13	27^*	51^*	92^*	149^*
F_m	19	48	1	10	41^*	91^*	149^*
F_h	19	73	0	4	19	86^*	149^*

In these test cases, the same potential sites are available and transmitter capacity remains fixed (58 Erlangs). However traffic demand progressively increases. Total demand in test case F_l is 1406.35 Erlangs. This increases to 2734.31 Erlangs in test case F_m and test case F_h has 4176.83 Erlangs of traffic. It is clearly shown in Figures 2.12, 2.13, 2.14 that coverage suffers (particularly in Figure 2.14) as only small cells can be commissioned. Larger cells would lead to overloading and dropped calls. This can also be seen in the independent set bound (Table 2.6), where there is a reduction in the number of possible sites which can be commissioned at high maximum power values.

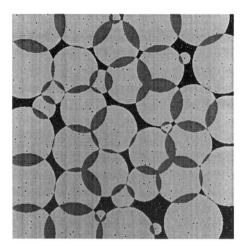

Figure 2.12.   Cell plan produced for test case F_l.

5.   Conclusions

When designing cellular wireless communication networks, the location and configuration of transmission infrastructure is a fundamental problem. In this paper we have considered and focussed on the problem when omni-directional equipment is used. A graph theoretic model has been used to derive improved lower bounds on the minimum number of sites, taking into account coverage, traffic and interference objectives. Such lower bounds are useful in estimating the required financial commitment prior to cell planning and can be used to assess operational cell plans. The approach proposed takes into account the topology of the network. Additionally, a framework based on independent sets from a graph based model has been proposed. Detailed computational results have been presented for a variety of test problems.

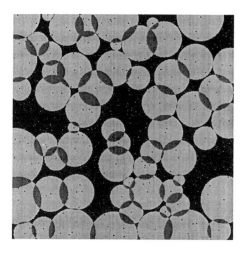

Figure 2.13. Cell plan produced for test case F_m.

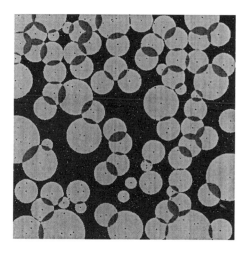

Figure 2.14. Cell plan produced for test case F_h.

References

Allen, S., Hurley, S., Taplin, R., and Whitaker, R. (2001). Automatic cell planning of broadband fixed wireless networks. In *Proceedings of the IEEE VTC Conference (Spring)*, pages 2808–2812, Rhodes, Greece.

Allen, S., Hurley, S., and Whitaker, R. (to appear, 2002). Cell planning and network design. In Hurley, S. and Leese, R., editors, *Methods and Algorithms for Radio Channel Assignment*, chapter 7. Open University Press.

Borndorfer, R., editor (1998). *Aspects of set packing, partitioning and covering*. Shaker, Aachen.

Borndorfer, R., Eisenblatter, A., Grotschel, M., and Martin, A. (1998). Frequency assignment in cellular phone networks. *Annals of Operations Research*, 76:73–93.

Carraghan, R. and Pardalos, P. (1990). An exact algorithm for the maximum clique problem. *Operations Research Letters*, 9:375–382.

Chamaret, B. and Condevaux-Lanloy, C. (1997). Graph based modeling for automatic transmitter location in cellular networks.

Chamaret, B., Josselin, S., Kuonen, P., Pizarroso, M., Salas-Manzanedo, B., Ubeda, S., and Wagner, D. (1997). Radio network optimization with maximum independent set search. In *Proceedings of the IEEE VTC'97 Conference*, pages 770–774, Phoenix, AZ.

Fortune, S. J., Gay, D. M., Kernighan, B. W., Landron, O., Valenzuela, R. A., and Wright, M. H. (1995). Wise design of indoor wireless systems. *IEEE Computational Science and Engineering*, 2(1):58–68.

Hurley, S. (2002). Planning effective cellular mobile radio networks. *IEEE Transactions on Vehicular Technology*, 51(2):243–253.

Ibbetson, L. and Lopes, L. (1997). An automatic base station placement algorithm. In *Proceedings of the IEEE VTC'97 Conference*, pages 770–774, Phoenix, AZ.

Ikegami, F., Yoshida, S., Takeuchi, T., and Umehira, M. (1984). Propagation factors controling mean field strength on urban streets. *IEEE Transactions on Antennas and Propagation*, AP-32:822–829.

Macario, R. (1996). *Modern Personal Radio Systems*. IEE, London.

Mathar, R. and Niessen, T. (2000). Optimum positioning of base stations for cellular radio networks. *Wireless Networks*, 6:421–428.

Molina, A., Athanasiadou, G., and Nix, A. (1999). The automatic location of base-stations for optimised cellular coverage: A new combinatorial approach. In *Proceedings of the IEEE VTC'99 Conference*, pages 606–610.

Molina, A., Athanasiadou, G., and Nix, A. (2000). Optimised base-station location algorithm for next generation microcellular networks. *Electronics Letters*, 36(7):668–669.

Murphey, R., Pardalos, P., and Resende, M. (1999). Frequency assignment problems. In Du, D. and Pardalos, P., editors, *Handbook of Combinatorial Optimization*, chapter 6. Kluwer Academic Publishers, Netherlands.

Pardalos, P. and Xue, J. (1994). The maximum clique problem. *Journal of Global Optimization*, 4:301–328.

Redl, S., Weber, M., and Oliphant, M. (1995). *An Introduction to* GSM. Artech House.

Reininger, P. and Caminada, A. (1998a). Connectivity management on mobile network design. In *10th Conference of the European Consortium for Mathematics in Industry ECMI-98*, Goteborg, Sweden.

Reininger, P. and Caminada, A. (1998b). Model for GSM radio network optimisation. In *2nd ACM International Conference on Discrete Algorithms and Methods for Mobility*, Dallas USA.

Sherali, H., Pendyala, C., and Rappaport, T. (1996). Optimal location of transmitters for micro-cellular radio communication system design. *IEEE Journal on Selected Areas in Communications*, 14(4):662–673.

Tutschku, K. (1998). Interference minimization using automatic design of cellular communication networks. In *Proceedings of the IEEE VTC'98 Conference*, pages 634–638.

Walfish, J. and Bertoni, H. (1988). A theoretical model of UHF propagation in urban environments. *IEEE Transactions on Antennas and Propagation*, AP-38:1788–1796.

Zoellner, J. and Beall, C. (1977). A breakthrough in spectrum conserving frequency assignment technology. *IEEE Transactions on Electromagnetic Compatability*, EMC-19:313–319.

Chapter 3

OPTIMAL DESIGN OF WIRELESS AD-HOC NETWORKS

Shin-yi Wu and G. Anandalingam
Operations and Information Management Department, The Wharton School, University of Pennsylvania, 500 Jon M. Huntsman Hall, Philadelphia, PA 19104-6340, USA, shinwu@wharton.upenn.edu

Decision and Information Technologies Department, Robert H. Smith School of Business, University of Maryland, Van Munching Hall, College Park, MD 20742, USA, ganand@rhsmith.umd.edu

Abstract   This paper investigates the optimal design and deployment of wireless ad-hoc networks. Wireless ad-hoc networks are a new form of wireless communications that do not rely on any fixed infrastructure like wired base stations to keep the network up and running. Instead, hosts in a wireless ad-hoc network rely on each other to keep the network connected over either radio or infrared. Since direct communication is allowed only between adjacent nodes, distant nodes in an ad-hoc network communicate over multiple hops. We examine the optimal design of such networks by modeling the problem as a mixed integer mathematical program, and deriving solution procedures based on Lagrangean Relaxation (LR). Using the LR, we were able to decompose the network design problem into two fairly-easy-to-solve sub-problems. We present algorithms for each sub-problem, and an overall heuristic based on LR to solve the design problem. From the computational experiments we have done, our Lagrangean relaxation based algorithms can generate solutions within 2.20-13.16% of optimality. In addition, our algorithm also solves the design problem very rapidly, within a few minutes in the most complex case.

Keywords   Wireless Ad-hoc Network, Network Design, Integer Programming, Lagrangean Relaxation, Subgradient Method, Heuristic

1. INTRODUCTION

When it comes to wireless networking, most people think of cell phones and wireless cellular networks. However, a new wireless networking paradigm is emerging that has vast ranging implications: wireless ad-hoc networks. Unlike traditional wireless cellular networks, wireless ad-hoc networks do not rely on any fixed infrastructure like wired base stations to keep the network up and running. Instead, hosts in a wireless ad-hoc network rely on each other to keep the network connected over either radio or infrared. Since direct communication is allowed only between adjacent nodes, distant nodes in an ad-hoc network communicate over multiple hops.

Although military tactical and other security-sensitive operations are still the main applications of ad-hoc networks, there is a trend to adopt ad-hoc networks for commercial uses, from the conventional narrow-band applications up to the emergent broadband services, due to their unique properties. Examples where ad-hoc networking can affect significant benefits include but are not limited to the following applications (Corson et al. 1999):

- *The digital battlefield*: soldiers who need to communicate with each other are deployed over an unfamiliar terrain where no fixed network infrastructure exists or has failed.
- *Disaster relief*: a large amount of disposable sensors are scattered into an unlivable circumstance to collect background data in the events like earthquakes, nuclear disasters, airplane disasters, etc. The sensors coordinate to establish a communications network and then send the data back to the master-site which has abundant power supply and computation capability for more intensive analysis.
- *Wireless office LAN connections*: different office entities (intelligent devices like PCs, notebooks, mobile phones, PDAs etc.) that want to communicate with each other form a temporary network without cabling, and use each participating node as both host and router to facilitate the process.

There has been considerable amount of work on wireless ad-hoc networks (Corson et al. 1999), and most of it has focused on routing protocols. Traditionally these routing protocols are evaluated in terms of packet loss rates, routing message overhead, and routing length (Iwata et al. 1999, Gafni and Bertsekas 1981, Chlamtac and Farago 1999, Sharony 1996). However, since most of the communication devices in wireless ad-hoc networks rely on batteries for energy, power consumption should be a critical design criterion as well. The main idea is that significant reductions in energy consumption can be achieved if wireless networks are designed specifically for minimum energy consumption.

There have been some studies on energy conserving routing as well (Lal and Sousa 1999, Rodoplu and Meng 1999). Nevertheless, all of these algorithms are conducted in a "local" fashion. While the local nature of the algorithms makes them robust because route discovery is done through local interactions, localized algorithms may utilize more energy than necessary. Sub-optimal energy consumption happens because nodes in a localized algorithm inherently "see" only local states, and thus may be forced into local maxima or minima. This may result in inefficient use of the limited power that is a particularity of wireless ad-hoc networking devices.

In fact, distributed resource allocation algorithm for wireless ad-hoc networks is not a necessity but only one of the alternatives. For example, in a multi-sensor network, if the master-site has a chance to know the locations of the sensors in the network, it can keep track of the whole system and a globally optimal resource allocation can be done in a centralized manner.

In this paper, we present an optimization-based algorithm to set up and maintain a wireless multi-sensor ad-hoc network. We assume that battery-powered sensors are scattered over a two-dimensional area and all of them are assumed to have transmission and reception capabilities. In addition, each of these sensors is assumed to come with a low-power global positioning system (GPS) receiver, which enables the sensor to provide accurate position information about itself. The recent low-power implementation of a GPS receiver makes its presence a viable option (Rodoplu and Meng 1999).

There are two major design issues in our research: First, the choice of active sensor nodes in the ad-hoc network. Since the locations of the air-scattered sensors can't be determined in advance and some of the sensors may be dropped in a "dead zone" where no useful data is available or they are simply out of order after the airdrop, we have to decide which sensors are going to be included in the final network. This could be done based on the node value at each sensor. In a situation where sensors have been dropped into an earthquake-damaged area, the node value could depend on factors like battery life remaining, distance from the nearest sensor, the distance from the epicenter etc. Second, we also have to decide the global optimal routing to forward the data back to the master-site.

The key point here is that only those sensors which can play a positive role (either those which can collect useful data or those which are critical in forwarding useful data to the master-site) should be included in the final network. Remember that, in a multi-sensor ad-hoc network, a sensor consumes its battery power not only when it is collecting background data but also when it is forwarding the data packets for its neighbor nodes. Clearly, we don't want to waste our limited energy to forward the data packet from those not so important nodes.

In this paper, we consider the following scenario: after the airdrop, those surviving sensors report their accurate locations via GPS to the master-site (this could be done by some algorithms like flooding and is beyond the scope of this paper). The master-site collects the location data, calculates the optimal routing of the whole network, distributes the notices to those on-duty sensors and starts to collect useful background data from those subordinate sensors.

This paper is organized as follows: In Section 2 we describe the mathematical model for designing ad-hoc networks. In Section 3, we present the solution approach for solving the different sub-problems and the overall problem. In Section 4 we present a method for getting some feasible solution to the problem using simple heuristics. We present the results of our algorithmic approach for solving both a simple problem and a number of different design problems in Section 5. We end the paper with some concluding remarks in Section 6.

2.   PROBLEM FORMULATION

As mentioned in the introduction, the design objective of the ad-hoc network in this paper is to maximize the net benefit of the data collected by the sensors in the network. This net benefit could be calculated as the difference between the data value and the cost of obtaining the data (e.g. energy consumption). In this section, we present the mathematical model for designing such ad-hoc networks.

2.1   Notation

Before we present the mathematical programming formulation of the wireless ad-hoc network design problem, we will provide a definition of the variables and parameters used in the model.

Given Parameters:
D_{ij}: physical distance between surviving node i and j
N: the set of all surviving nodes
n: the number of nodes in N besides master site (node 0)
p: path loss exponent
R: the largest power radius of the node (assumed to be the same for each node)
r: power consumption (in mW) at a node to receive and store a packet from another node. It is assumed to be a fixed number in this paper.
t: the predetection threshold (in mW) at each node

V_i: value of each data packet collected by node i. In this paper, we assume this value is a function of the node location (e.g. the reciprocal of the distance between this node and the epicenter) and once we know the location of the node, the node value is determined.

W: a weight to convert energy (in mW) to the unit of V_i.

Decision Variables:

b_0: a dummy variable that is interpreted as the amount of data packets that flow out of the network through the master-site (node 0) in each time unit

b_i: a dummy variable which is interpreted as the number of data packets (0 or 1) generated at node i ($i \neq 0$) in each time unit

c_i: the cost (power consumption in mW) to include surviving node i into the final network

f_{ij}: the amount of data packets transmitted from node i to node j in each time unit

x_i: the decision variable that is 1 if node i is included in the final network and 0 otherwise

y_{ij}: the decision variable which is 1 if there is a connection between node i and node j in the final network and 0 otherwise. Note that y_{ij} and y_{ji} have the same meaning and y_{ii} is meaningless in this model.

2.2 Mathematical Model of the Design Problem

By using mathematical programming techniques, we can transform the optimal design problem for wireless ad-hoc networks as the following mathematical formulation (Wu and Lin 1999, Wu and Anandalingam 2002).

Primal Problem IP:

$$\text{Max} \sum_{i \in N} (V_i - W c_i) x_i \quad or \quad \text{Min} \sum_{i \in N} (W c_i - V_i) x_i \quad (1)$$

s.t.

$$D_{ij} y_{ij} \leq R, \quad \forall i, j \in N \tag{2}$$

$$y_{ij} \leq x_i, \quad \forall i, j \in N \tag{3}$$

$$y_{ij} \leq x_j, \quad \forall i, j \in N \tag{4}$$

$$x_i \leq \sum_{j \in N} y_{ij}, \quad \forall i \in N \tag{5}$$

$$\sum_{i \in N} \sum_{j \in N} y_{ij} = 2 \left(\sum_{i \in N} x_i - 1 \right) \tag{6}$$

$$b_0 = -\sum_{i \in N} x_i + 1 \qquad (7)$$

$$-n \le b_0 \le 0 \qquad (8)$$

$$b_i = x_i, \quad \forall i \in N, i \ne 0 \qquad (9)$$

$$b_i + \sum_{j \in N} f_{ji} = \sum_{j \in N} f_{ij}, \quad \forall i \in N \qquad (10)$$

$$0 \le f_{ij} \le n y_{ij}, \quad \forall i, j \in N \qquad (11)$$

$$c_i = \sum_{j \in N} \left(f_{ij} \cdot t D_{ij}^{\ p} \right) + r \sum_{j \in N} f_{ji}, \quad \forall i \in N \qquad (12)$$

$$0 \le c_i \le n \left(t R^p + r \right), \quad \forall i \in N \qquad (13)$$

$$x_i = 0 \text{ or } 1, \quad \forall i \in N, i \ne 0 \qquad (14)$$

$$x_0 = 1 \qquad (15)$$

$$y_{ij} = 0 \text{ or } 1, \quad \forall i, j \in N, i \ne j \qquad (16).$$

The objective function is to maximize the sum of the net benefit in each time unit by including the nodes in the final network. Because the unit of the node value V_i may be different from the unit of the node cost c_i (in mW), we put a weight W in front of c_i to adjust it. This setting has the following benefits. If we want our network to work in a power-conserving mode and work longer, we can achieve this by enhancing the weight W. Otherwise, if we are eager to get real time data regardless how much power consumption will be, we can simply lower the weight W. In other words, W is an application-dependent parameter. In addition, we can calculate c_i in the following way. Assume each sensor collects just one data packet in each time unit and sends it back to the master-site for processing. Then for node i in this specific position in the network, c_i is the amount of energy it must consume to receive and forward the packets passing through it in this time unit.

We will now explain each constraint in detail. Constraint (2) ensures that the physical distance between node i and node j is shorter than the largest power radius of the nodes before we can connect them in the final network. Constraint (3) and (4) ensure that we have included node i and j into the final network before we can connect them together.

Constraint (5) ensures that if node i is included in the final network, it must be connected to some other node in the network; in other words, it cannot be isolated. Constraint (6) ensures the tree structure in the final network (# of arcs is equal to # of nodes in the network minus one). Although the tree structure is not a very reliable topology, it is indeed a very cost efficient one.

Constraint (7) guarantees that if we assume each node (except node *0*) in the network collects just one data packet in each time unit and sends it to node *0* through the network structure, then the amount of data packets that flow out of the network through the master-site (node *0*) in this time unit is equal to "# of nodes in the final network except node *0*."

Constraint (8) sets the boundaries of dummy variable b_0. Constraint (9) ensures that if we include node *i* in the final network, we assume it will contribute one data packet into the network in each time unit (This assumption facilitates the energy consumption calculation later).

Constraint (10) ensures that for each node in the network, # of total inflow packets is equal to # of total outflow packets in each time unit. Constraint (11) ensures that one connection must exist before we can have some packets flow through it.

Constraint (12) ensures that total energy consumption on a node is equal to total transmitting power (each packet with variable cost tD_{ij}^p) plus total receiver power (each packet with fixed cost *r*). Constraint (13) sets the boundaries of total energy consumption on a node.

Constraint (14) enforces the integer property of the decision variables with respect to node inclusion. Constraint (15) makes sure that we always include master-site (node *0*) in the final network. Constraint (16) enforces the integer property of the decision variables with respect to node connection.

3.   SOLUTION APPROACH

3.1   Lagrangean Relaxation

By using the Lagrangean relaxation method, we can transform the primal problem (IP) mentioned above into the following Lagrangean relaxation problem (LR) where constraint (3), (4), (5), (6), (10) and (12) are relaxed. The Lagrangean relaxation problem is generated by multiplying the relaxed constraints by a vector of multipliers, and adding them to the objective function.

Problem LR

$$\psi(a, d, e, g, h, k) =$$

$$\text{Min} \sum_{i \in N} \left(W c_i - V_i \right) x_i + \sum_{i \in N} \sum_{j \in N} a_{ij} \left(y_{ij} - x_i \right) + \sum_{i \in N} \sum_{j \in N} d_{ij} \left(y_{ij} - x_j \right) +$$

$$\sum_{i \in N} e_i \left(x_i - \sum_{j \in N} y_{ij} \right) + g \left(\sum_{i \in N} \sum_{j \in N} y_{ij} - 2 \sum_{i \in N} x_i + 2 \right) +$$

$$\sum_{i \in N} h_i \left(b_i + \sum_{j \in N} f_{ji} - \sum_{j \in N} f_{ij} \right) + \sum_{i \in N} k_i \left[c_i - \sum_{j \in N} \left(f_{ij} \cdot tD_{ij}^{\,p} \right) - r \sum_{j \in N} f_{ji} \right]$$

s.t.

$$D_{ij} y_{ij} \le R, \, \forall i, j \in N \tag{2}$$

$$b_0 = -\sum_{i \in N} x_i + 1 \tag{7}$$

$$-n \le b_0 \le 0 \tag{8}$$

$$b_i = x_i, \, \forall i \in N, i \ne 0 \tag{9}$$

$$0 \le f_{ij} \le n y_{ij}, \, \forall i, j \in N \tag{11}$$

$$0 \le c_i \le n \left(tR^p + r \right), \forall i \in N \tag{13}$$

$$x_i = 0 \text{ or } 1, \, \forall i \in N, i \ne 0 \tag{14}$$

$$x_0 = 1 \tag{15}$$

$$y_{ij} = 0 \text{ or } 1, \forall i, j \in N, i \ne j \tag{16}.$$

Since we relax six constraints here, we have six corresponding Lagrangean Multipliers a_{ij}, d_{ij}, e_i, g, h_i and k_i. Among them, g, h_i and k_i are not confined to be nonnegative because constraint (6), (10) and (12) are equality constraints. All other multipliers a_{ij}, d_{ij}, and e_i have to be nonnegative. Note that we have kept the same set of constraint numbers as in the previous case.

We can further decompose the Lagrangean relaxation problem into two independent sub-problems in (x_i, b_i, c_i) and (y_{ij}, f_{ij}). These sub-problems are fairly easy to solve.

Sub-problem 1: for x_i, b_i and c_i

$$\text{Min} \sum_{i \in N, i \neq 0} \left[(Wx_i + k_i)c_i + \left(-V_i - \sum_{j \in N} a_{ij} - \sum_{j \in N} d_{ji} + e_i - 2g \right) x_i + h_i b_i \right] +$$

$$(Wx_0 + k_0)c_0 + \left(-V_0 - \sum_{j \in N} a_{0j} - \sum_{j \in N} d_{j0} + e_0 - 2g \right) x_0 + h_0 b_0 + 2g$$

s. t.

$$b_0 = -\sum_{i \in N} x_i + 1 \tag{7}$$

$$-n \leq b_0 \leq 0 \tag{8}$$

$$b_i = x_i, \forall i \in N, i \neq 0 \tag{9}$$

$$0 \leq c_i \leq n(tR^p + r), \forall i \in N \tag{13}$$

$$x_i = 0 \text{ or } 1, \forall i \in N, i \neq 0 \tag{14}$$

$$x_0 = 1 \tag{15}.$$

Sub-problem 2: for y_{ij}, and f_{ij}

$$\text{Min} \sum_{i \in N} \sum_{j \in N} \left[\left(a_{ij} + d_{ij} - e_i + g \right) y_{ij} + \left(h_i - k_i r \right) f_{ji} - \left(h_i + k_i \cdot t D_{ij}^{\,p} \right) f_{ij} \right]$$

s. t.

$$D_{ij} y_{ij} \leq R, \forall i, j \in N \tag{2}$$

$$0 \leq f_{ij} \leq n y_{ij}, \forall i, j \in N \tag{11}$$

$$y_{ij} = 0 \text{ or } 1, \forall i, j \in N, i \neq j \tag{16}.$$

For Sub-problem 1, we can substitute constraint (7) and (9) into the objective function (i.e. substituting all b_i with x_i) and the problem can be further decomposed into $n+1$ independent small problems in (x_i, c_i) for each $i \in N$ respectively.

$$\text{Min} \sum_{i\in N,\ i\neq 0}\left[(Wx_i + k_i)c_i + \left(-V_i - \sum_{j\in N}a_{ij} - \sum_{j\in N}d_{ji} + e_i - 2g + h_i - h_0\right)x_i\right] +$$

$$(Wx_0 + k_0)c_0 + \left(-V_0 - \sum_{j\in N}a_{0j} - \sum_{j\in N}d_{j0} + e_0 - 2g - h_0\right)x_0 + h_0 + 2g$$

s.t.

$$-n \leq b_0 \leq 0 \tag{8}$$

$$0 \leq c_i \leq n(tR^p + r),\ \forall i \in N \tag{13}$$

$$x_i = 0 \text{ or } 1,\ \forall i \in N, i \neq 0 \tag{14}$$

$$x_0 = 1 \tag{15}.$$

In the small problem when $i = 0$, it is a trivial one thanks to constraint (15). For other small problems when $i \neq 0$, we can simply compare the minimal objective function value when $x_i = 0$ and $x_i = 1$, and decide the optimal value of x_i and c_i correspondingly.

Based on the analysis above, the following algorithm can be applied to find the optimal solutions of Sub-problem 1:

Algorithm 1:
Step 1. Set $x_0 = 1$;
Step 2. If $(W+k_0) > = 0$, set $c_0 = 0$,
       Else set $c_0 = nr$;
Step 3. For each i in N, $i \neq 0$,
      {
        If $(W+k_i) > = 0$, set $u = 0$,
        Else set $u = n(tR^p+r)$;
        If $k_i > = 0$, set $v = 0$,
        Else set $v = n(tR^p+r)$;
        If $[(W+k_i)u-V_i-\Sigma a_{ij}-\Sigma d_{ji}+e_i-2g+h_i-h_0] <= k_iv$,
          set $x_i = b_i = 1$ and $c_i = u$,
        Else set $x_i = b_i = 0$ and $c_i = v$
      };
Step 4. Set $b_0 = -\Sigma x_i + 1$.

As to Sub-problem 2, based on constraint (11), it is equivalent to the following problem and can be further decomposed into $(n-1)^2/2$ independent small problems.

$$\text{Min} \sum_{i<j} \begin{bmatrix} \left(a_{ij} + d_{ij} - e_i + g\right)y_{ij} + \left(h_i - k_i r\right)f_{ji} - \left(h_i + k_i \cdot tD_{ij}^{\,p}\right)f_{ij} \end{bmatrix} + \\ \begin{bmatrix} \left(a_{ji} + d_{ji} - e_j + g\right)y_{ji} + \left(h_j - k_j r\right)f_{ij} - \left(h_j + k_j \cdot tD_{ji}^{\,p}\right)f_{ji} \end{bmatrix}$$

s.t.

$$D_{ij}y_{ij} \le R, \ \forall \, i, j \in N \tag{2}$$

$$0 \le f_{ij} \le ny_{ij}, \ \forall \, i, j \in N \tag{11}$$

$$y_{ij} = 0 \text{ or } 1, \ \forall \, i, j \in N, i \ne j \tag{16}.$$

Again, for each such small problem, we can easily solve it by comparing the optimal objective function value when $y_{ij} = y_{ji} = 1$ or $y_{ij} = y_{ji} = 0$.

Based on the analysis above, we design the following algorithm to find the optimal solution of Sub-problem 2:

Algorithm 2:
Step 1. For every i, j in N $(i < j)$,
    {
      If $D_{ij} <= R$
      {
       If $[(h_i - k_i r) - (h_j + k_j * tD_{ji}^p)] >= 0$, set $u = 0$,
       Else set $u = n$;
       If $[(h_j - k_j r) - (h_i + k_i * tD_{ij}^p)] >= 0$, set $v = 0$,
       Else set $v = n$;
       If $[\,a_{ij} + d_{ij} - e_i + g + a_{ji} + d_{ji} - e_j + g + (h_i - k_i r)u - (h_j + k_j * tD_{ji}^p)u + (h_j - k_j r)v - (h_i + k_i * tD_{ij}^p)v\,] <= 0$,
         set $y_{ij} = y_{ji} = 1$, $f_{ji} = u$, and $f_{ij} = v$,
       Else set $y_{ij} = y_{ji} = f_{ji} = f_{ij} = 0$
      }
      Else set $y_{ij} = y_{ji} = f_{ji} = f_{ij} = 0$
    }.

3.2 The Dual Problem and the Subgradient Method

Following the algorithms proposed above, we could successfully solve the Lagrangean relaxation problem. According to the weak Lagrangean duality theorem (for a given set of Lagrangean multipliers, the optimal objective function value of the corresponding Lagrangean relaxation problem is a lower bound on the optimal objective function value of the primal problem), ψ is a lower bound on the optimal objective function value of the Primal Problem (IP). We then construct the following dual problem to calculate the tightest lower bound and solve the dual problem by using the subgradient method. More details about the subgradient method can be found in (Bertsekas 1999).

Max $\psi(a, d, e, g, h, k)$ (D)
s.t. $a, d, e >= 0$.

Let the vector (Sa, Sd, Se, Sg, Sh, Sk) be a subgradient of $\psi(a, d, e, g, h, k)$ at (a, d, e, g, h, k). In iteration m of the subgradient optimization procedure, the multiplier for each (a, d, e, g, h, k) is updated by

$$
\begin{bmatrix}
a^{m+1} \\
d^{m+1} \\
e^{m+1} \\
g^{m+1} \\
h^{m+1} \\
k^{m+1}
\end{bmatrix}
=
\begin{bmatrix}
a^{m} \\
d^{m} \\
e^{m} \\
g^{m} \\
h^{m} \\
k^{m}
\end{bmatrix}
+ \alpha^{m}
\begin{bmatrix}
Sa^{m} \\
Sd^{m} \\
Se^{m} \\
Sg^{m} \\
Sh^{m} \\
Sk^{m}
\end{bmatrix}
$$

where $Sa^{m} = y_{ij} - x_i$
$Sd^{m} = y_{ij} - x_j$
$Se^{m} = x_i - \sum_{j \in N} y_{ij}$
$Sg^{m} = \sum_{i \in N} \sum_{j \in N} y_{ij} - 2\sum_{i \in N} x_i + 2$
$Sh^{m} = b_i + \sum_{j \in N} f_{ji} - \sum_{j \in N} f_{ij}$
$Sk^{m} = c_i - \sum_{j \in N} (f_{ij} * tD_{ij}^{P}) - r\sum_{j \in N} f_{ji}$

The step size α^{m} is determined by

$$
\alpha^{m} = \beta \frac{\phi^{h} - \phi\left(a^{m}, d^{m}, e^{m}, g^{m}, h^{m}, k^{m}\right)}{\left\|Sa^{m}\right\|^2 + \left\|Sd^{m}\right\|^2 + \left\|Se^{m}\right\|^2 + \left\|Sg^{m}\right\|^2 + \left\|Sh^{m}\right\|^2 + \left\|Sk^{m}\right\|^2}
$$

where ϕ^{h} is the primal objective function value, which we get from a heuristic solution (an upper bound on the optimal primal objective function value), and β is a constant, $0 \le \beta \le 2$. In our implementation, we divide the whole iterations we want to run to several groups. In each group, we initialize β to $(2 - 0.25q)$, where q is the indicator of the group and we half β whenever the dual objective function value do not improve in s iterations, where s is refereed to as the improvement counter limit. The initial value of the multiplier vector (a,d,e,g,h,k) is chosen to be the 0 vector, and is reset to the best multiplier vector we can get so far whenever we reach the boundary of each iteration groups or β is halved. In addition, ϕ^h is updated to the best upper bound we can get so far.

After the implementation of the subgradient optimization procedure mentioned above, we got a lower bound on the optimal objective function value of the primal problem. However, no primal feasible solution was found in the process. In order to get the primal feasible solutions, we try to utilize the optimal dual solutions to develop some heuristic algorithms for the primal problem.

4. GETTING PRIMAL FEASIBLE SOLUTIONS

Because we relax constraints (3), (4), (5), (6), (10), and (12) above, the solutions we get for the Lagrangean relaxation problems may not be feasible for the original primal problem. To get the primal feasible solutions, we have to decide the following decision variables by some heuristic:

b_0: a dummy variable that is interpreted as the amount of data packets that flow out of the network through the master-site (node *0*) in each time unit

b_i: a dummy variable which is interpreted as the number of data packet (0 or 1) generated at node i ($i \neq 0$) in each time unit

c_i: the cost (power consumption in mW) to include surviving node i into the final network

f_{ij}: the amount of data packets transmitted from node i to node j in each time unit

x_i: the decision variable that is 1 if node i is included in the final network and 0 otherwise

y_{ij}: the decision variable which is 1 if there is a connection between node i and node j in the final network and 0 otherwise. Note that y_{ij} and y_{ji} have the same meaning and y_{ii} is meaningless in this model.

In the process of the Lagrangean dual search procedure, we have set some x_i and y_{ij} to 1. We can utilize these determined variables to design the following heuristic algorithm. This heuristic guarantees a feasible solution.

Algorithm "adhoc":

Step 1. If $y_{ij}=1$, set the corresponding x_i and x_j to 1. This enforces constraint (3) and (4).

Step 2. Try to connect isolated nodes to the network. If it is infeasible, simply remove the node from our list. This ensures constraint (5).

Step 3. Construct the tree network. Start from the master-site and stretch out one level at an iteration through those $y_{ij}=1$ connection. If there is going to be a cycle, reset that $y_{ij}=1$ to 0 to avoid it.

Step 4. Remove those x_i and y_{ij} which are not in the tree structure. Together with Step 3, this ensures constraint (6).

Step 5. Trim the tree by removing those branches whose total value is smaller than their total cost.

Step 6. Reconstruct the tree by repeating Step 3 and Step 4.

Step 7. Set b_i according to x_i. Calculate the flow f_{ij} on each connection according to the tree structure and the flow conservation law. Calculate c_i accordingly as well. This assures constraint (10) and (12).

5.   COMPUTATIONAL EXPERIMENTS

In this section, ten test examples are used to test the algorithms proposed above. All experiments are performed on a Pentium 200 PC running Microsoft® Windows 95 with 48MB DRAM. The code is written in ANSI C and is compiled by Microsoft® Visual C++ 5.0. The performance is analyzed in the following section. Due to the space constraint, we can only report a simple test example in detail in subsection A. Other nine test examples will be shown in subsection B, but only final results are presented.

5.1   A Simple Problem

We will first illustrate our method by presenting a simple example (Figure 1 and Table 1). The major assumptions and parameters used in this experiment are shown as following:

1. Node *0* serves as the master-site and takes the responsibility of coordination. The power supply is always sufficient here.
2. *n*, the number of surviving nodes besides node *0*, is 12.
3. *p*, path loss exponent, is 4.
4. *R*, the largest power radius of the node, is 500 m.
5. *r*, power consumption at a node to receive and store a packet from another node, is 20 mW.
6. *t*, the predetection threshold at each node, is 10^{-7} mW.
7. *W*, a weight to convert energy (in mW) to the unit of V_i, is 0.1.

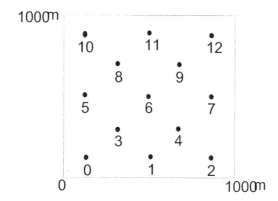

Figure 1. The Distribution Of The Surviving Nodes After The Airdrop

Table 1. Surviving Node Information

	Location (X m, Y m)	Power Radius (m)	Node Value V_i
Node [0]	(100, 100)	500	30
Node [1]	(500, 100)	500	30
Node [2]	(900, 100)	500	2000
Node [3]	(300, 300)	500	3000
Node [4]	(700, 300)	500	3000
Node [5]	(100, 500)	500	3000
Node [6]	(500, 500)	500	3000
Node [7]	(900, 500)	500	30
Node [8]	(300, 700)	500	3000
Node [9]	(700, 700)	500	3000
Node [10]	(100, 900)	500	30
Node [11]	(500, 900)	500	2000
Node [12]	(900, 900)	500	30

Figure 2 and Table 2 illustrate the final wireless ad-hoc network we get from our heuristic algorithm. The connections between nodes show the routes from each node to the master-site. Note that some nodes (1, 7, 10 and 12) are not included in the network because the values of the nodes are considered too low by the optimization routine.

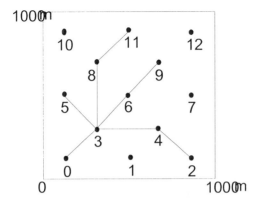

Figure 2. Final Wireless Ad-hoc Network

Table 2. Node Cost

	Node Cost c_i (mW)
Node [0]	160
Node [1]	0
Node [2]	640
Node [3]	5260
Node [4]	5140
Node [5]	640
Node [6]	1300
Node [7]	0
Node [8]	5140
Node [9]	640
Node [10]	0
Node [11]	640
Node [12]	0

In addition, the best objective function value of the primal problem *IP* we can get is $f^* = -20074$ and the best objective function value of the dual problem *D* we can get is $q^* = -22150$. (We have changed the maximization problem to a minimization one, so the objective function values are negative now.) The relative gap between them is only $(f^* - q^*) / |q^*| = 9.37$ %; i.e. the solution is near-optimal.

5.2 Other Test Results

Due to the space constraint, only the final results of the other nine test examples are presented in Table 3; detailed results are available upon request. From the results shown below, we can see that the relative duality gaps we get are only a few percents; thus it is clear that our solutions are almost optimal.

Table 3. Final Result Of Some Test Examples

	Original # of nodes	Final # of nodes	Target area	Largest power radius of the node	Node value V_i	Weight W	$f^\bullet$	$q^\bullet$	Relative gap $\dfrac{(f^\bullet - q^\bullet)}{\lvert q^\bullet \rvert}$	Computational time for 2000 iterations
Case 1	13	12	1 km²	500 m	0 ~ 50	10^{-3}	-307.17	-334.93	8.29 %	21 secs
Case 2	13	12	1 km²	500 m	0 ~ 50	10^{-3}	-299.15	-327.01	8.52 %	20 secs
Case 3	13	12	1 km²	500 m	0 ~ 50	10^{-3}	-280.31	-307.75	8.92 %	23 secs
Case 4	25	24	100 km²	3 km	0 ~ 50	10^{-7}	-762.09	-779.25	2.20 %	34 secs
Case 5	25	24	100 km²	3 km	0 ~ 50	10^{-7}	-516.16	-534.23	3.38 %	37 secs
Case 6	25	24	100 km²	3 km	0 ~ 50	10^{-7}	-658.48	-675.57	2.53 %	44 secs
Case 7	100	99	400 km²	4 km	0 ~ 1200	10^{-6}	-56369	-64050	11.99 %	395 secs
Case 8	100	98	400 km²	4 km	0 ~ 1200	10^{-6}	-54828	-63138	13.16 %	433 secs
Case 9	100	99	400 km²	4 km	0 ~ 1200	10^{-6}	-58649	-67166	12.68 %	508 secs

6.   SUMMARY AND CONCLUSIONS

This paper investigates the optimal design and deployment of wireless ad-hoc networks. We modeled the problem as a mixed integer program, and derived solution procedures based on Lagrangean relaxation. Using the Lagrangean relaxation, we were able to decompose the network design problem into two fairly-easy-to-solve sub-problems. Effective solution procedures of the Lagrangean relaxation problem are developed and the

Lagrangean-based solutions are further improved using subgradient optimization procedures. These Lagrangean solutions provide lower bounds on the optimal solutions to the primal problem. A heuristic is developed to generate feasible solutions to the primal problem. From the computational experiments we have done, our Lagrangean relaxation based algorithms can generate solutions within 2.20-13.16% of optimality. In addition, our algorithm also solves the design problem very rapidly, within a few minutes in the most complex case. Further, to the best of our knowledge, this is the first time this wireless ad-hoc network design problem has been formulated using mathematical programming techniques and solved to near optimality. Note also that it is feasible to periodic redesign the topology of the ad-hoc network by reapplying the algorithm dynamically and distribute the usage of power across all nodes. This would increase the time over which data can be collected from valuable sources as currently some nodes remain unused but have battery power available.

REFERENCES

Bertsekas, DP. 1999. *Nonlinear Programming.* Athena Scientific, pp. 609-618.

Chlamtac, I., A. Farago. 1999. A new approach to the design and analysis of peer-to-peer mobile networks. *Wireless Networks* 5:3 149-156.

Corson, M.S., J. P. Macker, G. H. Cirincione. 1999. Internet-based mobile ad-hoc networking. *IEEE Internet Computing* 3:4 63-70.

Gafni, E.M., D. P. Bertsekas. 1981. Distributed algorithms for generating loop-free routes in networks with frequently changing topology. *IEEE Transactions on Communications* 29:1 11-18.

Iwata, A., C. Chiang, G. Pei, M. Gerla, T. Chen. 1999. Scalable routing strategies for ad-hoc wireless networks. *IEEE Journal on Selected Areas in Communications* 17:8 1369-1379.

Lal, S., E. S. Sousa. 1999. Distributed resource allocation for DS-CDMA-based multimedia ad-hoc wireless LAN's. *IEEE Journal on Selected Areas in Communications* 17:5 (1999) 947-967.

Rodoplu, V., T. H. Meng. 1999. Minimum energy mobile wireless networks, *IEEE Journal on Selected Areas in Communications* 17:8 1333-1344.

Sharony, J. 1996. An architecture for mobile radio networks with dynamically changing topology using virtual subnets. *Mobile Networks & Applications* 1:1 75-86.

Wu, S., G. Anandalingam. 2002. Optimal Infrastructure Expansion of Wireless Networks. *Sixth INFORMS Telecommunications Conference, Boca Raton, Florida.*

Wu, S., Y. Lin. 1999. Design and management of wireless communications networks. *Proceedings of INFORMS 4th Conference on Information Systems and Technology, Cincinnati, Ohio* 284-306.

Chapter 4

SURVIVABLE NETWORK DESIGN: ROUTING OF FLOWS AND SLACKS

Deepak Rajan

Department of Industrial Engineering and Operations Research
University of California, Berkeley 94720–1777
deepak@ieor.berkeley.edu

Alper Atamtürk*

Department of Industrial Engineering and Operations Research
University of California, Berkeley 94720–1777
atamturk@ieor.berkeley.edu

Abstract   We present a new mixed–integer programming model and a column generation method for the survivable design of telecommunication networks. In contrast to other failure scenario models, the new model has almost the same number of constraints as the regular network design problem, which makes it effective for large instances. Even though the complexity of pricing the exponentially many variables of the model is $\mathcal{NP}$–hard, in our computational experiments, we are able to produce capacity–efficient survivable networks with dense graphs up to 70 nodes.

Keywords: Column generation, p–cycles, pricing complexity, survivable network design.

1.   Introduction

In this paper we consider the survivable design of telecommunication networks. Given an undirected graph $G = (N, E)$, where N is the set of nodes and E is the set of links, i.e., tuples of nodes, and demand of each node from every other node, the *telecommunication network design problem* is to install integer multiples of a capacity unit on the links and route the flow of demands so that

*Supported, in part, by NSF grant DMII–0070127.

the total capacity installation cost is minimized. In many telecommunication networks (e.g. Asynchronous Transfer Mode networks), the capacity installed on a link between two nodes allows running of flow up to the capacity in both directions. Thus capacity is undirected even though flow is directed.

A network is said to be *survivable* if all of the demands can be met under the failure of any one of its links. In this paper, we define link failure as the event of decreasing the capacity of the link to zero. Since in telecommunication networks the probability of two components failing simultaneously is very small, designing a network protected against single component failures is considered satisfactory. Two edge–connectedness of the underlying graph G is a necessary condition for the survivability of the network, but is clearly not sufficient. In order to ensure that the flow on the network can be rerouted in case of a failure, sufficient spare (excess) capacity must be available on the working links of the network. However, over–provisioning of capacity is a major concern for telecommunication companies due to the high investment costs required in installing capacity. Therefore designing capacity–efficient survivable networks (i.e., networks with low capacity installation cost) is a critical problem.

Various heuristic and exact approaches have been developed for designing survivable networks. The reader is referred to [19] for an overview of survivable network design problems and a synthesis of related literature. One of the simplest techniques for protecting a network against failures is the so–called $1+1$ *Diverse Protection* (DP) switching [7], which uses dedicated link–disjoint backup routes for each demand pair. Although rerouting disrupted flow to an alternative route can be done very fast in $1+1$ DP networks and operating such networks is quite easy, allocating capacity for demand–dedicated link–disjoint routes results in a network that is highly capacity–inefficient.

With the advent of add/drop multiplexers, a new protection technique known as the *Self–Healing Rings* (SHR) [2, 11, 17, 19] has been introduced. The topology of SHR networks is a set of rings (undirected cycles) covering the nodes of the graph. Due to the ring topology, SHR networks are inherently survivable. If a link of a ring fails, flow on the link is sent along the ring in the reverse direction. SHR networks deliver very fast rerouting times in the event of a failure while achieving lower spare capacity requirements than $1+1$ DP networks, since spare capacity on a ring is shared by all demand flows using that ring. Even though SHRs provide good survivability characteristics and extremely fast reconfiguration of flow, imposing a ring topology on the telecommunication network still leads to inefficient capacity utilization and therefore high cost.

A significant increase in the capacity efficiency of survivable networks can be achieved by allowing a general network topology and global rerouting of flows in the case of link failures. This requires provisioning link capacities that will allow rerouting under every link failure scenario [3]. Unfortunately, the size of failure scenario based global link restoration models grows very rapidly with the size of the graph and render such models unfit for tackling practical problems. Furthermore, implementation of global rerouting of all flows – whether disrupted or not – in the event of a failure requires much more complex hardware and software packages and is inherently slower than the SHR and $1 + 1$ DP networks.

Consequently, hierarchical restoration schemes are popular for designing survivable networks in practice. In the first stage, link capacities are determined for the no–failure scenario without survivability concerns. In the second stage, sufficient spare capacity is assigned to the links of the network so that the disrupted flow can be safely rerouted in the case of failures [4, 5, 12, 13, 14]. The reader may refer to [21] for a detailed comparison of various restoration strategies.

In this paper we introduce a new mixed–integer programming model for de-signing survivable networks. This model considers routing of no–failure flows and failure flows simultaneously by installing slacks on the directed cycles of the network so as to ensure survivability in the case of link failures. In a failure, only disrupted flow is rerouted. However, since failure and no–failure flows are considered simultaneously when determining link capacities, the model de-livers survivable networks with capacity–efficiency very close to global link restoration. The model builds upon [12] and improves capacity efficiency by using *directed* p-cycles for routing disrupted flow. Furthermore, since only dis-rupted flow is rerouted, reconfiguration of the network can be done quickly. Of significant note, the number of the constraints of the formulation is almost the same as the regular network design problem, which makes the model effective for large instances. The number of the variables is exponential in the number of links of the graph; however, the variables are treated implicitly by a column generation approach.

Outline. In Section 2, in addition to the new model, we describe two others: global link restoration and spare capacity assignment using p–cycles, that are used for comparison. In order to tackle large instances, in Section 3 we develop a column generation approach and show that the pricing complexity of the variables is $\mathcal{NP}$–hard. In Section 4 we present results of computational experiments that compare the capacity–efficiency and ease of solvability of these models. Using a polynomial–time pricing heuristic, we solve the model by column generation and report successful computational experiments with dense graphs up to 70 nodes.

2.   Link restoration

2.1   Global link restoration

Here we present a mathematical model of the minimum cost survivable network design problem. We refer to this model as the global link restoration, since it allows rerouting *all* flows, even those that are not disrupted under a link failure. In order to differentiate between undirected capacities and directed flow, we let $[ij]$ denote the undirected link between nodes i and j, and (ij) and (ji) denote the two directed arcs corresponding to link $[ij]$. We define the arc set A of the network as the set of all arcs corresponding to E, that is, $A = \{(ij), (ji) : [ij] \in E\}$. Let S be the set of failure scenarios. For simplicity of notation, we represent the no–failure scenario with $0 \in S$; thus $S = E \cup \{0\}$ ($0 \notin E$), and let $A \setminus [ij] = A \setminus \{(ij), (ji)\}$. We define commodities by aggregating all of the flow originating from a node. So, the demand associated with commodity $k \in K \subseteq N$ is the sum of demands d_{ik} from node k to every other node i. Let $b_i^k = \sum_{j \neq k} -d_{jk}$ if i is the origin node of commodity k, $b_i^k = d_{ik}$ if i is a destination node of commodity k and $b_i^k = 0$ otherwise. Also let g_{ij}^k and h_e be the cost of routing commodity k on arc (ij) and installing a capacity unit on link e, respectively, and finally let c_e be the existing (previously installed) capacity on link $e \in E$. Then the *Global Link Restoration Model* is

$$\min \quad \sum_{(ij) \in A} \sum_{k \in K} g_{ij}^k x_{ij}^{k0} + \sum_{e \in E} h_e y_e$$

$$\sum_{j:(ji) \in A} x_{ji}^{ks} - \sum_{j:(ij) \in A} x_{ij}^{ks} = b_i^k \quad \forall i \in N, \forall k \in K, \forall s \in S \quad (4.1)$$

$$\text{(GLR)} \qquad \sum_{k \in K} x_{ij}^{ks} \leq c_e + y_e \qquad \forall (ij) \in A \setminus \{s\}, \ \forall s \in S, \ e = [ij] \quad (4.2)$$

$$y_e \in \mathbf{Z}_+ \quad \forall e \in E$$

$$x_{ij}^{ks} \in \mathbf{R}_+ \quad \forall (ij) \in A, \forall k \in K, \forall s \in S.$$

where x_{ij}^{ks} is the amount of commodity k routed through arc (ij) in failure scenario s and y_e is the capacity installed on link e. Constraints (4.1) guarantee that the all demands are satisfied in all failure scenarios. Constraints (4.2) ensure that the capacity installed on a link is large enough to accommodate flow routed through that link for all failure scenarios.

(GLR) imposes no restrictions on either the network structure or the routing of flow. Hence, it delivers the most capacity–efficient survivable network possible (by letting $g_{ij}^k = 0$) if it can be solved to optimality. Note, however, that formulation (GLR) has $|N||K||S| + |A||S|$ constraints and $|A||K||S| + |E|$ variables. For a complete graph of $|N|$ nodes with complete demand, $|K| = |N|$, $|A| = |N|(|N| - 1)$, and $|S| = |N|(|N| - 1)/2 + 1$. So, for instance, when $|N| = 20$, (GLR) has 148,980 constraints and 1,451,790 variables. Even when the network is not as dense, (GLR) can easily have tens of thousands of constraints and millions of variables for even medium–sized networks, making it virtually impossible to load into the computer memory, let alone solve it to optimality. Also note that the size of (GLR) is larger than the regular network design problem (NDP) by an order of magnitude $|S|$ ((NDP) is the special case of (GLR) with the single no–failure scenario $S = \{0\}$). Since solving (GLR) optimally is exceedingly difficult except for very small instances, researchers have adopted heuristic approaches to solve it and its variants [9, 16]. Polyhedral cutting planes are given in [3, 6] for (GLR).

2.2   Spare Capacity Assignment

Even though the global link restoration scheme described in the previous section achieves the lowest capacity requirement, it carries several disadvantages. The first is the size of the formulation. A second disadvantage is that rerouting of disrupted as well as undisrupted flow in case of a failure is harder to implement than rerouting only disrupted flow. It requires sophisticated and expensive hardware and software and longer reconfiguration times. On the other hand, rerouting disrupted demand on rings in SHR networks requires much simpler equipment and control mechanisms at the nodes, and is much easier and faster to implement.

As a result, recently there has been an interest in developing hybrid networks which are capacity–efficient and at the same time are easy to restore under failure. This is accomplished in an hierarchical manner. In the first stage a capacity–efficient solution (flows and link capacities) is found for the network design problem without survivability concerns. In the second stage, given the working capacities, a minimum cost allocation of spare capacity on the links is determined so that flow on each arc can be routed, in case of a link failure. This second stage problem is referred to as the *Spare Capacity Assignment Problem* (SCA).

Grover and Stamatelakis [12] introduce the concept of utilizing (undirected) predefined cycles (*p-cycles*) of links for the configuration of spare capacity. In this scheme sufficient spare capacity is installed on the cycles of the graph so that the working capacity on any link is covered by the cycles that the link is either on or is a chord of. Figure 4.1 illustrates the way in which an individual p–cycle may be used for restoration. In (i), an example of a p–cycle is shown in bold links. Note that a p–cycle is just an undirected cycle which is used to cover working link capacities. In (ii), link $[AB]$ on the p–cycle fails, and the remaining links of the cycle are used for rerouting the flow on link $[AB]$. In (iii), we see how the p–cycle can also be used for restoring the flow on a link that is a chord of the p–cycle. Here link $[CD]$ fails, and the p–cycle provides two restoration paths between C and D. Thus installing half the working capacity

Figure 4.1.   An undirected p–cycle

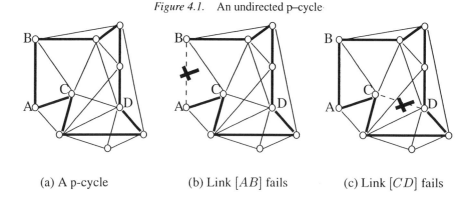

(a) A p-cycle   (b) Link $[AB]$ fails   (c) Link $[CD]$ fails

of $[CD]$ on the p–cycle as spare capacity covers link $[CD]$. Further inspection of Figure 4.1 shows that this particular p–cycle provides restoration paths for nine *on–cycle* failures and for ten *chord* failures.

Let $(\bar{x}, \bar{y})$ be a solution for the regular network design problem (NDP) and P be the set of simple undirected cycles of G. Grover and Stamatelakis [12] give the following integer set covering model for the capacity assignment problem with p–cycles:

$$\min \quad \sum_{e \in E} h_e \sum_{p \in P} r_{pe} w_p$$

$$\text{(SCA)} \qquad \sum_{p \in P} q_{pe} w_p \geq c_e + \bar{y}_e \qquad \forall e \in E \qquad (4.3)$$

$$w_p \in \mathbf{Z}_+ \qquad \forall p \in P.$$

The decision variable w_p denotes the number of spare capacity units assigned to p–cycle $i \in P$. Here r_{pe} is 1 if link e is on cycle p and 0 otherwise; q_{pe} is 2 if link e is a chord of cycle p, 1 if e is on cycle p, and 0 otherwise. Thus $\sum_{p \in P} r_{pe} w_p$ is the spare capacity installed on link e.

Naturally, solving first a network design problem and then assigning spare capacity to cover the working links is less capacity–efficient than solving (GLR) directly. However, this hierarchical approach breaks the task of designing a survivable network into two problems that are much easier to tackle computationally than global link restoration (GLR) and therefore is often preferred in practice. The hierarchical spare capacity assignment (SCA) approach using p–cycles has been reported to achieve much better capacity–efficiency than ring architectures as well as very quick recovery times by several authors [12, 18, 20].

2.3   Routing of Flows and Slacks

In this section, we present a mixed–integer programming model for routing failure flows and no–failure flows simultaneously. Rather than using undirected p–cycles to cover working link capacities from (NDP), we utilize *directed* p–cycles of arcs to introduce sufficient slack on top of the no–failure flows, so that the flow on each arc can be rerouted along these slacks. We refer to this scheme as the routing of flows and slacks. Let x_{ij}^k be the amount of commodity k flowing through arc $(ij) \in A$ in the no–failure scenario. Let C be the set of *directed* cycles of the network. Define a cycle–slack variable z_c to denote the amount of slack routed on cycle $c \in C$. For directed cycle $c \in C$ and arc $(ij) \in A$ let α_{ij}^c be 1 if c includes (ij), 0 otherwise, and let ρ_{ij}^c be 1 if (ij) is a chord to cycle c, 0 otherwise. Then the *Routing of Flows and Slacks* can be formulated as

$$\min \sum_{(ij)\in A}\sum_{k\in K} g_{ij}^k x_{ij}^k + \sum_{e\in E} h_e y_e$$

$$\sum_{j:(ji)\in A} x_{ji}^k - \sum_{j:(ij)\in A} x_{ij}^k = b_i^k \qquad \forall i \in N, \forall k \in K \qquad (4.4)$$

(RFS) $$\sum_{k\in K} x_{ij}^k - \sum_{c\in C} \rho_{ij}^c z_c - \sum_{c\in C} \alpha_{ji}^c z_c \le 0 \qquad \forall (ij) \in A \qquad (4.5)$$

$$\sum_{k\in K} x_{ij}^k + \sum_{c\in C} \alpha_{ij}^c z_c \le c_e + y_e \quad \forall (ij) \in A, \ e = [ij] \ (4.6)$$

$$y_e \in \mathbf{Z}_+ \qquad\qquad \forall e \in E$$

$$z_c \in \mathbf{R}_+ \qquad\qquad \forall c \in C$$

$$x_{ij}^k \in \mathbf{R}_+ \qquad\qquad \forall (ij) \in A, \forall k \in K.$$

Constraints (4.5) ensure that for each arc (ij) the total slack installed on the directed cycles that (ji) is on or a chord is at least the total flow on (ij). Observe that a directed cycle–slack provides coverage for flows in the reverse direction for the arc on the cycle; see arc (ba) in Figure 4.2. A directed cycle–slack provides only *one* recovery path for the flow on a chord arc; see arc (cd) in Figure 4.2. However, slack introduced for the directed cycle in the reverse direction also provides coverage for the flow on arc (cd) as well. Constraints (4.6) ensure that capacity installed on link $[ij]$ is large enough to accommodate the flow routed on arc (ij) as well as the slack introduced on the arc. In order to emphasize the importance of routing slacks through directed p–cycles, rather than covering working link capacities with undirected p–cycles as in [12], we give the example in Figure 4.3. Here, capacity is available in units of c and the flow on each arc (x, z), (z, y), and (y, x) equals c. Since installed capacity on a link allows flow in both directions up to capacity, the network in Figure 4.3 is survivable with a total of $3c$ capacity. However, covering

Figure 4.2.   A directed p–cycle

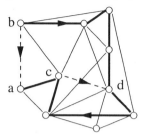

installed capacities with undirected p–cycles would require installing additional
c units on each link and would double the installed capacity. However routing
a cycle–slack of c units in the counter–clockwise direction (from x to y to z)
covers all of the flow on the network and requires no additional capacity. We
note that routing slacks to cover failure–flows will lead to lower capacity than
covering no–failure capacity even without the assumption that installed capacity
on a link allows flow in both directions up to capacity. Consequently, (RFS)

Figure 4.3.   A small survivable network

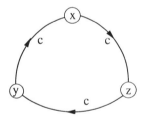

produces survivable networks that are more capacity–efficient than (SCA) for
two reasons: (1) (RFS) routes slacks rather than using undirected p–cycles to
cover working link capacities, and (2) (RFS) considers the routing of no–failure
flows when determining excess capacity installation. Indeed our computational
experiments indicate that the capacity–efficiency delivered by (RFS) is very
close to (GLR) for small instances.

Interestingly, in contrast to (GLR), (RFS) requires only one additional constraint for each arc than the regular network design problem (NDP) without
survivability requirement. However, the number of cycles in a graph, hence
cycle–slack variables in the formulation, is exponential in the number of the
arcs.

3. A column generation approach

Since (RFS) has exponentially many cycle–slack variables, all of the variables cannot be included in the model when solving large instances. Selecting a small subset of the variables a priori and solving the model with these variables can result in suboptimal solutions. Therefore, we develop a column generation [8] approach and introduce the cycle–slack variables into (RFS) with a restricted number of variables as they are needed. In order to solve larger instances efficiently, we also reformulate (RFS) using path–flow variables, rather than the arc–flow variables. This reduces the number of constraints, introduces an exponentially many path–flow variables, which can also be generated, as needed, via column generation.

Because the column generation algorithms for multicommodity flow problems converge to an optimal LP solution faster when commodities are disaggregated [15], we use pairwise demands as commodities in the formulation. Let K be the set of node pairs with positive demand and P_k denote the set of s_k–t_k paths for commodity $k \in K$. For $(ij) \in A$ and $p \in P_k$, let δ_{ij}^p be 1 if path p includes arc (ij), 0 otherwise. For $p \in P_k$, defining the path–flow variables x_p as the fraction of commodity k routed through path p under the no–failure scenario, we reformulate the problem of routing of flows and slacks as

$$\min \quad \sum_{(ij)\in A} \sum_{k\in K, p\in P_k} d_k \delta_{ij}^p g_{ij}^k x_p + \sum_{e\in E} h_e y_e$$

$$(w_k) \qquad \sum_{p\in P_k} x_p = 1 \ \forall k \in K \qquad (4.7)$$

$$(u_{ij}) \sum_{k\in K, p\in P_k} d_k \delta_{ij}^p x_p - \sum_{c\in C} \rho_{ij}^c z_c - \sum_{c\in C} \alpha_{ji}^c z_c \le 0 \ \forall (ij) \in A \qquad (4.8)$$

$$(v_{ij}) \qquad \sum_{k\in K, p\in P_k} d_k \delta_{ij}^p x_p + \sum_{c\in C} \alpha_{ij}^c z_c \le c_e + y_e \ \forall (ij) \in A, e = [ij] \ (4.9)$$

$$\text{(RFS–P)} \qquad\qquad x_p \in \mathbf{R}_+ \qquad \forall p \in P_k, \ \forall k \in K$$

$$y_e \in \mathbf{Z}_+ \qquad \forall e \in E$$

$$z_c \in \mathbf{R}_+ \qquad \forall c \in C.$$

where u, v, w are the corresponding dual variables of the LP relaxation of (RFS–P). Constraints (4.7) ensure the demand for each commodity is satisfied for the no–failure scenario. Constraints (4.8) ensure that sufficient slack is allocated to directed cycles to cover all no–failure flow on each arc. Constraints (4.9) ensure that for each edge, sufficient capacity is installed for routing the slack introduced and the no–failure flow on the arcs in either direction.

3.1   Pricing of cycle–slack variables

Given an LP–relaxation solution to (RSF–P) that has a restricted set of cycle–slack variables, we are interested in finding a cycle–slack variable z_c with negative reduced cost, if one exists. For a dual solution (u, v, w) the reduced cost of the cycle–slack variable z_c is

$$\sum_{ij \in A} ((u_{ji} - v_{ij}) \alpha_{ij}^c + u_{ij} \rho_{ij}^c).$$

A negative reduced cost z_c can be identified by finding a negative weight directed cycle that has at least three arcs on $G = (N, A)$, where weight of an arc (ij) on the cycle is $f_{ij}^a = u_{ji} - v_{ij}$ and the weight of an arc (ij) that is a chord of the cycle is $f_{ij}^h = u_{ij}$. Observe that f^a is unrestricted in sign, but $f^h \leq 0$ since $u \leq 0$.

A negative weight directed cycle could be found in polynomial time, for instance, by the Bellman–Ford algorithm [1] if the cycles did not carry a weight for their chords. The presence of weights for the chords complicates the problem significantly.

Pricing Problem of P–cycles.   Let us formally define the Pricing Problem of P–cycles (PPP) as: Given the arc weights $f^a \in \mathbf{R}^A$ and chord weights $f^h \in \mathbf{R}^A$, either find a negative cost p–cycle or conclude that no such p–cycle exists.

Theorem 1 *The Pricing Problem of P–cycles (PPP) is $\mathcal{NP}$–hard.*

PROOF: We prove the theorem by reducing PPP to the decision version of TSP [10]: Given a complete directed graph $G = (N, A)$, weights $d : A \mapsto \mathbf{Z}_+$, and a positive integer k, does there exist a Hamiltonian cycle in G with total weight $< k$? In order to answer TSP, we construct the following instance of PPP. Let $n = |N|$. For $(ij) \in A$, let $f_{ij}^a = d_e + (M(n-3) - 2k)/(n(n-1))$ and $f_{ij}^h = -(M+k)/(n(n-1))$, where $M > nk$. Let $h(c)$ denote the set of chords of p–cycle c in G. Any p–cycle on G with ℓ arcs has exactly $\ell^2 - 3\ell$ directed chords. Hence the weight of p–cycle c with ℓ arcs is equal to

$$
\begin{aligned}
\sum_{(ij) \in c} f_{ij}^a + \sum_{(ij) \in h(c)} f_{ij}^h &= d(c) + \frac{\ell(M(n-3) - 2k)}{n(n-1)} - \frac{\ell(\ell - 3)(M+k)}{n(n-1)} \\
&= d(c) + M \frac{\ell(n-3) - \ell(\ell - 3)}{n(n-1)} - k \frac{2\ell + \ell(\ell - 3)}{n(n-1)} \\
&= d(c) + M \frac{\ell(n - \ell)}{n(n-1)} - k \frac{\ell(\ell - 1)}{n(n-1)} \quad (4.10)
\end{aligned}
$$

where $d(c)$ is the weight of the cycle c for the TSP. When M is chosen as above, (4.10) is positive unless $\ell = n$. Hence, PPP has an affirmative answer only if the p–cycle is Hamiltonian. However, since the weight of any Hamiltonian p–cycle c on G is $d(c) - k$ (the second term in (4.10) vanishes when $\ell = n$), PPP has an affirmative answer if there exists a Hamiltonian cycle c of weight $d(c) < k$. Hence, TSP has an affirmative answer if and only if PPP has an affirmative answer. ◇

A polynomial–time heuristic. When all chord weights f^h of p–cycles are zero, PPP reduces to finding a negative weight (f^a) directed cycle with at least three arcs. This can be accomplished in $O(|A||N|^2)$ with a simple modification to the Bellman–Ford label–correcting algorithm for finding shortest paths in a directed graph.

Since chord weights f^h are nonpositive, if we find a negative weight cycle c by assuming that f^h is zero, we also find a negative weight p–cycle. Therefore, in order to find negative reduced cost cycle–slack variables, we first find negative weight directed cycles using f^a and add the corresponding cycle–slack variables to the restricted formulation of (RFS–P). When we exhaust all such negative weight cycles, there can still be other negative reduced cost cycle–slack variables with $f^a_{ij} < 0$, that could not be found this way.

Note that the longer the p–cycle is, especially for dense graphs, the more the number of chords it has. Thus, longer p–cycles have a higher tendency of having a negative weight. Therefore, we could potentially get "good" p–cycles by changing the weights f^a in such a way that we get longer cycles when we solve the polynomial–time negative weight cycle problem. One possible way of accomplishing this is by reducing all arc weights f^a by a certain constant so that the longer cycles will be in favor. We incorporate this idea in the column generation algorithm for pricing cycle–slack variables that do not correspond to negative weight cycles.

3.2   Pricing of path–flow variables

The pricing problems of the path–flow variables are disjoint for each commodity $k \in K$ and therefore can be solved separately. Given a dual solution (u, v, w) to the LP relaxation of the restricted (RFS–P), the reduced cost of a path–flow variable x_p $p \in P_k$ is

$$\sum_{ij \in A} (g^k_{ij} - u_{ij} - v_{ij}) d_k \delta^p_{ij} - w_k$$

Since $u, v \le 0$, $\zeta = \min\{\sum_{ij \in A}(g^k_{ij} - u_{ij} - v_{ij})d_k\delta^p_{ij} : p \in P_k\}$ is an s_k–t_k shortest path problem with nonnegative weights, and can be solved efficiently using Dijkstra's algorithm [1]. If $\zeta < w_k$, then the flow–path variable corresponding for an optimal s_k–t_k path has a negative reduced cost, and is added to the restricted formulation.

4.   Computational Results

Here we present our computational experiments performed to compare the capacity–efficiency and ease of solvability of the models (NDP), (GLR), (SCA), (RFS), and (RFS–P). Our goal is to determine whether the new method of routing flow and slacks is a viable alternative for designing survivable telecommunication networks.

While (GLR) produces the most capacity–efficient survivable networks, the size of the formulation, which essentially carries a copy of the regular network design problem for each failure scenario, makes it unfit for tackling problems unless they are very small. Nevertheless, in our experiments we run the (GLR) model for small instances in order to find the lowest capacity requirement for the purpose of comparison. In order to have a fair comparison for the capacity–efficiency of (SCA) and (RFS), we solved these models with the same set of cycles that are selected a priori. For these experiments we created small instances of randomly generated graphs with 75% link density and 50% demand density. In Table 4.1 we present the number of constraints and variables in the four formulations for the graph with 14 nodes. (NDP) is the regular network design problem with no survivability constraints. In Table 4.1, we see that the formulations of (NDP) and (RFS) are about the same size. The formulation of (GLR) is orders of magnitude bigger than the rest of the models. For (RFS), the restricted set of p–cycles is chosen as follows: First, we calculate the minimum cost spanning tree (T - using edge weights proportional to h_e). Then, for every edge e on the tree, we find the minimum cost cycle that uses edge e and exactly one edge $\notin T$. Cycle–slack variables (both directions) corresponding to these undirected cycles are added to the formulation. We also add these cycle–slack variables a priori to (RFS–P).

Table 4.1.   Problem size

$n = 14$	*(NDP)*	*(GLR)*	*(SCA)*	*(RFS)*
Cons	342	27352	133	488
Vars	2117	151329	105	2173

All of the models, are solved with CPLEX7.5 MIP solver on an Intel Pentium4 2GHz Linux workstation with 1GB main memory with one hour CPU time limit. In Table 4.2 we report the solution times in CPU second (Time) and the best IP solutions found (IPsoln) for the four models. Optimality gap (End Gap) of the best IP solution is reported in place of time if the branch–and–bound computation is not finished in one hour time limit. In Figure 4.4 we show ratio of installed capacity for the solutions provided by (GLR), (SCA), and (RFS) to the capacity of the regular (nonsurvivable) network design model (NDP). Here

Table 4.2. Comparison of the models

| Size | Time/(End Gap) | | | | IP soln | | | |
n	(NDP)	(GLR)	(SCA)	(RFS)	(NDP)	(GLR)	(SCA)	(RFS)
5	0.03	0.57	0.00	0.04	50.5	90.7	131.7	110.5
6	0.16	1.27	0.00	0.19	129.5	192.0	323.9	230.8
7	0.27	23.6	0.00	1.00	103.4	143.8	210.0	160.1
8	2.88	577.1	0.00	4.18	146.6	176.8	281.2	236.0
9	517.1	(3.5)	0.00	2.88	172.7	223.9	361.7	257.3
10	(1.6)	(13)	0.00	2.47	235.8	308.0	495.8	372.2
11	1216	(-)	0.00	42.5	289.3	(-)	533.9	384.7
12	(3.0)	(-)	0.00	61.2	326.0	(-)	689.0	570.9
13	(1.6)	(-)	0.00	2967	366.1	(-)	683.7	577.4
14	(1.9)	(-)	0.00	(0.6)	443.0	(-)	896.2	695.5
15	(1.8)	(-)	0.00	(0.9)	554.9	(-)	1164	896.4

Figure 4.4. Relative capacity–efficiency of the survivability models

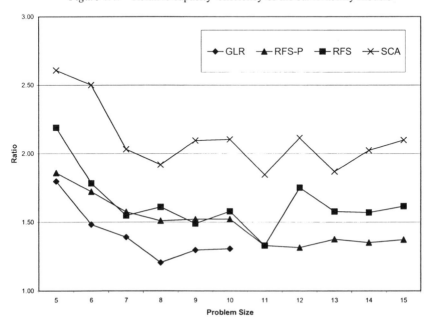

we see that survivable networks produced by (SCA) have about 100% more capacity installed compared with the nonsurvivable networks (NDP), whereas (RFS) requires only about 50% increase in the capacity. Moreover, when compared with (GLR), which provisions the lowest possible capacity for survivable networks, we see that (RFS) requires only an additional 20 % capacity, whereas (SCA) provisions 59% excess capacity over (GLR).

When we compare the models in terms of ease of solvability, we see that the (SCA) model is the easiest to solve; it takes negligible time. We should recall, however, that (SCA) requires the solution of (NDP) as an input. So one should take into consideration of the solution time of (NDP) for designing survivable networks with (SCA). Surprisingly, we observe in Table 4.2 that (RFS) is solved more easily than (NDP) and we were able to obtain optimal solutions or feasible solutions within 1% of optimal (for the subset of cycle–slack variables used in the formulation) for all instances in Table 4.2. It was not possible to solve even the LP relaxations of (GLR) for instances with more than 14 nodes within an hour of CPU time. No feasible solution is found by CPLEX for instances with more than 10 nodes.

Table 4.3.   The effect of column generation

Size	(RFS)			(RFS–P)			Paths	Cycles
n	(1)	(2)	(3)	(1)	(2)	(3)		
5	0.00	0.04	110.5	0.01	0.05	93.8	23	8
6	0.00	0.19	230.8	0.01	0.19	222.9	36	6
7	0.01	1.00	160.1	0.01	0.41	162.8	51	4
8	0.01	4.18	236	0.01	2.55	221.3	107	14
9	0.02	2.88	257.3	0.02	6.03	262.8	143	14
10	0.04	2.47	372.2	0.02	4.99	358.9	182	10
11	0.10	42.5	384.7	0.06	88.0	384.5	282	26
12	0.05	61.2	570.9	0.17	2337	428.6	499	38
13	0.08	2967	577.4	0.24	(1.4)	503.4	567	50
14	0.12	(0.6)	695.5	0.31	(0.2)	598.4	702	46
15	0.19	(0.9)	896.4	0.42	(0.2)	761.3	839	46

(1) LP Soln time, (2) Time (End Gap), (3) IP soln.

In Table 4.3 we compare (RFS–P) with (RFS) to see the effect of generating variables as needed rather than solving (RFS) on a subset of the variables selected a priori. A comparison of columns (3) indicate that the capacity–efficiency of the networks improve significantly by pricing the cycle–slack variables based on their LP reduced costs. The networks produced by (RFS–P) have about 15% more capacity than the ones from (GLR), whereas (RFS) has 20% excess and (SCA) has 59% excess capacity. The LP solution times for (RFS–P), which include the time for pricing variables, indicate that columns can be generated very efficiently. Observe in the last two columns of Table 4.3 that only a small number of the variables are generated.

Finally in Table 4.4 we report the results of the our experiments with the column generation approach for large instances. Table 4.4 demonstrates that relatively large instances could be effectively solved by the new survivability model (RFS–P) with a column generation approach. These computational experiments suggest that the method of routing flows and slacks is quite effective in designing survivable networks.

Table 4.4. Experiments with large instances

Size	LP time	(EndGap)	IP Soln	Paths	Cycles
20	3.97	(0.7)	1641	2171	100
30	27.8	(1.4)	3567	3549	190
40	123.4	(2.8)	6245	7262	262
50	186.3	(1.1)	12212	10643	352
60	2315	(0.6)	28754	14251	366
70	1333	(1.4)	24121	23490	390

5.   Conclusions and research directions

In this paper, we have presented a new method (RFS) for designing capacity–efficient survivable telecommunication networks. This method differs from the hierarchical link capacity covering methods such as (SCA) [12], in that we route no–failure flows and slacks for disrupted flow through directed cycles of the network. Therefore, capacity–efficiency achieved by (RFS) is always at least as high as (SCA). Our computational experiments show that (RFS) delivers consistently about 30% more capacity–efficient networks than (SCA) does. In fact, (RFS) compares well with global link restoration (GLR), which gives theoretically the most capacity–efficient survivable networks possible (see Figure 4.4). In order to solve large instances we developed a column generation approach. We showed that the pricing problem for the cycle–slack variables problem is $\mathcal{NP}$–hard, and gave an efficient heuristic to price them effectively. Judicious selection of cycle–slack variables seems to be very important in increasing the capacity–efficiency of the networks. Pricing the variables based on their LP reduced costs, even with a heuristic method, improved capacity–efficiency of the networks over selecting them a priori significantly. Our computational experiments suggest that the method of routing flows and slacks is an effective way for designing survivable telecommunication networks.

There are several directions for further research. We are currently working on developing other efficient ways of pricing the cycle–slack variables. We plan to study the weighted p–cycle problem in detail. In a subsequent paper, we will perform a polyhedral analysis of the new model, in order to develop strong cutting planes for the problem. A challenging issue is how to integrate column and cut generation schemes.

Finally the method of routing flows and slacks can be easily adapted to other failure scenarios, such as simultaneous failure of links or node failures and to particular technologies, such as WDM, VWP, WP networks.

References

[1] Ahuja, R. K., Magnanti, T. L., and Orlin, J. B. (1993). *Network Flows: Theory, Algorithms, and Applications.* Prentice-Hall, Englewood Cliffs, NJ.

[2] Altinkemer, K. (1994). Topological design of ring networks. *Computers and Operations Research*, 21:421–431.

[3] Alevras, D., Grötschel, M., and Wessäly R. (1998). Cost-efficient network synthesis from leased lines. *Annals of Operations Research*, 76:1–20.

[4] Balakrishnan, A., Magnanti, T. L., Sokol, J. S., and Wang, Y. Modeling and solving the single facility line restoration problem. *Operations Research*, to appear.

[5] Balakrishnan, A., Magnanti, T. L., Sokol, J. S., and Wang, Y. (2001). Telecommunication link restoration planning with multiple facility types. *Annals of Operations Research*, 106:127–154.

[6] Bienstock, D. and Muratore, G. (2000). Strong inequalities for capacitated survivable network design problems. *Mathematical Programming*, 89:127–147.

[7] Chung, S. H, King, H. G., Yoon Y. S., and Tcha, D. W. (1996). Cost–minimizing construction of a unidirectional SHR with diverse protection. *IEEE Transactions on Networking*, 4:921–928.

[8] Chvátal, V. (1983). *Linear Programming.* W. H. Freeman and Company, New York.

[9] Dahl, G. and Stoer, M. (1998). A cutting plane algorithm for multicommodity survivable network design problems. *INFORMS Journal on Computing*, 10:1–11.

[10] Garey, M. R. and Johnson, D. S. (1979). *Computers and Intractability: A Guide to the Theory of NP-Completeness.* W. H. Freeman and Company, New York.

[11] Goldschmidt, O., Laugier, A., and Olinick, E. V. SONET/SDH ring assignment with capacity constraints. *Discrete Applied Mathematics*, to appear.

[12] Grover, W. D. and Stamatelakis, D. (1998). Cycle-oriented distributed pre-configuration: ring-like speed with mesh-like capacity for self-planning network restoration. *Proceedings of IEEE International Conference on Communications 1998*, 537–543.

[13] Herzberg, M., Bye, S. J., and Utano, A. (1995). The hop-limit approach for spare capacity assignment in survivable networks . *IEEE/ACM Transactions on Networking* 3:775–784.

[14] Iraschko, R., MacGregor, M., and Grover, W. (1998). Optimal capacity placement for path restoration in STM or ATM mesh survivable networks. *IEEE/ACM Transactions on Networking* 6:325–336.

[15] Jones, K. L., Lustig, I. J., Farvolden, J. M., and Powell, W. B. (1993). Multicommodity network flows: the impact of formulation on decomposition. *Mathematical Programming* 62:95–117.

[16] Lisser, A., Sarkissian, R., and Vial, J. P. (1995). Survivability in telecommunication networks. Technical Report 1995.3, Department of Management Studies, University of Geneva, Switzerland.

[17] Luss, H., Rosenwein, M. B., and Wong. R. T. (1998). Topological network design for SONET ring architecture. *IEEE Transactions on Systems, Man and Cybernetics*, 28:780–790.

[18] Schupke, D. A., Gruber, C. G., and Autenrieth, A. (2002). Optimal configuration of p–cycles in WDM networks. *IEEE International Conference on Communications 2002*.

[19] Soriano, P., Wynants, C., Séguin, R., Labbé, M., Gendreau, M., and Fortz, B. (1998). Design and dimensioning of survivable SDH/SONET networks. In Sansò, B. and Soriano, P., editors, *Telecommunications Network Planning*, pages 147–168. Kluwer Academic Publishers, Netherlands.

[20] Stamatelakis, D. and Grover, W. D. (2000). Theoretical underpinnings for the efficiency of restorable networks using pre-configured cycles ("p-cycles"). *IEEE Transactions on Communications*, 48:1262–1265.

[21] Xiong, Y. and Mason, L. G. (1999). Restoration strategies and spare capacity requirements in self-healing ATM networks. *IEEE/ACM Transactions on Networking*, 7:98–110.

Chapter 5

PLANNING SELF-HEALING RING CAPACITY UNDER DEMAND UNCERTAINTY

Steven Cosares

Hofstra University, Hempstead, New York, USA

Abstract   We describe an approach to planning the capacity for self-healing rings in a survivable network when there is uncertainty about the demands that will be served. When detailed, reliable forecast data is not available, network plans based on stochastic methods that consider multiple demand scenarios are usually superior to those based on single point-estimates. However, a large number of potential realizations usually have to be considered before a reasonable plan can be developed. In addition, information regarding the distribution of the point-to-point demands may be elusive. In this paper, we show that when survivable components, like self-healing rings, are placed into the network some robustness to demand uncertainty is naturally provided, so the planning process can be simplified. We present an approach to sizing these components that uses the information available, like the total demand in a geographic area or the total demand terminating at each location. These data are often more reliable and easier to obtain than individual point-to-point demand values. We describe the differences between sizing unidirectional and bidirectional rings in the presence of demand uncertainty. Unlike unidirectional rings, where the capacity depends only on the total demand, the capacity requirement for bidirectional rings varies with the values of the individual demands and their locations. However, bidirectional rings are often more economical and more robust to demand uncertainty. In our approach, we employ a fast routing heuristic that find the capacity of bidirectional rings under a variety of demand scenarios. The scheme allows for a more accurate comparison between ring alternatives and the risks inherent to each. We describe how this approach to sizing can be incorporated into existing decision support for survivable network planning.

Keywords   Network Planning, Self-Healing Rings, Survivability, Uncertainty

1.   BACKGROUND

Survivable architectures like self-healing rings and re-configurable meshes are incorporated into optical communication networks to provide protection for the demands they serve. Each is planned with appropriate topology and sufficient capacity to satisfy most or all of the expected demand, even in the event of some equipment or cable failure(s). The equipment, which are compliant with optical networking standard like SONET, SDH, or WDM, have the ability to immediately redirect traffic and use available capacity to avoid a failed location. Network plans that incorporate these architectures said to be *robust* to uncertainty about the future condition of the network elements. That is, the planned network would remain capable of satisfying the customers' demand, even under a wide variety of unforeseen occurrences that would temporarily alter the topology of the network. Thus the severe economic consequences associated with disconnecting customers, even for short periods of time, are avoided. Such robust plans are thought to be superior to those that do not provide demand protection, even if their associated capital costs are marginally higher.

A question arises as to whether survivable network plans are inherently robust in other ways. For instance, do they naturally hedge against the risks associated with demand uncertainty? Could the same mechanisms that allow traffic to be redirected in the event of some unforeseen equipment failure be used to establish a connection for some unforeseen demand between a pair of locations, or to accommodate some unexpected increase in overall demand volume?

We believe the answer to these questions is a resounding "Yes". Further, we believe that there is considerable value in establishing plans that contain a measure of robustness to demand uncertainty. First, planners want to design capable networks, even if they can't predict the future well enough to produce precise forecasts. Second, because the demand between any particular pair of locations is likely to fluctuate during the planning horizon, it would be beneficial to be able to quickly switch capacity from one pair to another in response. Third, because there are costs associated with setting capacity levels either too low or too high; the planner would like a plan that avoids these costs wherever possible.

Very few decision support systems for network planning, if any, explicitly consider both forms of robustness. Those designed for planning under uncertainty often rely on some large-scale stochastic programming approach, (see [9]), in which all of the possible demand scenarios are either implicitly or explicitly represented. These systems use information from each of the scenarios to generate a single network plan that is expected to perform well when the actual demand is realized. For example, in [12], the authors present an approach for setting the link capacities in a network with the objective of minimizing the average number of unserved demands over the scenarios considered. The issue of demand protection never arises, even though the nodes in their network are assumed to have cross-connection capability, (i.e., for switching of traffic). Ironically, the networks produced by their approach often have the same topology and equipment as survivable meshes. It may be possible to build a better network by considering scenarios for network failure in addition to those concerning possible demand values. Wholesale changes would be required, however, if systems of this type are to consider a wider variety of survivable architecture alternatives.

Decision support systems that are designed to produce survivable networks usually find good locations for point-to-point systems and self-healing rings as well as survivable meshes. Rings, like meshes, not only provide demand protection, but also are capable of accommodating demands between *any* pairs of its nodes, so they can adapt to unexpected changes in the demands. Most planning systems for survivable networks do not exploit this property. They usually require a single point-estimate forecast for the demands, so are not equipped to provide solutions when the demands are uncertain. This is unfortunate because such systems often consider thousands of potential placements of rings and other survivable architectures, before arriving at a proposed solution, (see [5]), so they are irreplaceable in the network planning process.

We point out that both types of planning system are sufficiently complex, so we look for some reasonable alternative before attempting to develop some super-complex hybrid system that combines both approaches. Rather, we suggest a phased approach, where some base survivable network plan is established first. This plan is likely to find ideal locations for self-healing rings and survivable mesh subnetworks, even if its decisions are based on some small sample of the potential demand scenarios. In the second phase, the capacities of each of the survivable components is altered, to account for a wider set of feasible possibilities, thus making them more robust to uncertainty in the demands that are assigned to them. For mesh subnetworks, the methods described in [12] can be used to adjust the capacities of the associated links. In this paper, we address the adjustments that a planner would make to the self-healing rings identified in the base plan.

In the next section we describe ring type selection and ring capacity determination when the point-to-point demands are given. We discuss how the problems are complicated when some demand information is missing. We describe an *opportunity cost* model that measures the penalty associated with placing either too much or too little ring capacity. In Section 3, we describe a simulation experiment that helps a planner determine a ring capacity and ring type appropriate to the demand information available. We demonstrate the approach on a baseline model for demands that represents fairly limited knowledge. The results associated with the baseline model are compared to those for demand models representing other levels of planner knowledge. We demonstrate how, as one would expect, greater knowledge results in lower expected opportunity costs. We conclude with additional recommendations regarding the process of planning under demand uncertainty.

2.   SELF-HEALING RING SELECTION

When a survivable network plan is finalized, the decisions to place components like self-healing rings at locations throughout the network are as much based on guidelines enforced by the planner as they are based on economic comparisons. Such guidelines may be established through company policy or by empirical observations from a variety of optimal network plans. For example, planners have found that self-healing rings are an economical alternative when the underlying network topology is amenable and/or there is a large amount of demand volume expected between and among the locations served by the ring. The requirements for restoration speed may dictate that rings be used, rather than some other survivable architecture, like a mesh. In some cases, a planner may have already decided on the locations of some rings prior to consulting a decision support system. In the system described in [5], such planner decisions are considered before any system generated options. Guidelines have been embedded into the system heuristics wherever possible.

The decisions regarding the *locations* of the self-healing rings are not likely to be reviewed by the planner during the process of adjusting for demand uncertainty. Rather, it would be the job of the planner to determine, for each ring location, whether the type and capacity adequately provide the desired robustness. He or she would determine if more (or less) capacity should be purchased and whether the type (e.g., unidirectional, two-fiber or four-fiber bidirectional) is capable of weathering the possibility that the actual demand will be different than what was assumed. These decisions are different from those described in [6], where the capacity and type are selected based solely on cost.

2.1 Unidirectional vs. Bidirectional Rings

The following nomenclature is used in a model for ring type and capacity selection. The parameter n represents the number of multiplexer locations (*nodes*) on the ring. While the route of the fiber used to support the ring may pass through a larger number of locations in the network, it is only these n nodes from which contain the equipment that allows traffic to originate or terminate. The term *link* refers to the span of fiber between a pair of adjacent nodes on a ring. We let $d(i,j)$ represent the number of units of demand between nodes i and j that are to be satisfied on the ring (or stack of rings). In a model for demand uncertainty, $d(i,j)$ is a random variable from some (known or unknown) probability distribution. We let $t(i)$ represent the total demand originating at node i; D represents the total demand among all of the nodes. These too are random variables. However, because they are aggregates of the $d(i,j)$ variables, and are hence less sensitive to individual fluctuation, it is reasonable to expect that the planner has more reliable forecasts for these values. See [14] for a discussion of how such estimates may be obtained.

All of the links in a self-healing ring must have the same capacity. Thus in a ring with capacity C, it would be possible to number the units of capacity in the links: $1,2,...,C$. *Slot c* refers to the unit of capacity around the ring associated with the number c. A number of options are available for how a ring utilizes its slots to satisfy (and, when necessary, protect) the demands. Vendor equipment implementing different routing and protection options would come at different costs per unit of capacity. They would also require different amounts of capacity to guarantee protection for all of the demands. The procedure for selecting the most cost-effective ring solution for a given set of demands would be to perform the following steps for each vendor option available:

1. Based on the equipment's characteristics, solve an appropriate version of the *Ring Routing and Slotting* problem, which finds the minimum capacity C required to route and protect the demands. (See, e.g., [3] and [6] for details.)

2. Solve a version of the *Ring Stacking* problem, which uses the available equipment sizes to provide an optimal mix of rings to stack, thus meeting the demand requirement C. Apportion the demands among these rings and calculate the total cost. (See, e.g., [1] and [5])

The vendor option having the minimum total cost would be selected.

With unidirectional rings, each demand unit is assigned to its own slot. Because a ring is two-connected, this same slot can also be used to provide protection if one of the links or nodes fails. Hence the total capacity required for rings of this type is equal to the total demand D. Insofar as the value of D is reliably forecast, this type of ring is robust to demand uncertainty; the capacity requirement is relatively insensitive to the individual variations in the values of $d(i,j)$, as long as the total remains stable.

With bidirectional rings, on the other hand, the capacity requirement is quite sensitive to the individual $d(i,j)$ values and cannot be directly mapped to a function of D. In these rings, one or more demand units are allowed to share slots, as long as their routes do not overlap at any link. Additional capacity is made available to provide the required demand protection. In many cases, it would be possible to select routes (directions) for the demands to pack them in a way that requires considerably less total capacity than the unidirectional alternative. This is traded off against the higher cost of equipment.

Based on the equipment options considered for the bidirectional rings, some version of the *Route and Slot* problem (RSP) models the task of optimally packing the demands to require the minimum total capacity (number of slots). In [3] the authors describe various versions of the problem that model some common options available for bidirectional ring equipment. Most of them are NP-Hard. Some equipment allows the demand units to change slots at an intermediate node in its route on the ring. The associated version of RSP is described in [6] and [11]. Some equipment allows the units from a demand to be split between the clockwise and counter-clockwise directions on the ring instead of just one direction. The associated version of RSP is described in [4] and [10]. The simplest version of RSP arises when both options are available, (see [13]). The most complex version arises when neither option is available (see [3]). In this case, (associated with a two-fiber bidirectional ring), each demand is assigned a direction and each demand unit is packed into one of K (working) slots. K additional slots are required to provide an avenue for those demands that might be impacted by a link or node failure. It is this type of ring we will focus on in the remainder of the paper. It requires the largest capacity of all of the bidirectional ring alternatives and it is most similar to unidirectional rings in both cost and function, so it would serve best for the purpose of comparison. A fast and effective heuristic to find a value for K is described in [2]. It will be a useful routine in the simulation experiments described in the next sections.

2.2   The Impact of Demand Uncertainty

Most forecasting models for $d(i,j)$ use some past data to represent future scenarios. However, a reliable set of deterministic values for every pair of locations often remains elusive for a variety of reasons. The popularity of newly created services may make it difficult to anticipate the volume of demand. Models based on the past may vastly under-estimate or over-estimate the volume of demand these new services will place on the network. Even if the aggregate volume of demand on the network is accurately anticipated, the specific locations generating the demand may not be known. In addition, the actual traffic over the network may fluctuate over time and may migrate between locations during the planning horizon.

Since the capacity requirement for a bidirectional ring is sensitive to the individual $d(i,j)$, even if the total demand D is fixed, one might expect bidirectional rings to be less robust to demand uncertainty than unidirectional rings. Indeed, even if the demand volume D were known, the following characteristics may not be:

– *The demand topology*: describing which pairs of nodes (on the ring) require connection,
– *The demand values*: the values of the individual (non-zero) $d(i,j)$.

The planner takes on some risk when placing a bidirectional ring if the demand characteristics turn out to be quite different from what was expected. If the capacity he or she selected is too high, then the money spent on the unused slots will have been wasted. If the capacity is set too low, then some potential customers will not be served. If the planner chooses to satisfy the unexpected demand volume by using the slots reserved for protection, then the guarantee for 100% protection will not be met if some link or node fails. High-cost, emergency capacity placements may have to be made in order to rectify the situation.

In either of these cases, a cost of lost opportunity is incurred. The parameter r represents the unit penalty from under-capacitating the ring. This includes the lost revenue that would have been earned from each slot. It also includes a (large) penalty factor that represents the impact to customer satisfaction when the network is unable to provide protected services when requested. The parameter c represents the unit penalty from over-capacitating the ring. This is equal to the marginal cost of each (unused) slot in the ring. Finding a value for c can be as straightforward as taking the total equipment cost of some available ring type and dividing by its capacity. A more sophisticated approach would entail running some simulation experiment to represent more typical levels of utilization and performing regression analysis on the results to obtain marginal cost information, (see [7]). An exact value for the revenue parameter r is a bit more elusive. A single slot may serve a variety of demands over the planning horizon; penalty values are quite subjective. For the remainder of this paper, we will assume that r is described as a multiple of c, e.g., $r = 20\ c$. This better represents a planner's evaluation of the trade-off between the two types of planning errors.

3.   A SIMULATION FOR RING SIZING

To measure the extent to which a planner is liable for the cost of some lost opportunity when he or she places a bidirectional ring, we recommend a simulation experiment where a large variety of demand scenarios are generated. In each of these scenarios, values for $d(i,j)$ are set that are consistent with the available information about the demand volume, the total demand at the nodes, the demand topology, and the demand values. Then a heuristic is run to find the optimal capacity requirement associated with each scenario. A histogram representing the distribution of these capacity values is used to help the user select an appropriate capacity and to measure the expected opportunity costs associated with his or her selection.

The process is illustrated on some baseline demand model. In this case, we consider a ring with $n = 15$ nodes and a fixed demand volume $D = 200$. To represent limited knowledge about the demand topology, in each scenario we randomly select $m = 50$ node pairs to have non-zero demand, then the 200 demand units are randomly partitioned among these 50 node pairs. The baseline model represents a very limited amount of planner knowledge. Clearly, if more specific information were available, it would be used in the generation of values for $d(i,j)$. As we shall see, the results of our analysis are not specific to the values we selected for n and D.

In the simulation experiment, we generate 1000 instances consistent with the baseline model. In each of these instances, the unidirectional ring capacity is obviously 200. For bidirectional rings, the *Route then Slot* heuristic described in [2] is run and the value obtained for the number of (working) slots K is doubled to generate the ring capacities C. The distribution of these C values is described with the histogram in Figure 1.

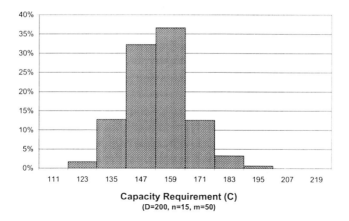

Figure 1. Distribution of Capacity Values for the Baseline Demand Model

The mean capacity in the baseline model is 153.9; the standard deviation is 12.5; the smallest value is 118, the largest is 200. The histogram shows that for all of the scenarios generated, a bidirectional ring of capacity 200 would be sufficient to satisfy the expected demands. As a matter of fact, placing a bidirectional ring with that much capacity may be a waste of money! The histogram also shows that, despite the variability of C under the baseline model, bidirectional rings are a more robust choice than unidirectional rings of the same capacity. This is further evidenced by the graph in Figure 2, which gives the percentage of demands that can be accommodated by a ring of capacity 200, for larger values of D.

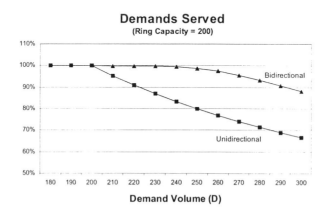

Figure 2. Comparing the Robustness to Total Demand (D)

To develop the graph in Figure 2, we note that a unidirectional ring of capacity 200 can accommodate 200 demand units, so as D increases, a smaller percentage of demand is satisfied. To measure the robustness of bidirectional rings to uncertainty in D, we generate 500 scenarios from the baseline model for each value of D. We calculate the average, over the scenarios, of the proportion of demands that were satisfied. Which is shown on the graph. It turned out that for each value of D represented in the graph, over 99.5% of the scenarios were such that the bidirectional ring served more demand than the unidirectional ring.

It should come as no surprise that as D, the demand volume, increases the required ring capacity would increase linearly with D. As a matter of fact, for each value of D examined in the experiment above, the shapes of the associated histograms are the same. A regression analysis of the results suggests that not only is the average capacity linearly related to D, (i.e., $.76*D$), but the median and other ordinals are as well. Our analysis also shows that the distribution parameters are relatively insensitive to the value of n, the size of the ring. This implies that the histogram in Figure 1, associated with a particular demand volume, ($D=200$), can be translated to situations with a similar demand model but different levels of demand volume. As we shall see, however, these results are not applicable to situations with different demand models.

3.1   Determining Ring Capacity

Given a distribution for C associated with a particular demand model, like the histogram for the baseline model in Figure 1, the planner must now select an appropriate capacity for the ring, which we refer to as C^*. One may interpret the distribution as describing the relative likelihood that a choice for C^* is robust to demand uncertainty. One can also interpret the histogram as describing how the value of the optimal ring capacity may fluctuate throughout the planning horizon. Based on the planner's objectives for the network with regards to costs, the quality of service, and robustness, some selection criteria can be applied through which an appropriate value for C^* can be determined. For instance, if the planner wishes to be 99% sure that the ring will be large enough to accommodate the demands, then he or she could set C^* to the 99th percentile of the distribution, which is $0.91*D$ under the baseline demand model.

If the planner's objective is to minimize the expected opportunity costs from over-sizing or under-sizing the ring, then the problem of finding C^* is equivalent to the *Newsvendor* problem (described in [8]). In that model, a newsstand owner must determine how many newspapers to order each morning to maximize profit in an environment of fluctuating or uncertain customer demand. The revenue parameter r represents the unit (opportunity) costs from under-capacitating; the cost parameter c represents the unit cost of over-capacitating. The model suggests setting C^* to the value where the cumulative relative frequency in the sizing distribution is equal to $((r-c) / r)$.

Suppose, for instance, that the planner establishes that $r = 20^*c$. Then the value of C^* suggested by the model is at the 95th percentile of the distribution, (which is 0.87^*D under the baseline demand model). We point out that the value for C^* is very sensitive to the cost parameters set by the planner.

Once a value for C^* is selected, then the average cost of lost opportunity is calculated from the simulation results as follows. For each of the demand scenarios, the required capacity C is determined. If $C < C^*$, then the cost of over-capacitating is $((C^* - C) * c)$; otherwise the cost of under-capacitating is $((C - C^*) * r)$. For the baseline model, with $D = 200$ and $r = 20^*c$, the Newsvendor model suggests a ring of capacity 174, having a cost of 174^*c. The average opportunity cost is calculated to be 28.6^*c.

3.2 Comparison of Demand Models

The baseline demand model represents a fairly modest level of knowledge about the demand topology and the demand values. As such, a wide variety of demand scenarios can be generated that are consistent with the model. The limited knowledge about demand values is reflected by allowing the demand units to be randomly assigned to any of the node pairs in the topology. For demand models representing a higher level of knowledge about the demand values, e.g., where some $t(i)$ and/or $d(i,j)$ are known, the demand scenarios are drawn from a smaller domain. Hence the variance of the distribution of C values is smaller, so the expected opportunity costs will be lower. A similar argument can be made for demand models which maintain an individual probability distribution for each $d(i,j)$. The parameters assumed for each distribution (e.g., the mean, the standard deviation, the distribution function), betray knowledge about the demand values as well as knowledge about the demand topology, so would result in decisions that have a lower opportunity cost.

The impacts of uncertainty about the demand topology on the opportunity costs are not as easily reasoned. The baseline model represents limited knowledge about the demand topology by specifying that *any* 50 of the 105 possible node pairs (or approximately 50%) require a connection. The effect of this density selection is described in Table 1.

Table 1. Comparison of Demand Models by Topology Density

Demand Model	Description	Mean C	Standard Deviation	Ring Size	Opportunity Cost
Baseline	*50% Density (m=50)*	154	12.4	174	28.6 * c
Sparse	*25% Density (m=25)*	154	15.7	180	34.0 * c
Dense	*75% Density (m=75)*	154	10.9	172	23.6 * c

For each demand model, D is 200 and $r = 20*c$. In the Sparse model, any 25 node pairs can have demand; in the Dense model, 75 node pairs are selected at random. In all three cases, the average value of the required capacity C is 154. The table shows that the sparser models represent a lower level of knowledge and a higher opportunity cost. Since any 25 links can be a part of the topology, a wider variety of demand patterns are generated. This results in a commensurately higher standard deviation for the distribution of C values The Newsvendor model suggests a larger ring capacity (180) to hedge against the inherent risk of under-capacitating.

In a Two Hub model, the demand topology has $2*n$ node pairs. There is a connection between node h and every other node and between node k and every other node. This model represents greater knowledge about the topology than the baseline model. Table 2 describes the impact of the missing information about the locations of hubs h and k.

Table 2. Comparison of Demand Models by Hub Location

Demand Model	Description	Mean C	Standard Deviation	Ring Size	Opportunity Cost
Two Hubs	*Hubs Far Apart*	126	7.4	140	17.6 * c
Two Hubs	*Hubs at Avg Distance*	150	8.7	164	22.6 * c
Two Hubs	*Hubs Adjacent*	192	6.6	204	18.2 * c
Two Hubs	*Hub Locs Unknown*	152	24.3	192	46.7 * c

In the first three cases, where the relative distance between the hubs is known, the average opportunity cost is smaller than that of the baseline model. The average distance in a ring with 15 nodes is four links; the furthest apart a pair of hubs can be is seven links. The simulation experiment shows that a smaller ring is required when the hubs are known to be far apart. This implies a new guideline: if the planner has the option, he or she should choose a physical routing for a ring that keeps the demand centers at a distance. For the case where the hubs are adjacent, the total cost of the bidirectional ring solution is estimated to be *222.2*c*. The unidirectional alternative would cost about *200*c*. This implies another guideline: when the hubs are close to each other, or when there is only one hub on the ring, it may be economical to place unidirectional rings instead of a bidirectional rings. When information about the locations of the hubs is missing the simulation experiment generates all possible scenarios. Clearly, this situation comes with the highest expected opportunity cost.

In a Complete demand model, any of the node pairs can be part of the demand topology. The 200 demand units are randomly spread throughout the network. While may seem that this model reflects the most uncertainty about the demand topology and should replace the baseline model for comparison purposes, it turns out this model is too optimistic. The mean value for the capacity requirement C is only 122. The standard deviation is a relatively small 5.8. The suggested ring capacity is 132 and the associated opportunity cost is a modest *14.2*c*. We explain this phenomenon by pointing out that, in this model, most of the scenarios generated are isomorphic to each other; each node pair is eligible and is likely to receive a very small percentage of the total demand volume. So most of the demand scenarios would require a ring capacity in a relatively small range of values. Therefore any use of this demand model to represent a high level of uncertainty should be reconsidered.

4.   CONCLUSIONS

The simulation-based approach to sizing described in this paper is made possible because of the special properties peculiar to rings. All of the links in a self-healing ring require the same capacity, which includes the capacity for demand protection. The availability of fast heuristics to find the capacity makes it possible to examine a large number of scenarios in a relatively short period of time. If the routines for finding capacities had been more time consuming or if they involved more decision variables, as is the case for mesh networks, then some other approaches must be considered, e.g., variants to those described in [12]. In these approaches, some initial survivable (base) design would be developed; the simulation experiments would identify appropriate changes to the base capacities. The locations where demands are consistently left unserved *or unprotected* would receive increases in capacity; the portions of the network that are consistently under-utilized by working *or protection* traffic would be reduced.

Each of the demand models presented in this document represents a family of similar situations from which the associated distribution can be used to determine a ring capacity. Recall that the distribution parameters of the capacity values are linear in D and somewhat insensitive to n. So it is not necessary to run a new simulation for every ring in the network. Rather, it might be useful for a planner to maintain a repository of representative demand models, having a variety of topologies, along with their associated distributions, which is consulted whenever necessary. Such a repository may also be consulted by a decision support system to replace the thousands of runs of the capacity determination heuristic they presently perform.

The reduction in opportunity costs associated with knowledge about demands suggests that it may be worth the expense to improve the forecasting procedures presently employed in network planning. It may also be worthwhile to develop enhancements to the decision support systems to allow for more flexible modeling of demand information. In cases where the data is imprecise or incomplete, the system could automatically generate a set of demand scenarios that are consistent with the information provided. A reasonable approach would be to develop a mechanism through which planners could articulate their knowledge by answering an adaptive sequence of questions; then the system could narrow down the domain from which to generate demand scenarios. The simulation experiments drawing from this smaller domain would generate a distribution of capacity values having a smaller variance. Hence the opportunity costs would be reduced. Such a system could address the uncertainty in any planning problem requiring information about demands.

ACKNOWLEDGEMENTS

This research was partially supported by a research grant from the Frank G. Zarb School of Business at Hofstra University.

REFERENCES

[1]   Armony, Klincewicz, Luss, and Rosenwein, "Design of Stacked Self-Healing Rings Using a Genetic Algorithm". Fourth INFORMS Telecom Conference, Boca Raton, 1998, to appear in Journal of Heuristics.

[2]   Carpenter, T. and Cosares, S., "A Comparison of Heuristics for Routing and Slot Assignment on Ring Networks", Fifth INFORMS Telecom Conference, Boca Raton, 2000, to appear in Telecom. Systems.

[3]   Carpenter, Cosares, Saniee, "Demand Routing and Slotting on Ring Networks", DIMACS Technical Report 97-02, 1997.

[4]   Cheng, C., "A New Approximation Algorithm for the Demand Routing and Slotting Problem with Unit Demands on Rings", Proc. 2nd Intl Workshop on Approximation Algorithms for Combinatorial Optimization Problems, Berkeley, CA, August 1999.

[5]   Cosares, Deutsch, Saniee, Wasem, "SONET Toolkit: A Decision Support System for the Design of Robust and Cost-Effective Fiber-Optic Networks", Interfaces 25, pp. 20-40, 1995.

[6]   Cosares, S. and Saniee, I. "An Optimization Problem Related to Balancing Loads on SONET Rings", Telecom. Systems 3, pp. 165-181, 1994.

[7]   Cox, Bell, Popken, "What is the Cost of a DS3?," Sixth INFORMS Telecom Conference, Boca Raton, 2002.

[8]   Gass, S. and Harris, C., ed., *Encyclopedia of Operations Research and Management Science*, Kluwer Academic Publishers, 1996.

[9]   Infager, G., *Planning Under Uncertainty*, Boyd & Fraser Publishing, 1994.

[10] Kumar, V., "Approximating Circular-arc Coloring and Bandwidth Allocation in All-optical Ring Networks", Proc. First Intl Workshop on Approximation Algorithms for Combinatorial Optimization Problems, Aalborg, July, 1998.

[11] Schrijver, Seymour, Winkler, "The Ring Loading Problem", SIAM J. Disc. Math 11, pp. 1-14, 1998.

[12] Sen, Doverspike, Cosares, "Network Planning with Random Demands", Telecommunications Systems 3, pp. 11-30, 1994.

[13] Vachani, Shulman, Kubat, Ward, "Multicommodity Flows in Ring Networks", INFORMS Journal on Computing, 8, pp. 235-242, 1996.

[14] Wasem, Gross, Tlapa, "Forecasting Broadband Demand Between Geographic Areas" IEEE Communications Magazine, pp. 50-57, February 1995.

Chapter 6

AN EVOLUTIONARY APPROACH TO THE MULTI-LEVEL CAPACITATED MINIMUM SPANNING TREE PROBLEM

Ioannis Gamvros
The Robert H. Smith School of Business
University of Maryland, College Park, MD 20742
igamvros@rhsmith.umd.edu

S. Raghavan*
The Robert H. Smith School of Business
University of Maryland, College Park, MD 20742
raghavan@umd.edu

Bruce Golden
The Robert H. Smith School of Business
University of Maryland, College Park, MD 20742
bgolden@rhsmith.umd.edu

Abstract   Capacitated network design is a crucial problem to telecommunications network planners. In this paper we consider the Multi-Level Capacitated Minimum Spanning Tree Problem (MLCMST), a generalization of the well-known Capacitated Minimum Spanning Tree Problem. We present a genetic algorithm, based on the notion of grouping, that is quite effective in solving large-scale problems to within 10% of optimality.

Keywords: Network Design, Capacitated Minimum Spanning Tree, Multi-Level, Genetic Algorithms.

*Partially supported by Center for Satellite and Hybrid Communication Networks, University of Maryland.

1.   Introduction

One problem that arises often in practice in the design of local access communications networks is the Terminal Layout Problem. This problem is typically referred to in the Operations Research literature as the Capacitated Minimum Spanning Tree Problem (CMST) and has been extensively studied by many researchers over the years (see [9] for an extensive review). In the CMST problem, we are given a set of customer locations or terminals, each with its own traffic requirements that we wish to transport to a given *central* location (node). Furthermore, a single type of facility with a fixed capacity K is available for installation on a link. Each link can only have a single facility installed, and we wish to design a feasible minimum cost tree network—as defined by the links that have facilities installed on them—to carry the traffic. In practice, it seems unreasonable to assume that only a single type of facility is available to the network planner. Consequently, in this paper, we deal with a generalization of the CMST problem that we believe reflects the practical concerns that arise in the design of local access networks more closely. In our problem, we allow for the installation of multiple types of facilities with differing capacities. This problem we call the Multi-Level Capacitated Minimum Spanning Tree Problem (MLCMST).

Formally, the MLCMST is defined as follows: Given a graph $G = (N, E)$, with node set $N = \{0, 1, 2, \ldots, n\}$, where node 0 represents the central facility and the rest are customer locations, and edge set E, W_i the traffic requirement (or weight) of node i to be transported to the *central node* 0, facility types $0, 1, \ldots, L$ with capacities $Z_0 < Z_1 < \ldots < Z_L$ and cost function C_{ij}^l denoting the cost of a facility of type l installed between nodes i and j; we wish to find a minimum cost tree network on G to carry the traffic.

Figure 6.1 gives an example of the MLCMST problem. In Figure 6.1(a), the square node in the center is the central node to which traffic must be transported. There are 3 types of links with capacities $Z_0 = 1, Z_1 = 3$, and $Z_2 = 6$, and the traffic generated from each node is 1 unit. Figure 6.1(b) shows a feasible multi-level capacitated spanning tree. Notice, the topology of the network is a tree, and traffic on any link is less than or equal to the capacity of the facility installed on the link.

In general, the traffic requirements for each of the terminal nodes can be different. However, in this paper we restrict our attention to unit demand problems: i.e., problems with $W_i = 1$ for all customer nodes. Additionally, we restrict our attention to (realistic) cost functions that exhibit economies of scale that usually exist in communication networks. In other words, the cost function satisfies the relationship

$$C_{ij}^y \leq \frac{Z_y}{Z_x} C_{ij}^x$$

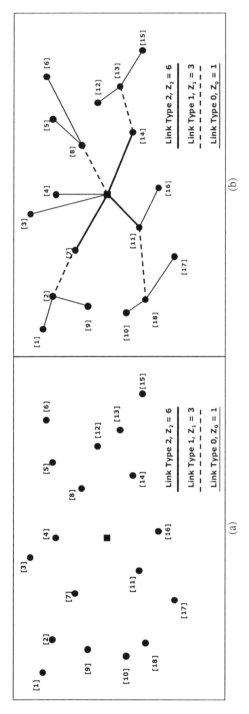

Figure 6.1. Multi-Level Capacitated Minimum Spanning Tree. (a) Nodes in the network. (b) Feasible Multi-Level Capacitated Spanning Tree.

for every edge $\{i, j\} \in E$, and $x < y$. We also impose the restriction that only a single facility type is permitted to be installed on a link. This condition is actually not restrictive. If multiple facilities can be installed on a link, Salman et al. [19] point out, in the context of a related problem, that by applying a dynamic programming algorithm one can convert the problem to one where only a single facility type is installed on a link. This is done by determining the optimal combinations for all traffic levels, and creating new link types each representing one of the optimal combinations.

1.1   Related Literature

The MLCMST does not appear to have been given much attention by researchers previously. The most closely related problem is the so called Local Access Network Design (LAND) problem [3, 19] or the so-called Telpak problem [18]. In the LAND problem, as in the MLCMST, we are given traffic demand from nodes in a network that need to be transported to a central node, varying facility types with differing costs and capacities, and we wish to design a minimum cost network to transport this traffic. However, the topology of the underlying network is not restricted to be a tree. Herein lies the distinction between the MLCMST problem and the LAND problem. In a survey paper, Gavish [9] describes the Telpak problem, but restricts it to a tree. He presents a formulation for this problem, and also points to the lack of attention given to this important problem by researchers.

Berger et al. [3] propose a tabu search procedure for the LAND problem to obtain good heuristic solutions for problems with up to 200 nodes, and 9 cable types. In their problem, the demand from a node must travel to the central node along the same path (i.e., demand splitting is not allowed). Salman et al. [19] study the version of the LAND problem that allows demand splitting, and propose a branch and bound procedure using a technique called search by objective relaxation. Using this technique, they solve to optimality problems with 10 nodes, and up to 9 cable types.

On the other hand, the CMST problem has attracted a lot of attention from the research community over the years. The most well-known heuristic for the problem is the Esau-Williams heuristic [5] that starts with a feasible star solution and uses a savings calculation to create and merge subtrees. This heuristic is still used as a benchmark against which other techniques are evaluated. Sharma [21] and McGregor at al. [15] propose algorithms based on a clustering (grouping) approach. They first assign the nodes into groups and then find a Minimum Spanning Tree (MST) for each group. Karnaugh [13], Kershenbaum et al. [14], and Gouveia and Lopes [12] describe so-called Second Order Greedy Algorithms (SOGA). These are local search heuristics that start with an initial solution generated typically by the Esau-Williams heuristic and try to improve it by either restricting the solution to include or exclude some links. Gavish and Altinkemer [10] describe a parallel savings heuristic that adds to the solution multiple links per iteration.

More recently, metaheuristic approaches such as simulated annealing and tabu search have been successfully used to obtain high-quality solutions for the CMST problem space. Sharaiha et al. [20] present a tabu search approach for the problem. Bourjolly et al. [4] use simulated annealing in order to search the solution space. With the help of a modified version of Esau-Williams and a neighborhood description, they were able to generate effective solutions using the simulated annealing approach. They compared their results with Sharaiha et al.'s tabu search algorithm for 40, 50, 80, and 100 node size problems, both with unit demand and non-unit demand, and for the cases where the central node is at the center and at the edge of the graph. The simulated annealing algorithm outperformed the tabu search algorithm for smaller size non-unit demand problems, and on unit demand problems for which the central node was located at the center. Amberg et al. [2] compare a simulated annealing approach and three tabu search approaches with the Esau-Williams algorithm for different parameters for the metaheuristics. They tested their algorithms for 40 and 80 node size unit-demand problems with the central node either at the center or at the edge and achieved 1% to 7% improvements over Esau-Williams when the parameters of the metaheuristics were optimized. Recently, Ahuja et al. [1] present an improved neighborhood structure for the CMST problem, which they use in conjunction with a tabu search algorithm to generate solutions. They present improvements over the best known solutions for different sets of problems. For non-unit demand problems, their algorithm improved the best-known solution in terms of cost by 3% on average. Patterson and Pirkul [17] have embedded different heuristic processes into the topological design of a neural network and have used this network to generate solutions. They reported that the neural network that was based on the Esau-Williams algorithm was able to find solutions that were, on average, 0.5% away from the optimum with running times close to one hour for 150 node problems.

1.2   Overview of our Approach

In this paper, we present a genetic algorithm for the MLCMST. Conceptually, our approach splits this problem into two parts: a grouping problem and a network design problem. The grouping problem aims at finding the best assignment of the nodes into groups that correspond to subtrees of the central node. Consequently, it makes sure that the sum of the weights in a group does not exceed the capacity of the highest capacity link. In other words, for every group we require that $\sum W_i \leq Z_L$. The cost of an assignment to the grouping part is determined by solving the network design subproblem. It requires the construction of a minimum cost multi-level tree network that will connect all the nodes in each of the groups with the central node. Notice that this problem is identical to the MLCMST, but defined on each of the groupings. We apply our genetic algorithm (GA) to the grouping problem. Consequently, the GA calls upon the construction heuristic to construct subtrees on the groupings and provide the cost (fitness) of the solution to the problem.

The notion of determining groupings (or nodes in a subtree) has been used previously by some researchers for the CMST problem [1, 2, 15, 20, 21]. Observe that, in the case of the CMST problem, interconnecting nodes that belong to the same subtree is quite simple as it is the Minimum Spanning Tree problem. While, in the case of the MLCMST it is identical to the original problem, albeit on a smaller graph.

1.3   Organization of this Paper

The rest of the paper is organized as follows. Section 2 describes our genetic algorithm procedure. Next, Section 3 describes the construction heuristic that the genetic algorithm uses to construct a multi-level tree with unit degree at the root. Then, Section 4 describes a mixed integer programming formulation for the problem. We used the LP-relaxation of this model to obtain lower bounds for our problem. We present our computational experiments in Section 5. Section 6 outlines some directions where, we believe, some improvements may be obtained for the solution procedure.

2.   Genetic Algorithm

A genetic algorithm is a powerful evolutionary local search algorithm that typically consists of a few basic steps as shown in Figure 2. At first, an initial population of feasible solutions (chromosomes) $P(t)$ has to be created. After the creation of the initial population, we evaluate the fitness of all the individuals in that population. This evaluation is required to check the termination condition and at the selection step. Usually, genetic algorithms terminate when there are no improvements in a number of successive populations (generations) or after a predefined number of generations. The selection step chooses different chromosomes from the old population $P(t - 1)$ for reproduction. After the chromosomes are selected, they reproduce (crossover) to create children. The next population $P(t)$ is determined by taking some fraction of the best children, and some fraction of the best (elite) parents (this process is called elitism). At this stage, random mutations can arbitrarily change the genetic material found in the population. The purpose of mutations is to divert the search process to places that it wouldn't have examined otherwise. In the following sections, we elaborate on each of the steps of our genetic algorithm. Prior to that, we discuss

Begin
       $t \longleftarrow 0$
       initialize $P(t)$
       evaluate $P(t)$
       while (not termination-condition) **do**
            $t \longleftarrow t + 1$
            select parents from $P(t-1)$
            reproduce parents
            Determine $P(t)$ from children and elite parents
            $P(t)$: mutations
            evaluate $P(t)$
       end
end

Figure 6.2.   Steps of a Genetic Algorithm.

the data structure or *representation* that we use to represent chromosomes in our GA.

We use a representation proposed by Falkenauer [6] in the context of bin packing. This representation, as shown in Figure 6.3, breaks up the chromosome representing the solution into two parts. An item part and a group part. In the item part, the nodes are assumed to be ordered in increasing order, and the characters represent the group (subtree of the central node) that the node belongs to. The group part contains a list of groups (subtrees) that make up the tree solution. The representation shown in Figure 6.3 indicates that nodes $1, 3, 4$, and 7 are in a group (group **A**), nodes $2, 5$, and 6 are in a group (group **B**), nodes $8, 9$, and 10 form a group (group **C**), and node 11 forms a group (group **D**). The group part lists the four groups **A, B, C,** and **D**. Observe that the order of the groups in the group part does not alter the grouping represented by the chromosome. Further, the mnemonic used to identify groupings is largely irrelevant (other than they be distinct from each other). Also note that since the number of subtrees of the root node will vary by solution, the length of the group part of the chromosome will vary.

The advantage of this representation is that it allows for a focus on the groups in a solution (via the group part), which is how we have approached the problem. Further, in the context of the bin packing problem, Falkenauer [6] indicates that this representation has short, low-order, high-performance schemata, which

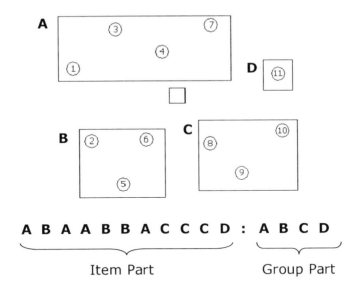

Figure 6.3.   Representation of a solution in the Genetic Algorithm.

according to the Building Block Hypothesis [11] typically results in high quality solutions.

2.1   Initial Population

Since any genetic material - apart from mutations - found in the final solution will come from the individuals in this population, the choice of the initial population is a very important aspect of the whole search procedure. If it is too specific, then the search will be limited to a small region of the solution space leading to a local optimum. On the other hand, if the initial population is very diverse then the algorithm will spend valuable computational resources exploring a variety of promising areas of the search space.

To create the initial population, we use the Esau-Williams heuristic [5] to solve a CMST problem on our graph by setting the (subtree) capacity constraint to Z_L, the maximum capacity in our problem. For convenience we state the Esau-Williams algorithm below. Since the Esau-Williams heuristic gives a unique solution for a given graph, and we need our initial population to be diverse, we multiply the cost of each edge, C_{ij}^L by a uniformly distributed random variable in the range $[(1 - \epsilon), (1 + \epsilon)]$. Varying the value of ϵ trades off between increased diversity of the initial population (for large ϵ) and early termination to a solution further away from the global optimum (for small ϵ).

To create increased variety in the initial population, we also experimented with changing the capacity constraint K of the Esau-Williams algorithm. Specifically, we configured the capacity constraint as a uniformly distributed integer random variable in the range $[Z_L - \delta, Z_L]$. Each time we run the Esau-Williams heuristic to determine an initial solution, we also varied the capacity constraint in this manner.

Esau-Williams Heuristic.   In the CMST problem, we are given a root node r, a link facility with capacity K, and facility costs C_{ij} for installing a facility on link $\{i, j\}$. The Esau-Williams heuristic is applied to the CMST on a complete graph. It starts with a feasible star network by connecting each node directly to the root node. It then computes the savings obtained by merging two subtrees of the root node for every pair of subtrees of the root node. It does this by computing a savings value

$$S_{ij} = \min_{k \in T(i)} C_{kr} - C_{ij}$$

where $T(i)$ denotes the nodes in i's subtree ($T(i)$ does not include the root node). This represents the savings obtained by connecting node i to j, and deleting the connection from node i's subtree to the root node. By definition $S_{ij} = \infty$ when nodes i and j are in the same subtree, or if the demand in the subtree obtained by merging i's subtree and j's subtree is greater than K. The algorithm selects the highest (positive) savings, merges the two subtrees corresponding to this savings to obtain a new feasible tree. Next, the savings function is updated, and the procedure continues until no savings can be obtained by merging subtrees (i.e., all $S_{ij} \leq 0$).

2.2 Crossover

The crossover operator is responsible for combining two chromosomes so that a new offspring chromosome can be generated. It is important to note here that the crossover operator should not only guarantee that the offspring chromosome will be a valid one (i.e., it will satisfy the constraints imposed by the problem) but it should also make sure that meaningful genetic material (i.e., building blocks) is passed on from the parents to the children.

Our crossover operator is identical to that of Falkenauer [6], with a small change specific to the MLCMST problem. It is applied to the group part of the chromosome structure, and is able to work with chromosomes of varying length. It consists of the following steps:

1 Select at random two crossing sites, which define the crossing section, on the group part of the two parent chromosomes.

2 Inject the contents between the two crossing sites of the first parent just before the first crossing site of the second parent.

3 Update the membership of the items as follows. All items will belong to the group specified in the second parent, unless the group to which the item belongs in the first parent is injected into the second parent. In that case, the item would have a new membership specified by the group of the first parent. If any group is empty as a result, remove it from the group part.

4 Finally, if a group from the second parent has lost items and it now has less than k items, we reassign these items to other groups with probability p_{cr}. If any group is empty as a result, remove it from the group part. (This step differs from Falkenauer [6].)

We illustrate the procedure with the example shown in Figure 6.4. Consider the two chromosomes shown in Figure 6.4(a). To perform a crossover, we generate at random two crossing sites for each chromosome. They are just prior to and after group **B** for the first parent, and just prior to group **a** and after group **b** for the second parent as shown below.

$$
\begin{array}{cccccccccc}
A & B & A & A & B & B & A & C & C & C & D \\
a & b & a & c & b & b & c & b & b & d & c
\end{array}
\quad : \quad
\begin{array}{cccc}
A & |B| & C & D \\
 & |a \quad b| & c & d
\end{array}
$$

Injecting the contents of the crossing section of the first parent ($|\mathbf{B}|$) to the second parent at the first crossing site of the second parent, we obtain **Babcd** as the new grouping for the child. The group membership of the nodes in the child follow from the second parent, unless the group that the node belongs to in the first parent has been injected into the group part. Since **B** is the only group injected from the first parent, the item part of the child is **aBacBBcbbdc**. Consequently, we obtain the chromosome **aBacBBcbbdc** : **Babcd** from the crossover (as shown in Figure 6.4(b).

The final step in the crossover procedure is specifically designed for our problem and it aims at improving the result of the crossover operator. In other grouping problems, like the bin packing problem, for example, it is desired that all the bins are close to or at their maximum capacity. Thus, usually a heuristic like First Fit Decreasing is applied to reassign nodes in groups with fewer items. In our case, however, it is not wise to reassign nodes to any group just because it has available capacity. Actually it is not certain that there will be any gains by reassigning these nodes at all. Consequently, we design our reassignment procedure as follows. Observe that the membership in the groups is either identical to the group in the first parent, or is a subset of the group in the second parent. Our reassignment procedure focuses on such groups (i.e., where the group is inherited from the second parent but has fewer members than in the parent). If the number of items in such a group is less than a parameter k,

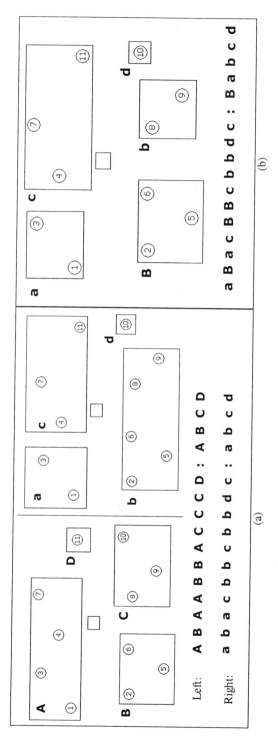

Figure 6.4. Crossover Operator in Genetic Algorithm. (a) Parents, (b) Offspring.

then, with probability p_{cr}, each item is assigned to the group that the closest node not in its group belongs to.

For example, suppose $k = 3$, and $p_{cr} = 0.5$ and consider the result in Figure 6.4(b). The only group that qualifies and must be considered for reassignments is group b. Then, with probability 0.5, we reassign node 9 to the group that node 10 (assuming 10 is closest to it and the group has sufficient capacity to accommodate node 9), and with probability 0.5 we reassign 8 to the group that node 6 is in (assuming that 6 is closest to it).

2.3   Mutation Operator

Our mutation operator aims at shuffling some of the items among groups. Specifically, our mutation operator is applied with probability p_μ to each node (item) of every chromosome and it searches for alternative groups that this node can be assigned to. The search is done by finding a set of nodes M for which $C_{im}^0 < C_{m0}^0$, where m is the node that the operator acts on, i are the nodes in M and 0 is the central node. We then consider the nodes i, one by one, starting with the one with the smallest C_{im}^0 and check to see if the group that this node i belongs to has available capacity. If there is available capacity and the group that i belongs to is different from the current group that m belongs to we reassign m to the new group. Otherwise we move on to the next node in M. If no node in M satisfies these constraints, node m is not reassigned.

Consider the chromosome shown in Figure 6.4(b). Suppose we apply the mutation operator to node 4. For node 4, $M = \{3, 7\}$. Since 3 is closest node to 4 in M, it is considered first; and since it belongs to a different group, node 4 is assigned to that group creating the chromosome **aBaaBBcbbdc : Babcd**.

2.4   Selection

The selection procedure is an important step in the genetic algorithm. If the selective pressure is too strong (i.e., only the fittest individuals are selected for reproduction), then it is possible that some very fit chromosomes are going to dominate early in the search process and lead the algorithm to a local optimum, thus terminating the search. On the other hand, if the selective pressure is too weak (i.e., even individuals with low fitness have a high probability of being selected for reproduction), then the algorithm is going to traverse the solution space aimlessly. We employ the classical roulette wheel mechanism [16] to select the chromosomes that will participate in reproduction and create subsequent generations.

In the GA structure presented in Figure 2, we did not specify how many children to generate. Some options are to generate as many children as the population size, or to generate more offspring than the population size and select only the best of those to make up the next generation. Additionally, we

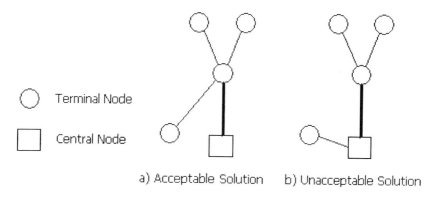

a) Acceptable Solution   b) Unacceptable Solution

Figure 6.5.   Construction heuristic must generate a solution where the central node has degree 1.

employ elitism. We ensure that a percentage E of each generation is made up of selected individuals (i.e., the alive chromosomes) from the previous generation. We select these *elite* individuals by evaluating and selecting the best parents.

3.   Construction Heuristic

The GA uses the construction heuristic to construct subtrees on the groupings in order to evaluate them. Given that the GA will repeatedly call the construction heuristic and use the solutions generated by it to evaluate the groupings, it is crucial that the construction heuristic is fast and provides near-optimal solutions.

The problem at hand is almost identical to the overall problem, except that it is defined on a smaller network (the subgraph defined by the grouping). However, for the construction heuristic, we impose the additional restriction that the degree of the central node is 1. The notion is that each grouping represents a subtree of the central node and, thus, when the subtree is viewed in isolation it has degree 1 at the central node. Notice that as a consequence, we ignore solutions that may be slightly better where the central node has a degree greater than 1. Figure 6.5 illustrates this point. Our rationale for keeping the degree of the central node 1 is that if a better solution exists where the degree of the central node is greater than 1, then that corresponds to new groupings which we leave for the GA to identify.

In our heuristic, we assume the graph is complete. The first step of our heuristic consists of determining the node that is to be connected directly to the central node (i.e., the node in the subtree that will be directly connected to the root). For each node, we calculate the sum of distances to each node in the grouping including the central node, and select the node with the minimum value (we call this node the *centroid* node), to be in the set of candidate nodes

N_C that would be considered for connection to the central node. To this set, we add all nodes in the grouping that are closer to the central node than the "centroid node".

Initially, all nodes are connected to the node that is to be directly connected to the central node with the lowest capacity link (link type 0). Thus, if we ignore the connection to the central node, then this node takes the role of a central node for the subtree, and all nodes are connected directly to it using the lowest capacity links in a star configuration. Our construction heuristic considers the savings obtained by upgrading the capacity of a link to the node that is directly connected to the central node, and connecting other nodes through this upgraded link. Specifically, our construction heuristic solves the following *core problem*.

We are given a complete graph with node set N^*, a root node r, two link types, 0 and l, with capacities $Z_0 < Z_l$, costs C_{ij}^0 and C_{ij}^l respectively, and an initial tree network that is constructed as a star with r at the center using link type 0. We would like to determine where to upgrade the connections in the star network to facilities of type l, and reconnect some of the links with capacity Z_0 to this connection instead of their direct connection to the root node. Obviously, upgrading the capacity of the connection will increase the cost, but if the cost of the lower capacity connections is reduced, that might reduce the overall cost. Figure 6.6 illustrates the core problem.

Our solution approach to the core problem consists of the following steps. We start with the star network and construct a savings value $d_{ij} = C_{jr}^0 - C_{ij}^0$, where r denotes the root node for the problem. This represents the savings in connecting node j to node i. We then compute for each node D_i the overall savings in upgrading link $\{i, r\}$ to a facility of type l. We compute

$$D_i = C_{ir}^0 - C_{ir}^l + \max_{\{J:|J|<Z_l\}} \sum_{\{j:d_{ij}>0, j\in J\}} d_{ij}$$

for each node i directly connected to the root r by a facility of type 0. The first two terms represent the change in cost by upgrading link $\{i, r\}$ from a facility of type 0 to a facility of type l. The third term represents the greatest savings obtained by changing the connections $\{j, r\}$ to the connections $\{j, i\}$ ensuring that the capacity of facility l is not violated. We then select the largest D_i. This represents the largest savings obtained by upgrading link $\{i, r\}$ and implementing it. We repeatedly apply this procedure, recomputing the savings d_{ij} and D_i in the core problem until there are no more savings (i.e., $D_i \leq 0$). Note that once we construct a subtree of the root by this savings procedure, we will not consider the nodes it contains in computing further savings.

Our overall procedure starts with the highest capacity level that is greater than or equal to the size of the group. For example if the group size is 4, and the smallest capacity that is greater than or equal to 4 is one with a capacity of 5, the procedure starts with the facility of type, say k, with the capacity of 5. We

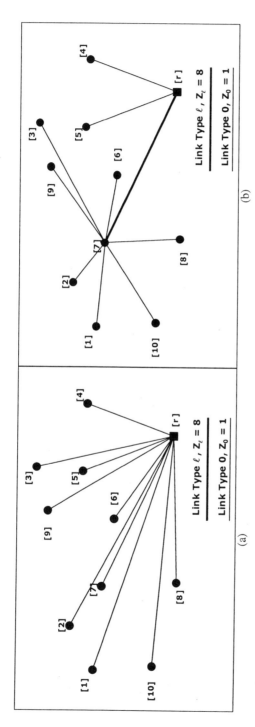

Figure 6.6. Core problem in construction heuristic for constructing tree on grouping. (a) All nodes are connected to a "root" node via links of capacity Z_0. (b) Determine savings by upgrading links connected to the "root" to capacity Z_l and redirecting the connections to the "root" to the node whose connection to the root has been upgraded (i.e., in this example, node 7).

identify the set of candidate nodes N_C that will connect the group to the central node. We select a node in N_C and create a star network connecting the nodes in the grouping to it with facilities of type 0. We then consider the core problem with facilities of type $l = k - 1$ (one lower than what we started with). We apply the savings procedure until there are no more savings. We then consider the network defined by the lowest capacity facilities in the current solution. For each of the stars in this network, we consider the core problem with facilities of type $l = k - 2$, and apply the savings heuristic. We repeat this procedure, constructing the network defined by the lowest capacity facilities in the current solution, and solving the core problem, lowering the value of l by 1 each time, until we are left with $l = 0$. The final level (i.e., when $l = 0$) deals with the lowest capacity levels. If the lowest level facility has capacity 1, we stop. Otherwise, our last step is to perform the familiar Esau-Williams heuristic on each of the star networks defined by the lowest capacity links. We perform these steps for each of the nodes in N_C, and so have $|N_C|$ different solutions. Consequently, we select as the solution of the construction heuristic the one that is of lowest cost among these $|N_C|$ solutions.

Figure 6.7 gives an example of our construction heuristic procedure. Figure 6.7(a) shows the set of nodes and the set N_C consisting of nodes $6, 7, 13$, and 18. As shown in Figure 6.7(b), we select node 7, as it is in N_C, and create a star connecting all nodes to 7 (except the central node) with link type 0. We solve the core problem on this star network with $l = 2$, to obtain the network shown in Figure 6.7(c). Observe link $\{2, 7\}$ has been upgraded to a facility of type 2, and nodes $1, 11, 15, 16, 17, 19$, and 20, are directly connected to node 2. Also, link $\{5, 7\}$ has been upgraded, and nodes $3, 4, 6, 9, 13, 14$, and 18, are directly connected to node 5. We now lower the value of l to 1, and consider the star networks defined by the lowest capacity facilities. There are three star networks: one at node 2 with direct links to nodes $1, 11, 15, 16, 17, 19$, and 20; one at node 7 with direct links to nodes $8, 10$, and 12; and one at node 5 with direct links to nodes $3, 4, 6, 9, 13, 14$, and 18. We solve the core problem on these three star networks to obtain the solution shown in Figure 6.7(d). We lower l to 0. Since $l = 0$ and $Z_0 = 1$ we stop.

4.   Mixed-Integer Programming Model

We now describe a strong Mixed-Integer Programming Model for the ML-CMST. We obtained lower bounds to evaluate our Genetic Algorithm by solving the Linear Programming relaxation of the model. A related paper [8] provides additional details on the strength of the formulation.

We model the problem on a directed graph. To do this, we replace each edge $\{i, j\}$ in the graph by two directed arcs (i, j) and (j, i). We denote the set of directed arcs by A. The cost of installing a facility of type l on an arc (i, j), C_{ij}^l,

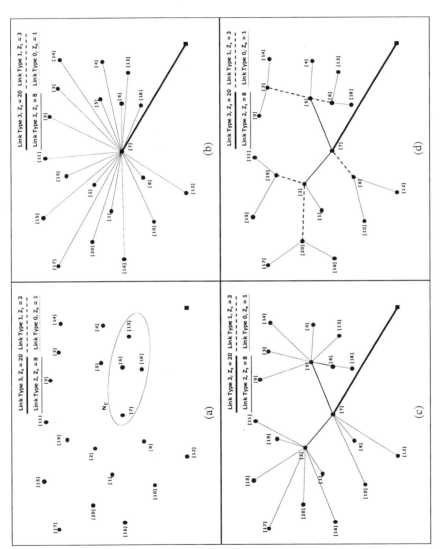

Figure 6.7. Construction heuristic example.

is identical to the cost of installing a facility of type l on edge $\{i, j\}$. We will introduce two types of arc variables in our model. Let x_{ij} denote whether a facility is installed on arc (i, j), being 1 if a facility is installed on the arc, and 0 otherwise. Let y_{ij}^k be 1 if a facility of type k is installed on arc (i, j), and 0 otherwise. Thus, it identifies the type of facility installed on arc (i, j).

We create a commodity for each terminal node, with a supply of 1 at the terminal node, and a demand of 1 at the central node. In our notation, the origin of commodity k is node k and the destination of commodity k is node 0. We let f_{ij}^k denote the flow of commodity k on arc (i, j). Our multicommodity directed flow formulation (MCF) for the problem is:

$$(\text{MCF}) \quad \min \sum_{(i,j) \in A} \sum_{l=0}^{L} C_{ij}^l y_{ij}^l \tag{6.1}$$

$$\text{s.t.} \quad \sum_{j \in N} f_{ji}^k - \sum_{l \in N} f_{il}^k = \begin{cases} -1 & \text{if } i = k; \\ 1 & \text{if } i = 0; \quad \forall i \in N, k \in K \\ 0 & \text{otherwise}; \end{cases} \tag{6.2}$$

$$\sum_{k \in K} f_{ij}^k \leq \sum_{l=0}^{L} Z_l y_{ij}^l \quad \forall (i, j) \in A, \tag{6.3}$$

$$\sum_{l=0}^{L} y_{ij}^l = x_{ij} \quad \forall (i, j) \in A, \tag{6.4}$$

$$f_{ij}^k \leq x_{ij} \quad \forall (i, j) \in A, k \in K, \tag{6.5}$$

$$\sum_{j \in N} x_{0j} = 0 \tag{6.6}$$

$$\sum_{j \in N} x_{ij} = 1 \quad \forall i \in N, i \neq 0, \tag{6.7}$$

$$x_{ij} + x_{ji} \leq 1 \quad \forall (i, j) \in A, \tag{6.8}$$

$$x_{ij} \in \{0, 1\} \quad \forall (i, j) \in A, \tag{6.9}$$

$$y_{ij}^l \in \{0, 1\} \quad \forall (i, j) \in A, l = 0, \dots, L, \tag{6.10}$$

$$f_{ij}^k \geq 0 \quad \forall (i, j) \in A, k \in K. \tag{6.11}$$

Constraints 6.2, 6.5, 6.6, 6.7, and 6.8 ensure that the topology of the underlying network is a tree that is directed towards the central node. Constraint 6.4 ensures that only one type of facility is installed on an arc, and only if the arc is selected to be in the multi-level capacitated tree (i.e., only if $x_{ij} = 1$). Constraint 6.3 ensures that the flow sent on a link is less than the capacity installed on the link.

Table 6.1. Genetic Algorithm Parameters.

Category	Description	Name	Value
General	Population Size	-	100
	Num. of Offspring	-	300
Selection	Selection of parents	-	Roulette
	Elitism	E	50%
Mutation	Classic Mutation Rate	p_μ	1%
Initial Population	Cost Matrix Perturbation	ϵ	0.1
	Group size Range	δ	0
Stopping Criteria	Maximum Number of Generations	-	50
	Num. of generations without improvement	-	10
Crossover	Probability of Reassignment	p_{cr}	1
	Num. of nodes for Reassignment	k	< 6

5. Computational Experiments

We now report on several computational experiments with the GA for the MLCMST problem. We coded our GA and construction heuristic in Visual C++. We conducted all runs on a Dual Processor Pentium III PC running Windows 2000, 1GHz clock speed, and with 512MB RAM.

We generated three sets of 50 terminal node problems—one with the root node in the center, one with the root node in the corner, and one where the root node is located randomly—each containing 50 problem instances (together with the root node there are a total of 51 nodes in these problem instances). We label these three sets 50c, 50e, and 50r respectively. The points in these problems are generated randomly on a 20×20 grid. We also generated one 100 terminal node problem set—containing 50 problem instances—with the root node in the center. We label this set of problems 100c. For all test problems, we used three link types with capacities 1, 3, and 10 respectively. The cost of link type 0, C_{ij}^0, is equal to the Euclidean distance between the two end points of the link (all instances were on complete graphs). The cost of link type 1 is equal to twice the cost of link type 0, and the cost of link type 2 is equal to six times the cost of link type 0.

To compare the results of the GA to a lower bound, we solved the LP relaxation of the multicommodity directed flow formulation presented in Section 4. We coded this formulation in the ILOG OPL Studio programming language and ran it on the same computer as the GA. Our version of ILOG OPL Studio uses CPLEX 7.1 to solve the optimization problems.

Table 6.2. Computational results for GA on 50 and 100 node problems. Results are a summary over 50 instances for each case.

Problem group	GA solutions		GA running time		Gap	
	Ave	Range	Ave (sec)	Range (sec)	Ave %	Range %
50c	598.858	543.987–657.207	33.3	19.0–56.4	9.95%	6.86%–12.67%
50e	1081.767	955.497–1173.596	78.8	57.0–99.0	5.90%	4.15%–7.28%
50r	764.060	551.855–1081.390	65.4	43.0–88.8	8.08%	5.37%–12.27%
100c	1111.776	1014.684–1219.632	66.6	48.8–92.6	7.68%	6.43%–9.95%

Table 6.3. Lower bound results for 50 and 100 node problems. Results are a summary over 50 instances for each case.

Problem group	Lower bounds		LP running time	
	Ave	Range	Ave (sec)	Range (sec)
50c	544.688	499.420–601.044	252.3	149.8–612.2
50e	1021.578	897.726–1117.859	3454.9	1941.2–6158.3
50r	707.656	507.171–1019.981	1488.3	234.8–3496.4
100c	1032.446	953.365–1135.519	7121.2	4212.7–15563.3

After significant computational testing on the different GA parameters [7] we selected the values shown in Table 6.1.

Tables 6.2 and 6.3 summarize the results of our computations for the 50 node and 100 node problems. The gap shown in Table 6.2 represents the difference between the GA solution and the lower bound divided by the lower bound, expressed in percentage terms. This gap provides an upper bound, or a guarantee, on how far the GA solution is from optimality.

Comparing the results for the 50 node problems we find that the average gap is about 9.95% (with a range of 6.86%-12.67%) and average running time of the GA is 34 seconds for 50 node problems with the central node in the center. When the central node is in the corner, the running time of the GA goes up to an average of 79 seconds, but the quality of the solutions improves, with an average gap of 5.90% (with a range of 4.15%-7.28%). When the central node is selected randomly, the results are in between these two cases. Examining the results for the set of 100 node problems with the central node in the center, we find the average running time of the GA has doubled to about 67 seconds. Surprisingly, as the problem size has increased, the quality of the solutions has improved with an average gap of 7.68% (with a range of 6.43%-9.95%). It is not clear why this is the case, but it appears that as the problem size increases the GA does well in finding good groupings that are close to the maximum link capacity.

In Table 6.3, we report on the value of the lower bound and the running time for CPLEX to solve the LP relaxation of our multicommodity directed flow formulation (i.e., to obtain the lower bound). Observe that the average running time increases from about 252 seconds to 3455 seconds when the central node is moved from the center to the corner. In other words when the central node is in the corner the linear program becomes harder to solve. Additionally when the problem size increase from 50 nodes to 100 nodes (with central node in the center) the running time increases from an average of 252 seconds to 7121 seconds. This is due to the size of the formulation which grows quite rapidly (it has $\mathcal{O}(|N|^3 + L|N|^2)$ variables and $\mathcal{O}(|N|^3)$ constraints).

We wanted to get a better assessment of the gap between the GA solution and our lower bound. For this reason we tried solving to optimality smaller instances of the MLCMST problem. Surprisingly, we found that the following single commodity directed flow model (SCF) that is weaker than the multicommodity directed flow model proposed in Section 4 solves faster with CPLEX (as an MIP) than the MCF model.

(SCF) $\min \sum_{(i,j) \in A} \sum_{l=0}^{L} C_{ij}^l y_{ij}^l$

s.t. $\sum_{j \in N} f_{ji} - \sum_{l \in N} f_{il} = \begin{cases} -1 & \text{if } i \neq 0; \\ |N| - 1 & \text{if } i = 0; \end{cases}$ for all $i \in N$,

$$f_{ij} \leq \sum_{l=0}^{L} Z_l y_{ij}^l \qquad \forall (i,j) \in A,$$

$$f_{ij} \geq 0 \qquad \forall (i,j) \in A,$$

$$(6.4), (6.6), (6.8), (6.9), (6.10).$$

Consequently, we used this model to obtain optimal solutions to small instances of the MLCMST problem. However, even solving this model to optimality is computationally challenging, and it can only solve problems with about 34 nodes with the central node in the center in about 2 hours of CPU time.

Table 6.4 summarizes the results of our experiments on small instances with 20 and 30 nodes. These are labeled 20c, 20e, and 20r for 20 node instances with the central node at center, corner, and random location respectively. We only solved to optimality 30 node instances with the central node in the center (problem group 30c). Even using SCF, CPLEX is unable to solve to optimality, within 10 hours of CPU time, 30 node problems with the central node at the corner. Note that the lower bound (LB) is obtained by solving the LP relaxation of the strong multicommodity directed flow formulation. We see that the LB-OPT Gap is generally about 6% on average indicating the LB is reasonably good and fairly consistent (on average). The GA-OPT Gap varies significantly. The GA appears to do better on instances with the central node in the corner. Also, as the size of the instance goes up, the GA-Opt Gap decreases and the GA does better.

Comparing these results with our results in Table 6.2, we believe that there is significant room to improve the lower bound on all instances. For problems with the central node in the corner we believe the GA does quite well (with respect to optimal), while there is room to improve the GA solution when the central node is in the center.

Finally, we wanted to assess the gains achieved by using a genetic algorithm approach. Consequently, we compared the solutions obtained by the GA to the following Modified Esau-Williams heuristic that we propose.

Modified Esau-Williams Heuristic.   The modified Esau-Williams (EW) heuristic first applies the Esau-Williams for the CMST with capacity constraint Z_L and edge cost function C_{ij}^L to get groupings. It then applies the construction

Table 6.4. Comparison of lower bound and GA to optimal solution for small instances. Results are a summary over 50 instances for each case.

Problem group	Opt	GA Soln	LB	GA-Opt Gap $= \frac{GA}{Opt} - 1$		LB-Opt Gap $= 1 - \frac{LB}{Opt}$	
	Ave	Ave	Ave	Ave(%)	Range (%)	Ave (%)	Range (%)
20c	249.626	275.038	235.335	10.08%	0.85%-23.87%	5.70%	2.86%-9.83%
20e	451.538	460.546	427.252	1.98%	0%-7.28%	5.38%	4.01%-7.66%
20r	320.139	336.137	300.257	5.27%	0.21%-12.74%	6.26%	1.94%-9.15%
30c	366.866	392.848	344.935	7.02%	1.73%-15.87%	5.97%	4.00%-8.91%

Table 6.5. Comparison of GA to modified Esau-Williams heuristic. Results are a summary over 50 instances for each case.

Problem group	GA Solution	Modified EW	GA Improvement $= (1 - (GA\ Soln/Modified\ EW\ Soln))$	
	Ave	Ave	Ave (%)	Range (%)
50c	598.858	641.246	7.1%	0.9% - 13.5%
50e	1081.767	1111.581	2.8%	0.1% - 9.5%
50r	764.060	804.073	5.4%	0.5% - 13.1%
100c	1111.776	1160.999	4.4%	1.6% - 10.3%

heuristic described in Section 3 to each of the groupings found by the Esau-Williams heuristic to find a heuristic solution to the MLCMST problem.

We applied the modified EW heuristic to the 50 and 100 node problems that we had applied our GA to. In all cases the GA found strictly better solutions than the modified EW heuristic. The GA improves the modified EW solution by an average of 7.1% (with a range of 0.9%-13.5%) when the central node is in the center and by an average of 2.8% (with a range of 0.1%-9.5%) when the central node is in the corner. For 100 node problems the GA improves upon the modified EW by an average of 4.4% (with a range of 1.6%-10.3%).

6.   Conclusions

In this paper, we presented a genetic algorithm for the MLCMST problem. The genetic algorithm generates solutions very rapidly, and we have been able to solve up to 100 node problems to within 10% of optimality.[1] As noted earlier, the actual performance of the GA is significantly better, as these lower bounds are obtained by solving the LP relaxation of an MIP formulation for the problem.

There are several directions in which we are pursuing our ongoing research on the MLCMST. Recall, the construction heuristic constructs a subtree on a grouping with the restriction the degree of the central node is 1. We conducted computational experiments (generating groupings of Z_L or fewer nodes) and compared the solutions obtained by the construction heuristic to the optimal solution of the following two problems:[2] (1) Find a minimum cost subtree on a grouping with the restriction that the degree of the central node is 1, (2) Find a minimum cost subtree on a grouping (no restriction on degree of central node). We found that the solutions generated by the construction heuristic on groupings is within 0.5% (on average) of the optimal solution to the problem where the degree of the central node is 1. And the solution generated by the construction heuristic on groupings is within 2.5% (on average) of the optimal solution to the problem where there is no degree restriction on the central node. Thus, one direction of our research is to try to improve the construction heuristic, allowing it to generate solutions on groupings where the degree of the central node is greater than 1. This would result in improvements in the overall GA solution. Another direction is the development of alternate heuristic solution procedures to the genetic algorithm approach for the MLCMST problem. A third direction is the improvement of the genetic algorithm operators and parameters.

We also believe we should perform our computational tests on a wider variety of problems. These problems should not only vary in size (i.e., number of

---

[1] The GA can solve larger problems quite easily. The bottleneck is solving the LP relaxation of the formulation that provides us with lower bounds.

[2] Optimal solutions were obtained by solving MIP formulations to the two problems.

nodes) and number of link types, but should also cover a wide variety of cost function combinations. One additional challenge concerning the construction heuristic would be to make it capable of dealing with non-unit demands. This capability is in a way already "built-in" in the case of the genetic algorithm since the representation we used is, as we mentioned earlier, popular with grouping problems that attempt to partition items with non-unit weights. However, this might not be as easy for the construction heuristic and it will definitely add more complexity to the procedure.

References

[1] Ahuja, R. K., J. B. Orlin, D. Sharma, "Multi-Exchange Neighborhood Structures for the Capacitated Minimum Spanning Tree Problem," *Mathematical Programming*, **91**, pp. 71–97, 2001.

[2] Amberg, A., W. Domschke, S. V. Darmstadt, "Capacitated Minimum Spanning Trees: Algorithms Using Intelligent Search," *Combinatorial Optimization: Theory and Practice*, **1**, pp. 9–40, 1996.

[3] Berger, D., B. Gendron, J. Y. Potvin, S. Raghavan, P. Soriano, "Tabu Search for a Network Loading Problem with Multiple Facilities," *Journal of Heuristics*, **6**(2), pp. 253–267, 2000.

[4] Bourjolly, J., D. Tomiuk, G. H. M. Kapantow, "Using Simulated Annealing to Minimize the Cost of Centralized Telecommunications Networks," *INFOR*, **37**(3), 1999.

[5] Esau, L. R., K. C. Williams, "On Teleprocessing System Design: Part II," *IBM System Journal*, **5**(3), pp. 142–147, 1966.

[6] Falkenauer, E., "A Hybrid Grouping Genetic Algorithm for Bin Packing", *Journal of Heuristics*, pp. 5–30, 1996.

[7] Gamvros, I., "An Evolutionary Approach for the Multi-Level Capacitated Minimum Spanning Tree," M.S. in Telecommunications' Project, University of Maryland, 2001.

[8] Gamvros, I., B. L. Golden, S. Raghavan, "The Multi-Level Capacitated Spanning Tree Problem," *In preparation*, 2002.

[9] Gavish, B. "Topological Design of Telecommunications Networks - Local Access Design Methods," *Annals of Operations Research*, **33**, pp 17–71, 1991.

[10] Gavish, B., K. Altinkemer, "A Parallel Savings Heuristic for the Topological Design of Local Access Tree Networks," *Proc. IEEE-INFOCOM*, pp. 130–139, 1986.

[11] Goldberg, D. E., *Genetic Algorithms in Search, Optimization and Machine Learning*, Addison-Wesley, Reading, MA, 1989.

[12] Gouveia, L., M. J. Lopes, "Using Generalized Capacitated Trees for Designing the Topology of Local Access Networks," *Telecommunication Systems*, **7**, pp. 315–337, 1997.

[13] Karnaugh, M., "A New Class of Algorithms for Multipoint Network Optimization," *IEEE Transactions on Communications*, **24**(5), pp. 500–505, 1976.

[14] Kershenbaum, A., R. Boorstyn, R. Oppenheim, "Second-Order Greedy Algorithms for Centralized Network Design," *IEEE Transactions on Communications*, **22**(11), pp. 1835–1838, 1980.

[15] McGregor, P. M., D. Shen, "Network Design: An Algorithm for Access Facility Location Problems," *IEEE Trans. Comm.*, **25**, pp. 61–73, 1977.

[16] Michalawicz, Z., *Genetic Algorithms (+) Data Structures = Evolution Programs*, Springer-Verlag, New York, 1996.

[17] Patterson, R., H. Pirkul, "Heuristic Procedure Neural Networks for the CMST Problem," *Computers & Operations Research*, **27**, pp. 1171–1200, 2000.

[18] Rothfarb, B., M. C. Goldstein, "The One-Terminal Telepak Problem," *Operations Research*, **19**, pp. 156–169, 1971.

[19] Salman F. S., R. Ravi, J. Hooker, "Solving the Local Access Network Design Problem," Working Paper, Krannert Graduate School of Management, Purdue University, 2001.

[20] Sharaiha Y. M., M. Gendreau, G. Laporte, I. H. Osman, "A Tabu Search Algorithm for the Capacitated Minimum Spanning Tree Problem," *Networks*, **29**, pp. 161–171, 1997.

[21] Sharma R. L., "Design of an Economical Mutlidrop Network Topology with Capacity Constraints," *IEEE Trans. Comm. COM*, **31**, pp. 590–591, 1983.

Chapter 7

OPTIMIZED TRAFFIC LOAD DISTRIBUTION IN MPLS NETWORKS

G. Haßlinger
Deutsche Telekom, T-Systems
D-64307 Darmstadt, Germany
gerhard.hasslinger@telekom.de

S. Schnitter
Deutsche Telekom, T-Systems
D-64307 Darmstadt, Germany
stefan.schnitter@t-systems.com

Abstract   Multiprotocol label switching (MPLS) has been developed by the IETF in order to support traffic engineering for a balanced and higher network-wide utilization of resources as a main objective. Meanwhile MPLS has been extended towards a generalized common control plane (GMPLS) for resource provisioning including optical networks. Traffic demands for each source to destination pair can be directed through a MPLS network on predefined paths (LSP: label switched path), whereas routing in IP networks is based on the shortest path first principle and does not allow to establish direct control of the load balance with a per flow or per demand granularity. We investigate optimization algorithms that compute a LSP design for a given traffic matrix with regard to the following goals:

(i) Minimize the maximum link utilization corresponding to the considered path design and

(ii) minimize the length of paths without affecting the first goal (i).

We evaluate the obtainable traffic engineering gain using a heuristic algorithm, whose performance is compared to bounds obtained by linear programming and the max-flow-min-cut principle. The implications of MPLS traffic engineering in the context of network planning, failure recovery and quality of service (QoS) provisioning are outlined.

Keywords: Traffic engineering, flow optimization, LSP design, resource utilization, shortest versus explicit path routing, MPLS, QoS.

1.   Introduction

Interior gateway protocols for routing in IP networks (OSPF [21], IS-IS [6]) use the shortest path to forward the traffic on network links, with regard to routing weights assigned to each link on a path. This may lead to an unbalanced distribution of the traffic with higher utilization of some links while others remain underutilized. When the mean utilization on a link over a relevant period, e.g. a busy hour, exceeds a threshold below the link capacity then quality of service guarantees are violated due to statistical variance of the traffic in time causing delay and data loss. In the IP backbone of service providers, thresholds of the link load for providing sufficient QoS can be estimated based on statistical multiplexing [14, 15], which leads to smoothed traffic variation and a higher level of the allowable utilization. Therefore QoS is also improved by network-wide balancing of the link loads such that the highest load is kept as small as possible.

Naturally, the network planning process has main influence on the traffic loads in a topology design according to a forecast for the traffic matrix. But traffic demand forecasts prior to the operational state of a network are usually inaccurate and even during the operational phase the demands in IP networks are highly variable with a steep increase to twice the traffic volume in less than a year. Even when topology adaptation is possible later on, there are often further constraints to be taken into account, which may be in conflict with a proper load balancing.

Approaches to adjust the load distribution in pure IP networks with fixed topology make use of modifications of the link weights with regard to the load in order to redirect the shortest paths [8, 9, 10]. But when path selection is based only on link specific attributes and is done without knowledge of the end-to-end paths and the intensities of traffic flows then a general network-wide optimization of the traffic load may become a difficult task. Anyway, the granularity of modifying the traffic load per link is coarser than by an arbitrary choice of the path of each demand.

MPLS allows to specify the paths for traffic demands from each source to destination where a demand can even be distributed over several routes through the network with each of them carrying a predefined portion. Label switched paths (LSP) usually build a full mesh among all edge nodes of a network. For scalability in large networks, MPLS can be organized in hierarchical layers with aggregation of traffic flows into a common forwarding equivalence class in a higher layer. On each layer, direct influence can be enforced on the composition of traffic on the links with additional support being offered by measurement statistics for each LSP. Therefore we presume the traffic demand matrix to be known, which is usually not available in IP networks without underlying MPLS [4, 20]. The demands have to be measured in a time frame of interest like a daily busy hour. We assume the path design to be updated in a daily or weekly time schedule. More dynamic approaches are considered by [8, 26], based on measurement of performance characteristics like the delay or loss rate and adaptation steps for load balancing in a shorter time frame.

The improved load control mechanisms of MPLS enable standard methods of operations research and flow theory to maximize the network-wide throughput [1, 2, 5, 27]. Nevertheless, traffic engineering remains a non-trivial task. We study MPLS traffic engineering for efficient resource utilization in a fixed network topology. As the main optimization criterion for a LSP design, we aim at minimizing the highest utilization on the network links in terms of the ratio of the aggregated traffic rate of all flows directed over a link to a capacity threshold ensuring proper QoS characteristics. The thresholds are obtained by dimensioning rules [14, 15], such that traffic rates in excess of the threshold indicate a bottleneck and trigger an extension or redesign of the network topology or at least a redistribution of the traffic load. Provided that all traffic rates remain below the corresponding thresholds by a factor $1/\lambda$, the criterion allows to increase the overall traffic equally by the factor λ until the currently provided bandwidth is regarded as insufficient within the given topology.

While generalized (G-)MPLS is developing as a control plane for convergence of the IP layer and the underlying optical network layer [13], optimization of resource allocation is more complex in the optical layer, since the source to destination demands presently can be switched only at the granularity of large bandwidth units, each carried on a wavelength of an optical fiber [3, 7, 16, 18, 19, 24, 25]. Packet switching on the IP layer can make use of statistical multiplexing whereas circuit switching on the optical layer cannot provide shared use of the complete link bandwidth by all traffic flows. As a consequence, MPLS traffic engineering on IP layer is less restricted and can be optimized using standard algorithms to make more efficient use of resources.

We measure the gain achieved by an optimization method as the factor of the maximum allowable linear increase of the traffic matrix until a threshold at one of the network links is reached in comparison to other allocation methods for traffic e.g. the shortest path first principle. The previous optimization criterion usually does not lead to a unique solution, but some degree of freedom remains to direct traffic over a number of non-critical links with low load. For those cases we prefer solutions with as small as possible detours from shortest path routing as a secondary goal, when the previously defined traffic engineering gain is still fully exploited. This is again QoS motivated since shortest paths can be expected to minimize the delay and the probability of failure on the path.

The extent to which the routers allow for load balancing by splitting up source-to-destination traffic demands over multiple paths is decisive for the achievable traffic engineering gain as well as for the complexity of the optimization algorithms. When e.g. a single traffic demand is larger than the threshold of each link then a feasible allocation must split up the demand over several links connected to the source. This demonstrates the potential impact of limited flexibility, although in service provider networks source-to-destination traffic flows are typically at least an order of magnitude smaller than link bandwidths.

Assuming that arbitrary load balancing and splitting of demands is possible, an optimum LSP design can be found by means of linear programming being available in several efficient standard tools. Otherwise, when each demand has to be delivered on a single path, then the bin-packing problem is included and the optimization becomes NP-hard [12]. Therefore we suggest an heuristic algorithm based on simulated annealing to compute a LSP design. Although options for load balancing over multiple paths are foreseen in MPLS [22], they may not be fully implemented in present equipment for routing and label switching. In addition, using multiple paths may have an impact on the quality of service since larger delay variation and a larger portion of out-of-sequence packets can be expected. Router performance presently seems to be another obstacle for multi path load balancing in normal operation mode.

We proceed with notations for the optimization problem and goals in sections 2. In section 3 we present a heuristic algorithm to compute the LSP design together with a brief outline of the alternatives of linear programming and the max-flow-min-cut principle. Results of the application to a case study including the impact of link failures are presented in section 4. We conclude with a discussion of the implications of traffic engineering in the context of network planning and operation.

2.   Notations and specification of traffic engineering objectives

The network is represented by a strongly connected and directed graph $D = (V, A)$ with a set $V = \{v_1, \ldots, v_n\}$ of edges and arcs $A \subset V \times V$. For each arc $a \in A$ let $h(a), t(a) \in V$ be the head and tail nodes of $a = (h(a), t(a))$. We denote the traffic matrix by $T = (t_{ij}) \in \mathbb{R}^{n \times n}$ with elements t_{ij} characterizing the traffic demand from node v_i to v_j.

In addition, the functions $cap : A \to \mathbb{R}_0^+$ and $c : A \to \mathbb{R}_0^+$ are introduced to assign a *capacity* and a *cost* to each arc. A *path* p in the directed graph is a sequence of arcs $p = (a_1, \ldots, a_r)$ of length $r \in \mathbb{N}_0$ such that $a_i \neq a_j$ for $i \neq j$ and $t(a_i) = h(a_{i+1})$ for $i = 1, \ldots, r - 1$. An (i, j)-*path* denotes a path with $h(a_1) = v_i$ and $t(a_r) = v_j$.

In a considered network topology D, a LSP design is given by a matrix $P = (p_{ij})$ of paths, where p_{ij} is an (i, j)-path carrying the traffic demand t_{ij} provided that $t_{ij} > 0$ and that a unique path is associated with each demand. In general, a source to destination demand may be delivered on a set of (i, j)-paths.

In order to evaluate the performance of a LSP design P, the resulting utilization of the links is essential. Thus we define the utilization or *load* (both terms will be used synonymously) as a function $l_{P,T} : A \to \mathbb{R}_0^+$, which determines the ratio of the traffic rate to the capacity on each link:

$$l_{P,T}(a) := \sum_{i,j=1}^{n} \frac{t_{ij}(a)}{cap\,(a)} \quad \text{where} \quad t_{ij}(a) := \begin{cases} t_{ij} & \text{if } a \in p_{ij} \\ 0 & \text{else.} \end{cases} \quad (7.1)$$

$T_P(a) = (t_{ij}(a)) \in \mathbb{R}^{n \times n}$ is the portion of per demand traffic which is routed via $a \in A$ when the LSP design P is applied. In general p_{ij} is extended to a set $p_{ij}^{(1)}, \cdots, p_{ij}^{(k)}$ of (i,j)-paths associated with portions $t_{ij}^{(1)}, \cdots, t_{ij}^{(k)}$ of the traffic demand t_{ij} to be carried on them, such that

$$\forall m : t_{ij}^{(m)} > 0; \quad \sum_m t_{ij}^{(m)} = t_{ij} \quad \text{and} \quad t_{ij}(a) := \sum_{m:\, a \in p_{ij}^{(m)}} t_{ij}^{(m)}.$$

Finally a LSP design P is *feasible* if the resulting loads do not exceed the capacities, i.e. we have

$$\forall a \in A : \qquad l_{P,T}(a) \leq 1.$$

2.1   Optimization goals

As the main criterion for the LSP design, the highest utilization of a link in the network should be made as small as possible. The load level on a link is decisive for the probability to enter overload situations with impact on the delay and loss performance. Therefore the objective of a maximum distance to full utilization correlates with QoS support. Moreover, the capacity $cap(a)$ of a link is set to a threshold that can guarantee sufficient QoS. A LSP design computed to minimize the utilization in relation to these thresholds at the same time maximizes the potential of scaling the traffic matrix T by a factor λ_{max}, such that an increased load $\lambda_{max} T = (\lambda_{max} t_{ij})$ is still feasible in the constructed LSP design. In particular, let

$$M(P,T) := \max_{a \in A} l_{P,T}(a)$$

be the maximum load resulting from a traffic matrix T and a corresponding LSP design P. Then we state the following optimization problem:

> For a given traffic matrix T find a LSP design P such that
> $$M(P,T) \to \min.$$
> (OPT1)

The assumption of a linear increase of the traffic demands in T by the same factor is not crucial for the optimization algorithms, which also apply for the case of different increase factors for each demand.

The optimization problem OPT1 usually does not provide a unique solution for the LSP design. Often there are traffic demands that may take one of several paths over non-critical links without impact on OPT1.

Therefore we adopt the shortest path principle as a secondary optimization goal as far as it does not detract from OPT1 for load balancing:

> For a given traffic matrix T find a LSP design P such that
> $$\sum_{a \in A} l_{P,T}(a) \to \min.$$
> (OPT2)

OPT2 specifies the shortest path by the hop count. In general, other cost functions determined by the link weights may be included. OPT2 again is motivated by supporting QoS since shorter paths lead to lower end-to-end delay.

3. Algorithms for traffic engineering

3.1 Overview

There are at least three methods to be considered for balancing the load distribution by an appropriate LSP design and to compute the achievable traffic engineering gain:

- heuristic optimization,

- linear programming and

- the max-flow-min-cut principle.

Heuristic algorithms represent the most flexible and scalable means for off-line optimization when approximate solutions are sufficient. While linear programming presumes that traffic demands can be arbitrarily distributed on multiple paths, we use heuristics for the case that each demand must be directed on a unique path [23]. The latter assumption introduces an additional constraint for load balancing. We can estimate the significance of the flexibility in branching traffic flows over several paths by comparing the traffic engineering gain for both alternatives. The delivery of each traffic demand t_{ij} on a unique path leads to a NP-hard optimization problem including the NP-complete bin-packing problem already for a balanced assignment of a number of demands on two parallel links [12]. This is illustrated in the example of figure 7.1, where the paths for a number of traffic demands have to pass two common nodes, which are connected via two routes. Then the question how to allocate the demands on both alternative routes between the nodes in order to achieve a predefined load balance already represents the basic bin-packing problem.

Therefore no scalable exact solution can be expected under that assumption and we prefer a heuristics, which is based on the search for paths minimizing

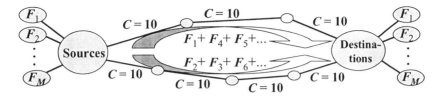

Figure 7.1. Example of a flow allocation equivalence to the bin-packing problem

the weighted costs for the links in a network-wide view. The cost function is increasing with the load on each link, leading to a tendency to shift paths away from highly utilized links. Initially, the paths for traffic demands are allocated sequentially in a predefined order until a feasible solution is reached. Differences in the performance of shortest or largest demand first as well as random order as sequential solution strategies for bin-packing [12] turned out to be relevant in the optimization of MPLS traffic engineering. Afterwards we proceed with stepwise improvement of the initial solution using simulated annealing.

3.2 The max-flow-min-cut principle

The max-flow-min-cut principle can be used to determine a minimum cut through the network, such that the sum of capacities of the links on the cut represents a bottleneck for the maximum achievable traffic load $\lambda_{max}T$, see figure 7.2.

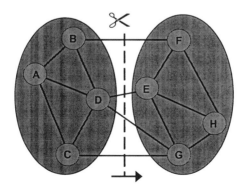

Capacity of a cut: $C_{Cut} = C_{BF} + C_{DE} + C_{DG} + C_{CG}$

Flow demands: $F_{Cut} = F_{\{A, B, C, D\}} \rightarrow \{E, F, G, H\}$

Figure 7.2. Example of the Max-flow-min-cut principle

A bound $B(T)$

$$B(T) \leq \min_{P \in \mathcal{P}(T)} M(P,T)$$

on the optimum solution of problem (OPT1) can be obtained by means of the max-flow-min-cut theorem, as a basic approach in network flow theory [1, 2]. A cut $C = (V_S, V_D)$ through the network is defined by a partition of the nodes into a set $V_S \subset V$ of source nodes and a complementary set $V_D = V \setminus V_S$ of destinations. The set of arcs from a node in V_S to a node in V_D is then denoted by $A(V_S, V_D)$, i.e.

$$A(V_S, V_D) = \{a \in A : h(a) \in V_S \text{ and } t(a) \in V_D\}.$$

On the other hand, the subset of demands $T_C \subset T$ with sources in V_S and destinations in V_D inevitable has to pass through one of the links on the cut. Consequently, for each cut C

$$R_C := \sum_{v_k \in V_S} \sum_{v_l \in V_D} t_{kl} \Big/ \sum_{a \in A(V_S, V_D)} cap\,(a) \leq 1 \qquad (7.2)$$

must hold for the ratio R_C of the sum of all flows demanded in the traffic matrix from a source in V_S to a destination in V_D to the sum of capacities available on all arcs of the cut in a feasible solution.

The reciprocal of the maximum of the ratios R_C for all cuts C limits the increase factor of the traffic matrix until the admissible traffic load faces a bottleneck of link capacities on the corresponding cut. Thus

$$B(T) := \max_C R_C \leq \min_{P \in \mathcal{P}(T)} M(P,T) \qquad (7.3)$$

provides a bound for an optimum LSP design, which in general is only achievable when demands can be distributed on multiple paths.

3.3   Linear programming

Linear programming determines the maximum admissible traffic load under the same precondition as for the max-flow-min-cut principle and in addition constructs a corresponding LSP design of paths for each traffic demand t_{ij}.

Therefore variables are introduced to represent the flow on the edges distinguished by each originating source. They are related by equations expressing flow conservation at each node, such that the rate of all incoming traffic equals the rate of the traffic departing from a node, including the input from sources and the output at destinations. The capacity of each link is also included as a constraint for the traffic rates. For the resulting set of linear boundary equations the simplex algorithm is available as a standard method to obtain an exact solution for the optimum load distribution and a corresponding LSP design. The method is flexible in the consideration of alternative cost functions as optimization objectives [11].

In addition, explicit restrictions can be imposed on the set of possible paths for traffic demands from a source instead of including all paths through the network. In this way the complexity of the state space may be reduced when storage or time consumption in the computation become too expensive. On the other hand, the set of paths can be chosen e.g. to exclude all paths of length $\geq k$ or in general to exclude all paths which do not meet a delay bound or another QoS criterion. In this way constraint based routing can also be regarded by selecting a corresponding set of admissible paths for each flow demand.

3.4 Heuristic optimization algorithm

As pointed out in section 3.1, we address the LSP design problem with demand allocation on a single path by a heuristic algorithm, which computes an approximate solution of (OPT1) and as a secondary goal keeps the length of the paths as small as possible (OPT2). We start with an empty LSP design P. The paths corresponding to the non-zero entries of the traffic matrix t_{ij} are then computed sequentially by the following steps:

---

1. Select a new traffic demand $t_{ij} > 0$ and initialize the arc costs e.g. by $c(a) := 1$ for all $a \in A$.

2. Compute an (i, j)-path with minimal arc costs to be added to P.

3. Update the arc loads $l_{P,T}(a)$ for all $a \in A$ using equation (7.1) and the resulting maximum arc load $M(P,T)$.

4. If $M(P,T) > B(T) + tol \qquad (tol \in \mathbb{R}^+)$

   (a) Identify $A_M := \{a \in A : l_{P,T}(a) = M(P,T)\}$

   (b) Set $c(a) := c(a) + \kappa$ for all $a \in A_M$. $\qquad (\kappa \in \mathbb{R}^+)$

   (c) Go to step 2.

5. Go to step 1 until all demands are allocated.

For the calculation of cost minimal paths in step 2 we apply a suitable version of Dijkstra's algorithm. The main ideas of this algorithm are:

- As far as the maximum arc load does not exceed the lower bound $B(T)$ we direct the traffic demands on shortest paths and, in case of unique arc costs, on paths with a minimum number of arcs.

- If the maximum arc load of the current LSP design exceeds $B(T) + tol$, we increase the arc costs of those arcs which are utilized most by a predefined constant $\kappa \in \mathbb{R}$ and recalculate the last path to minimize the altered arc costs. Thus lower utilized arcs are preferred in the following path searches. The procedure in step 4 is carried out only a fixed number of times because it is obvious that there may be no LSP design that fulfills the inequality in step 4 ($B(T)$ is a lower bound to the optimum). If we exceed κ we will increase tol.

- Increasing selected arc costs will result in paths that are not the shortest possible. But by increasing only the costs of those arcs which have the highest load and by resetting the arc costs before the next traffic demand is treated, the algorithm tends to avoid detours from the shortest path.

The result of the proposed algorithm obviously depends on the order for treating the traffic demands and thus on the initial sequence in the processing of demands. The impact of different sequencing alternatives is regarded as follows:

- The *Largest Traffic Demands First* is favorable.

  This corresponds to the *First Fit Decreasing Order* strategy, which is proven to provide solutions to the bin packing problem in a range essentially closer to the optimum than a *First Fit* strategy with random or increasing order [12] pp. 124-127. *First Fit Decreasing Order* solutions for bin packing are bounded within about 22% relative deviation from the optimum whereas in general worst cases are subject to relative deviations of up to 70% from optimum.

- A stochastic optimization method is used to improve the solution.

  In particular we apply simulated annealing as a stochastically relaxed local search method that searches a predefined neighborhood $N(x)$ of a given solution x, i.e. a sequence for the traffic demands in this context. A candidate $y \in N(x)$ is accepted if it yields an improvement in the objective function and otherwise may still be accepted with a certain probability in case that it becomes worse. In this way the strategy is capable of escaping from regions with a local optimum and of reaching a global optimum depending on an appropriate choice of the involved parameters, although usually no bound on the time consumption can be given until the optimum solution is approached.

  The convergence time of simulated annealing depends on the initial solution, where the largest demand first strategy can save a considerable amount of running time. Knowledge about the bound $B(T)$ which can be gained e.g. from a calculation the non-constructive max-flow-min-cut bound also helps to adapt $B(T) + tol$ and to improve the convergence.

Since the computation effort for each single step of the above algorithm is small, a large set of candidate sequences can be included in a reasonable time span. For further applications of simulated annealing to sequencing problems see e.g. [17].

4.   A case study for optimized load balancing

In this section we show results of the optimization for traffic engineering carried out for the network topology depicted in figure 7.3. The network consists of four inner core nodes and twelve outer core nodes, each of the latter being connected to two different inner core nodes. All links in figure 7.3 are bidirectional providing the same capacity C, with the exception of the links between v_1 and v_5 which have twice the capacity $2\,C$.

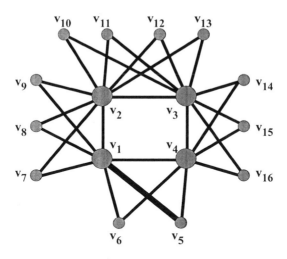

Figure 7.3.   Graph of an example network topology

The traffic matrix includes two main parts, one for local traffic which is exchanged in an almost uniform pattern between most of the nodes in a set S, and another part for external input being distributed from a few nodes where e.g. peering points are concentrated. In particular, v_1 and v_5 are sources of large demands and the traffic matrix is determined by

$$t_{ij} = \begin{cases} s_1 \, d_j & \text{for } i = 1 \text{ and } j \neq i, \\ s_5 \, d_j & \text{for } i = 5 \text{ and } j \neq i, \\ t_1 & \text{for } i \in S; \quad j \in \{1, 5\}, \\ t_2 & \text{for } i \in S; \quad j \in S \text{ and } j \neq i, \\ 0 & \text{else}, \end{cases}$$

where $s_1 = 170$; $s_5 = 150$; $t_1 = 30$; $t_2 = 20$;

$(d_1, \cdots, d_{16}) =$

$(0.2, \ 0.2, \ 1, \ 0.25, \ 0.2, \ 0.25, \ 0.2, \ 0.2, \ 1, \ 0.2, \ 0.2, \ 0.25, \ 0.25, \ 1, \ 1, \ 1)$

and $S = \{2, \ 3, \ 7, \ 8, \ 9, \ 10, \ 11, \ 14, \ 15, \ 16\}$.

Table 7.1 shows some results concerning the traffic engineering gain and optimized LSP design computed by the heuristic algorithm of section 3.4 with the largest demands first strategy. The maximum arc load can be reduced to 35% as compared to 51.5% for shortest path routing with unique link weights, i.e. over paths with a smallest possible number of links. In this case the max-flow-min-cut bound is reached and thus the traffic engineering gain is fully exploited by the heuristics.

The difference in the allowable linear increase of the traffic matrix is about a factor 1.47. The initial solution by allocating largest demands first already achieves 38.6% as the maximum utilization and thus most of the gain.

The total number of arcs counted over the single paths of all demands increases by 15 in the initial solution and by only three after simulated annealing. In this and many other cases there are only few detours from the shortest path required to obtain the optimized load distribution.

	$M(P,T)$	λ_{max}	no. of arcs
Shortest path routing	0.515	1.941	267
Initial solution (largest demands first)	0.386	2.591	282
Optimized solution (simulated annealing)	0.35	2.857	270
Bounds	≥ 0.35	≤ 2.857	≥ 267

Table 7.1. Maximum utilization, scale factor and number of arcs for LSP design methods

We extend the evaluation of the example considering single link failures and the corresponding shifts in the maximum link load. For each of the 28 links in the network we computed

- the lower bound of the maximum link utilization by the max-flow-min-cut principle,

- the maximum link utilization achieved for a LSP design using single paths for each demand as constructed by the heuristic algorithm and

- the maximum link utilization obtained by shortest path routing with a minimum number of links in the path for each demand.

The results in figure 7.4 show that the LSP design obtained by the heuristics exploits most of the traffic engineering gain and is within 6.5% relative deviation of the bound $B(T)$ except for two cases of 16.6% and 18.9% respectively. On the other hand, shortest path first without optimization often leads to unbalanced traffic distribution of about twice the maximum load on a link and even varying up to 2.94 times the lower bound when (v_1, v_4) fails. In the latter case, the traffic of all demands from the sources v_1 and v_5 to the destinations v_4, v_{14}, v_{15} and v_{16} and in addition t_{53} is routed via the link (v_5, v_4). There are alternative paths e.g. from v_1 via v_6 to v_4 which obviously can detract load from the bottleneck on (v_4, v_5). But following standard routing policy, the bottleneck path is preferred from v_1 to v_4, since a smaller link weight is usually assigned to (v_1, v_5) reciprocal to the higher capacity of this link. There are often multiple shortest paths available in the considered topology and we have chosen one of them by some random rule without optimizing a path design in the set of all possible shortest paths.

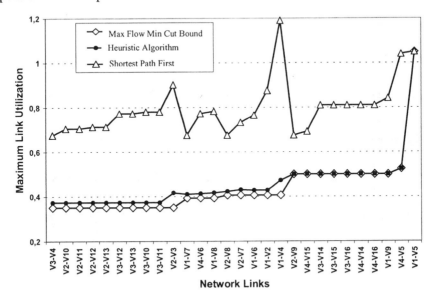

Figure 7.4. Maximum link utilization for single bi-directional link failures

Figure 7.4 indicates that the topology can tolerate a number of single link failure cases without impact on the maximum link load. A failure of the link

(v_5, v_1) on the other hand even rises the lower bound to an overload situation, which can only be prohibited by a change in the topology. In this way traffic engineering results also identify insufficient failure protection.

5.   Implications for MPLS traffic engineering in service provider networks

We studied the efficiency of MPLS traffic engineering in Deutsche Telekom's IP backbone consisting of a full mesh of LSPs between several dozen edge routers. Changing traffic profiles and some changes in the topology have been observed over a one year time frame. Applying the optimization algorithms, which have been outlined in the previous section in an operational scenario under varying preconditions, our main conclusions are:

- The traffic engineering gain has been evaluated as the difference of the feasible traffic load for shortest path first routing compared to the LSP design by off-line optimization. We observed that an additional load of 50% - 100% can be admitted due to traffic engineering still satisfying the constraints for maximum load on the network links.

- The difference in the achievable gain between the linear programming results for possible distribution of a traffic demand t_{ij} on multiple paths and the heuristics restricted to a single path per demand was always below 5%. The option of branching traffic flows over several routes seems to have minor impact on the efficiency. A reason for that can be seen in the presence of many small traffic demands in the traffic matrix T, which allow for a fine granularity in load balancing already for single paths.

- The LSP design obtained by optimization due to both goals of section 2.1 exhibits only a small number of paths, which deviate from the shortest route. Therefore an off-line computed LSP design can be configured without much effort starting from established shortest path routes, and may in an initial phase be done without the help of automatic configuration tools.

5.1   Traffic engineering and quality of service

As mentioned earlier, the link capacities $cap(a)$ considered for traffic engineering should not be set to the full line speed, but should correspond to thresholds with regard to quality of service demands [14, 15] or even including further constraints for provisioning and reliability. The quality of service surely benefits when the maximum utilization in a network is reduced. In a next step this improvement can be transferred into higher utilization of resources such that a predefined sufficient level for QoS is preserved in the tradeoff with a cost efficient solution.

In some cases traffic engineering selects longer paths than IP routing. The delay introduced by such detours has to be controlled or the optimization algorithms should already exclude paths that violate delay constraints. The ongoing development of MPLS by the IETF and the equipment manufacturers enables a broad variety of QoS support mechanisms ranging from reservation of bandwidth after admission control for strict QoS guarantees to differentiated services (DiffServ). The DiffServ concept classifies traffic to be treated by different forwarding strategies in routers and switches, which is supported in MPLS using experimental bits for distinguishing traffic classes or using multiple LSPs between a source and destination, each of them carrying one traffic class. Therefore traffic engineering has to take into account the underlying QoS concept.

5.2 Traffic engineering and reliability, path protection

When optimized load balancing is employed in normal operation of a network leading to a higher network-wide utilization of resources, then link and node failures can lead to more serious degradation of the throughput than for non-optimized routing, since then there are less under-utilized capacities available which may help to work around a breakdown.

Therefore the most likely failure situations and their consequences should be carefully taken into account. The traffic engineering algorithms can be applied to modified network topologies and may precompute an optimized LSP design e.g. for each case of a single link or node failure as discussed in the case study of section 4. But even with a precomputed LSP design at hand, the problem of a fast restoration in a failure situation is difficult to solve in this way. Moreover, restoration is usually handled on the optical network level in SDH/SONET and WDM systems [3, 7, 13, 18, 24] such that an integrated concept for restoration with regard to path assignment on the optical layer, MPLS label switching as well as IP routing has to be established.

5.3 Traffic engineering and network planning

The achievable gain by traffic engineering depends on network planning. If network planning and traffic engineering would be carried out independent of each other without mutual knowledge about possible modifications then the complete solution may be far from optimum. Again the optimization algorithms of section 3 can be used to study proposed topology alternatives in order to estimate their behavior including shifts of traffic paths for load balancing. Especially the max-flow-min-cut principle is appropriate to find bottlenecks in a proposed network topology as well as alternatives.

Hierarchic structures without cross connections reduce the set of source to destination paths even to a unique path in a strict hierarchy. Meshed network topologies, which can be found in various types in parts of the Internet allow for a higher traffic engineering gain, with multiple choices available for traffic path allocation.

6.   Conclusion

MPLS traffic engineering can be optimized by basic methods of operations research such that the overall utilization of network resources can be essentially improved.

A heuristic algorithm using simulated annealing, linear programming and the max-flow-min-cut principle have been successfully applied to compute bounds for the optimization. The first two methods also construct a corresponding path design. From our experience in traffic engineering, linear programming and the max-flow-min-cut principle predict the same traffic engineering gain. The heuristic optimization also comes close to that limit of the gain even under the additional restriction to select a single path per source-to-destination demand.

The traffic engineering gain is related to network planning and should not be completely exploited for economizing, since then more serious reliability and QoS concerns have to be taken into account.

References

[1] R.K. Ahuja, T.L. Magnanti and J.B. Orlin, *Network flows: Theory, algorithms and applications*, Prentice Hall (1993)

[2] V.K. Balakrishnan, *Network optimization*, Chapman & Hall, London (1995)

[3] G. Bernstein, E. Mannie and V. Sharma, *Framework for MPLS-based control of optical SHD/SONET networks*, IEEE Network (July 2001) 20-26

[4] N. Benameur and J.W. Roberts, *Traffic matrix interference in IP networks*, Proc. NETWORKS, Munich (2002) 151-156

[5] D. Bienstock, *New developments in solving multicommodity flow problems*, Proc. 6. INFORMS Telecom. Conf. TC4.1, Boca Raton (2002)

[6] R.W. Callon, *Use of OSI IS-IS for routing in TCP/IP and dual environments*, RFC 1195, proposed IETF standard (1990)

[7] R. Doverspike and J. Yates, *Challenges for MPLS in optical network restoration*, IEEE Communications Magazine (Febr. 2001) 89-96

[8] A. Elwalid, C. Lin, S. Low and I. Widjaja, *MATE: MPLS Adaptive Traffic Engineering*, Proc. IEEE INFOCOM (2001)

[9] A. Feldmann, A. Greenberg, C. Lund, N. Reingold and J. Rexford, *NetScope: Traffic engineering for IP networks*, IEEE Network, special issue on Internet traffic engineering, Ed. Z. Wang (March 2000) 11-19

[10] B. Fortz and M. Thorup, *Internet traffic engineering by optimizing OSPF weights*, Proc. IEEE INFOCOM (2000)

[11] M. Franzke and A. Pönitz, *Global shortest path solutions for the traffic engineering problem*, Proc. NETWORKS, Munich (2002) 275-278

[12] M.R. Garey and D.S. Johnson, *Computers and intractability: A guide to the theory of NP-completeness*, Freeman, NY (1979)

[13] L. Gouveia, P. Patricio, A. de Sousa and R. Valadas, *Multi-layer network dimensioning for MPLS over WDM networks*, Proc. 6. INFORMS Telecom. Conf. TE1.3, Boca Raton (2002)

[14] F. Hartleb and G. Haßlinger, *Comparison of link dimensioning methods for IP networks*, Proc. IEEE Globecom (2001) 2240-247

[15] G. Haßlinger, *Quality-of-service analysis for statistical multiplexing with Gaussian and autoregressive input modeling*, Telecommunication Systems 16 (2001) 315-334

[16] J.Q. Hu and B. Leida, *Traffic grooming, routing and wavelength assignment in optical networks*, Proc. 6. INFORMS Telecom. Conf. ME1.4, Boca Raton (2002)

[17] M. Kolonko, *Some new results on simulated annealing applied to the job shop scheduling problem*, Europ. J. Operational Research, 113 (1999) 123-136

[18] A. Koster and A. Zymolka, *Cost-efficient design of optical networks I & II: Dimensioning and routing & Wavelength assignment*, Proc. 6. INFORMS Telecom. Conf. MA1.3-4, Boca Raton (2002)

[19] Y. Liu, *Spare capacity allocation: Model, analysis and algorithm*, Proc. 6. INFORMS Telecom. Conf. TB1.1, Boca Raton (2002)

[20] A. Medina, C. Fraleight, N. Taft, S. Bhattacharyya and C. Diot, *Taxonomy of IP traffic matrices*, Proc. SPIE, Vol. 4868, Boston (2002) 200-211

[21] J. Moy, *Open shortest path first Version 2*, RFC 2328, IETF standard (1998)

[22] E. Rosen, A. Viswanathan and R. Callon, *Multiprotocol label switching architecture*, RFC 3031, Proposed IETF standard (2001)

[23] S. Schnitter and G. Haßlinger, *Heuristic Solutions to the LSP-design for MPLS Traffic Engineering*, Proc. NETWORKS 2002, Munich (2002) 269-273

[24] S. Sengupta and R. Ramamurthy, *From network design to dynamic provisioning and restoration in optical cross-connect mesh networks: An architectural and algorithmic overview*, IEEE Network (July 2001) 46-54

[25] R. Wessaely, A. Bley and A. Kroller, *A component-resource model for the design of communication networks*, Proc. 6. INFORMS Telecom. Conf. TC1.1, Boca Raton (2002)

[26] I. Widjaja, I. Saniee, A. Elwalid and D. Mitra, *Online Traffic Engineering with Design-based Routing*, Proc. 15th ITC Specialist Seminar, Wuerzburg, Germany (2002)

[27] R.D. Wollmer, *Optimal investment in capacity expansion of arcs in stochastic multicommodity network flows*, Proc. 6. INFORMS Telecom. Conf. WA1.4, Boca Raton (2002)

Chapter 8

SCHEDULING OF A GENERALIZED SWITCH: HEAVY TRAFFIC REGIME

Alexander L. Stolyar

Bell Labs, Lucent Technologies
Murray Hill, NJ 07974, USA
stolyar@research.bell-labs.com

Abstract

We consider a *generalized switch* model, which is a natural model of scheduling multiple data flows over a shared time-varying wireless environment. It also includes as special cases the input-queued cross-bar switch model, and a discrete time version of a parallel server queueing system.

Input flows, $n = 1, \ldots, N$, are served in discrete time by a switch. Switch *state* follows a finite discrete time Markov chain. In each state m, the switch chooses a *scheduling decision* k from a finite set $K(m)$, which has the associated service rate vector $(\mu_1^m(k), \ldots, \mu_N^m(k))$.

We study the MaxWeight discipline which always chooses a decision

$$k \in \arg\max_k \sum_n \gamma_n \mu_n^m(k) Q_n ,$$

where Q_n's are the queue lengths, and γ_n's, are arbitrary positive parameters. It has been shown in previous work, that MaxWeight discipline is optimal in terms of system stability, i.e. it stabilizes queues if it is feasible to do all.

We show that MaxWeight also has striking optimality and "self-organizing" properties in the *heavy traffic* limit regime. Namely, under a non-restrictive additional conditions, MaxWeight minimizes system *equivalent workload* $X = \sum_n \nu_n^* Q_n$, where $\nu^* = (\nu_1^*, \ldots, \nu_N^*)$ is some fixed vector with positive components; moreover, in the limit, vector $(\gamma_1 Q_1, \ldots, \gamma_N Q_N)$ is always proportional to ν^*. These properties of MaxWeight discipline can be utilized in applications to optimize various system performance criteria.

Keywords: Queueing, MaxWeight, scheduling, heavy traffic, wireless, generalized switch

1.   Introduction

In this paper, we study the heavy traffic regime in the following model. Multiple input flows, indexed by $n = 1, \ldots, N$, each with its own queue, are served in discrete time by a *generalized switch*. Switch *states* are random, and follow a finite discrete time Markov chain. Each state m of the switch has an associated set $K(m)$ of *scheduling decisions*; if a decision $k \in K(m)$ is chosen, then the maximum number of customers of each flow which can be served in the corresponding time slot is given by the (service rate) vector $(\mu_1^m(k), \ldots, \mu_N^m(k))$.

Our primary motivation for considering this model is the problem of scheduling multiple data flows over a wireless environment (see [11, 1, 16]). As an example of this setting, the N input flows represent data flows which need to be transmitted to N mobile users from a single or multiple antennas. An assignment of transmission data rates and powers by the antennas, must satisfy certain constraints, in particular constraints on Signal-to-Noise ratios, mutual interferences, etc.; it is an assumption of the model that all those constraints are incorporated into a finite number of transmission rate vectors that can be chosen in each "state" of the radio environment. The assumption that the state follows a finite Markov chain corresponds to the assumption that the radio environment changes with time in a random, but "sufficiently stationary" way.

The generalized switch model also includes as a special case the much studied input-queued cross-bar switch, with L input and output ports (see for example [12, 13]). The $N = L^2$ flows represent input-output port pairs (l_1, l_2). A scheduling decision k is an input-output "matching," i.e. a subset of L pairs such that each value of l_1 and l_2 appears only once. When a matching k is chosen, only flows from it are served at a certain (usually constant) rate.

Finally, we note that our model also includes a discrete time version of a parallel server system (see [9, 23]). In this model, N input flows are served by L servers. In each time slot, a server l can choose to serve one of the queues, and if it chooses queue n, it serves it at the rate $\mu_{nl} > 0$. A "switch" scheduling decision k is then a combination of the decisions for the individual servers, $k = (n_1, \ldots, n_L)$, and the service rates by different servers are summed up.

The issue of *stability* for the different versions of the generalized switch model is very well studied ([18, 19, 12, 13, 11, 2, 5, 1, 16]). The maximum stability region of such system (i.e., the set of input flows' rate vectors $\lambda = (\lambda_1, \ldots, \lambda_N)$ such that there exists a scheduling rule making the system stable) is easily characterized in terms of a linear program. One of the principal stability results for this type of models (due originally to Tassiulas-Ephremides [18, 19]) is the fact that a simple MaxWeight scheduling discipline attains the maximum stability region.

In the setting of this paper, the MaxWeight discipline is defined as follows. *In each switch state m, choose a scheduling decision*

$$k \in \arg \max_{k \in K(m)} \sum_n \gamma_n \mu_n^m(k) Q_n \;,$$

where $Q_1, \ldots, Q_N$, are the current queue lengths, and $\gamma_1 > 0, \ldots, \gamma_N > 0$, are an arbitrary set of parameters.

We remark that, in the special case of (discrete time) parallel server system, the MaxWeight reduces to a particularly simple scheduling rule: each server l serves a queue n which maximizes $\gamma_n \mu_{nl} Q_n$.

We consider a *heavy traffic* regime, when the vector λ of flow input rates converges to some point v^* on the boundary of the system stability region. We assume that this point v^* is such that a *Complete Resource Pooling (CRP)* condition is satisfied. If CRP condition holds, associated with it there is a unique (up to a scaling) vector $\nu^* = (\nu_1^*, \ldots, \nu_N^*)$ with all positive components. The linear combination $X = \sum_n \nu_n^* Q_n$ is called *equivalent workload*.

Our main result Theorem 3 is that

In the heavy traffic limit, under the CRP condition, MaxWeight scheduling rule (a) minimizes the equivalent workload among all scheduling rules at any time t, and in addition, (b) vector $(\gamma_1 Q_1, \ldots, \gamma_N Q_N)$ is always proportional to ν^*.

Property (a) in particular means that (in heavy traffic) MaxWeight discipline produces a Pareto optimal set of queue lengths - no other discipline can make *all* the queue lengths shorter than MaxWeight. The "self-organizing" property (b) is usually called State Space Collapse. This notion goes back to the papers of Whitt [20] and Reiman [14, 15]. Recently a quite general theory of the heavy traffic state space collapse in multiclass queueing networks has been developed by in [3] and [22]. The generalized switch model is not within the framework of multiclass networks. However, the general approach of [3] and [22], and some key constructions can be applied for our model.

Our main result demonstrates that MaxWeight rule is very attractive for applications. Indeed, it is an extremely simple "on-line" rule, which does *not* require a priori knowledge of the input rates or statistics of the switch states. It only "needs to know" the current queue lengths and the current set of available service rate vector choices. Moreover, as outlined at the end of Section 6, with some additional work the CRP condition can be weakened to a Resource Pooling (RP) condition, which is satisfied in virtually any practical application. And yet, if system becomes heavily loaded it "automatically" minimizes equivalent workload. In addition, (due to the state space collapse property (b)) the choice of parameters γ_n allows one to "distribute" equivalent workload among the queues in any desired way, to satisfy a desired optimality criterion. For example, if c_n is the "cost rate" of holding a customer in queue n, then the holding cost can be (approximately) minimized by moving (almost) all workload into the queue with the minimal value of c_n/ν_n^*; this is achieved by setting this γ_n to a small value. Moreover, MaxWeight allows one to *estimate* ν^* from periodic measurements of the queue lengths - again, by the state space collapse property (b), in heavy traffic vector $(\gamma_1 Q_1, \ldots, \gamma_N Q_N)$ is approximately proportional to ν^*.

Several heavy traffic models, related to ours, have been considered in the literature. A continuous time parallel server model was studied in [7, 9, 23]. In [7, 9] the optimal solutions of associated Brownian control problems were found, in the sense of minimizing the expected discounted holding cost. Based on these solutions, the *discrete review* policies considered which are conjectured to be asymptotically optimal in heavy traffic. *Continuous review threshold rules* for this model were proposed and studied in [23]. With these rules, vector ν^* (in our notation) has to be precomputed based on the input rates, and queue length thresholds, which are control parameters, need to be set for appropriate queues. Also, the values of the thresholds depend on the system load - increase as the load converges to critical. Asymptotic optimality of the threshold rules has been proved both in the sense of equivalent workload minimization and (more strongly) in the expected discounted cost.

A multiuser variable channel scheduling model in heavy traffic (motivated by a scheduling problem in wireless systems) has been considered in [4]. This model has a constraint that "one user can be served at a time," although possible generalizations mentioned. The controls proposed in [4] require that most of the service resources be "preallocated" based on the input rates, and only a small portion of the resources is used for dynamic control. The asymptotic optimality under various criteria is proved.

The paper is organized as follows. In Section 2 we introduce basic notations and definitions. We describe the formal model in Section 3. In Sections 4 and 5 we briefly discuss previous work on stability for the models related to ours, in particular MaxWeight stability results. We describe the Complete Resource Pooling (and a weaker Resource Pooling) condition in Section 6. Section 7 contains the statement of our main heavy traffic result, Theorem 3, and a plausible conjecture on the asymptotics of stationary distributions. Sections 8 and 9 contain a sketch of the main result proof. (A detailed proof can be found in [17].)

2.   Notation

We will use standard notations R and R_+ for the sets of real and real nonnegative numbers, respectively; and a not quite standard notation R_{++} for the set of strictly positive real numbers. Corresponding N-times product spaces are denoted R^N, R_+^N, and R_{++}^N. The space R^N is viewed as a standard vectorspace, with elements $x \in R^N$ being row-vectors $x = (x_1, \ldots, x_N)$. The dot-product (scalar product) of $x, y \in R^N$, is

$$x \cdot y \doteq \sum_{n=1}^{N} x_n y_n \;;$$

and the norm of x is

$$\|x\| \doteq \sqrt{x \cdot x} \;.$$

We define the scaling operators Γ^r and $\tilde{\Gamma}^r$, $r > 0$, for a scalar function $h = (h(t), \; t \in C), \; C \subseteq R$, as follows:

$$(\Gamma^r h)(t) \doteq \frac{1}{r} h(rt), \; t \in C/r \doteq \{y/r \mid y \in C\}, \tag{8.1}$$

and

$$(\tilde{\Gamma}^r h)(t) \doteq \frac{1}{r} h(r^2 t), \; t \in C/r^2. \tag{8.2}$$

For a scalar c, $\Gamma^r c = \tilde{\Gamma}^r c \doteq c/r$. For any set of functions (or functions and scalars) the operators Γ^r and $\tilde{\Gamma}^r$ are applied componentwise.

We denote by $D([0, \infty), R)$ the standard Skorohod space of right-continuous left-limit (RCLL) functions defined on $[0, \infty)$ and taking real values. (See, for example, [6] for the definition of this space and associated topology and σ-algebra.)

The symbol $\overset{w}{\to}$ denotes convergence in distribution of random processes (or other random elements), i.e. the weak convergence of their *distributions*. Typically, we consider convergence of processes in $D([0, \infty), R)$ or its N-times product space $D^N([0, \infty), R)$ equipped with product topology and σ-algebra.

We reserve symbol $\Rightarrow$ for the weak convergence of *elements* of the Skorohod space $D([0, \infty), \bar{R})$ (the space of RCLL functions which may take infinite values $+\infty$ and $-\infty$); namely, "$\Rightarrow$" means convergence in every point of continuity of the limit *except maybe point* 0. The symbol $\overset{u.o.c.}{\to}$ (or the abbreviation *u.o.c.* after a convergence statement) means *uniform on compact sets* convergence of *elements* of $D([0, \infty), \bar{R})$ or its N-times product $D^N([0, \infty), \bar{R})$.

3.   The Model

Consider the following queueing system. There is a finite set $N = \{1, \ldots, N\}$ of input flows (or customer types) served by a *switch*. (We will use the same symbol N for both the set and its cardinality.) Each input flow consists of discrete *customers*. Customers of each flow waiting for service are queued in a buffer of infinite capacity.

The system operates in discrete time $t = 0, 1, 2, \ldots$. By convention, we will identify an (integer) time t with the unit time interval $[t, t+1)$, which will sometimes be referred to as the *time slot* t; and we will assume that all system variables we consider are constant within each time slot.

The switch has a finite set of *switch states* M. In each time slot, the switch is in one of the states $m \in M$; and the sequence of states $m(t)$, $t = 0, 1, 2, \ldots$, forms an irreducible (finite) Markov chain with stationary distribution $\{\pi^m, m \in M\}$,

$$\pi^m > 0, \ \forall m \in M, \quad \sum_{m \in M} \pi^m = 1 .$$

When switch is in state $m \in M$, a finite number of *scheduling decisions* can be made, which form a finite set $K(m)$; if a decision $k \in K(m)$ is chosen at time t, then $\mu_n^m(k) \geq 0$ customers of flow $n \in N$ are served and depart the system at time $t + 1$ (or all flow n customers present at time t, if their number was less than $\mu_n^m(k)$). We will denote $\mu^m(k) \doteq (\mu_1^m(k), \ldots, \mu_N^m(k)) \in R_+^N$ the corresponding vector of service rates, and assume that $\mu^m(k) \neq 0$ for all $m \in M$ and $k \in K(m)$.

New customer arrivals occur at times $t = 1, 2, \ldots$. Denote by $A_n(t)$, $t \geq 1$, the number of type n customers arrived at time t, and assume by convention that these customers are immediately available for service at time t. We assume that each input process A_n is an ergodic (discrete time) Markov chain with countable space, and the input processes are mutually independent. Let us denote by λ_n, $n \in N$, the mean arrival rate for flow n, i.e., the mean number of type n customers arriving in one time slot when the Markov chain A_n is in stationary regime. (Main results of this paper, pertaining to the *heavy traffic* asymptotic regime, will require additional assumptions on the input flows. We will introduce those assumption later when we define the heavy traffic regime.)

The random process describing the behavior of the entire system is $S = (S(t), \ t = 0, 1, 2, \ldots)$, where

$$S(t) = \{(U_{n1}(t), \ldots, U_{nQ_n(t)}(t)), \ A_n(t+1), \ n \in N; \ m(t) \},$$

$Q_n(t)$ is the type n queue length at time t (including new arrivals at time t), and $U_{nl}(t)$ is the current *delay* of the l-th type n customer present in the system at time t. (Within each type, the customers are numbered in the order of their arrivals.)

A mapping G which takes a system state $S(t)$ in a time slot into a fixed probability distribution $G(S(t))$ on the set of scheduling decisions $K(m)$ (with $m = m(t)$) will be called a *scheduling rule*, or a *queueing discipline*. With a fixed discipline G, the scheduling decision at time t is chosen randomly according to the distribution $G(S(t))$. If scheduling decision $k \in K(m(t))$ is chosen at time t, then $D_n(t+1) = \min\{Q_n(t), \mu_n^{m(t)}(k)\}$ of type n customers are served and depart the system at time $t + 1$. According to our conventions, for each flow n,

$$Q_n(t) = Q_n(t-1) - D_n(t) + A_n(t), \ t = 1, 2, \ldots .$$

Our assumptions imply that with any scheduling rule, S is a discrete time countable Markov chain. To avoid trivial complications, we make an additional (not very restrictive) technical assumption that we will only consider scheduling rules G such that the Markov chain S is irreducible and aperiodic. By *stability* of the Markov chain S (and stability of the system) we understand its ergodicity, which (in case of irreducibility and aperiodicity) is equivalent to the existence of a stationary probability distribution.

4. Necessary and Sufficient Stability Condition. Static Service Split Rule

Suppose, for each of its states $m \in M$, a sub-probability measure $\phi_m = (\phi_{m,k}, k \in K(m))$, is fixed, which means that $\phi_{m,k} \geq 0$ for all $k \in K(m)$, and $\sum_k \phi_{m,k} \leq 1$.

Consider a *Static Service Split* (SSS) scheduling rule, parameterized by the set of measures $\phi \doteq (\phi_m, m \in M)$. When the switch is in state m, the SSS rule chooses one scheduling decisions $k \in K(m)$ randomly with probability $\phi_{m,k}$, and with the probability $1 - \sum_k \phi_{m,k}$ does not serve any of the queues. Then, clearly, the long-term service rate allocated to flow $n \in N$ is equal to

$$v_n = \sum_{m \in M} \pi^m \sum_{k \in K(m)} \phi_{mk} \mu_n^m(k) \, .$$

Sometimes, the set ϕ itself we will call an SSS rule. Thus,

$$v \doteq (v_1, \ldots, v_N) = v(\phi) \, ,$$

where $v(\cdot)$ is the function of an SSS rule ϕ, defined by the above expressions.

The following simple stability result is quite standard (see for example [1]).

Theorem 1 *A scheduling rule G under which the system is stable exists if and only if there exists an SSS rule such that*

$$\lambda_n < v_n, \ \forall n \in N \, . \tag{8.3}$$

5. The MaxWeight Discipline

It has been shown relatively recently that there are scheduling rules which (unlike SSS) do not use a priori information about input rates λ_n and the stationary distribution π of the server state, and yet ensure system stability as long as the necessary and sufficient stability condition (8.3) is satisfied. In particular, the MaxWeight discipline, which we define shortly, has this property. (There are numerous results on MaxWeight stability for different special cases of our model. The first results of this type were obtained probably in [18, 19]. For the model we consider in this paper, the MaxWeight stability was proved in [1].)

Let us call the value

$$W_n(t) \equiv U_{n1}(t)$$

(with $W_n(t) = 0$ if $Q_n(t) = 0$ by convention) the *delay* of flow n at time t.

MaxWeight Discipline. Let a set of positive constants γ_n, $n \in N$, be fixed. When switch is in state $m \in M$ (in a time slot t), a scheduling decision k is chosen from the following subset:

$$k \in \arg \max_{k \in K(m)} \sum_{n \in N} \gamma_n V_n(t) \mu_n^m(k) \ ,$$

where for each n, $V_n(t) = \eta_n^Q Q_n(t) + \eta_n^W W_n(t)$, with fixed constants $\eta_n^Q \geq 0$ and $\eta_n^W \geq 0$, $\eta_n^Q + \eta_n^W > 0$. (The "ties" are broken arbitrarily; for example, in favor of the largest index n.)

Theorem 2 *[1] Let an arbitrary set of positive constants γ_n, $n \in N$, be fixed. Then MaxWeight scheduling rule is throughput optimal, i.e. it makes the system stable if it is feasible to do at all, with any other rule.*

Proof is a straightforward extension of the proof of Theorem 3 in [1].

To simplify the exposition, in the rest of this paper we consider the MaxWeight rule with $V_n(t) \equiv Q_n(t)$, although all results (appropriately adjusted) hold for the more general MaxWeight rule defined above.

6.   Resource Pooling and Complete Resource Pooling Conditions

6.1   Definition

Our notion of Complete Resource Pooling (CRP) defined in this section can be viewed as a natural extension of this notion introduced in [9] (see also [23]) for a parallel server model. (It is somewhat more general simply because the generalized switch model is more general). We use a simple geometric interpretation of the CRP in the definition.

Let us denote by V the set of all service rate vectors $v(\phi)$ corresponding to all possible SSS rules ϕ. In our case, V is a polyhedron in R_+^N (as a linear image of the polyhedron of possible values of ϕ). Polyhedron V may turn out to be degenerate, i.e., have dimension less than N.

An SSS rule ϕ^* and the corresponding vector $v^* = v(\phi^*) \in V$ of service rates we will call *maximal* if the vector v^* is not dominated by any other $v \in V$. (We say that vector $v^{(1)}$ is dominated by vector $v^{(2)}$ if $v_n^{(1)} \leq v_n^{(2)}$ for all $n \in N$, and the strict inequality $v_n^{(1)} < v_n^{(2)}$ holds for at least one n.)

We will denote by $V^* \subset V$ the subset of all maximal $v \in V$.

Note that the set

$$\bar{V} = \{y \in R_+^N \mid y \le v \in V\} = \{y \in R_+^N \mid y \le v \in V^*\}$$

is the closure of the system *stability region*. The stability region is defined as the set of all input rate vectors λ such that the system can be made stable under at least one scheduling discipline (in which case MaxWeight also makes it stable).

Definition. *We will say that a Resource Pooling (RP) condition holds for a non-zero vector $v^* \in \bar{V}$, if*
(i) $\bar{V}$ is non-degenerate (i.e. has dimension N);
(ii) v^* lies on the boundary of $\bar{V}$, in the interior of one of its $N-1$-dimensional faces.
If, in addition, (iii) $v^* \in V^*$, then we say that Complete Resource Pooling (CRP) condition holds

Since $\bar{V}$ is a polyhedron, if RP condition holds, then a unique (up to scaling) outer normal vector ν^* to $\bar{V}$ at point v^* exists and $\nu^* \in R_+^N$. If the stronger CRP condition holds, then, in addition, $\nu^* \in R_{++}^N$, i.e., all components of ν^* are strictly positive. By convention, we assume that ν^* is the vector defined uniquely by the normalizing condition

$$\|\nu^*\| = 1 . \tag{8.4}$$

6.2   Constructive Definition of the Sets V and $\bar{V}$

The constructive definition of V and $\bar{V}$ for the generalized switch model, which we describe here, is *not* used in our analysis (and obviously *not* involved in any way in the definition of the MaxWeight scheduling rule). It may however help the understanding of the model, in particular, the example presented in the next subsection.

The polyhedron V is the convex hull formed by the points

$$\sum_m \pi_m \mu^m(k_m) ,$$

corresponding to all possible combinations $(k_1, \ldots, k_M)$, with $k_m \in K(m)$ for each $m \in M$. These points are $v(\cdot)$-images of the corner points of the polyhedron of possible values of ϕ.

Now, let us extend this set of points by their projections to all $2^N - 2$ (proper, non-degenerate) subspaces of R^N, and the point 0. The polyhedron $\bar{V}$ is the convex hull formed by this extended set of points.

6.3   Example

Consider the following example. We have two flows ($N = 2$) and two switch states $m = 1, 2$ with stationary probabilities $\pi_1 = 1/3$ and $\pi_2 = 2/3$,

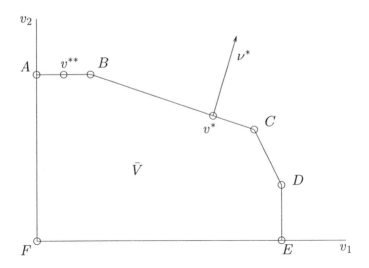

Figure 8.1.   The RP and CRP conditions.

respectively. There are two scheduling decisions corresponding to state $m = 1$, with the service rate vectors $(5, 2)$ and $(2, 8)$. And there are two scheduling decisions corresponding to state $m = 2$, with the service rate vectors $(11, 2)$ and $(2, 5)$. The polyhedron $\bar{V}$ can be constructed using the procedure described in the previous subsection, and is shown on the Figure 8.1. Its corner points are $A = (0, 6)$, $B = (2, 6)$, $C = (8, 4)$, $D = (9, 2)$, $E = (9, 0)$, and $F = (0, 0)$.

All the points lying on the (A, B, C, D, E) boundary, *except the corner points themselves*, satisfy the RP condition. The set V^* of maximal elements is (B, C, D). Therefore, points satisfying the CRP condition are those in the interior of segments (B, C) and (C, D). Thus, for example, the point v^* satisfies both the RP and the stronger CRP condition. The point v^{**} satisfies the RP, but not the CRP condition.

6.4   Discussion

Results we present in this paper (and their proofs in [17]) assume CRP condition. However, the proofs can be extended to cover the RP case. The basic intuition is that the input flows corresponding to indices n such that $v_n^* = 0$, become "irrelevant" in the heavy traffic regime (described below in the paper): their queue lengths become 0 in the limit. If we look at the subset of "bottleneck" flows (those with $v_n^* > 0$), and remove "irrelevant" components from vectors v^*, ν^*, and the service rate vectors $\mu^m(k)$, we obtain a bottleneck subsystem (of lower dimension) for which the CRP condition does hold.

Consequently, it can be shown that all the results presented in this paper hold *as is* under the RP condition. We also note that the RP condition is very non-restrictive: a typical ("arbitrarily chosen") point v^* on the "north-east" boundary of $\bar{V}$ satisfies this condition with probability 1.

In the rest of the paper we assume the stronger CRP condition.

7. Heavy Traffic Regime. Main Results

Consider a fixed vector v^* satisfying the CRP condition, and the corresponding vector ν^*. The quantity

$$X(t) \doteq \sum_{n=1}^{N} \nu_n^* Q_n(t) = \nu^* \cdot Q(t) \, ,$$

where $Q(t) = (Q_1(t), \ldots, Q_N(t))$ is the queue length vector at time t, will be referred to as *equivalent workload* of the switch.

Consider a sequence of systems, indexed by $r \in \mathcal{R} = \{r_1, r_2, \ldots\}$, where $r_i > 0$ for all i and $r_i \uparrow \infty$ as $i \to \infty$. (Hereafter in this paper "$r \to \infty$" means that r goes to infinity by taking values from the sequence $\mathcal{R}$, or some subsequence of $\mathcal{R}$; the choice of a subsequence will be clear in each case from context.)

Assume that for each flow n the mean input rate parameter λ_n^r is such that

$$r(\lambda_n^r - v_n^*) \to b_n \, , \tag{8.5}$$

where $b_n \in R$ is a fixed constant. Obviously, vector v^* is the limit of the sequence of input rate vectors. For this reason, from this point on in the paper, we will denote $\lambda = v^*$.

We make the following additional assumptions on the input flows, which are a form of assumptions introduced in [3]. For each $n \in N$ and each r,

$$A_n^r(t), \ t = 1, 2, \ldots, \ \text{are i.i.d.} \, , \tag{8.6}$$

with

$$Var[A_n^r(0)] \to \sigma_n^2 \geq 0, \ r \to \infty \, , \tag{8.7}$$

and

$$E[A_n^r(0)]^2 I\{A_n^r(0) > z\} \leq \eta(z) \, , \tag{8.8}$$

where $\eta(\cdot)$ is a fixed function, $\eta(z) \to \infty$ as $z \to \infty$, and $I\{\cdot\}$ is the indicator function. These assumptions imply the functional central limit theorem (FCLT) for each input flow:

$$\{r^{-1}(F_n^r(r^2 t) - \lambda_n^r r^2 t), \ t \geq 0\} \xrightarrow{w} \{\sigma_n B(t), \ t \geq 0\} \, , \tag{8.9}$$

where

$$F_n^r(t) \doteq \sum_{l=1}^{\lfloor t \rfloor} A_n^r(l)$$

is the cumulative number of flow n customers arrived by time t (i.e. in the interval $[0, t]$, excluding customers present at time 0), B is a standard (zero drift, unit variance) Brownian motion, and $\overset{w}{\to}$ here denotes convergence in distribution of the processes in the Skorohod space $D([0, \infty), R)$.

The Markov chain describing the switch state process does not change with r. Let us introduce the following function of a switch state:

$$\bar{\mu}^m \doteq \max_{k \in K(m)} \nu^* \cdot \mu^m(k), \ m \in M \, ,$$

and denote

$$\bar{\mu} \doteq \sum_{m \in M} \pi^m \bar{\mu}^m = \nu^* \cdot \lambda \, ,$$

where the last equality easily follows from the definition of $\nu^* = \lambda$. (Obviously, $\bar{\mu}$ is the maximum possible average rate at which the equivalent workload can be processed by the switch.) Then, from the FCLT for Markov chains, for any initial state of the (switch state) Markov chain, we have the following convergence as $r \to \infty$:

$$\{r^{-1}(\sum_{l=1}^{\lfloor r^2 t \rfloor} \bar{\mu}^{m(l-1)} - \bar{\mu} r^2 t), \ t \geq 0\} \overset{w}{\to} \{\sigma_s B(t), \ t \geq 0\} \, , \tag{8.10}$$

where

$$\sigma_s^2 = \lim_{n \to \infty} n^{-1} E[\sum_{t=1}^{n} \bar{\mu}^{m(t-1)} - \bar{\mu} n]^2 \, . \tag{8.11}$$

We will denote

$$\sigma^2 \doteq \sigma_s^2 + \sum_n [\nu_n^*]^2 \sigma_n^2 \, .$$

For each value of scaling parameter r, let $Q^r(\cdot)$ and $X^r(\cdot) = \nu^* \cdot Q^r(\cdot)$ be the corresponding (vector) queue length and the *equivalent workload* processes. Let us apply the *diffusion* scaling to $Q^r(\cdot)$ and $X^r(\cdot)$ to define the following scaled processes:

$$\tilde{q}^r(t) \doteq r^{-1} Q^r(r^2 t) \, , \ t \geq 0,$$
$$\tilde{x}^r(t) \doteq r^{-1} X^r(r^2 t) \, , \ t \geq 0.$$

We assume that the initial states of the scaled processes converge as follows:

$$\tilde{q}^r(0) \to \tilde{q}(0) = \tilde{x}(0)\nu^\circ \, ,$$

where $\tilde{x}(0) \geq 0$ is a fixed constant, and

$$\nu^\circ \doteq [\sum_n (\nu_n^*)^2 / \gamma_n]^{-1} (\nu_1^*/\gamma_1, \ldots, \nu_N^*/\gamma_N) \, .$$

This of course also means that $\tilde{x}^r(0) \to \tilde{x}(0)$.

Let us denote $a \doteq \nu^* \cdot b$.

Consider the following one-dimensional reflected Brownian motion process $\tilde{x} = (\tilde{x}(t), \ t \geq 0)$:

$$\tilde{x}(t) = \tilde{x}(0) + at + \sigma B(t) + \tilde{y}(t) , \qquad (8.12)$$

where

$$\tilde{y}(t) \doteq -[0 \wedge \inf_{0 \leq u \leq t} \{\tilde{x}(0) + au + \sigma B(u)\}] . \qquad (8.13)$$

Theorem 3 *Consider the system in heavy traffic, under CRP condition.*

1 *Suppose, the scheduling rule in the system is MaxWeight. Then, as* $r \to \infty$,

$$\tilde{x}^r \overset{w}{\to} \tilde{x} , \qquad (8.14)$$

and, moreover,

$$\tilde{q}^r \overset{w}{\to} \tilde{q} \doteq \tilde{x}\nu^\circ . \qquad (8.15)$$

2 *The MaxWeight is asymptotically optimal in that it minimizes the equivalent workload process. More precisely, the equivalent workload process* $\tilde{x}^r_G$ *corresponding to an arbitrary scheduling discipline* G *is such that for any time* $t \geq 0$ *and any* $u \geq 0$,

$$\liminf_{r \to \infty} P\{\tilde{x}^r_G(t) > u\} \geq P\{\tilde{x}(t) > u\} . \qquad (8.16)$$

Suppose, the drift $a < 0$. Then, it follows from Theorems 1 and 2 that for all sufficiently large r, the system is stable, and therefore has a stationary distribution. The following is a very natural conjecture about the asymptotics of stationary distributions.

Conjecture. *Consider the system with MaxWeight discipline in heavy traffic, under CRP condition. Suppose* $a < 0$. *Then, as* $r \to \infty$,

$$\tilde{q}^r(\infty) \overset{w}{\to} \tilde{x}(\infty)\nu^\circ ,$$

where $\tilde{q}^r(\infty)$ *and* $\tilde{x}(\infty)$ *are random vector and random variable with distributions equal to stationary distributions of the processes* $\tilde{q}^r$ *and* $\tilde{x}$, *respectively. It is well known that*

$$P\{\tilde{x}(\infty) > u\} = \exp\{(2a/\sigma^2)u\}, \ u \geq 0 .$$

8.   Process Behavior under Fluid Limit Scaling

In this section we introduce and study the sequence of processes introduced in the previous section under the *fluid limit* scaling and under MaxWeight discipline. The attraction property of the sample paths of the limiting process, which is key for the proof of our main (diffusion limit) results in the next section, is presented below in Theorem 4. It basically means that any such sample path converges to a "fixed point" (a vector q^* such that $(\gamma_1 q_1^*, \ldots, \gamma_N q_N^*)$ is proportional to ν^*), uniformly on the initial state (up to a scaling by the initial state norm).

First, we need to define the following additional (random) functions associated with the system for each value of the scaling parameter r. (The functions $F_n^r(t)$, $Q_n^r(t)$, and $X^r(t) = \nu^* \cdot Q^r(t)$, have already been defined earlier.)

Let

$$\hat{F}_n^r(t) \doteq \sum_{l=1}^{\lfloor t \rfloor} D_n^r(l)$$

denote the number of type-n customers that were served and have departed by time $t \geq 0$. Also, denote by $G_m^r(t)$ the total number of time slots by (and including) time $t - 1$, when the server was in state m; and by $\hat{G}_{mk}^r(t)$ the number of time slots before (and including) time $t - 1$ when the server state was m and the scheduling decision $k \in K(m)$ was chosen.

We will denote for $t \geq 0$,

$$H^r(t) \doteq \sum_{l=1}^{\lfloor t \rfloor} \bar{\mu}^{m(l-1)} ,$$

$$Y^r(t) \doteq H^r(t) - \nu^* \cdot \hat{F}^r(t) \equiv \sum_{l=1}^{\lfloor t \rfloor} [\bar{\mu}^{m(l-1)} - \nu^* \cdot D^r(l)] ,$$

and

$$W^r(t) \doteq X^r(0) + \nu^* \cdot F^r(t) - H^r(t).$$

The following relations obviously hold for all $t \geq 0$ and any $n \in N$:

$$F_n^r(0) = \hat{F}_n^r(0) = 0 ,$$

$$Q_n^r(t) = Q_n^r(0) + F_n^r(t) - \hat{F}_n^r(t) , \qquad (8.17)$$

$$X^r(t) = W^r(t) + Y^r(t) . \qquad (8.18)$$

We will consider the process $Z^r = (Q^r, X^r, W^r, Y^r, F^r, \hat{F}^r, G^r, H^r, \hat{G}^r)$, where

$$Q^r = (Q^r(t) = (Q_1^r(t), \ldots, Q_N^r(t)), \quad t \geq 0),$$

$$X^r = (X^r(t), \ t \geq 0),$$
$$W^r = (W^r(t), \ t \geq 0),$$
$$Y^r = (Y^r(t), \ t \geq 0),$$
$$F^r = (F^r(t) = (F_1^r(t), \ldots, F_N^r(t)), \ t \geq 0),$$
$$\hat{F}^r = (\hat{F}^r(t) = (\hat{F}_1^r(t), \ldots, \hat{F}_N^r(t)), \ t \geq 0),$$
$$G^r = ((G_m^r(t), \ m \in M), \ t \geq 0),$$
$$H^r = (H^r(t), \ t \geq 0),$$
$$\hat{G}^r = ((\hat{G}_{mk}^r(t), \ m \in M, \ k \in K(m)), \ t \geq 0),$$

Recall our convention that all component functions, as functions of t, are defined for $t \in R_+$ and are constant within each time slot $[t, t+1)$, $t = 0, 1, 2, \ldots$.

Now, for each r consider the scaled process

$$\Gamma^r Z^r \doteq z^r = (q^r, x^r, w^r, y^r, f^r, \hat{f}^r, g^r, h^r, \hat{g}^r) .$$

From (8.17) we get:

$$q_n^r(t) \equiv f_n^r(t) - \hat{f}_n^r(t), \ t \geq 0, \ n = 1, 2, \ldots, N. \tag{8.19}$$

Definition. A fixed set of functions $z = (q, x, w, y, f, \hat{f}, g, h, \hat{g})$ we will call a *fluid sample path* (FSP), or just a fluid path, if there exists a sequence $\mathcal{R}_f$ of values of r, and a sequence of *sample paths* (of the corresponding *processes*) $\{z^r\}$ such that, as $r \to \infty$ along sequence $\mathcal{R}_f$,

$$z^r \to z, \ u.o.c. \ ,$$

and in addition

$$\|q(0)\| < \infty ,$$
$$(f_n^r(t), t \geq 0) \to (\lambda_n t, t \geq 0) \ u.o.c. \ ,$$
$$(g_m^r(t), t \geq 0) \to (\pi^m t, t \geq 0) \ u.o.c. \ .$$

Remark. A sequence $\mathcal{R}_f$ existence of which is required in the above definition, may be completely unrelated to the sequence $\mathcal{R}$ we introduced earlier in the definition of the heavy traffic regime.

The following simple lemma establishes some basic properties of fluid sample paths. We omit a trivial proof.

Lemma 1 *For any fluid sample path z, all its component functions are Lipschitz continuous and, in addition,*

$$f_n(t) = \lambda_n t , \ t \geq 0 , \ n \in N,$$

$$g_m(t) = \pi^m t \, , \, t \geq 0 \, m \in M,$$
$$q_n(t) = q_n(0) + f_n(t) - \hat{f}_n(t) \, , \, t \geq 0 \, , \, n \in N,$$
$$w(t) = w(0) = x(0) \, , \, t \geq 0 \, ,$$
$$x(t) = \nu^* \cdot q(t) = x(0) + y(t) \, .$$

Since all component functions of an FSP are Lipschitz, they are absolutely continuous, and therefore almost all points $t \in R_+$ (with respect to Lebesgue measure) are such that all component functions of z have derivatives; we will call such point *regular*. The vector $q(t)$ corresponding to an FSP we will call its *state* at time t. The dynamics of the state q is therefore governed by the differential (vector) equation

$$\frac{d}{dt} q(t) = \lambda - v(t) \, , \tag{8.20}$$

which holds at every regular point t, and where $v(t) \doteq \hat{f}'(t)$.

Consider a fixed FSP with non-zero initial state $q(0)$. For each $t \geq 0$, consider a "moving fixed point" $q^*(t) = x(t)\nu^\circ$ (which is the point y in the hyperplane $\nu^* \cdot y = x(t)$ such that $(\gamma_1 y_1, \ldots, \gamma_N y_N)$ is proportional to ν^*). Let us introduce the following Lyapunov function:

$$G^*(q(t)) = \frac{1}{2x(t)^2} \sum_n \gamma_n (q_n(t) - q_n^*(t))^2 \, .$$

The following uniform convergence result holds. (See [17] for the proof.)

Theorem 4 *There exist fixed constants $T_1 > 0$ and $C_1 \geq 1$ such that any fixed fluid sample path z with $\|q(0)\| > 0$, is such that the equivalent workload $x(t) = \nu^* \cdot q(t)$ is a continuous non-decreasing bounded function which attains its limit value $x^* = \lim x(t)$ within time $\|q(0)\| T_1$, and $x^* \leq C_1 x(0)$. (This, of course, implies that*

$$x(t) = x^*, \quad q^*(t) = q^*, \quad \lambda(t) = \lambda, \quad \forall t \geq \|q(0)\| T_1 \, ,$$

where $q^* \doteq \lim_{\xi \to \infty} q^*(\xi)$.)
In addition, $G^*(q(t))$ is a non-increasing function of t, converging to 0:

$$\lim_{t \to \infty} G^*(q(t)) = 0 \, . \tag{8.21}$$

Moreover, the convergence in (8.21) is uniform in the following sense. For any $\epsilon_2 > 0$ there exists $T_2 = T_2(\epsilon_2)$ such that

$$G^*(q(t)) \leq \epsilon_2, \quad \forall t \geq \|q(0)\| T_2 \, . \tag{8.22}$$

Finally, there exists $\epsilon_3 > 0$ such that

$$G^*(q(0)) \leq \epsilon_3, \quad \text{implies} \quad x^* = x(0) \, , \tag{8.23}$$

i.e., $x(t) = x(0)$, $\forall t \geq 0$.

9.   Proof of Theorem 3

We only sketch the proof in this section (due to space constraints). The detailed proof, in which Theorem 4 plays key role, can be found in [17]. (See remarks after Lemma 2.)

For each $r \in \mathcal{R}$ consider the following process, obtained by a diffusion scaling:

$$\tilde{\Gamma}^r(Q^r, X^r, W^r, Y^r, F^r, H^r) \doteq (\tilde{q}^r, \tilde{x}^r, \tilde{w}^r, \tilde{y}^r, \tilde{f}^r, \tilde{h}^r) .$$

To prove properties (8.14)-(8.16), it will suffice to show that for any subsequence $\mathcal{R}_1 \subseteq \mathcal{R}$ there exists another subsequence $\mathcal{R}_2 \subseteq \mathcal{R}_1$ such that these properties hold when $r \to \infty$ along $\mathcal{R}_2$. And one of the standard ways to do this is to choose subsequence $\mathcal{R}_2$ and construct all processes (for all $r \in \mathcal{R}_2$) on the same probability space in a way such that the desired properties hold with probability 1 (or are implied by a certain probability 1 properties). In this section we do just that.

Let us fix an arbitrary subsequence $\mathcal{R}_1 \subseteq \mathcal{R}$ of indices $\{r\}$. According to Skorohod representation theorem (see, for example, [6]), for each n, the sequence of the input processes $\{F_n^r\}$ can be constructed on a probability space such that the convergence in (8.9) holds u.o.c. with probability 1 (w.p.1). Similarly, the sequence of switch state processes (Markov chains) $\{m^r\}$ can be constructed on a probability space such that the convergence in (8.10) holds u.o.c. w.p.1., which can be written as

$$(\tilde{h}^r(t) - \bar{\mu}rt, \ t \geq 0) \overset{u.o.c.}{\to} (\sigma_s^2 B(t), \ t \geq 0) . \tag{8.24}$$

We can and do assume that the underlying probability space $\Omega = \{\omega\}$ is a direct product of those $N + 1$ probability spaces.

Using Large Deviations estimates for Markov chains and Borel-Cantelli lemma, it is easy to show (as for example in [16]) that the following properties also hold with probability 1, for any fixed $T_3 > 0$:

$$\max_{0 \leq l \leq T_3 r^{3/2}} |\sqrt{r}\, g_m^r(\frac{l+1}{\sqrt{r}}) - \sqrt{r}\, g_m^r(\frac{l}{\sqrt{r}}) - \pi^m| \to 0, \ m \in M , \tag{8.25}$$

$$\max_{0 \leq l \leq T_3 r^{3/2}} |\sqrt{r}\, h^r(\frac{l+1}{\sqrt{r}}) - \sqrt{r}\, h^r(\frac{l}{\sqrt{r}}) - \bar{\mu}| \to 0, \tag{8.26}$$

where (8.26) follows from (8.25).

Now, from Bramson's weak law estimates ([3], Proposition 4.2), we know that for any $T_3 > 0$ and any $\epsilon > 0$ and any $n \in N$, for all large r, we have

$$P\{\max_{0 \leq l \leq T_3 r} \sup_{0 \leq \xi \leq 1} |f_n^r(l+\xi) - f_n^r(l) - \lambda_n \xi| \geq \epsilon\} < \epsilon .$$

This allows us to choose a subsequence $\mathcal{R}_2 \subseteq \mathcal{R}_1$, such that as $r \to \infty$ along $\mathcal{R}_2$, with probability 1, for any $T_3 > 0$ and any $n \in N$, we have

$$\max_{0 \leq l \leq T_3 r} \sup_{0 \leq \xi \leq 1} |f_n^r(l + \xi) - f_n^r(l) - \lambda_n \xi| \to 0 . \tag{8.27}$$

Then we have

$$\tilde{x}^r(t) = \tilde{w}^r(t) + \tilde{y}^r(t), \ t \geq 0,$$

and

$$(\tilde{w}^r(t), \ t \geq 0) \overset{u.o.c.}{\to} (\tilde{w}(t), \ t \geq 0) ,$$

where

$$\tilde{w}^r(t) \doteq \tilde{x}^r(0) + \nu^* \cdot \tilde{f}_n^r(t) - \tilde{h}^r(t) ,$$

and

$$\tilde{w}(t) \doteq \tilde{x}(0) + at + \sigma B(t)$$

is a continuous function.

In the rest of this section, we restrict ourselves to a (measurable, probability 1) subset $\Omega_2 \subseteq \Omega$ of elementary outcomes w, such that all the specified above "probability 1" properties hold, when $r \to \infty$ along $\mathcal{R}_2$.

For each $r \in \mathcal{R}_2$, $\tilde{y}^r$ is a non-decreasing RCLL function. Therefore, for any fixed $w \in \Omega_2$, from any subsequence $\mathcal{R}_3(w) \subseteq \mathcal{R}_2$ (which may depend on w!) it is always possible to find a further subsequence $\mathcal{R}_4(w) \subseteq \mathcal{R}_3(w)$ such that

$$\tilde{y}^r \Rightarrow \tilde{y} , \tag{8.28}$$

where $\tilde{y}$ is a non-decreasing RCLL function, which may take the values $+\infty$. (In other words, $\tilde{y} \in D([0,\infty), \bar{R})$. We also remind that "$\Rightarrow$" means the convergence in every point of continuity of the limit function except maybe point 0.) We note that (8.28) implies that

$$\tilde{x}^r \Rightarrow \tilde{x} \doteq \tilde{w} + \tilde{y} , \tag{8.29}$$

and therefore $\tilde{x}(t) < \infty$ if and only if $\tilde{y}(t) < \infty$.

The following lemma contains the key observation which will be used repeatedly in the proof of Theorem 3.

Lemma 2 *Suppose, $w \in \Omega_2$ and a subsequence $\mathcal{R}_4(w) \subseteq \mathcal{R}_2$ are fixed such that, along this subsequence, (8.28) holds. Suppose, a sequence $\{\tilde{t}^r, \ r \in \mathcal{R}_4(w)\}$ is fixed such that*

$$\tilde{t}^r \to t' \geq 0 ,$$

and

$$\tilde{x}(\tilde{t}^r) \to C > 0 .$$

Let $\delta > 0$ be fixed, and

$$\epsilon = \epsilon(\delta, t') = \sup_{\xi_1, \xi_2 \in [t'-\delta, t'+\delta] \cap R_+} |\tilde{w}(\xi_1) - \tilde{w}(\xi_2)| < C .$$

Then,
(a) $\tilde{y}$ (and $\tilde{x}$) is finite in $[0, t' + \delta)$;
(b) $\tilde{y}$ does not increase in $(t', t' + \delta)$, i.e., $\tilde{y}(t' + \delta-) - \tilde{y}(t') = 0$;
(c) the following bound holds

$$C - \epsilon \leq \tilde{x}(t) \leq CC_1 + \epsilon , \quad \forall t \in [t', t' + \delta) ,$$

with C_1 defined in Theorem 4;
(d) for any $\alpha > 0$,

$$(\tilde{q}^r(t), \ t \in [t' + \alpha, t' + \delta - \alpha]) \overset{u.o.c.}{\to} (\tilde{q}(t), \ t \in [t' + \alpha, t' + \delta - \alpha]) ,$$

where $\tilde{q}(t) = \tilde{x}(t)\nu^\circ$.
  If, in addition, $\tilde{t}^r = t'$ for all r, and $\tilde{q}^r(t') \to \tilde{q}(t')$, then
(b') $\tilde{y}$ does not increase in $[t', t' + \delta)$, i.e., $\tilde{y}(t' + \delta-) - \tilde{y}(t'-) = 0$, where $\tilde{y}(0-) = 0$ by convention;
(d') the following holds:

$$(\tilde{q}^r(t), \ t \in [t', t' + \delta]) \overset{u.o.c.}{\to} (\tilde{q}(t), \ t \in [t', t' + \delta]) .$$

Proof is presented in [17]. It employs the general approach developed in [3] to show that the fluid sample path attraction property (Theorem 4) implies State Space Collapse: roughly speaking, the properties (d) and (d'). This in turn is used to show the equivalent workload conservation properties (b) and (b'). ∎

9.1   Proof of Statement 1

To prove the convergences (8.14) and (8.15) in Statement 1 of the theorem, it will suffice to prove the following

Proposition 1 *As $r \to \infty$ (along $\mathcal{R}_2$), for any $w \in \Omega_2$ (i.e. with probability 1), we have the following convergences*

$$(\tilde{y}^r(t), \ t \geq 0) \overset{u.o.c.}{\to} (\tilde{y}(t), \ t \geq 0) , \tag{8.30}$$

where $\tilde{y}$ is defined by (8.13), and

$$(\tilde{q}^r(t), \ t \geq 0) \overset{u.o.c.}{\to} (\tilde{q}(t), \ t \geq 0) , \tag{8.31}$$

where $\tilde{q} = \tilde{x}\nu^\circ$.

Proof of Proposition 1. Let us fix $\omega \in \Omega_2$. As explained earlier, for an arbitrary subsequence $\mathcal{R}_3(\omega) \subseteq \mathcal{R}_2$ there exists another subsequence $\mathcal{R}_4(\omega) \subseteq \mathcal{R}_3(\omega)$ such that the convergence (8.28) holds along this subsequence. Then, the proof of Proposition 1 will be complete if we can prove the following statements (for the chosen ω, with $r \to \infty$ along $\mathcal{R}_4(\omega)$).

Step 1. *The limit function $\tilde{y}$ is finite everywhere in $[0, \infty)$.*

Step 2. *Function $\tilde{y}$ is continuous.*

Step 3. *If $\tilde{x}(t) > 0$, then t is* not *a point of increase of $\tilde{y}$.*

Step 4. *The function $\tilde{y}$, defined above as a limit, satisfies equation (8.13).*

Step 5. *Convergence (8.31) holds.*

Proof of Step 1. Suppose the statement does not hold. Denote $t_* = \inf\{t \geq 0 \mid \tilde{y}(t) = \infty\}$. The inf is attained because $\tilde{y}$ is RCLL. There are two possible cases:

(a) $t_* = 0$;

(b) $0 < t_* < \infty$.

Case (a). Let us fix small $\delta > 0$ and let $\epsilon = \epsilon(\delta, 0)$ be as defined in Lemma 2. Consider some fixed $C > \tilde{x}(0) + \epsilon$, and define

$$\tilde{t}^r = \min\{t \mid \tilde{x}^r(t) \geq C\} .$$

Then we must have $\tilde{t}^r \to t_* = 0$ and $\tilde{x}^r(\tilde{t}^r) \to C$. (The latter follows from the property (8.27).) Now, if we set $t' = t_* = 0$, then all conditions of Lemma 2 are satisfied. According to Lemma 2, $\tilde{y}$ is bounded in $[t', t' + \delta]$, which contradicts to the assumption (a), since $t' + \delta > t^*$.

The contradiction for the case (b) is obtained very similarly. We choose a small $\delta \in (0, t^*)$ and denote

$$\epsilon_5 = \sup_{\xi_1, \xi_2 \in [t^* - 2\delta, t^* + 2\delta] \cap R_+} |\tilde{w}(\xi_1) - \tilde{w}(\xi_2)| .$$

Then we choose a small $\delta^* \in (0, \delta)$ and a large $C > \tilde{x}(t^* - \delta^*) + \epsilon_5$. We define

$$\tilde{t}^r = \min\{t \geq t^* - \delta^* \mid \tilde{x}^r(t) \geq C\} ,$$

and choose a further subsequence of $\{r\}$ such that

$$\tilde{t}^r \to t' \in [t^* - \delta^*, t^*] .$$

The conditions of Lemma 2 are satisfied, so $\tilde{y}$ is bounded in $[t', t' + \delta]$, which contradicts to the assumption (b), since $t' + \delta > t^*$. Step 1 has been proved.

The proofs of Steps 2 and 3 are also easily proved by using statements (a)-(c) and (b') of Lemma 2 - we omit details.

Proof of Step 4 follows from the statements of Steps 2 and 3, and the standard properties of the one-dimensional Skorohod problem (see, for example, [21]).

Finally, the proof of the convergence (8.31) (Step 5) is easily obtained by contradiction by using statements (d) and (d') of Lemma 2.

Thus, the proof of Proposition 1, and with it the proof of the Statement 1 of the theorem, is complete.

9.2 Proof of Statement 2.

To prove Statement 2 we use the same construction of the probability space Ω, the subsequence $\mathcal{R}_2$, and the probability 1 subset Ω_2. Consider an arbitrary discipline G. For $\omega \in \Omega_2$, consider paths of $\tilde{x}_G^r$, $\tilde{y}_G^r$, and $\tilde{w}_G^r$, corresponding to the discipline G. Since these paths are constructed on the same probability space as the paths corresponding to MaxWeight discipline, we have $\tilde{w}_G^r = \tilde{w}^r$ and therefore $\tilde{w}_G^r \to \tilde{w}_G = \tilde{w}$ u.o.c. For any subsequence $\mathcal{R}_4(\omega) \subseteq \mathcal{R}_2$ such that $\tilde{y}_G^r \Rightarrow \tilde{y}_G$, where $\tilde{y}_G$ is some non-decreasing RCLL function, we must have $\tilde{y}_G(t) \geq \tilde{y}(t)$ for all $t \geq 0$; this follows from the properties of the one-dimensional Skorohod problem. This immediately implies that, along subsequence $\mathcal{R}_2$,

$$\liminf_{r \to \infty} \tilde{y}_G(t) \geq \tilde{y}(t), \quad t \geq 0 ,$$

and the desired statement easily follows.

Proof of Theorem 3 is complete.

10. Conclusions

The results demonstrate that the MaxWeight discipline not only provides maximum system stability region (as has been shown in numerous previous work), but also has striking optimality (equivalent workload minimization) and self-organizing (state space collapse) properties when system is under heavy traffic. These properties and the parsimonious nature of MaxWeight rule, make it very attractive in practical applications. MaxWeight also allows to *efficiently* control system, namely, distribute workload among queues in any desired way.

A new important theoretical insight is that *it is feasible to efficiently control a system as complex as generalized switch by a very parsimonious rule* not requiring any "precomputation" of rule parameters or any "preallocation" of the service resources. We conjecture that the class of scheduling rules which "automatically" minimize equivalent workload in heavy traffic is very large, and probably roughly "coincides" with the class of "on-line" rules having the maximum stability region.

References

[1] M. Andrews, K. Kumaran, K. Ramanan, A. L. Stolyar, R. Vijayakumar, P. Whiting. Scheduling in a Queueing System with Asynchronously Varying Service Rates. 2000. (Submitted.)

[2] M. Armony, N. Bambos. Queueing Networks with Interacting Service Resources. 2000. (Submitted.)

[3] M. Bramson. State Space Collapse with Applications to Heavy Traffic Limits for Multiclass Queueing Networks. *Queueing Systems*, Vol. 30, (1998), pp. 89-148.

[4] R. Buche, H.J. Kushner. Control of Mobile Communications with Time-Varying Channels in Heavy Traffic. 2001. Preprint.

[5] J.G.Dai, B.Prabhakar. The Throughput of Data Switches with and without Speedup. *Proceedings of the INFOCOM'2000*, 2000.

[6] S. N. Ethier and T. G. Kurtz. *Markov Process: Characterization and Convergence.* John Wiley and Sons, New York, 1986.

[7] J. M. Harrison. Heavy Traffic Analysis of a System with Parallel Servers: Asymptotic Optimality of Discrete Review Policies. *Annals of Applied Probability*, Vol. 8, (1998), pp. 822-848.

[8] J. M. Harrison. Brownian Models of Open Processing Networks: Canonical Representation of Workload. *Annals of Applied Probability*, Vol. 10, (2000), pp. 75-103.

[9] J.M.Harrison, M.J.Lopez. Heavy Traffic Resource Pooling in Parallel-Server Systems. *Queueing Systems*, To appear.

[10] J. M. Harrison, J.A.Van Mieghem. Dynamic Control of Brownian Networks: State Space Collapse and Equivalent Workload Formulations. *Annals of Applied Probability*, Vol. 7, (1997), pp. 747-771.

[11] N.Kahale and P.E.Wright. Dynamic Global Packet Routing in Wireless Networks. *Proceedings of the INFOCOM'97*, 1997, pp. 1414-1421.

[12] N.McKeown, V.Anantharam, and J.Walrand. Achieving 100% Throughput in an Input-Queued Switch. *Proceedings of the INFOCOM'96*, 1996, pp. 296-302.

[13] A.Mekkittikul and N.McKeown. A Starvation Free Algorithm for Achieving 100% Throughput in an Input-Queued Switch. *Proceedings of the ICCCN'96*, 1996, pp. 226-231.

[14] M.I.Reiman. Some Diffusion Approximations with State Space Collapse. In *Proc. of the Internat. Seminar on Modeling and Performance Evaluation Methodology*, Lecture Notes in Control and Information Sciences. Springer, New York, 1984, pp. 209-240.

[15] M.I.Reiman. A Multiclass Feedback Queue in Heavy Traffic. *Advances in Applied Probability*, Vol. 20, (1988), pp. 179-207.

[16] S.Shakkottai, A.Stolyar. Scheduling for Multiple Flows Sharing a Time-Varying Channel: The Exponential Rule. To appear in *Analytic Methods in Applied Probability: In Memory of Fridrih Karpelevich,* Y.Suhov (ed.), American Mathematical Society, 2002.

[17] A. L. Stolyar. MaxWeight Scheduling in a Generalized Switch: State Space Collapse and Equivalent Workload Minimization under Complete Resource Pooling. *Bell Labs Technical Report*, July 2001.

[18] L. Tassiulas, A. Ephremides. Stability Properties of Constrained Queueing Systems and Scheduling Policies for Maximum Throughput in Multishop Radio Network. *IEEE Transactions on Automatic Control*, Vol. 37, (1992), pp. 1936-1948.

[19] L.Tassiulas, A.Ephremides. Dynamic Server Allocation to Parallel Queues with Randomly Varying Connectivity. *IEEE Transactions on Information Theory*, Vol. 39, (1993), pp. 466-478.

[20] W.Whitt. Weak Convergence Theorems for Priority Queues: Preemptive Resume Discipline. *Journal of Applied Probability*, Vol. 8, (1971), pp. 74-94.

[21] R.J.Williams. An Invariance Principle for Semimartingale Reflecting Brownian Motions in an Ortant. *Queueing Systems*, Vol. 30, (1998), pp. 5-25.

[22] R.J.Williams. Diffusion Approximations for Open Multiclass Queueing Networks: Sufficient Conditions Involving State Space Collapse. *Queueing Systems*, Vol. 30, (1998), pp. 27-88.

[23] R.J.Williams. On Dynamic Scheduling of a Parallel Server System with Complete Resource Pooling. *Fields Institute Communucations*, (1998).

Chapter 9

ASYMPTOTIC ANALYSIS OF RATE ADAPTIVE MULTIMEDIA STREAMS

Steven Weber and Gustavo de Veciana

Department of Electrical and Computer Engineering
The University of Texas at Austin
{sweber,gustavo}@ece.utexas.edu

Abstract   We investigate dynamic adaptation policies for rate adaptive multimedia streams in a network where each route traverses at most one bottleneck link. Dynamic adaptation allows clients to dynamically adapt the stream subscription level, i.e., time-average stream rate, in response to changes in available link capacity, and allows the system to maintain a lower blocking probability than is possible with non-adaptive streams. We define the quality of service for rate adaptive streams using the metrics of time-average subscription level, rate of adaptation, i.e., change in subscription level, and blocking probability. We investigate two baseline policies, namely, fair share adaptation and two rate randomized adaptation, and show that each suffers from significant implementation drawbacks. We then show that the adaptation policy which maximizes the mean subscription level overcomes these drawbacks, although streams with a duration near a critical threshold may experience unacceptably high rates of adaptation. This motivates the investigation of admission policies for rate adaptive streams where a stream is given a static subscription level at the time of admission which it maintains throughout its lifetime. We identify the asymptotically optimal admission policy for rate adaptive streams and show that it achieves an expected subscription level equal to that under the optimal dynamic adaptation policy. We also show that it maintains the asymptotic zero blocking property achievable using dynamic rate adaptation but does not incur the implementation overhead and QoS drawbacks of dynamic rate adaptation. The conclusion is that near optimal QoS can be obtained using a simple admission policy which gives the maximum subscription level to short duration streams and the minimum subscription level to long duration streams.

Keywords: multimedia streams, rate adaptation, multi-service loss networks

1.   Introduction

Streaming connections allow clients to play multimedia content in real time as it is transferred over the network, and therefore streams require strict service guarantees, e.g., bandwidth, delay and loss, to guarantee satisfactory client perceived performance. Rich multimedia content may consume large amounts of network resources relative to other applications—resources that may well be available on certain routes at certain times. During congestion, however, these streams lack the ability to adjust their resource consumption in response to heavier traffic. This results in heavy loss, if service is not guaranteed, or unfairness, if service is guaranteed and non-preemptive. Multimedia data, however, is adaptive in the sense that satisfactory playback may be obtained over a large range of compression levels. This fact has motivated the investigation of rate adaptive multimedia streams which offer the client the ability to dynamically change the compression/resolution of the stream during playback in response to network congestion. The canonical service model for rate adaptive streams is hierarchical encoding, e.g., McCanne, 1996; Vishwanath and Chou, 1994, where multimedia content is simultaneously encoded into a set of subscription levels offering a range of stream resolutions with a commensurate range of required bandwidth. Clients may subscribe to as many subscription levels as their available bandwidth permits and may adapt their resolution by adding or dropping levels in response to changing network congestion.

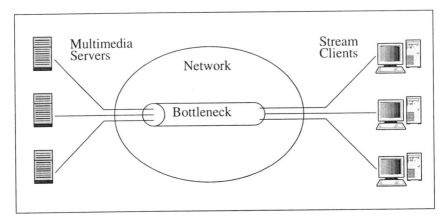

Figure 9.1.   A network consisting of multimedia servers providing streaming content to clients, where stream routes traverse at most one bottleneck link.

The setup for the paper is shown in Figure 9.1 which depicts a network with stream content being transmitted from multimedia servers to clients. We assume all active streams travel routes comprising at most one bottleneck link. The restriction to a single bottleneck link is required for purposes of obtaining closed form expressions for the mean subscription level and rate of adaptation. The policies themselves, however, are similar for general networks, see Weber and de Veciana, 2002. We assume a network protocol, e.g., DiffServ or IntServ, that guarantees a fixed amount of bandwidth is available for these streams, i.e., streams will not incur any loss.

In this paper, extending previous work in Weber and de Veciana, 2002, we investigate the critical issue of adaptation policies, i.e., when should streams adjust their subscriptiou level, which streams should adjust, to which subscription level should they adjust, etc. Our approach is unique in that we provide a system level, as opposed to a client level, analysis of various adaptation policies in a dynamic network, i.e., where streams come and go. We investigate three aspects of quality of service associated with rate adaptive streams: the mean subscription level, the rate of adaptation, and the blocking probability. We identify three dynamic adaptation policies: fair share adaptation, two rate randomized adaptation, and an optimal adaptation policy that maximizes the time average subscription level. Although the optimal dynamic adaptation policy maximizes the mean subscription level, investigation of the rate of adaptation as a function of stream duration identifies that streams with a duration within a critical interval will experience an unacceptably high rate of adaptation. The threshold nature of the optimal dynamic adaptation policy suggests that a near optimal mean subscription level may be obtained by a duration dependent admission policy that does not dynamically adapt streams, thereby reducing the rate of adaptation to zero. That is, instead of using a single class admission policy and setting subscription levels using a given dynamic adaptation policy, we use a multi-class admission policy that sets static subscription levels for streams at the time of admission based on stream durations, which are assumed to be known a priori, and then we do not make use of dynamic adaptation. The price paid for reducing the rate of adaptation to zero is a higher blocking probability because streams may no longer adapt their subscription level to make room for new streams, but it is shown that this increase in blocking probability is negligibly small for large capacity links. The conclusion is that duration dependent admission policies obtain near optimal mean subscription levels, zero rate of adaptation, marginally higher blocking probabilities, all without the protocol and complexity overhead of dynamic rate adaptation.

Relevant work includes Saparilla and Ross, 2000; Argiriou and Georgiadis, 2002; Rejaie et al., 1999; Gorinsky and Vin, 2001; Gorinsky et al., 2000; Kar et al., 2000; B.Vickers et al., 2000. The work in Saparilla and Ross, 2000 investigates optimal policies to dynamically adapt the fraction of the available bandwidth given to a base and enhancement layer. Their work differs from ours in that it takes is a client-centric view while ours is a system-centric view. Recent work in Argiriou and Georgiadis, 2002 uses an almost identical model for QoS as ours, but pursues a very different line of analysis. Their approach doesn't seem to permit an investigation of optimal adaptation policies, which is a major focus of our work. A different tack on the problem is taken in Rejaie et al., 1999 which proposes a TCP-friendly congestion control scheme for rate adaptive video which makes smart use of buffering to absorb short time scale congestion. This paper also takes a client-centric view. The work in Gorinsky and Vin, 2001; Gorinsky et al., 2000 investigates many of the same issues, but with notably different results, particularly with respect to suggesting the benefit of providing additional encoding levels. The work in Kar et al., 2000 offers a system level analysis of rate adaptive streams, but in a static context, i.e., a fixed number of streams. Finally, B.Vickers et al., 2000 investigates a model where the server dynamically adjusts the number and rate of each subscription layer in response to congestion feedback.

The paper is organized as follows. Section 2 specifies the model and notation. Section 3 defines the three aspects of QoS that we deem most important for rate adaptive streams. Section 4 analyzes all three aspects of QoS for three dynamic adaptation policies. Section 5 analyzes admission policies for rate adaptive streams that identify subscription levels for streams at the time of stream initiation, but don't make use of dynamic adaptation. Section 6 concludes the paper.

2.   Model and Notation

Let stream durations be independent random variables, denoted D, with a common distribution F_D, and a mean $\mathbb{E}[D] = \mu^{-1}$. We will use d to denote a known stream duration, and will write $D \sim exp(\mu)$) to denote $F_D(x) = 1 - exp(-\mu x)$. Let new stream requests arrive as a Poisson process with parameter λ. Let $\rho = \frac{\lambda}{\mu}$ denote the offered load to the link and let c be the capacity of the bottleneck link.

We abstract stream compression and encoding by considering the resulting time average mean of the compressed stream. That is, if we consider a VBR multimedia stream of duration d encoded so that the instantaneous transmission rate is $(b(t), 0 \le t \le d)$ and the time average mean is

$$s = \frac{1}{d} \int_0^d b(t)dt,$$

then we speak of the stream as having a *subscription level s*. We will also speak of s as a *rate*, although this is not to be confused with the instantaneous rate $b(t)$.

Let $\bar{s}$ denote the maximally useful subscription level and $\underline{s}$ denote the minimally acceptable subscription level. The maximum subscription level corresponds to the coarsest resolution such that any finer resolution yields a negligible increase in user perception, while the minimum subscription level corresponds to the coarsest resolution deemed acceptable. Thus the interval $[\underline{s}, \bar{s}]$ defines the range of acceptable subscription levels for the stream. We define the *adaptivity* β of a stream as the ratio of its minimum and maximum subscription levels, i.e., $\beta \equiv \underline{s}/\bar{s} \in (0, 1]$.

We define the set of supported subscription levels as $\mathcal{S} \equiv \{\bar{s} = s_1 > ... > s_K = \underline{s}\}$ for $K \geq 2$. Clients may adapt their subscription level over the course of stream playback in response to changing network congestion, where the choice of the instantaneous subscription level is dictated by the enforced adaptation policy. Note that for the case of hierarchical encoding a subscription level s corresponds to subscribing to a set of layers such that the aggregate subscription is s. We abstract away the layering aspect and just consider the set of feasible subscription levels.

Let $N(t)$ denote the number of streams that are active at time t. The maximum number of streams that can be admitted without use of adaptation is $m \equiv \lfloor \frac{c}{\bar{s}} \rfloor$ and the maximum number of streams that can be admitted with adaptation is $\bar{m} \equiv \lfloor \frac{c}{\underline{s}} \rfloor$. We require $N(t) \leq \bar{m}$, i.e., we guarantee that all admitted streams receive sufficient bandwidth to subscribe to the minimum rate or higher.

We will make use of two distinct admission policies. In Section 4 we employ a dynamic adaptation policy and a single class full sharing admission policy. That is, admission policies have no bearing on the rate received by the stream, which is handled by the adaptation policy, and a stream is admitted at time t if $N(t) < \bar{m}$. Under this assumption the process $\{N(t)\}$ has an invariant distribution $P(N(t) = n) \equiv p_{\bar{m}}(n), 0 \leq n \leq \bar{m}$ of an $M/GI/\bar{m}/\bar{m}$ queue.

In Section 5 we employ admission policies for rate adaptive streams which are a special form of multi-class stochastic knapsacks with full sharing, i.e., an arriving stream of a given class is always admitted if there is sufficient capacity for an additional stream at the subscription level associated with that class. Thus the stream class determines the subscription level, which it maintains throughout its duration in the system, i.e., no dynamic adaptation.

Let $D_1, ..., D_{N(t)}$ be the durations of the $N(t)$ streams active at time t. An adaptation policy π identifies instantaneous subscription levels for all active streams subject to the subscription feasibility constraint

$$S_i^\pi(t) \in \mathcal{S}, i = 1, ..., N(t),$$

and the link capacity constraint

$$\sum_{i=1}^{N(t)} S_i^\pi(t) \leq c,$$

where $S_1^\pi(t), ..., S_{N(t)}^\pi(t)$ denotes the random variables associated with the instantaneous stream subscription levels of the active streams at time t under policy π. We will concentrate on dynamic adaptation policies that always make maximum use of the available capacity. This implies that admitting streams when $N(t) \geq \underline{m}$ requires that existing streams adapt their subscription levels to accommodate the newly admitted stream, i.e., for $\underline{m} \leq N(t) \leq \bar{m}$ we assume $\sum_{i=1}^{N(t)} S_i(t) = c$.

Thus, under dynamic adaptation, clients may experience streams encoded with a time-varying subscription level. We denote the client *subscription schedule* under the dynamic adaptation policy π as the random process $(S^\pi(t), 0 \leq t \leq D)$.

3.   Quality of Service

We consider three aspects of the overall client perceived performance when viewing a stream encoded with a time-varying instantaneous subscription level: the time-average mean subscription level, the rate of adaptation, and the blocking probability.

The normalized time-average mean subscription level is defined as:

$$Q^\pi \equiv \frac{1}{D} \int_0^D \frac{S^\pi(t)}{\bar{s}} dt \in [\beta, 1],$$

where $Q^\pi = \beta$ corresponds to a stream that receives rate $\underline{s}$ throughout its duration, and $Q^\pi = 1$ corresponds to a stream that receives rate $\bar{s}$ throughout its duration.

The time-average mean subscription level is not a complete characterization of client perceived performance. The time-average mean does not incorporate the number of changes of subscription level nor the size of those changes. Work by Girod, 1992 demonstrates that frequent changes in image resolution have deleterious effects on overall client perceived performance. The metric also is valuable from the standpoint of implementation. Real dynamic adaptation protocols will have an upper bound on the minimum time between subscription changes. We can analyze the feasibility of a suggested protocol by analyzing its rate of adaptation to see if it falls below the specified bound. To this end we suggest a second QoS metric, the rate of adaptation, defined as

$$R^\pi \equiv \frac{1}{D} \sum_{t \in C^\pi} |S^\pi(t^+) - S^\pi(t^-)|,$$

where $C^\pi \equiv \{t \mid 0 < t < D, S^\pi(t^+) \neq S^\pi(t^-)\}$ is the set of times at which the client subscription level changes. Thus the rate of adaptation is the time-average rate of change of the subscription level.

The third aspect of overall client perceived performance is the probability that a client is denied service, i.e., blocked. We consider only full sharing admission policies, i.e., a client is admitted whenever there exist adequate resources to support the client. In Section 4 we consider single class admission policies, and so the blocking probability is given by the Erlang B blocking formula

$B(\rho, \bar{m}) = p_{\bar{m}}(\bar{m})$. In Section 5 we consider multi-class admission policies, where the blocking probability depends on the class to which the stream is assigned. In that case we will use as our metric the overall blocking probability, i.e., if streams of class k arrive at rate λ_k and have a blocking probability B_k then the overall blocking probability is $\sum_{k=1}^{K} \frac{\lambda_k}{\lambda} B_k$.

Previous work Weber and de Veciana, 2002 identified an appropriate joint load and capacity scaling regime for rate adaptive streams, and showed that non-trivial asymptotic expressions for the mean subscription level were obtainable. We define the rate adaptive scaling regime as choosing $c(\lambda) \equiv \alpha \bar{s} \rho$, for $\alpha > 0$ the rate adaptive scaling parameter, and investigating QoS as $\lambda \to \infty$ and $c = c(\lambda)$. We define

$$q^{\alpha,\pi} \equiv \lim_{\lambda \to \infty, c=c(\lambda)} \mathbb{E}[Q^\pi], \qquad r^{\alpha,\pi} \equiv \lim_{\lambda \to \infty, c=c(\lambda)} \mathbb{E}[R^\pi],$$

as the asymptotic mean subscription level and rate of adaptation under the policy π with a rate adaptive scaling parameter α. Note that $\alpha = \frac{c}{\rho \bar{s}}$ represents the capacity divided by the desired overall workload. In Weber and de Veciana, 2002 we identify $\alpha \leq \beta$ as an overloaded regime, characterized by a high blocking probability of $1 - \frac{\alpha}{\beta}$ and minimum $q^{\alpha,\pi} = \beta$. We also identify $\alpha \geq 1$ as an under-loaded regime, characterized by zero blocking and maximum $q^{\alpha,\pi} = 1$. The regime $\beta < \alpha < 1$ corresponds to the critically loaded regime with zero blocking, but a policy dependent asymptotic value for q.

Finally, a note about utility functions. Our previous work Weber and de Veciana, 2002 uses a utility function $u(s)$ giving the utility of a given subscription level, and the definition of Q is correspondingly changed to the time average mean utility. Recent work by Kimura Kimura, 1999 on MPEG-2 encoding demonstrates that our assumption of an (implicitly defined) linear utility function may be reasonable.

4.   Dynamic Adaptation Policies

Throughout this section we assume a single class admission policy with full sharing as described in Section 2. Thus the blocking probability $B(\rho, \bar{m})$ is independent of the adaptation policy. We investigate three dynamic adaptation policies: fair share ($\pi = fs$), two rate randomized adaptation ($\pi = ra$), and optimal adaptation ($\pi = \pi^*$), defined as the policy which maximizes the expected mean subscription level $\mathbb{E}[Q]$. We identify the expected mean subscription level $\mathbb{E}[Q^\pi]$, the expected rate of adaptation $\mathbb{E}[R^\pi]$ for all three policies, and, when possible, identify their asymptotic analogues $q^{\alpha,\pi}$ and $r^{\alpha,\pi}$.

Fair Share Dynamic Adaptation

Under fair share adaptation, with n active streams in the system, each stream chooses subscription level

$$s_{fs}(n) \equiv \begin{cases} \bar{s}, & 0 < n \leq \underline{m} \\ \frac{c}{n}, & \underline{m} \leq n \leq \bar{m} \end{cases}.$$

That is, we assume $S = \{\underline{s}, \frac{c}{\bar{m}-1}, ..., \frac{c}{\underline{m}+1}, \bar{s}\}$, so that the number of required subscription levels grows linearly in c. The following lemma gives finite capacity and asymptotic expressions for the expected mean subscription level and expected rate of adaptation under the fair share adaptation policy.

Lemma 1 *Under the fair share* $(\pi = fs)$ *adaptation policy we have that*

$$\mathbb{E}[Q^{fs}] = \sum_{n=0}^{\bar{m}-1} p_{\bar{m}-1}(n) \frac{s_{fs}(n+1)}{\bar{s}}, \tag{9.1}$$

$$q^{\alpha,fs} = \begin{cases} \beta, & \alpha \leq \beta \\ \alpha, & \beta < \alpha < 1 \\ 1, & \alpha \geq 1 \end{cases}, \tag{9.2}$$

$$\mathbb{E}[R^{fs}] = 2\mu \sum_{n=\underline{m}}^{\bar{m}-1} p_{\bar{m}-1}(n) s_{fs}(n+1), \tag{9.3}$$

$$r^{\alpha,fs} = \begin{cases} 2\mu\underline{s}, & \alpha \leq \beta \\ 2\mu\bar{s}\alpha, & \beta < \alpha < 1 \\ 0, & \alpha \geq 1 \end{cases}. \tag{9.4}$$

Thus both $q^{\alpha,fs}, r^{\alpha,fs}$ are linear in α in the critical regime $\beta < \alpha < 1$. Figures 9.2 and 9.3 exhibit the above equations along with simulation results for $\lambda = 40$ and 320 versus α. The plots illustrate a good match between computational and simulation results, as well as the convergence to the asymptotic values.

Although $r^{\alpha,fs}$ is finite, the asymptotic expected number of adaptations is infinite. Straightforward manipulations show that the expected number of subscription level changes under the fair share policy is $2\lambda\mathbb{P}(\underline{m}-1 \leq N < \bar{m}-1)$ which goes to infinity as λ gets large. This result is easily understood: in a loss network the number of active streams changes at rate $2\lambda(1 - B(\rho, \bar{m}))$. The difference here is that no change in rate is required by a change in the number of streams when $n < \underline{m}$.

Two Rate Randomized Dynamic Adaptation

To realize fair share adaptation content servers must provide a large set of subscription levels. The idea behind two rate randomized dynamic adaptation

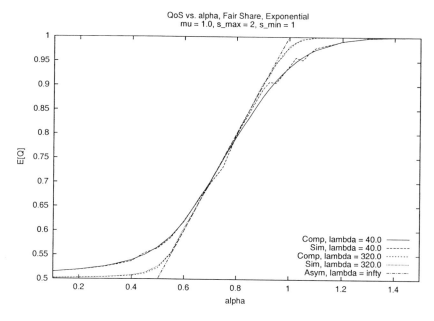

Figure 9.2. Simulation and computation results for the fair share dynamic adaptation policy: $\mathbb{E}[Q^{fs}]$ *and* $q^{\alpha,fs}$ *vs.* α *for* $\lambda = 40,320$, $\mu^{-1} = 1$, $\underline{s} = 1, \bar{s} = 2$, *and* $c(\lambda) = \alpha\bar{s}\rho$. *The overloaded regime is* $\alpha \le \beta = 0.5$, *the critically loaded regime is* $0.5 < \alpha < 1$, *and the under-loaded regime is* $\alpha \ge 1$.

is that instead of adapting all streams by a small amount we can do equally well on average by adapting a small set of streams by a larger amount. Under two rate randomized dynamic adaptation, when there are n active streams, we allocate a rate $\bar{s}$ to $\bar{n}(n)$ of the streams, chosen at random, and a rate $\underline{s}$ to the remaining $\underline{n}(n)$ streams. The functions $(\underline{n}(n), \bar{n}(n))$ are defined as

$$\left(\underline{n}(n), \bar{n}(n)\right) \equiv \begin{cases} (0,n), & 0 \le n \le m \\ \left(\left\lceil \frac{n\bar{s}-c}{\bar{s}-\underline{s}} \right\rceil, \left\lfloor \frac{c-n\underline{s}}{\bar{s}-\underline{s}} \right\rfloor\right), & m < n \le \bar{m} \end{cases}.$$

The quantity $\bar{n}(n)$ is the maximum number of streams that can be supported at subscription level $\bar{s}$ while leaving sufficient capacity for the remaining $\underline{n}(n)$ streams to maintain a subscription level $\underline{s}$. Note that $\mathcal{S} = \{\bar{s}, \underline{s}\}$, which is significantly smaller than the set of required supported subscription levels under fair share. The following lemma gives finite capacity and asymptotic expressions for the expected mean subscription level and expected rate of adaptation under the two rate randomized adaptation policy.

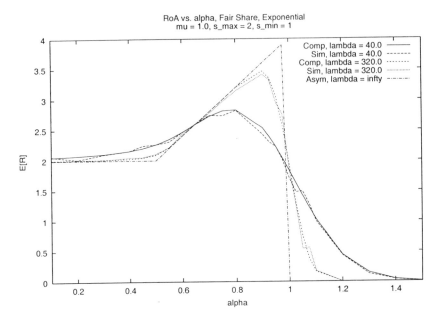

Figure 9.3.   Simulation and computation results for the fair share dynamic adaptation policy: $\mathbb{E}[R^{fs}]$ *and* $r^{\alpha,fs}$ *vs.* α *for varying* λ. *Same simulation parameters as Figure 9.2.*

Lemma 2 *Under the two rate randomized adaptation policy* $(\pi = ra)$ *we have that*

$$\mathbb{E}[Q^{ra}] = \sum_{n=0}^{\bar{m}-1} p_{\bar{m}-1}(n) \left[\frac{\underline{n}(n+1)}{n+1} \beta + \frac{\bar{n}(n+1)}{n+1} \right], \tag{9.5}$$

$$q^{\alpha,ra} = q^{\alpha,fs}, \tag{9.6}$$

$$\mathbb{E}[R^{ra}] = 2(\bar{s} - \underline{s})\mu \sum_{n=\underline{m}}^{\bar{m}-1} p_{\bar{m}-1}(n) \frac{\bar{n}(n)\underline{n}(n+1) + \bar{n}(n+1)\underline{n}(n)}{n+1} \tag{9.7}$$

$$r^{\alpha,ra} = \begin{cases} \infty, & \alpha \le \beta \\ \infty, & \beta < \alpha < 1 \\ 0, & \alpha \ge 1 \end{cases}. \tag{9.8}$$

Thus two rate randomized adaptation achieves an asymptotic mean subscription level equal to that under the fair share policy, but suffers from an infinite asymptotic infinite rate of adaptation for $\alpha < 1$.

Figures 9.4 and 9.5 exhibit the above equations along with simulation results for $\lambda = 40$ and 320 versus α. The plots illustrate a good match between computational and simulation results, as well as the convergence to the asymptotic values.

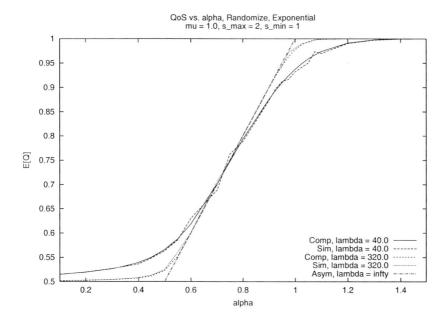

Figure 9.4. Simulation and Computation of $\mathbb{E}[Q^{ra}]$, $q^{\alpha,ra}$, $\mathbb{E}[R^{ra}]$ vs. α for varying λ. Same simulation parameters as Figure 9.2.

It can be shown that $\mathbb{E}[Q^{fs}] - \mathbb{E}[Q^{ra}] \leq \frac{\bar{s}-\underline{s}}{m}$, so that for large capacity links the expressions are nearly equal, and the difference goes to zero as the link capacity increases, i.e., $q^{\alpha,ra} = q^{\alpha,fs}$ Weber and de Veciana, 2002. The rate of adaptation, however, is drastically different for randomized adaptation than for fair share. The problem is that our formulation of the two rate randomized policy randomly selects a new set of the appropriate size to be adapted each time $N(t)$ changes and $N(t) \geq \underline{m}$. We have also investigated a randomized adaptation policy that keeps state information on stream subscription levels, and changes rate for as few streams as required by changes in $\bar{n}$ and $\underline{n}$. Under this policy we find equivalent expressions for $\mathbb{E}[Q^{ra}]$ but the values for $\mathbb{E}[R^{ra}]$ are on par with $\mathbb{E}[R^{fs}]$. The drawback to the fair share policy is that it requires a large number of supported subscription levels and requires a large number of adaptations, although the overall rate of adaptation is reasonably small. The two rate randomized adaptation policy either suffers from unacceptably high rate of adaptation or requires link state be kept to keep the rate of adaptation reasonably low.

The drawbacks to the fair share and two rate randomized adaptation policies are serious: the unacceptably high number of adaptations required by fair share and the unacceptably high rate of adaptation required by randomized adapta-

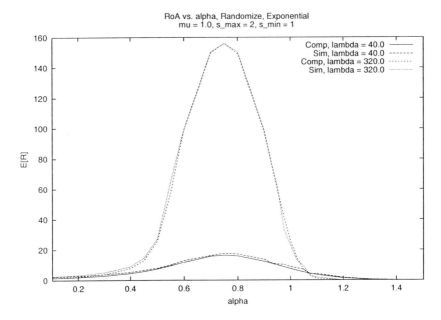

Figure 9.5.   Simulation and Computation of $\mathbb{E}[Q^{ra}], q^{\alpha,ra}, \mathbb{E}[R^{ra}]$ *vs.* α *for varying* λ*. Same simulation parameters as Figure 9.2.*

tion render these policies infeasible for large capacity links. These drawbacks motivate investigation of the optimal adaptation policy, which we explore next.

Optimal Dynamic Adaptation

We use the term optimal dynamic adaptation policy to denote the policy that maximizes $\mathbb{E}[Q^{\pi}]$ over all feasible policies. The following theorem, from Weber and de Veciana, 2002, identifies this policy as granting preference to short duration streams.

Theorem 1 *Order the streams active at time t by increasing duration so that* $D_1 < ... < D_{N(t)}$*. The dynamic adaptation policy* π^* *that maximizes* $\mathbb{E}[Q^{\pi}]$ *is*

$$S_i^{\pi^*}(t) = \begin{cases} \bar{s}, & i = 1, ..., \bar{n}(N(t)) \\ \underline{s}, & i = \bar{n}(N(t)) + 1, ..., N(t) \end{cases}.$$

The intuition behind this result is simple: we maximize the long term client average mean subscription level by giving priority to short duration streams since those streams consume fewer resources.

The optimal rate of an admitted stream depends on the number of other streams in the system as well as on their durations. Let D denote the duration of an arbitrary active stream, let N denote the number of other active streams, and let $D_1, ..., D_N$ be their durations. Define

$$Y_{N,D} \equiv \sum_{i=1}^{N} 1(D_i \leq D)$$

as the number of streams with shorter durations than the considered stream of duration D. The distribution of stream durations when viewed at an arbitrarily chosen time is not $F_D(d)$ because we are more likely to see longer duration streams than short duration streams at an arbitrary time. The distribution is $F_U(u) \equiv \mu \int_0^u z dF_D(z)$ for the $M/GI/\infty$ queue Walrand, 1988, which should approximate the distribution for the $M/GI/\bar{m}/\bar{m}$ queue when the blocking probability is low. In the sequel we consider approximations that are valid whenever $B(\rho, \bar{m})$ is acceptably small. In this regime, $Y_{N,D} \sim Bin(N, F_U(D))$ since $D_1, ..., D_N$ are i.i.d. with distribution $F_U(D)$. The following theorem gives approximate expressions for the expected mean subscription level and expected rate of adaptation under the optimal adaptation policy.

Theorem 2 *Under the optimal adaptation policy and in a low blocking regime*

$$\mathbb{E}[Q^{\pi^*}] \approx 1 - (1-\beta) \sum_{n=1}^{\bar{m}-1} p_{\bar{m}-1}(n) \int_0^\infty \mathbb{P}(Y_{n,d} \geq \bar{n}(n+1)) dF_D(d) \quad (9.9)$$

$$\mathbb{E}[R^{\pi^*}] \approx 2\lambda(\bar{s} - \underline{s}) \sum_{n=\underline{m}-1}^{\bar{m}-2} \left(p_{\bar{m}-1}(n) \times \right.$$

$$\left. \int_0^\infty \mathbb{P}\left(Y_{n,d} < \bar{n}(n+1), Y_{n+1,d} \geq \bar{n}(n+2) \right) dF_D(d) \right) \quad (9.10)$$

Under the optimal adaptation policy

$$q^{\alpha,\pi^*} = \begin{cases} \beta, & \alpha \leq \beta \\ 1 - (1-\beta)\bar{F}_D(F_U^{-1}(\frac{\alpha-\beta}{1-\beta})), & \beta < \alpha < 1 \\ 1, & \alpha \geq 1 \end{cases} \quad (9.11)$$

A simple expression for r^{α,π^*}, $\beta < \alpha < 1$ appears difficult to obtain, although it may be shown that $r^{\alpha,\pi^*} = \infty$ for $\alpha \leq \beta$, and $r^{\alpha,\pi^*} = 0$ for $\alpha \geq 1$.

Figures 9.6 and 9.7 exhibit the above equations along with simulation results for $\lambda = 40$ and 320 versus α for the case of exponentially distributed stream durations. The plots show a good match between computational and simulation results for the finite capacity case when the low blocking assumption is valid $\alpha \geq 0.5$, as well as the convergence to the asymptotic values. The region $\alpha \leq \beta$ illustrates the divergence between computed and simulated results due to the low blocking assumption being violated in this regime. Comparing the plot of $\mathbb{E}[Q^{\pi^*}]$ with $\mathbb{E}[Q^{fs}]$ in Figure 9.2 and $\mathbb{E}[Q^{ra}]$ in Figure 9.4, we see an increase in mean subscription level under the optimal policy of as much as 20% in the critical regime. The plot of $\mathbb{E}[R^{\pi^*}]$ shows that the rate of adaptation decreases in α. The intuition, made clear in the following discussion on client perceived performance, is that the optimal adaptation policy effectively creates a duration threshold and streams near that threshold experience high adaptation. For α near β that threshold is very short, so that short streams experience frequent adaptation, yielding a very high rate of adaptation, while for α near 1 the threshold is very long, so that only the very longest streams experience adaptation, which, when divided by their long stream duration, gives them a small rate of adaptation.

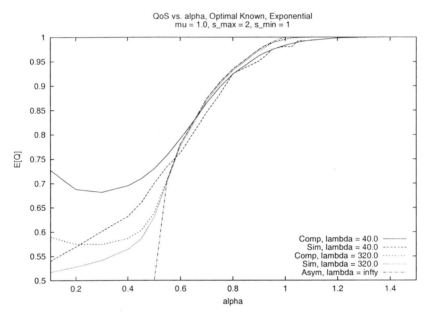

Figure 9.6.   Simulation and Computation of $\mathbb{E}[Q^{\pi^*}]$ and q^{α,π^*} vs. α for varying λ, $\beta = 0.5$,
$D \sim exp(1)$.

Client perceived performance measures may be obtained by considering the QoS metrics conditioned on a particular client stream duration d. The following lemma gives expressions for these quantities for both finite capacity and asymptotic cases. We use the following notation

$$q_d^{\alpha,\pi^*} \equiv \lim_{\lambda \to \infty, c=c(\lambda)} \mathbb{E}[Q^{\pi^*} \mid D = d], \quad r_d^{\alpha,\pi^*} \equiv \lim_{\lambda \to \infty, c=c(\lambda)} \mathbb{E}[R^{\pi^*} \mid D = d]$$

to denote the asymptotic mean subscription level and rate of adaptation for a stream with duration d.

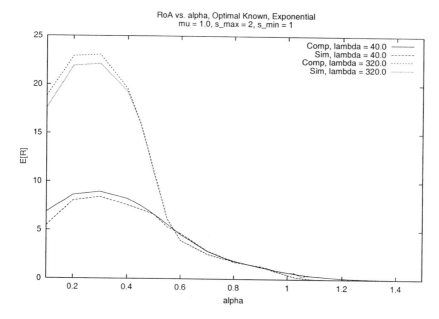

Figure 9.7. Simulation and Computation of $\mathbb{E}[R^{\pi^*}]$, *vs.* α *for varying* λ, $\beta = 0.5$, $D \sim exp(1)$.

Lemma 3 *Under the optimal adaptation policy and in a low blocking regime*

$$\mathbb{E}[Q^{\pi^*} \mid D = d] \approx 1 - (1 - \beta) \sum_{n=1}^{\bar{m}-1} p_{\bar{m}-1}(n) \mathbb{P}(Y_{n,d} \geq \bar{n}(n+1)) \quad (9.12)$$

$$\mathbb{E}[R^{\pi^*} \mid D = d] \approx 2\lambda(\bar{s} - \underline{s}) \sum_{n=\underline{m}-1}^{\bar{m}-2} \Big(p_{\bar{m}-1}(n) \ \times$$

$$\mathbb{P}\Big(Y_{n,d} < \bar{n}(n+1), Y_{n+1,d} \geq \bar{n}(n+2)\Big)\Big). \quad (9.13)$$

Under the optimal adaptation policy

$$q_d^{\alpha,\pi^*} = \begin{cases} \beta, & \alpha \leq \beta, \\ \beta, & \beta < \alpha < 1, d \geq F_U^{-1}(\frac{\alpha - \beta}{1 - \beta}) \\ 1, & \beta < \alpha < 1, d < F_U^{-1}(\frac{\alpha - \beta}{1 - \beta}) \\ 1, & \alpha \geq 1 \end{cases} \quad (9.14)$$

A simple expression for r_d^{α,π^*} appears difficult to obtain, although $r_d^{\alpha,\pi^*} = 0$ for $|d - F_U^{-1}(\frac{\alpha - \beta}{1 - \beta})| > \epsilon$, for some unspecified $\epsilon > 0$.

Figures 9.8 and 9.9 exhibit the above equations along with simulation results for $\lambda = 320$ versus d for $\alpha = 0.75$ and $\beta = 0.5$. The plots illustrate a good match between computational and simulation results, as well as the convergence to the asymptotic values. Several points are worth mentioning. First, it is easily seen from these plots that the optimal dynamic adaptation policy grants a constant subscription level of $\bar{s}$ for streams with durations significantly shorter than the threshold $F_U^{-1}(\frac{\alpha-\beta}{1-\beta})$, and a constant subscription level of $\underline{s}$ for streams with durations significantly longer than the threshold. Streams with durations in the vicinity of the threshold experience a mean subscription level in $(\beta, 1)$, and a relatively high rate of adaptation.

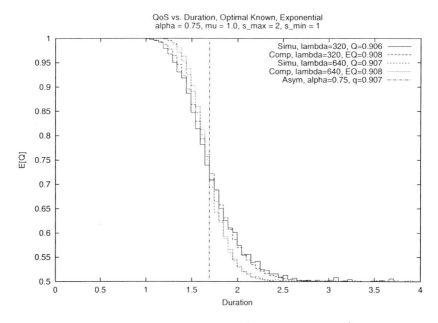

Figure 9.8.   Simulation and Computation of $\mathbb{E}[Q^{\pi^*} \mid D = d]$ *and* q_d^{α, π^*} *vs. d for* $\alpha = 0.75$ *and* $\lambda = 320, 640$, $\beta = 0.5$, $D \sim exp(1)$.

The main idea that is gleaned from these figures is that the optimal dynamic adaptation policy only utilizes dynamic adaptation for a small number of streams with duration near the threshold. These streams are the ones that are toggled between $\bar{s}$ and $\underline{s}$ as streams depart and arrive respectively. These observations suggest that near optimal mean subscription levels may be obtainable by an admission policy where streams are granted a fixed subscription level depending on their duration at the time of stream initiation. A fixed subscription level means $\mathbb{E}[R^{\pi}] = 0$ but that the blocking probability B would be higher because streams no longer can adapt their subscription levels to accommodate newly admitted streams. We investigate admission policies for rate adaptive streams in the next section.

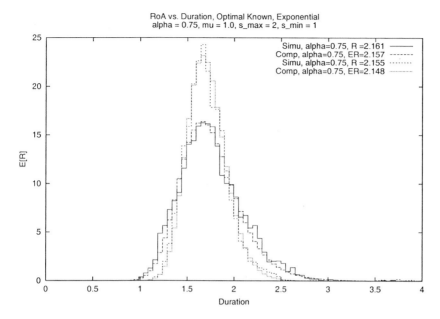

Figure 9.9. Simulation and Computation of $\mathbb{E}[R^{\pi^*} \mid D = d]$ *vs.* d *for* $\alpha = 0.75$ *and* $\lambda = 320, 640, \beta = 0.5, D \sim exp(1)$.

5. Admission Policies For Rate Adaptive Streams

We define an admission policy for rate adaptive streams as an admission policy that assigns a subscription level to a stream which that stream maintains throughout its lifetime in the system, i.e., the stream is not dynamically adapted. The previous section demonstrates that on large capacity links the optimal dynamic adaptation policy effectively creates a duration threshold and gives short duration streams the maximum subscription level and long duration streams the minimum subscription level. This suggests designing an admission policy for rate adaptive streams whereby streams are admitted at a duration dependent subscription level which they maintain throughout their lifetime. In this section we will show that such an admission policy can obtain an expected subscription level that is asymptotically equal to that under the optimal dynamic adaptation policy, and has the added benefit of not requiring dynamic adaptation. We make a slight abuse of notation and say $\pi = aa$ to refer to an admission policy for rate adaptive streams where dynamic adaptation is not employed.

Recall that $\mathcal{S} \equiv \{\bar{s} = s_1, ..., s_K = \underline{s}\}$ is the set of supported subscription levels, and that without loss of generality we assume $s_k > s_{k+1}$. Let $\mathcal{D} \equiv \{d_1, ..., d_{K-1}\}$ denote a set of duration thresholds where $d_k \geq d_{k-1} \geq 0$ for $k = 1, ..., K - 1$. A stream of duration d is assigned a static subscription level given by

$$S^{aa}(d) = s_{k^*}, \ k^* = \max\{0 < k \leq K \mid d_{k-1} \leq d < d_k\}.$$

We assume $d_0 = 0$ and $d_K = \infty$ in the above definition. The stream is admitted at time t provided

$$\sum_{k=1}^{K} s_k N_k(t) + S^{aa}(d) \leq c$$

where we redefine $N(t) \equiv (N_1(t), ..., N_K(t))$ as the number of active streams at each subscription level at time t.

This system is a K class stochastic knapsack with a full sharing admission policy Ross, 1995. The parameters of the stochastic knapsack are the capacity c, the class size s_k, and the class load $\rho_k = \frac{\lambda_k}{\mu_k}$ where λ_k is the class arrival rate and μ_k^{-1} is the mean class duration. We calculate the arrival rate, mean class duration, and class load as

$$\begin{aligned}
\lambda_k &= \lambda(F_D(d_k) - F_D(d_{k-1})), \\
\mu_k^{-1} &= \mathbb{E}[D \mid d_{k-1} \leq d < d_k] = \mu^{-1}\frac{F_U(d_k) - F_U(d_{k-1})}{F_D(d_k) - F_D(d_{k-1})}, \\
\rho_k &= \rho(F_U(d_k) - F_U(d_{k-1})),
\end{aligned}$$

for $k = 1, ..., K$. Recall $F_U(u) \equiv \mu u \int_0^u z f_D(z)dz$ is the distribution of stream durations when the system is viewed at an arbitrary time.

The blocking probabilities are class dependent and we write $B_k(\mathcal{D}) \equiv \mathbb{P}(\sum_{l=1}^{K} s_l N_l(t) + s_k > c)$ for $k = 1, ..., K$. We define the overall blocking probability as $B(\mathcal{D}) \equiv \sum_{k=1}^{K} \frac{\lambda_k}{\lambda} B_k(\mathcal{D})$. We can bound this as $B(\rho, \bar{m}) \leq B(\mathcal{D}) \leq B(\rho, \underline{m})$ since $B(\rho, \bar{m})$ corresponds to the single class system where all streams are admitted at rate $\underline{s}$ and $B(\rho, \underline{m})$ corresponds to the single class system where all streams are admitted at rate $\bar{s}$.

The expected subscription level under the admission policy for rate adaptive streams is defined as

$$\mathbb{E}[Q^{aa}] \equiv \sum_{k=1}^{K} \frac{\lambda_k(1 - B_k(\mathcal{D}))s_k}{\lambda(1 - B(\mathcal{D}))\bar{s}},$$

which can be thought of as a normalized revenue function, i.e., an admitted stream of class k earns revenue s_k, and so $\mathbb{E}[Q^{aa}]$ is the normalized rate at which revenue is earned. Similarly, we define the asymptotic expected subscription level under the admission policy for rate adaptive streams as

$$q^{\alpha,aa} \equiv \lim_{\lambda \to \infty, c = c(\lambda)} \mathbb{E}[Q^{aa}].$$

The following theorem identifies the asymptotically optimal admission policy for rate adaptive streams that maximizes the asymptotic expected subscription level subject to maintaining an asymptotic blocking probability of zero.

Theorem 3 *The two class admission policy for rate adaptive streams with duration threshold*

$$d^* = \begin{cases} 0, & \alpha \leq \beta \\ F_U^{-1}(\frac{\alpha-\beta}{1-\beta}), & \beta < \alpha < 1 \\ \infty, & \alpha > 1 \end{cases} \qquad (9.15)$$

maximizes the asymptotic expected subscription level $q^{\alpha,aa}$ *over all K class stochastic knapsacks that achieve an asymptotic blocking probability of 0 for $\alpha > \beta$. Moreover, this admission policy $\pi = aa^*$ achieves an asymptotic expected subscription level equal to that under the optimal dynamic adaptation policy, i.e., $q^{\alpha,aa^*} = q^{\alpha,\pi^*}$.*

Theorem 3 gives the asymptotically optimal admission policy for rate adaptive streams and, more importantly, tells us that there is no loss in asymptotic mean subscription level incurred by not using dynamic adaptation. Thus admission policies for rate adaptive streams obtain the equivalent mean subscription level as dynamic adaptation, have the benefit of a rate of adaptation of 0, and maintain the low blocking characteristic of dynamic adaptation. The cost paid is that the blocking probability using dynamic adaptation goes to 0 exponentially fast for $\alpha > \beta$ while the blocking probability using the optimal admission policy for rate adaptive streams goes to 0 like $O(\frac{1}{\sqrt{c}})$ for $\beta < \alpha \leq 1$, and exponentially for $\alpha > 1$.

Figures 9.10 and 9.11 provide a comparison between the optimal dynamic adaptation policy and the optimal admission policy for rate adaptive streams. Figure 9.10 provides computational and simulation results for the expected subscription level under the two class admission policy which maximizes the expected subscription level subject to an overall blocking probability of $B^* = 1\%$ for $\lambda = 40,320$. That is, the duration d^* solves

$$\max_d \{\mathbb{E}[Q^{aa}] \mid B(d) \leq B^*\}$$

making the slight abuse of notation by writing d for $\mathcal{D} = \{d\}$. A plot of $q^{\alpha,aa^*} = q^{\alpha,\pi^*}$ is also provided. The plot illustrates the convergence to the asymptotic expected subscription level.

Figure 9.11 gives the overall blocking probability for a two class admission policy where the duration threshold is chosen so that the expected subscription level equals that under the optimal dynamic adaptation policy, i.e., d^* is chosen as the unique d such that $\mathbb{E}[Q^{aa}] = \mathbb{E}[Q^{\pi^*}]$ for $\lambda = 40,320$. Plots of the computed and simulated overall blocking probability are given, along with a

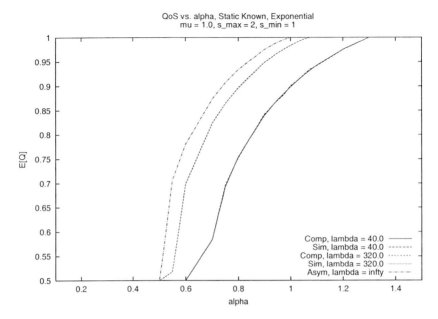

Figure 9.10.   *Simulation and computation of* $\mathbb{E}[Q^{aa^*}]$ *and* q^{α, aa^*} *vs.* α *for* $B^* = 1\%$, $\lambda = 40, 320$, $\beta = 0.5$, *and* $D \sim exp(1)$. *Not all lines are visible because the computed and simulation values being nearly equal.*

plot of the asymptotic blocking probability, i.e., $1 - \frac{\alpha}{\beta}$ for $\alpha \leq \beta$ and 0 for $\alpha > \beta$. The panel illustrates the convergence to the asymptotic blocking probability.

Finally, we offer a brief comment on implementation. The optimal adaptive admission policy requires that the bottleneck link identify its duration threshold (9.15), which depends on $F_D, \rho, c, \underline{s}, \bar{s}$. The distribution F_D could be analyzed and hard-coded, or could be estimated empirically by keeping track of stream durations. The load ρ could be estimated empirically by monitoring arriving service request times and service durations. Indeed, such a measurement would make the model more robust to the observed non-stationarities present in Internet traffic. The parameters $\underline{s}$ and $\bar{s}$ could be estimated by monitoring stream rate associated with long duration and short duration streams. The algorithm could easily be made to be distributed—stream service requests would traverse the route from client to server and at each node pick up the duration threshold for that link along with an admission decision. Upon returning to the client, provided all link admission decisions are positive, the client subscribes to the stream content provider at the maximum rate if the stream duration is smaller than the maximum duration threshold, and subscribes at the minimum rate otherwise.

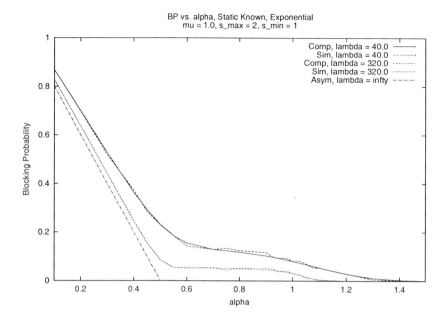

Figure 9.11. Simulation and computation of $B(d^*)$ *(see text) and asymptotic blocking probability vs α for $\lambda = 40, 320$, $\beta = 0.5$, and $D \sim exp(1)$.*

6. Conclusion

The rationale behind dynamic adaptation of rate adaptive streams is that by dynamically adjusting the subscription level we obtain the system benefit of a low blocking probability and the client benefit of making full use of all available capacity. The price paid for these gains is that clients incur a lowered perceived QoS both in terms of the mean subscription level and the rate of adaptation compared with non-adaptive streams admitted at their maximum subscription level $\bar{s}$. Our investigation of adaptive admission shows that, for large capacity links, a simple duration threshold two class admission policy obtains the asymptotic optimal mean subscription level, asymptotic zero blocking probability, and zero rate of adaptation. Thus, for large capacity links, the protocol, resource, and implementation overhead required by dynamic adaptation is not justifiable. Moreover, optimal QoS is obtainable using only two subscription levels—this has the significant implication that multimedia content providers gain little benefit from providing more than two encodings. Of course, this is assuming clients aren't access line limited, in which case additional encodings will be of use to such clients. Future work in this area will analyze the case of heterogeneous minimum and maximum subscription levels.

Appendix

Proof of Lemma 1 The proof of (9.1) and (9.2) is found in Weber and de Veciana, 2002.

Proof of (9.3). Conditioned on a stream being admitted, that stream sees the system with capacity $\bar{m} - 1$, i.e., the process $N(t)$ denoting the number of other streams has an invariant distribution $p_{\bar{m}-1}(n), 0 \leq n \leq \bar{m} - 1$, where n is the number of other streams in the system. By PASTA the conditioned stream sees the other streams in steady state. In steady state, when $N(t) = n$, the number of other streams changes due to arrivals and departures at rate $\lambda + n\mu$. The definition of the fair share rate implies that not all changes in the number of streams will change the fair share rate. When $n \in \{0, ..., \underline{m} - 2\}$ neither an arrival or departure causes a change in rate. When $n \in \{\underline{m} - 1, ..., \bar{m} - 2\}$ an arrival causes a change in rate from $\frac{c}{n+1}$ to $\frac{c}{n+2}$. When $n \in \{\underline{m}, ..., \bar{m} - 1\}$ a departure causes a change in rate from $\frac{c}{n+1}$ to $\frac{c}{n}$. Admissions occur at rate λ for $n < \bar{m} - 1$ and departures occur at rate $n\mu$ for $n > 0$. Putting these observations together we obtain

$$\mathbb{E}[R^{fs}] = \sum_{n=\underline{m}-1}^{\bar{m}-2} \lambda p_{\bar{m}-1}(n)\left(\frac{c}{n+1} - \frac{c}{n+2}\right) + \sum_{n=\underline{m}}^{\bar{m}-1} n\mu p_{\bar{m}-1}(n)\left(\frac{c}{n} - \frac{c}{n+1}\right).$$

Using detailed balance equations for $\pi_{\bar{m}-1}(n)$ and relabelling indices yields the result.

Proof of (9.4). We may write (9.3) as

$$\mathbb{E}[R^{fs}] = 2\mu\bar{s}\alpha\mathbb{E}\left[\frac{1}{N/\rho}\Big|\underline{m} < N \leq \bar{m}\right]\mathbb{P}\left(\underline{m} < N \leq \bar{m}\right).$$

Define the random process $\{N^{\alpha,\rho}(t)\}$ for the number of streams on the link at time t when the load is ρ and the capacity is $c(\lambda) = \alpha\bar{s}\rho$. The distribution of $N^{\alpha,\rho}(t)$ is that of an $M/GI/\bar{m}/\bar{m}$ queue with load ρ and capacity $\bar{m} = \frac{\alpha}{\beta}\rho$. By the Law of Large Numbers

$$\lim_{\lambda \to \infty} \mathbb{E}[\frac{N^{\alpha,\rho}}{\rho}] = \begin{cases} \frac{\alpha}{\beta}, & \alpha \leq \beta \\ 1, & \beta < \alpha < 1 \\ 1, & \alpha > 1 \end{cases}$$

and

$$\lim_{\lambda \to \infty} \mathbb{P}\left(\alpha < \frac{N^{\alpha,\rho}}{\rho} \leq \frac{\alpha}{\beta}\right) = \begin{cases} 1, & \alpha \leq \beta \\ 1, & \beta < \alpha < 1 \\ 0, & \alpha \geq 1 \end{cases}.$$

The asymptotic rate of adaptation is

$$r^{\alpha,fs} = \lim_{\lambda \to \infty, c=c(\lambda)} \mathbb{E}[R^{fs}]$$

$$= \lim_{\lambda \to \infty} 2\mu\bar{s}\alpha\mathbb{E}\left[\frac{1}{N^{\alpha,\rho}/\rho}\Big|\alpha < \frac{N^{\alpha,\rho}}{\rho} \leq \frac{\alpha}{\beta}\right]\mathbb{P}\left(\alpha < \frac{N^{\alpha,\rho}}{\rho} \leq \frac{\alpha}{\beta}\right).$$

Thus when $\alpha \leq \beta$ we have $r^{\alpha,fs} = (2\mu\bar{s}\alpha)(\frac{\beta}{\alpha})(1) = 2\mu\bar{s}\beta = 2\mu\underline{s}$. When $\beta < \alpha < 1$ we have $r^{\alpha,fs} = (2\mu\bar{s}\alpha)(1)(1) = 2\mu\bar{s}\alpha$. Finally, when $\alpha \geq 1$ we have $r^{\alpha,fs}(2\mu\bar{s}\alpha)(1)(0) = 0$. ∎

Proof of Lemma 2

The proof of (9.5) and (9.6) is found in Weber and de Veciana, 2002.

Proof of (9.7). The preliminary remarks in the proof of Lemma 1 apply here as well.

All changes in rate are of size $\bar{s} - \underline{s}$, but the number of streams that change rate depends on the number of streams and the new random selection of streams to be adapted. Let t denote a jump time, i.e., a stream arrival or departure, $S(t)$ the rate allocated to the stream we've conditioned on being present, and $S(t^-)$ the rate allocated to that stream immediately prior to the jump time. The probability that the conditioned stream changes rate is

$$\mathbb{P}(S^{ra}(t) \neq S^{ra}(t^-)) = \mathbb{P}(S^{ra}(t) = \bar{s})\mathbb{P}(S^{ra}(t^-) = \underline{s}) + \mathbb{P}(S^{ra}(t) = \underline{s})\mathbb{P}(S^{ra}(t^-) = \bar{s})$$

When $n \in \{0, ..., \underline{m} - 2\}$ no streams change rate for either an arrival or departure. When $n \in \{\underline{m} - 1, ..., \bar{m} - 2\}$ an arrival causes a stream to change rate with probability

$$g(n+1) \equiv \frac{\bar{n}(n+2)\underline{n}(n+1) + \underline{n}(n+2)\bar{n}(n+1)}{(n+1)(n+2)}.$$

When $n \in \{\underline{m}, ..., \bar{m} - 1\}$ a departure causes a stream to change rate with probability $g(n)$. This gives

$$\mathbb{E}[R^{ra}] = \sum_{n=\underline{m}=1}^{\bar{m}-2} \lambda p_{\bar{m}-1}(n)g(n+1) + \sum_{n=\underline{m}}^{\bar{m}-1} n\mu p_{\bar{m}-1}(n)g(n).$$

Detailed balance equations yield the result.

Proof of (9.8). We may rewrite (9.7) as

$$\mathbb{E}[R^{ra}] = 2(\bar{s} - \underline{s})\mu\mathbb{E}\left[\frac{\bar{n}(N)\underline{n}(N+1) + \bar{n}(N+1)\underline{n}(N)}{N+1}\Big| \underline{m} \leq N \leq \bar{m} - 1\right] \times$$
$$\mathbb{P}\left(\underline{m} \leq N \leq \bar{m} - 1\right)$$

The same developments found in the proof of Lemma 1 regarding $\mathbb{P}(\underline{m} \leq N \leq \bar{m} - 1)$ apply. Under the rate adaptive scaling this becomes

$$r^{\alpha,ra} = \lim_{\lambda \to \infty, c=c(\lambda)} \mathbb{E}[R^{ra}]$$
$$= \lim_{\lambda \to \infty} 4(\bar{s} - \underline{s})\mathbb{E}\left[\frac{\bar{n}(N^{\alpha,\rho})\underline{n}(N^{\alpha,\rho})}{N^{\alpha,\rho}}\Big| \alpha < \frac{N^{\alpha,\rho}}{\rho} \leq \frac{\alpha}{\beta}\right]\mathbb{P}\left(\alpha < N^{\alpha,\rho} \leq \frac{\alpha}{\beta}\right).$$

For $\alpha \leq 1$ $\mathbb{P}(\alpha < N^{\alpha,\rho} \leq \frac{\alpha}{\beta}) = 1$ and so $r^{\alpha,ra} = \infty$ since

$$\lim_{\lambda \to \infty} \mathbb{E}\left[\frac{\bar{n}(N^{\alpha,\rho})\underline{n}(N^{\alpha,\rho})}{N^{\alpha,\rho}}\right] = \infty.$$

For $\alpha > 1$, however,

$$\mathbb{P}\left(\alpha < N^{\alpha,\rho} \leq \frac{\alpha}{\beta}\right)$$

goes to 0 exponentially in λ while

$$\mathbb{E}\left[\frac{\bar{n}(N^{\alpha,\rho})\underline{n}(N^{\alpha,\rho})}{N^{\alpha,\rho}}\Big| \alpha < \frac{N^{\alpha,\rho}}{\rho} \leq \frac{\alpha}{\beta}\right]$$

grows linearly in λ, forcing $r^{\alpha,ra}$ to 0.
∎

Proof of Theorem 1 See Weber and de Veciana, 2002.
Proof of Theorem 2
Proof of (9.9). Consider an arbitrary time t.

$$\mathbb{E}[Q^{\pi^*}] = \mathbb{E}[\frac{S^{\pi^*}(t)}{\bar{s}}]$$
$$= 1\mathbb{P}(Y_{N,D} < \bar{n}(N+1)) + \beta\mathbb{P}(Y_{N,D} \geq \bar{n}(N+1))$$
$$= 1 - (1 - \beta)\mathbb{P}(Y_{N,D} \geq \bar{n}(N+1)).$$

The first equality follows by ergodicity. Simple conditioning yields the equation.

Proof of (9.10). Consider again an arbitrary time t. Similar to the proofs of Lemmas 1 and 2, we break down the analysis for different values of $N(t)$. For $n \in \{0, ..., \underline{m} - 2\}$ neither an arrival nor departure causes a change in rate. For $n \in \{\underline{m} - 1, ..., \bar{m} - 2\}$, an arrival causes a change in rate from $\bar{s}$ to $\underline{s}$ if $Y_{n,D} < \bar{n}(n+1)$ and $Y_{n+1,D} \geq \bar{n}(n+2)$. For $n \in \{\underline{m}, ..., \bar{m} - 1\}$, a departure causes a change in rate from $\underline{s}$ to $\bar{s}$ if $Y_{n,D} \geq \bar{n}(n+1)$ and $Y_{n-1,D} < \bar{n}(n)$. Putting these observations together we obtain

$$\mathbb{E}[R^{\pi^*}] = (\bar{s} - \underline{s}) \times$$
$$\left(\sum_{n=\underline{m}-1}^{\bar{m}-2} \lambda p_{\bar{m}-1}(n) \int_0^\infty \mathbb{P}(Y_{n,d} < \bar{n}(n+1), Y_{n+1,d} \geq \bar{n}(n+2)) dF_D(d) \right.$$
$$\left. + \sum_{n=\underline{m}}^{\bar{m}-1} n\mu p_{\bar{m}-1}(n) \int_0^\infty \mathbb{P}(Y_{n,d} \geq \bar{n}(n+1), Y_{n-1,d} < \bar{n}(n)) dF_D(d) \right).$$

Detailed balance equations yield the result.

Proof of (9.11) may be found in Weber and de Veciana, 2002.

■

Proof of Lemma 3 The proofs of (9.12), (9.13), and (9.14) are exactly the same as the proofs of (9.9), (9.10) and (9.11) respectively, but with $D = d$.

■

Proof of Theorem 3 The critical insight behind the proof is that the optimal asymptotic expected subscription level subject to the asymptotic zero blocking constraint is met when asymptotic load equals asymptotic capacity, i.e.,

$$\lim_{\lambda \to \infty, c=c(\lambda)} \frac{\sum_{k=1}^K \rho_k s_k}{c} = \frac{\sum_{k=1}^K (F_U(d_k) - F_U(d_{k-1})) s_k}{\alpha \bar{s}} = 1.$$

It is shown in Ross, 1995 that blocking is zero for this case, although the convergence is $O(\frac{1}{\sqrt{c}})$. We may then write the optimization problem as

$$\max_{\mathcal{D}} \left\{ \sum_{k=1}^K (F_D(d_k) - F_D(d_{k-1})) s_k \Big| \sum_{k=1}^K (F_U(d_k) - F_U(d_{k-1})) s_k = \alpha \bar{s} \right\}$$

The Lagrangian is

$$L(\mathcal{D}, z) = \sum_{k=1}^K (F_D(d_k) - F_D(d_{k-1})) s_k - z \left(\sum_{k=1}^K (F_U(d_k) - F_U(d_{k-1})) s_k - \alpha \bar{s} \right)$$

Taking derivatives yields

$$\frac{\partial L(\mathcal{D}, z)}{\partial d_k} = f_D(d_k) s_k - f_D(d_k) s_{k+1} - z(f_U(d_k) s_k - f_U(d_k) s_{k+1}).$$

Use of the fact that $f_U(d) = \mu d f_D(d)$ allows

$$\frac{\partial L(\mathcal{D}, z)}{\partial d_k} = (s_k - s_{k+1}) f_D(d_k)(1 - z\mu d_k)$$

Optimality requires $\frac{\partial L(\mathcal{D}, z)}{\partial d_k} = 0$ for $k = 1, ..., K - 1$; inspection shows this is only true for $d_k = \frac{1}{z\mu}$, i.e., $d_k = d^* \, \forall k$. This implies the optimal threshold policy uses only two classes, i.e., $\bar{s}$ and $\underline{s}$, and so the inclusion of additional subscription levels, i.e., $K > 2$, is unnecessary.

For a two class system the blocking constraint simplifies to

$$F_U(d)\bar{s} + \bar{F}_U(d)\underline{s} = \alpha\bar{s}.$$

Solving this for d yields (for $\beta < \alpha \leq 1$)

$$d^* = F_U^{-1}(\frac{\alpha - \beta}{1 - \beta}).$$

When $\alpha \leq \beta$ asymptotic zero blocking is impossible since the system is overloaded. We minimize blocking, however, by admitting all streams at $\underline{s}$, i.e., $d^* = 0$. When $\alpha > 1$ we obtain asymptotic zero blocking by admitting all streams at $\bar{s}$, i.e., $d^* = \infty$. Combining these notions gives the result.

The asymptotic expected subscription level under the adaptive admission policy with duration threshold d^* is

$$q^{\alpha,aa^*} = F_D(d^*) + \beta\bar{F}_D(d^*).$$

Rearranging gives the result.

∎

References

Argiriou, N. and Georgiadis, L. (2002). Channel sharing by rate adaptive streaming applications. In *Proceedings of Infocom*.

B.Vickers, Alburquerque, C., and Suda, T. (2000). Source-adaptive multi-layered multicast algorithms for real-time video distribution. *IEEE/ACM Transactions on Networking*.

Girod, B. (1992). Psychovisual aspects of image communications. *Signal Processing*, 28:239–251.

Gorinsky, S., Ramakrishnan, K. K., and Vin, H. (2000). Addressing heterogeneity and scalability in layered multicast congestion control. Technical report, Department of Computer Sciences, The University of Texas at Austin.

Gorinsky, S. and Vin, H. (2001). The utility of feedback in layered multicast congestion control. In *Proceedings of NOSSDAV*.

Kar, K., Sarkar, S., and Tassiulas, L. (2000). Optimization based rate control for multirate multicast sessions. Technical report, Institute of Systems Research and University of Maryland.

Kimura, J. (1999). Perceived quality and bandwidth characterization of layered MPEG-2 video encoding. In *Proceedings of the SPIE International Symposium on Voice, Video, and Data Communications*.

McCanne, S. (1996). *Scalable Compression and Transmission of Internet Multicast Video*. PhD thesis, University of California at Berkeley.

Rejaie, R., Handley, M., and Estrin, D. (1999). Quality adaptation for congestion controlled video playback over the internet. In *SIGCOMM*, pages 189–200.

Ross, K. (1995). *Multiservice Loss Models for Broadband Telecommunication Networks*. Springer-Verlag, London.

Saparilla, D. and Ross, K. (2000). Optimal streaming of layered video. In *Proceedings of Infocom*.

Vishwanath, M. and Chou, P. (1994). An efficient algorithm for hierarchical compression of video. In *Proceedings of the IEEE International Conference on Image Processing*.

Walrand, J. (1988). *An Introduction to Queueing Networks*. Prentice-Hall, New Jersey.

Weber, S. and de Veciana, G. (2002). Network design for rate adaptive multimedia streams. In Submission.

Chapter 10

NUMERICAL METHODS FOR ANALYZING QUEUES WITH HEAVY-TAILED DISTRIBUTIONS

John Shortle, Donald Gross
George Mason University, 4400 University Dr., MS 4A6, Fairfax, VA 22030

Martin J. Fischer, Denise M.B. Masi
Mitretek Systems, 3150 Fairview Park Drive South, Falls Church, VA

Abstract: In many queues associated with data traffic (for example, a buffer at a router), arrival and service distributions are *heavy-tailed*. A difficulty with analyzing these queues is that heavy-tailed distributions do not generally have closed-form Laplace transforms. A recently proposed method, the Transform Approximation Method (TAM), overcomes this by numerically approximating the transform. This paper investigates numerical issues of implementing the method for simple queueing systems. In particular, we argue that TAM can be used in conjunction with the Fourier-series method for inverting Laplace transforms, even though TAM is a discrete approximation and the Fourier method requires a continuous distribution. We give some numerical examples for an M/G/1 priority queue.

Key words: Heavy-tailed distributions, numerical methods, Laplace transform inversion

1.   INTRODUCTION

Data have strongly suggested that many random variables associated with Internet traffic are *heavy-tailed*. Fowler, 1999, observes that heavy-tailed distributions appear in most of the protocol layers of the OSI stack. For example, at the application layer, requested file sizes follow a Pareto distribution (heavy-tailed); at the session layer, session durations also have a Pareto tail; at the transport layer, the number of TCP connections per web session has a heavy-tail; at the network layer, the interarrival times of packets have a heavy-tail; and there are many other examples (Crovella et al., 1998; Willinger and Paxson, 1998; Leland et al., 1994; Naldi, 1999; Paxson and Floyd, 1995). Thus, to analyze queueing models associated with data networks, it is important to analyze queues with heavy-tailed distributions.

Roughly speaking, a heavy-tailed random variable has a non-trivial probability of being extremely large. Technically, a distribution function *G(x)* is *heavy-tailed* if and only if

$$\lim_{x \to \infty} \frac{G^c(x+y)}{G^c(x)} = 1, y \geq 0,$$

where $G^c(x)$ is the complementary distribution function: $G^c(x) = 1 - G(x) = P(X > x)$. These distributions have tails which decay more slowly than any exponential function ($e^{ax} G^c(x) \to \infty$ as $x \to \infty, a > 0$). Common examples are the Pareto, lognormal, and Weibull (with shape parameter less than one) distributions. In this paper, we consider the lognormal distribution with density function:

$$g(x) = \frac{1}{\sqrt{2\pi}x\sigma} \exp\left\{-\frac{1}{2}\left(\frac{\ln(x) - \mu}{\sigma}\right)^2\right\}, \quad 0 < x < \infty$$

(with σ > 0), and the one-parameter Pareto distribution:

$$G^c(x) = (1+x)^{-\alpha}, \quad 0 \leq x < \infty \tag{1}$$

where α > 0 is a shape parameter, and a smaller α corresponds to a heavier tail. Since the Pareto distribution decays as a power law, it is also called *power-tailed*, which is a stronger type of heavy-tailed behavior. The lognormal and Weibull distributions are heavy-tailed but not power-tailed.

One problem is that many heavy-tailed distributions do not have analytic Laplace transforms and hence have no closed-form representation. Since queueing analysis relies extensively on manipulating Laplace transforms, this makes analysis using heavy-tailed distributions numerically difficult.

There are several ways to get around this. One way is to approximate a heavy-tailed distribution with a phase-type distribution (e.g., Feldman and Whitt, 1998, Greiner et al., 1998). However, Feldman and Whitt point out that other methods should be investigated. For instance, their fitting method does not work well for distributions with increasing failure rate. Another solution, which works for the Pareto distribution, is to use a continued fractions representation for the Laplace transform (Abate and Whitt, 1999). But this technique only applies to Pareto-type distributions, and not, for example, to the lognormal distribution.

Harris and Marchal, 1998, have suggested a simple method of approximating a Laplace transform, called the Transform Approximation Method or TAM. The advantage of TAM is that it works for all distributions- for example, distributions with infinite higher moments, such as the Pareto, where conventional moment-matching methods may fail, or distributions with non-decreasing failure rate, such as the lognormal.

As a simple example, consider the M/G/1 queue. To find the queue waiting time distribution, one typically uses the well-known formula (e.g., Gross and Harris, 1998):

$$W_q^*(s) = \int_0^\infty e^{-st} dF(t) = \frac{(1-\rho)s}{s - \lambda(1 - B^*(s))}. \tag{2}$$

Here, $F(t) = P(W_q \leq t)$, $W_q^*(s)$ and $B^*(s)$ are the Laplace transforms of the queue waiting time and service time, respectively, ρ is the offered load, and λ is the arrival rate. If the service distribution is heavy-tailed, $B^*(s)$ may not exist in closed form. In this case, to find $P(W_q \leq t)$, one takes the following steps:

- Step 1. Approximate $B^*(s)$.
- Step 2. Calculate $W_q^*(s)$ using Eq. 2.
- Step 3. Invert $W_q^*(s)$ numerically.

The performance of the TAM approximation (Step 1) and its application to M/G/1 and G/M/c queues with heavy-tailed distributions has been evaluated in Shortle et al., 2002, 2003, and Harris et al., 2000. In this paper, we focus on Step 3. Typically, one uses the Fourier-series method (Abate and Whitt, 1992, 1995) to invert Laplace transforms. In this paper, we show numerically that the Fourier-series method can be used in conjunction with TAM for certain queueing problems, even though TAM is a discrete approximation and the Fourier method requires a continuous distribution. Although there is some loss in accuracy in using the Fourier method with TAM, we show that this loss in accuracy is small.

Finally, we illustrate the applicability of the methods to an M/G/1 priority queue. Successful application of the methods to these simple queues indicates that the methods will have broader applicability in more complicated queues – for example, queues with correlated or bursty arrival streams, which is more typical of packet arrival processes.

2.   REVIEW OF THE TRANSFORM APPROXIMATION METHOD

In this section, we review the transform approximation method (TAM). For further details, see Shortle et al., 2002, Harris et al., 2000. TAM is based on ideas in Harris and Marchal, 1998. To motivate the method, consider approximating the Laplace transform:

$$B^*(s) = \int_0^\infty e^{-sx} dG(x), \quad \text{with the finite sum:}$$

$$\hat{B}^*(s) \equiv \frac{1}{N} \sum_{i=1}^{N} e^{-sx_i}, \tag{3}$$

where the points x_i are evenly spaced quantiles of the CDF G. For example, if $N=99$, then $G(x_1) = .01$, $G(x_2) = .02$, ..., $G(x_{99}) = .99$. This is equivalent to approximating G with a discrete N-point distribution. More generally, the TAM approximation is:

$$\hat{B}^*(s) \equiv \sum_{i=1}^{N} p_i e^{-sx_i}. \tag{4}$$

where the points x_1, x_2, ..., x_N, are arbitrarily selected increasing points, $y_i = G(x_i)$, and

$$p_i = \frac{y_{i+1} - y_{i-1}}{2}, \quad i = 2,3,\text{K}, N-1,$$

$$p_1 = \frac{y_1 + y_2}{2}, \quad p_N = 1 - \frac{y_{N-1} + y_N}{2}.$$

The first equation assigns to x_i half of the probability between the points to the left and right of x_i. The second gives an exception at the boundaries where the leftover probability near zero and infinity must be counted so all probabilities add to 1.

Because the choice of points x_i is arbitrary, we can pick points x_i (or equivalently quantiles y_i) which are far out in the tail of the distribution. This is important for heavy-tailed distributions, since we want to capture the tail behavior. In this paper, we choose points according to the following parameterization:

$$y_i = 1 - q^i,$$

for some q in $(0,1)$. For example, if $q = 0.1$, the quantiles are $y_1 = .9$, $y_2 = .99$, $y_3 = .999$, and so forth. The idea is to quickly get out in the tail. Shortle et al., 2002, showed that this parameterization gives a substantial improvement in accuracy over evenly spaced quantiles given in Eq. 3. In addition, when the mean of G exists, we can pick q so that the mean of the TAM approximation matches the mean of G.

3. LAPLACE TRANSFORM INVERSION AND TAM

This section investigates numerical issues with inverting Laplace transforms which come from TAM approximations. That is, we investigate the accuracy of Step 3 in the introduction. In particular, we show numerically that the Fourier method accurately inverts the waiting time distribution of an M/G/1 queue where G is approximated using TAM, even though the TAM approximation is discrete and the Fourier method requires a continuous distribution as input. We conjecture that this result is true for any queueing system with a waiting time distribution that is continuous everywhere except at zero.

More specifically, the TAM approximation (Eq. 4) is a discrete N-point distribution. Thus, for the M/G/1 queue, using TAM to approximate a heavy-tailed distribution G amounts to studying the $M/D_N/1$ queue. The examples in this section deal with the accuracy of the Fourier method on the $M/D_N/1$ queue.

The *Fourier-series method* is a well-known method for inverting Laplace transforms of probability distributions (Abate and Whitt, 1992, 1995). It is based on the following inversion formula:

$$F(t) = \frac{2}{\pi} \int_0^\infty \text{Re}(\phi(u)) \frac{\sin(tu)}{u} du, \quad \text{where}$$

$$\phi(u) = \int_0^\infty e^{iut} dF(t).$$

Re($\phi(u)$) denotes the real part of $\phi(u)$. The inversion formula holds for any continuous CDF $F(t)$ on the positive real line. In this paper, we are interested in $F(t) = P(W_q \leq t)$. The Fourier method approximates the continuous integral with a finite sum:

$$F_{h,K}(t) \equiv \frac{ht}{\pi} + \frac{2}{\pi}\sum_{k=1}^{K} \text{Re}(\phi(kh))\frac{\sin(tkh)}{k}. \qquad (5)$$

The finite sum $F_{h,K}(t)$ converges to $F(t)$ as $h \to 0, hK \to \infty$, provided t is a continuity point of F. The method can also be used to efficiently calculate F over the entire distribution, not just at a single t (see Abate and Whitt, 1992).

Distributions which are *discontinuous* are problematic for the Fourier method. That is, when F has a discontinuity, the Fourier method goes through the middle of the discontinuity (Figure 1). That is, $F_{h,K}(t) \to [F(t) + F(t-)]/2$. In addition, a single discontinuity at t slows down the convergence of the method *across the whole distribution*. This is because Re($\phi(u)$) does not go to zero when F has a discontinuity, slowing down the convergence of Eq. 5 with respect to K.

Discontinuous *F(t)*   Discontinuous *Derivative*

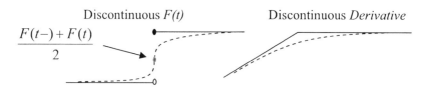

Figure 1. Potential problems inverting a CDF *F(t)* with the Fourier method.

Another potential problem is when the CDF F has a discontinuous *derivative*. Provided F is continuous at t, the Fourier method converges to the correct value. However, the convergence may be slower at the non-smooth point (Figure 1).

We now consider these issues in relation to the M/G/1 queue, where G is heavy-tailed and we approximate G with a TAM approximation. As we mentioned before, this is really an M/D$_N$/1 queue. Some properties of $F(t) = P(W_q \leq t)$ for the M/D$_N$/1 queue are:

1. $F(t)$ has an atom at 0 (discontinuity at 0), since there is a positive probability of an empty queue.
2. $F(t)$ is continuous everywhere else (see Brill, 2002). That is, even though the service distribution is discontinuous, the waiting time distribution is continuous everywhere except at 0.

3. *F(t)* has a *discontinuous derivative* at each of the *N* discrete points in the service distribution (see Brill, 2002).

For example, Figure 2 shows the CDF of an M/D/1 queue (*constant* service distribution). Here, the service time is 10 and the arrival rate is $\lambda = 0.01$. As shown, *F(t)* is continuous everywhere except at 0. *F(t)* has a discontinuous derivative at $t = 10$.

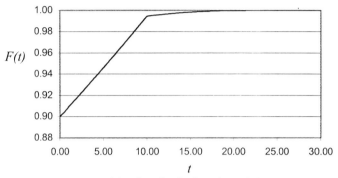

Figure 2. Waiting time distribution of an M/D/1 queue.

A potential problem in inverting the Laplace transform of the CDF in Figure 2 is the atom at 0. We can easily remove the atom as follows: Let

$$\widetilde{F}(t) = P(W_q \le t \mid W_q > 0) = (F(t) - (1 - \rho)) / \rho.$$

Now, $\widetilde{F}(t)$ is continuous everywhere. To find *F(t)*, we invert: $\widetilde{\phi}(u) = (\phi(u) - (1 - \rho)) / \rho$, the transform of $\widetilde{F}(t)$, using the Fourier method. This is fast since $\widetilde{F}(t)$ is continuous. Then we put the atom back to recover *F(t)* (solving the above equation for *F(t)*).

Following this procedure, the main problem is now the discontinuous derivative at $t = 10$. For the M/D/1 queue, we know the waiting time distribution exactly (Brill, 2002), so we can compare numerical inversion to the exact results. Figure 3 shows the accuracy of the Fourier method using two different parameter choices (Run 1: $h = 0.1$, $K = 600$; Run 2: $h = 0.001$, $K = 10,000,000$, Eq. 5). The y-axis is the logarithm of the fractional tail probability error (thus, lower values on the y-axis correspond to better accuracy). The figure shows that the accuracy is about five orders of magnitude worse at $t = 10$. The general upward trend is because the fractional error increases as the tail probability gets smaller.

Now, the M/D/1 queue is a worst-case scenario. Brill, 2002, has shown that the size of the jump in the derivative of the waiting time is proportional to the amount of probability at that discrete point in the service time. Thus, having all of the probability at a single point gives the biggest possible jump in the derivative of the waiting time. In general, to approximate a heavy-tailed distribution, we typically use a TAM approximation with many more points – for example, 100 or 1000 points. Because the probability is spread among many more points, the errors from the Fourier method at each of these points is much smaller.

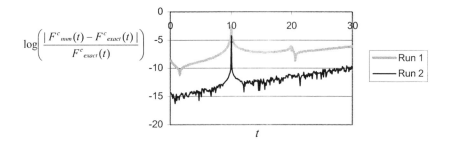

$$\log\left(\frac{|F^c_{mm}(t) - F^c_{exact}(t)|}{F^c_{exact}(t)}\right)$$

Figure 3. Accuracy of Fourier method for waiting time of M/D/1 queue.

Figure 4 illustrates this. The figure shows the accuracy of the Fourier method in calculating the waiting time distribution of an $M/D_N/1$ queue, where $N = 2, 5, 100$. The y-axis is the fractional tail error. As seen, there is a spike in the fractional error at each point in the discrete service distribution (2 spikes for $N = 2$, etc.). As N gets larger, the sizes of the spikes decrease. (We used the following parameters for the Fourier method, Eq. 5: $h = .01$, $K = 10,000$. Since we do not know the exact waiting time distribution for an $M/D_N/1$ queue, we estimated it by using much tighter parameters in the Fourier method: $h = 0.005$, $K = 1,000,000$.)

To get a sense for how these errors compare with typical problems, we compare the following three queues, each with hyper-exponential (or approximately hyper-exponential) service

$$G^c(t) = \frac{2}{3}e^{-2t} + \frac{1}{3}e^{-0.5t}$$

and arrival rate $\lambda = 0.75$:
1. Discontinuous $F(t)$. $F(t)$ is the waiting time of an $M/H_2/1$ queue. $F(t)$ has a discontinuity at 0, but is smooth everywhere else.
2. Discontinuous $F'(t)$. $F(t)$ is the waiting time of an $M/D_{100}/1$ queue, where D_{100} is a 100-point discrete TAM approximation to the H_2 distribution, removing the discontinuity at zero. $F(t)$ is continuous everywhere, but has a discontinuous derivative at 100 points.

3. Smooth *F(t)*. *F(t)* is the waiting time of M/H$_2$/1 queue, removing the
    discontinuity at zero.

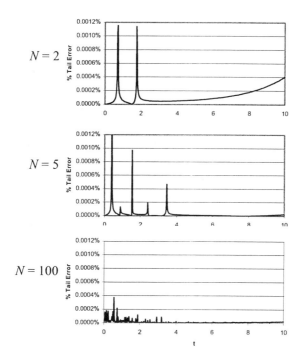

Figure 4. Accuracy of Fourier method for waiting time of M/D$_N$/1 queue.

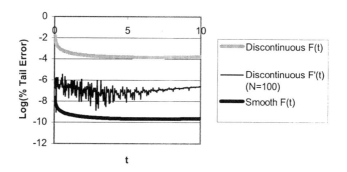

Figure 5. Accuracy of Fourier method for waiting time of M/D$_N$/1 queue.

In all cases, we ran the Fourier method with parameters $h = .01$, $K = 10,000$ (Eq. 5). In cases 1 and 3 we compared this to the exact waiting time distribution, given in Abate and Whitt, 1992. In case 2, we compared to an estimate for the exact distribution given by using tighter parameters in the Fourier method. Figure 5 shows the results of these calculations. (The y-axis is the logarithm of the tail probability error; thus, lower values on the y-axis correspond to better accuracy.) *Using the Fourier method to invert a distribution with discontinuous derivatives is substantially more accurate than inverting a distribution with atoms (discontinuities), but not as accurate as inverting a smooth distribution.*

4.   NUMERICAL EXAMPLES: M/G/1 PRIORITY QUEUE

We can use TAM in any queueing analysis involving Laplace transforms. In this section, we investigate using TAM on an M/G/1 *priority* queue: Consider a single server queue with two service classes. Type-1 customers have priority over Type-2 customers and service is preemptive. The priority class has service distribution G_1 and the secondary class has service distribution G_2. The Laplace transforms of these distributions are $g_1{}^*(s)$ and $g_2{}^*(s)$, respectively. Abate and Whitt, 1997, give the Laplace transform for the queue waiting time of Type-2 customers:

$$W_{q,2}{}^*(s) = \frac{\rho_1}{\rho_1 + \rho_2} h_0{}^*(s) + \frac{\rho_2}{\rho_1 + \rho_2} g_{2,e}{}^*(s + \rho_1 - \rho_1 b_1{}^*(s)), \qquad (6)$$

where ρ_1 and ρ_2 are the offered loads of the two customer types,

$$h_0{}^*(s) = \frac{1 - b_1{}^*(s)}{s + \rho_1 - \rho_1 b_1{}^*(s)}, \qquad (7)$$

$$b_1{}^*(s) = g_1{}^*\left(s + \rho_1 - \rho_1 b_1{}^*(s)\right), \qquad (8)$$

$$g_{2,e}{}^*(s) = \frac{1 - g_2{}^*(s)}{E(G_2)s}. \qquad (9)$$

$(g_{2,e}{}^*(s)$ is the Laplace transform of the equilibrium distribution for G_2.)

Like the M/G/1 queue, we have an expression for the Laplace transform of the queue waiting time $(W_{q,2}{}^*(s)$, Eqs. 6-9) in terms of the Laplace transforms of the service times $(g_1{}^*(s)$ and $g_2{}^*(s))$. Here, the expression is more complicated. In particular, because $b_1{}^*(s)$ is the *implicit* solution to Eq. 8, we must calculate it by iteratively evaluating Eq. 8.

If either service distribution G_1 or G_2 is heavy-tailed, then we nest the following three numerical procedures to calculate the waiting time distribution:

1. Approximate $g_1{}^*(s)$ and / or $g_2{}^*(s)$ in Eqs. 6-9 using the TAM approximation.
2. Numerically iterate Eq. 8 to get $b_1{}^*(s)$.
3. Use the Fourier method to invert $W_{q,2}{}^*(s)$.

Figure 6 shows the method applied to both Pareto and lognormal service distributions. We assume that priority customers have exponential service with mean 1. Secondary customers have (in the first case) lognormal service $(\mu = -1.15129, \sigma = 1.517427)$ with mean 1 and variance 9 or (in the second case) Pareto service $(\alpha = 2.25)$, scaled so that the mean is 1 and the variance is 9. Both customers have an arrival rate $\lambda = 0.4$. TAM and Fourier parameters are: $N = 2000$, $h = 0.007$, $K = 4500$. The figure shows that the tail of the waiting time for Pareto service does not dominate the tail for lognormal service until about $t = 250$.

To further test the accuracy of this procedure, we consider a special case where both customer classes have the same Pareto service distribution. In this case, the tail asymptotics of the Type-2 customers are known exactly. Specifically, Abate and Whitt, 1997, show that:

$$P(W_{q,2} > t) \sim \frac{\rho}{1-\rho} \cdot \left(\frac{1}{(1-\rho_1)t} \right)^{\alpha-1}, \qquad (10)$$

where α is the shape parameter of the common Pareto service distribution (Eq. 1), and $\rho = \rho_1 + \rho_2$ is the total offered load of both customer types. procedure.

Figure 7 shows the waiting time distribution calculated using the above. The x-axis is $\log(t)$. The y-axis is $\log\big(P(W_{q,2} > t)\big)$. On a log-log scale, the tail asymptote (Eq. 10) is a straight line. We have calculated the waiting time distribution three times using different accuracy parameters for the numerical methods. In the first run, $N = 500$, $h = 0.002$, $K = 600$. In the second run, $N = 2000$, $h = .002$, $K = 1200$. In the third run, $N = 8000$, $h = .0007$, $K = 3600$. The three runs took 20 seconds, 2 minutes, and 20 minutes, respectively, on a 500 MHz PC.

$F^c(t)$

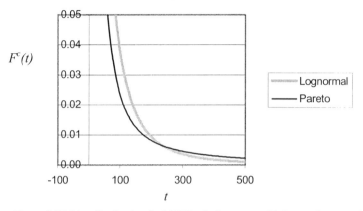

Figure 6. Waiting distribution for M/G/1 priority queue with Pareto, lognormal service.

$\log(F^c(t))$

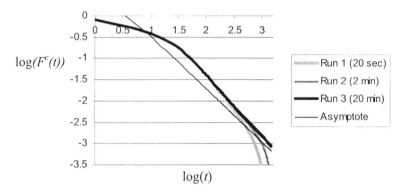

Figure 7. Waiting distribution for M/G/1 priority queue with common Pareto service.

From the figure, we observe the following:
1. Eventually, the numerically calculated tail probability $P(W_{q,2} > t)$ falls away from the power-law asymptote. This is because the TAM approximation is a finite distribution. By using more TAM points and more accurate parameters in the Fourier method, we can get the tail estimate to be accurate further out in the tail (Run 3).
2. The tail asymptote is not accurate until far out in the tail. In this case, at the 0.999 quantile, there is still a visible difference between the numerical estimate for $P(W_{q,2} > t)$, Run 3, and the tail asymptote. The fact that tail asymptotes are not accurate for heavy-tailed distributions until far out in the tail has been observed by several authors (e.g., Feldmann and Whitt, 1998).

5.   CONCLUSIONS

This paper investigated using a simple numerical procedure (TAM) to approximate Laplace transforms. Advantages of the method are that it is simple to implement, it works for any distribution, and it does not rely on moment matching (many heavy-tailed distributions have infinite moments). We acknowledge that other approximation methods may be more efficient for specific distributions. For example, a continued-fractions representation exists for the Laplace transform of a Pareto distribution (Abate and Whitt, 1999) - but it only works for Pareto and related distributions. TAM works for all distributions and can be implemented using a single piece of code.

We examined the accuracy of the Fourier-series method in conjunction with TAM. The Fourier method only works for continuous distributions, while TAM is a discrete distribution with a discontinuous CDF. We showed that this issue is not necessarily problematic: Even if the service distribution is discrete, the *waiting time* distribution is still continuous (but with discontinuous derivatives). While the accuracy of the Fourier method is decreased, it is not decreased substantially. Thus, it appears that TAM and the Fourier method can be successfully used together to solve queueing problems with heavy-tailed distributions.

In this paper, we applied concepts to the M/G/1 and M/G/1 priority queues. We acknowledge that a Poisson arrival process is generally not a good model for Internet data, since packets tend to arrive in bursts, and hence, are highly correlated. The purpose of this paper is to lay foundational work through simpler examples. Future work will investigate queues with correlated arrival processes.

ACKNOWLEDGEMENTS

The authors wish to thank the National Science Foundation for their support of this work under grant DMII 0140232. In addition, the authors would like to thank Ward Whitt who has provided insightful questions and direction for this work.

REFERENCES

Abate, J., G.L. Choudhury, W. Whitt. 1994. Waiting-time tail probabilities in queues with long-tail service distributions. *Queueing Systems* **16**, 311-338.

Abate, J., W. Whitt. 1992. The Fourier–series method for inverting transforms of probability distributions. *Queueing Systems* **10**, 5-88.

Abate, J., W. Whitt. 1995. Numerical inversion of Laplace transforms of probability distributions. *ORSA Journal on Computing* **7**, 36-43.

Abate, J., W. Whitt. 1997. Asymptotics for M/G/1 low-priority waiting-time tail probabilities. *Queueing Systems* **25**, 173-223.

Abate, J., W. Whitt. 1999. Computing Laplace transforms for numerical inversion via continued fractions. *INFORMS Journal on Computing* **11**, 394-405.

Brill, P.H. 2002. Properties of the waiting time in $M/D_n/1$ queues. Windsor Math Report, U. of Windsor, Ontario, Canada, April, 2002.

Crovella, M.E., M.S. Taqqu, A. Bestavros. 1998. Heavy-tailed probability distributions in the World Wide Web. *A Practical Guide to Heavy Tails: Statistical Techniques and Applications*. R. Adler, R. Feldman, and M.S. Taqqu, eds. Birkhaüser, Boston, MA, 3-25.

Feldman, A., W. Whitt. 1998. Fitting mixtures of exponentials to long-tail distributions to analyze network performance models. *Performance Evaluation* **31**, 245-279.

Fowler, T.B. 1999. A short tutorial on fractals and Internet traffic. *The Telecommunications Review* **10**, 1-14, Mitretek Systems, Falls Church, VA, http://www.mitretek.org/home.nsf/Telecommunications/TelecommunicationsReview.

Greiner, M., M. Jobmann, L. Lipsky. 1999. The importance of power-tail distributions for modeling queueing systems. *Operations Research* **47**, 313-326.

Gross, D. and C.M. Harris. 1998. *Fundamentals of Queueing Theory*, 3rd ed., John Wiley, New York.

Harris, C.M. and W.G. Marchal. 1998. Distribution estimation using Laplace transforms. *INFORMS Journal on Computing* **10**, 448-458.

Harris, C.M., P.H. Brill, M.J. Fischer. 2000. Internet-type queues with power-tailed interarrival times and computational methods for their analysis. *INFORMS Journal on Computing* **12**, 261-271.

Leland, W., M. Taqqu, W. Willinger, D. Wilson. 1994. On the self-similar nature of Ethernet traffic (extended version). *IEEE/ACM Transactions on Networking* **2(1)**, 1-13.

Naldi, M. 1999. Measurement-based modelling of Internet dial-up access connections. *Computer Networks* **31**, 2381-2390.

Paxson, V., S. Floyd. 1995. Wide-area traffic: The failure of Poisson modeling. *IEEE/ACM Transactions on Networking* **3**, 226-244.

Sigman, K. 1999. Appendix: A primer on heavy-tailed distributions. *Queueing Systems* **33**, 261-275.

Shortle, J., P. Brill, M. Fischer, D. Gross, D. Masi. 2002. An algorithm to find the waiting time for the M/G/1 queue. Conditionally accepted and re-submitted to *INFORMS Journal on Computing*, 2002.

Shortle, J., M. Fischer, D. Gross, D. Masi. 2003. Using the transform approximation method to analyze queues with heavy-tailed service. To appear in *Journal of Probability and Statistical Science* **1**, 17-30.

Willinger, W., V. Paxson. 1998. Where mathematics meets the Internet. *Notices of the American Mathematical Society* **45**, 961-970.

Chapter 11

PROVISIONING FOR BANDWIDTH SHARING AND EXCHANGE

Robert C. Hampshire

Princeton University, Department of Operations Research and Financial Engineering
Engineering Quadrangle, Princeton NJ 08544
rhampshi@princeton.edu

William A. Massey

Princeton University, Department of Operations Research and Financial Engineering
Engineering Quadrangle, Princeton NJ 08544
wmassey@princeton.edu

Debasis Mitra

Bell Laboratories, Lucent Technologies, 600 Mountain Avenue, Murray Hill, NJ 07974-0636
dmitra@lucent.com

Qiong Wang

Bell Laboratories, Lucent Technologies, 600 Mountain Avenue, Murray Hill, NJ 07974-0636
chiwang@lucent.com

Abstract   Customers of bandwidth services can be divided into two distinct groups: those customers requesting bandwidth for the future and those desiring bandwidth immediately. We develop a dynamic network provisioning methodology that minimally satisfies the QoS (blocking probability) requirements for the 'on-demand' customers. Our method is sufficiently general and captures time varying trends in the demand for services as well as different bandwidth requests for the multiple classes of customers. This allows a network provider to be efficient in reserving excess bandwidth for forward contracts. Asymptotic results and bounds for the Erlang loss system are invoked to obtain simple approximate solutions to this bandwidth provisioning problem.

Keywords: Bandwidth exchanges, network economics, network provisioning, Erlang B formula, heavy traffic limits, loss systems.

Introduction

In this paper, we develop a bandwidth provisioning scheme for a service network that satisfies the "on demand" customers. This sets the stage for providing bandwidth to serve customers with long-term contracts. Consider two broad categories of demand:

1 Immediate Demands

2 Forward Demands

Immediate Demand (ID) is the traditional category where customers make requests for bandwidth and expect the resources immediately. One advantage to traditional service is that there are historical records and statistical techniques for forecasting demand, which is expected to be stable, and describing its statistical properties, such as distributional information on arrivals and holding periods. One disadvantage however, is that there are corresponding expectations on the part of customers for a high quality of service, i.e., low blocking rates.

Forward Demand (FD), on the other hand, is the service category that is expected to grow rapidly with the increased availability of bandwidth in the Internet's infrastructure and universal high-capacity access to the Internet. Consider the following examples of application services that will create FD. Schools that offer distance learning, such as MIT or U.C. Berkeley, want to have bandwidth available from the campus to each learning site commencing at 10 am every Monday and Thursday during the term. Large corporations want contracts for guaranteed bandwidth supply for carrying internal communication traffic. Other carriers lease capacity for an extended period of time to defer capital investment in infrastructure.

We model the ID requests as multi-class Poisson. Say there are n ID classes, with class i characterized by (λ_i, μ_i, b_i), where λ_i is the Poisson rate of arrivals, $1/\mu_i$ is the mean holding time of individual demands, and b_i is the bandwidth demand on individual requests. We leave open for the present the matter of the distributions of the holding periods. An example of bandwidths demanded by differing classes is {64 kps, 128 kps, 256 kps, 384 kps}.

FD requests are indexed by i, and the j-th request is characterized by (R_j, S_j, T_j, b_j), where R_j is the time that the request is made, S_j is the start time of the bandwidth demand, T_j is its termination time, and b_j is the bandwidth requested.

We do not propose any specific statistical model for FD, in part because it is in a nascent stage, data is unavailable and also, as with any new service, the demand rates are unstable and unpredictable. It is our expectation that the holding times $T_j - S_j$ with be typically longer than in ID, and that the requested bandwidths b_j will also be larger.

Indeed if the holding times $T_j - S_j$ last for several hours or days, then there are important consequences on the modelling of ID. It becomes necessary to incorporate time dependencies, particularly in the arrival rates λ_i. We propose to consider time inhomogeneous Poisson processes, i.e., $\lambda_i \equiv \lambda_i(t)$ for $i = 1, \ldots, n$.

This paper focuses on a strategy to satisfy the ID customers. A provisioning methodology is developed to allocate the least amount of bandwidth needed to accommodate the QoS requirements of the ID customers, so that more capacity can be made available to serve the forward demand.

This provisioning scheme is developed first for a single customer class. Each member of this class requests a unit amount of resources and has identical demand characteristics that only depend on the current price. An asymptotic provisioning solution is obtained for the steady-state single class case. Next, the demand function for this single class case is allowed to depend on time. In this time-varying single class case an approximation technique is employed to develop a provisioning solution. The results for the single class steady-state and time-varying cases are then generalized to a multiple class case. This generalization allows for multiple customer classes each requesting distinct amounts of bandwidth and each having unique demand characteristics. Armed with the single class results and techniques of reversible systems, a multi-class provisioning solution is realized.

1. Canonical Design Problems for the Erlang Loss Model

Let us first investigate the single customer class case ($n = 1$). It is assumed that all the customers in this class request a unit amount of bandwidth ($b_i = 1$) and are governed by the same demand function that only depends on the price. Let customers arrive according to a Poisson process, where λ equals the mean *arrival rate*. Moreover, let the *holding time* for the unit bandwidth resource be random and assume that different customers have i.i.d. holding times, where $1/\mu$ equals the mean holding time. The unit amount of bandwidth requested by a customer is called a *channel* and we define L to equals the total number of channels. The resulting queueing model for this single class case is the classical Erlang loss model. Assuming a homogeneous Poisson arrival rate, it is typically denoted as an $M/G/L/L$ queue. When all channels are in use, the system is called *blocked* and we define ϵ to equal the probability that the system is blocked.

If there is an infinite amount of bandwidth available, then every customer requesting a channel receives it. The total number of channels *requested* by customers at a given time is called the *offered load* and we define q to equal its mean. It is a function of the aggregate demand for bandwidth. The $M/G/\infty$ (infinite server queue) is viewed as the offered load process for bandwidth requests. The steady state distribution for the $M/G/\infty$ queue length Q_∞ is Poisson where

$$\mathsf{Pr}(Q_\infty = i) = \frac{e^{-q}q^i}{i!} \qquad (11.1)$$

for all $i = 0, 1, \ldots$ and $q = \lambda/\mu$. Since $\mathsf{E}[Q_\infty] = \mathsf{Var}[Q_\infty] = q$, it follows that q equals the mean of Q_∞ and $\sqrt{q}$ equals the standard deviation of Q_∞.

In the context of this single class, unit bandwidth, classical Erlang loss model, we can discuss three canonical design problems:

1 The Quality of Service (QoS) Problem.

2 The Provisioning Problem.

3 The Pricing Problem.

In the next section, we generalize these basic problems to the case of a multi-class bandwidth model.

The first of three problems is the *quality of service (QoS) problem.* It can be described graphically by the following block diagram. Formally the problem

Figure 11.1.   The quality of service (QoS) problem.

statement is as follows: Given the number of channels L and the mean of the offered load q, what is the resulting probability of blocking ϵ experienced by the single customer class?

An exact solution to the QoS problem was obtained by Erlang [2]. The solution is the classical *Erlang blocking formula.* It states that if L is the total number of channels available and q is the mean of the offered load then the blocking probability equals:

$$\beta_L(q) = \frac{q^L}{L!} \left/ \sum_{i=0}^{L} \frac{q^i}{i!} \right. \qquad (11.2)$$

We can rewrite this formula as a conditional probability of the offered load process and obtain:

$$\beta_L(q) = P(Q_\infty = L \,|\, Q_\infty \le L) = P(L - 1 < Q_\infty \le L \,|\, Q_\infty \le L). \qquad (11.3)$$

What is *probabilistically* clear (using the theory of time reversible Markov chains, see Kelly [7]) but *physically* paradoxical is that the infinite server queue which experiences no congestion gives complete insight into the analysis of systems with blocking. Also this conditional form is quite useful in the heavy traffic analysis needed for the provisioning problem.

Now we relax the constraints on the arrival process and let customers arrive according to a non-homogeneous Poisson process where at time t, $\lambda(t)$ equals the mean rate of the non-homogenous Poisson process. The offered load process $\{\, Q_\infty(t) \mid t \geq 0 \,\}$ for this time varying case is the $M_t/G/\infty$ queue. At time t, the $M_t/G/\infty$ queue has a Poisson distribution or

$$P(Q_\infty(t) = i) = \frac{e^{-q(t)}q(t)^i}{i!}, \tag{11.4}$$

whenever $Q_\infty(0)$ has a Poisson distribution, which includes $Q_\infty(0) = 0$. Moreover, assuming that the holding times are exponential, the mean of the time varying offered load process is then:

$$\frac{d}{dt}q(t) = \lambda(t) - \mu \cdot q(t). \tag{11.5}$$

To model more general service distributions, we can numerically solve a similar set of ordinary differential equations for a phase type service. The total number of equations used for such distributions equals the number of service phases.

Now that the distribution of the time varying offered load process is known, how does one find a solution to the QoS problem? The modified offered load (MOL) approximation is employed to give an approximate solution to the time-varying QoS problem. Given L channels, if $Q_L(t)$ equals the number of channels in use at time t, then

$$\Pr(Q_L(t) = L) \approx \beta_L(q(t)) = P(Q_\infty(t) = L | Q_\infty(t) \leq L). \tag{11.6}$$

where $q(t)$ solves the above differential equation. This result can be found in Jagerman [5]. Error bounds for this approximation are given by Massey and Whitt [11]. The MOL approximation is at its best during periods of small blocking probabilities, which in practice is when such approximations are most useful.

The second canonical problem is the *provisioning problem*, which is the main thrust of this paper. Formally the problem statement is as follows: Given a mean offered load q, what is the smallest number L of channels needed to guarantee a QoS probability of blocking less than ϵ?

We use the work on server staffing in Jennings, Mandelbaum, Massey and Whitt [3] as motivation to develop a provisioning solution. If L is the amount of provisioned bandwidth that satisfies the single class QoS constraint, then L

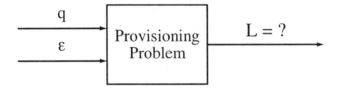

Figure 11.2. The provisioning problem.

should at least be as big as the mean of the offered load. It is also reasonable to add extra capacity to handle random demand fluctuations bigger than the mean. In this spirit we set the number of channels equal to the mean plus some multiple x of the standard deviation of the offered load or

$$L(q, x) = \lceil q + x\sqrt{q}\,\rceil, \tag{11.7}$$

where x is selected in [3] by computing the inverse of a Gaussian tail distribution. The inverse of the Gaussian tail distribution is useful for approximating solutions to provisioning problems for delay systems but not for loss systems. The more appropriate function to use in this paper is suggested by the work of Jagerman [6].

Recall that the probability of blocking ϵ equals the following conditional probability:

$$\beta_L(q) = \frac{P(Q_\infty = L)}{P(Q_\infty \leq L)} \tag{11.8}$$

where Q_∞ has a Poisson distribution. If we scale up the mean of the offered load, then we have the asymptotic result

$$\lim_{q \to \infty} \sqrt{q} \cdot \beta_{L(q,x)}(q) = \frac{\phi(x)}{\Phi(x)} = \text{``}P(N(0,1) = x \mid N(0,1) \leq x)\text{''} \tag{11.9}$$

where $N(0,1)$ has a normal distribution or formally

$$\phi(x) = \frac{1}{\sqrt{2\pi}} e^{-x^2/2} \quad \text{and} \quad \Phi(x) = \frac{1}{\sqrt{2\pi}} \int_{-\infty}^{x} e^{-t^2/2} dt. \tag{11.10}$$

This result can be found in Jagerman [6].

Now we define an important special function. Let ψ be the inverse function to ϕ/Φ, where for all $x > 0$

$$\frac{\phi(\psi(x))}{\Phi(\psi(x))} = x. \tag{11.11}$$

The properties of the ψ function are of utmost importance to our analysis of the provisioning problem. We now explore several of the key properties for ψ.

Theorem 1 *If ψ is the inverse of ϕ/Φ, then it is strictly decreasing with*

$$\psi(y) + y > 0 \qquad (11.12)$$

for all $y > 0$. Moreover, ψ is the unique solution to the nonlinear differential equation

$$\psi'(y) = \frac{-1}{(\psi(y) + y)y}, \qquad (11.13)$$

with the initial condition $\psi(\sqrt{2/\pi}) = 0$.

Proof: We first show that ψ solves the above differential equation. Starting with the identity

$$\frac{\phi(x)}{\Phi(x)} = \frac{e^{-x^2/2}}{\int_{-\infty}^{x} e^{-t^2/2} \, dt} = \frac{1}{\int_0^\infty e^{-t^2/2+xt} \, dt}, \qquad (11.14)$$

we obtain

$$\int_0^\infty e^{-t^2/2+\psi(y)t} \, dt = \frac{1}{y}. \qquad (11.15)$$

Now we differentiate both sides by y and get

$$\psi'(y) \cdot \int_0^\infty t e^{-t^2/2+\psi(y)t} \, dt = \frac{-1}{y^2}, \qquad (11.16)$$

which gives us

$$
\begin{aligned}
\frac{-1}{y^2} &= -\psi'(y) \cdot \int_0^\infty e^{\psi(y)t} \cdot \frac{d}{dt} e^{-t^2/2} \, dt \\
&= \psi'(y) \left(1 + \psi(y) \cdot \int_0^\infty e^{-t^2/2+\psi(y)t} \, dt \right) \\
&= \psi'(y) \left(1 + \frac{\psi(y)}{y} \right).
\end{aligned}
$$

and the differential equation for ψ follows from this identity.

Using the above identity (11.15) and integration by parts, we have

$$
\begin{aligned}
y + \psi(y) &= \frac{1}{\int_0^\infty e^{-t^2/2+\psi(y)} \, dt} + \psi(y) \qquad &(11.17) \\
&= \frac{1 + \psi(y) \int_0^\infty e^{-t^2/2+\psi(y)} \, dt}{\int_0^\infty e^{-t^2/2+\psi(y)} \, dt} \qquad &(11.18) \\
&= \frac{\int_0^\infty t e^{-t^2/2+\psi(y)} \, dt}{\int_0^\infty e^{-t^2/2+\psi(y)} \, dt} \qquad &(11.19)
\end{aligned}
$$

which shows that $y + \psi(y) > 0$ and completes the proof. ∎

The ψ function is the inverse of the hazard function. Because the ψ function solves a simple ordinary differential equation, we can easily compute it numerically. Moreover, ψ is a generic function so we can precompute a lookup table of values for $\psi(x)$ that can be used for all provisioning problems. We use a second order Runge-Kutta method to compute $\psi(x)$, based on the following approximation:

$$\psi(x+\Delta x) \approx \psi(x) - \frac{\Delta x}{(x + \Delta x/2)\left(x + \Delta x/2 + \psi(x) - \Delta x/\left(2x(x + \psi(x))\right)\right)} \tag{11.20}$$

Given the ψ function, we can construct an *asymptotic channel provisioning solution*. If $\epsilon = \beta_L(q)$ and we set $L = \lceil q + x\sqrt{q}\,\rceil$, then

$$\epsilon \approx \frac{1}{\sqrt{q}} \cdot \frac{\phi(x)}{\Phi(x)} \quad \text{implies} \quad x \approx \psi(\epsilon\sqrt{q}). \tag{11.21}$$

Making this approximation an equality gives us

$$L = \lceil q + \psi(\epsilon\sqrt{q})\sqrt{q}\,\rceil. \tag{11.22}$$

If we define $\ell(z) \equiv z + \psi(\epsilon\sqrt{z})\sqrt{z}$. We can show from the properties for ψ that

$$\ell(0) = 0 \quad \text{and} \quad \ell(L/(1 - \epsilon)) \geq L. \tag{11.23}$$

By the continuity of ℓ, there must exist some $0 < q \leq L/(1 - \epsilon)$ where $\ell(q) = L$. Given the properties of ψ, we have

$$L = q + \psi(\epsilon\sqrt{q})\sqrt{q} > q(1 - \epsilon). \tag{11.24}$$

Define the carried load to be the mean number of customers that are admitted for service. If L is the actual number of channels that gives a steady state offered load of q and a QoS of ϵ, then the carried load is $q(1 - \epsilon)$. This is consistent with the above inequality.

We now turn our focus to the time varying single class provisioning problem. An approximate provisioning solution can be realized via the modified offered load approximation combined with the ψ function. The solution takes the same form as above. The number of provisioned channels equals the mean of the offered load plus some multiple of the standard deviation of the offered load. The approximate time-varying provisioning solution is:

$$L(t) \approx q(t) + \psi\left(\epsilon\sqrt{q(t)}\right)\sqrt{q(t)} \tag{11.25}$$

where for the case of exponentially distributed service times, q solves the differential equation

$$\frac{dq}{dt}(t) = \lambda(t) - \mu \cdot q(t). \tag{11.26}$$

The provisioned number of channels, $L(t)$, is a continuous function of time due to the continuity of ψ and $q(t)$. Since $L(t)$ is set according to offered load $q(t)$, which is an expected value, it is possible that the actual number of users in the system exceeds the desired number of channels as specified by equation 11.25. This property is a unique by-product of the dynamic provisioning of network capacity. We define this scenario as a *ghost state*, and apply the following *non-preemptive service* discipline when the system reaches a ghost state:

- The excess channels process their last customers until their jobs are complete.

- During this period no new jobs are admitted.

Figure 11.3 is the state transition diagram for the single class customer case. It defines three distinct type of states: nonblocking states, blocking state and ghost states. If the system is in a nonblocking state then a transition to and from that state due to an arrival or service is allowed. While in a blocking state, any transition from this state due to an arrival is not permitted. In the ghost states a transition due to an arrival into a ghost state is forbidden. Only a transition due to a service from a ghost state is allowed.

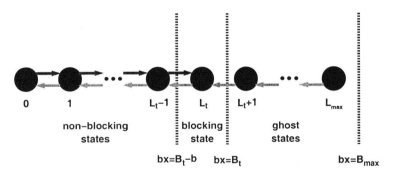

Figure 11.3. State transition diagram for the single class case.

Before concluding this section, should point out that there is a third design problem, called the *pricing problem*. Viewing price as a mechanism to control the offered load, this reduces to finding an offered load q that yields a QoS blocking probability ϵ given a total of L channels. This problem was addressed by Keon and Anandalingam [8] and for the case of a constant arrival rate, Courcoubetis and Reiman [1]. Also, a "Gaussian-distribution approximation based" approach is proposed by Lanning, Massey, Rider and Wang [9] for single-service models, and a "hazard function approximation" based approach is introduced for multi-service models in Hampshire, Massey and Wang [4].

2.   Generalization to the Multi-Class Bandwidth Model

The single class results can be generalized to a multiple customer class set-ting. Suppose that we have a heterogeneous set of customers, where each class requests differing amounts of bandwidth. Let $\lambda_1, \ldots, \lambda_n, 1/\mu_1, \ldots, 1/\mu_n$, and $b_1, \ldots, b_n$ be respectively, the call arrival rate functions, mean call holding times, and the amount of bandwidth requested for the n different classes of cus-tomers indexed by i. If there is an unlimited amount of available bandwidth, then all the classes behave like a collection of n-independent infinite server queues. We can then define an offered load model, where $Q_\infty^{(i)}(t)$ denotes the random number of customers simultaneously using b_i units of bandwidth. It follows that each $\left\{ Q_\infty^{(i)}(t) \mid t \geq 0 \right\}$ is an $M/G/\infty$ queueing process where each $Q_\infty^{(i)}(t)$ has a Poisson distribution whenever $Q_\infty^{(i)}(0)$ does. If we let R equal the offered load of the total requested bandwidth, then

$$R = \sum_{i=1}^{n} b_i Q_\infty^{(i)} \tag{11.27}$$

where in steady state $\mathsf{E}[Q_\infty^{(i)}] = \mathsf{Var}[Q_\infty^{(i)}] = q_i = \lambda_i/\mu_i$. Consequently,

$$\mathsf{E}[R] = \sum_{i=1}^{n} b_i q_i \quad \text{and} \quad \mathsf{Var}[R] = \sum_{i=1}^{n} b_i^2 q_i. \tag{11.28}$$

Let B be the total amount of available bandwidth. We can then formulate a carried load model where $Q_B^{(i)}(t)$ equals the random number of customers simultaneously using b_i units of bandwidth at time t, given an admission control policy that rejects any arriving customer requesting more bandwidth than is available.

We now reconsider the QoS problem for multiple customer classes. The

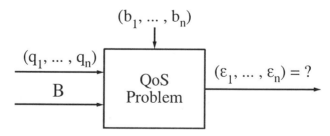

Figure 11.4.   The multi-class bandwidth quality of service (QoS) problem.

blocking for class j customers equals the probability of the event that $\sum_{i=1}^{n} b_i Q_B^{(i)}$ is greater than $B - b_j$.

Since the $Q_\infty^{(i)}(t)$'s are mutually independent Poisson random variables, we know that the probability given above is some generic function $\beta_B^{(i)} : \Re^n \to \Re$ of the $q_i(t)$'s where $q_i(t) = E[Q_\infty^{(i)}(t)]$. Let $\mathbf{q} = (q_1, ..., q_n)$ and $\mathbf{b} = (b_1, ..., b_n)$. In general, if $Q_1, ..., Q_n$ are a collection of mutually independent Poisson random variables with $q_i \equiv E[Q_i]$, if we define $\beta_B^{(i)}$ to be

$$
\begin{aligned}
\beta_B^{(i)}(\mathbf{q}, \mathbf{b}) &= \Pr\left(B - b_i < \sum_{j=1}^n b_j Q_B^{(j)} \right) \\
&= \Pr\left(B - b_i < \sum_{j=1}^n b_j Q_\infty^{(j)} \le B \,\middle|\, \sum_{j=1}^n b_j Q_\infty^{(j)} \le B \right) \\
&= \frac{\Pr\left(B - b_i < \sum_{j=1}^n b_j Q_\infty^{(j)} \le B \right)}{\Pr\left(\sum_{j=1}^n b_j Q_\infty^{(j)} \le B \right)},
\end{aligned}
$$

and $\mathbf{q} = (q_1, ..., q_n)$. Then this equals the steady state blocking probability for class i. This result follows from time reversibility as discussed in Kelly [7].

We now reconsider the capacity provisioning problem with time-varying arrival rates for multiple services. In this case, the blocking at time t for class j customers equals the probability of the event that $\sum_{i=1}^n b_i Q_B^{(i)}(t)$ is greater than $B(t) - b_j$. The modified offered load approximation for this probability is defined to be

$$
\begin{aligned}
&\Pr\left(B - b_i < \sum_{j=1}^n b_j Q_B^{(j)}(t) \right) \\
&\approx \Pr\left(B - b_i < \sum_{j=1}^n b_j Q_\infty^{(j)}(t) \,\middle|\, \sum_{j=1}^n b_j Q_\infty^{(j)}(t) \le B \right). \quad (11.29)
\end{aligned}
$$

One justification for this approximation is that it gives the exact answer when the arrival rates are constant and the system is in steady state. Thus an approximate QoS solution is :

$$
\begin{aligned}
\beta_B^{(i)}(\mathbf{q(t)}, \mathbf{b}) &= \Pr\left(B - b_i < \sum_{j=1}^n b_j Q_\infty^{(j)}(t) \le B \,\middle|\, \sum_{j=1}^n b_j Q_\infty^{(j)}(t) \le B \right) \\
&= \frac{\Pr\left(B - b_i < \sum_{j=1}^n b_j Q_\infty^{(j)}(t) \le B \right)}{\Pr\left(\sum_{j=1}^n b_j Q_\infty^{(j)}(t) \le B \right)}.
\end{aligned}
$$

We now reconsider the provisioning problem for multiple customer classes. If q_i is the mean offered load for customers requesting b_i units of bandwidth,

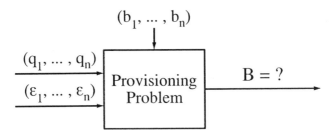

Figure 11.5. The multi-class bandwidth provisioning problem.

then the multiple class provisioning problem is to answer the question: What is the smallest amount B of bandwidth needed to guarantee a probability of blocking less than ϵ_i for each class i?

Recall that R is the offered load of the total requested bandwidth. If B is the amount of provisioned bandwidth that satisfies the multi-class QoS constraints, then B should be at least as big as the mean of the offered load R. It is also reasonable to add extra capacity to handle random demand fluctuations bigger than the mean. In this spirit we set the amount of bandwidth equal to the mean plus some multiple x of the standard deviation of the offered load. As in the single class case, we scale up the offered load of each class. In this limiting regime an asymptotic provisioning solution is found. If

$$B(\eta, x) \equiv \eta \cdot \sum_{i=1}^{n} b_i q_i + x \sqrt{\eta \cdot \sum_{i=1}^{n} b_i^2 q_i} \qquad (11.30)$$

where η is a scaling factor for the offered loads, then we have the limiting result:

$$\lim_{\eta \to \infty} \sqrt{\eta} \beta_{B(\eta,x)}^{(i)}(\mathbf{q}, \mathbf{b}) = \frac{b_i}{\sqrt{\sum_{i=1}^{n} b_i^2 q_i}} \cdot \frac{\phi(x)}{\Phi(x)}, \qquad (11.31)$$

where ϕ and Φ are defined the same as for the single class case. This limiting result can be found in the papers of Reiman [13] as well as Mitra and Morrison [12]. Since ψ is a decreasing function, then the constraint $\beta_B^{(i)}(\mathbf{q}, \mathbf{b}) \leq \epsilon_i$ asymptotically (using the value of $\sqrt{\eta} \beta_{B(\eta,x)}^{(i)}(\mathbf{q}, \mathbf{b})$ as $\eta \to \infty$ to approximate its value at $\eta = 1$) implies

$$\frac{b_i}{\sqrt{\sum_{i=1}^{n} b_i^2 q_i}} \cdot \frac{\phi(x)}{\Phi(x)} \leq \epsilon_i \quad \Rightarrow \quad x \geq \psi \left(\frac{\epsilon_i}{b_i} \sqrt{\sum_{i=1}^{n} b_i^2 q_i} \right). \qquad (11.32)$$

Our provisioned amount of bandwidth must satisfy the QoS conditions for all of the classes. Thus if x satisfies all the QoS conditions, then

$$x \geq \max_{1 \leq i \leq n} \psi \left(\frac{\epsilon_i}{b_i} \cdot \sqrt{\sum_{i=1}^{n} b_i^2 q_i} \right) \tag{11.33}$$

which is equivalent to

$$x \geq \psi \left(\min_{1 \leq i \leq n} \frac{\epsilon_i}{b_i} \cdot \sqrt{\sum_{i=1}^{n} b_i^2 q_i} \right). \tag{11.34}$$

Making this inequality an equality, we have the provisioning solution:

$$B = \sum_{i=1}^{n} b_i q_i + \psi \left(\min_{1 \leq i \leq n} \frac{\epsilon_i}{b_i} \cdot \sqrt{\sum_{i=1}^{n} b_i^2 q_i} \right) \sqrt{\sum_{i=1}^{n} b_i^2 q_i}. \tag{11.35}$$

This result leads to an asymptotic rule of thumb which states:

Asymptotic Rule of Thumb: The dominant QoS classes are the ones with the smallest ϵ_i / b_i ratio.

Satisfying their requirements provides more than enough bandwidth for all the other classes.

These results can be generalized to the time varying arrival case. The approximate time-varying provisioning solution at time t is

$$B(t) = \sum_{i=1}^{n} b_i q_i(t) + \psi \left(\min_{1 \leq i \leq n} \frac{\epsilon_i}{b_i} \cdot \sqrt{\sum_{i=1}^{n} b_i^2 q_i(t)} \right) \sqrt{\sum_{i=1}^{n} b_i^2 q_i(t)} \tag{11.36}$$

where if we assume that the service time for each class is exponentially distributed, then each $q_i(t)$ solves the differential equation

$$\frac{d}{dt} q_i(t) = \lambda_i(t) - \mu_i \cdot q_i(t). \tag{11.37}$$

These results are due to the modified offered load approximation. The bandwidth function $B(t)$ is a continuous function of time. Service discipline assumptions need to be made as in the single class case. During times of capacity reduction customers hold their resources until their job is complete. Also during this period no new customers of that class are admitted for service. Figure 11.6 is the state space transition diagram for a system with two classes of customers. It is assumed that class 2 customers request more bandwidth, b_i, than the first class. This figure defines four distinct type of states: nonblocking states, class 2 blocking states, class 1 and 2 blocking states and ghost states. If the system is

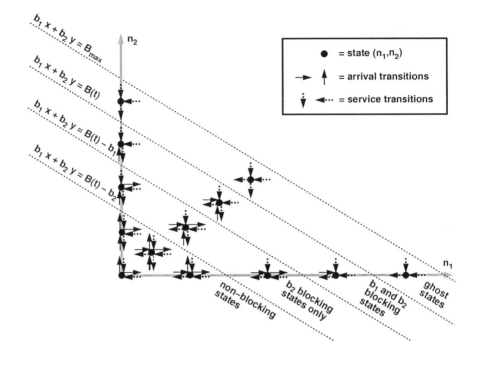

Figure 11.6.   State transition diagram for the two-class case.

in a nonblocking state then a transition to and from a state due to an arrival or a service is allowed for both classes. While in a class 2 blocking state, transitions from these states due to an arrival of a class 2 customer is not permitted. In the class 1 and 2 blocking states transitions from these states due to an arrival of a class 1 or class 2 customer is not permitted. In the ghost states a transition due to an arrival of either class into the ghost state is forbidden. Only a transition due to a service is allowed in ghost states.

Before we conclude this section, we state for completeness the general multiple class bandwidth version of the pricing problem. Given the desired QoS probability of blocking ϵ_i for each class i requesting b_i units of bandwidth and given the amount of bandwidth B, what is the largest offered load q_i that yields a QoS blocking probability less than ϵ_i? An approximate algorithm for solving this problem is explored in the paper Hampshire, Massey and Wang [4].

3.   Numerical Results

Numerical results are given for the provisioning problem with two customer classes. These two classes may have time varying arrival functions. The provisioning problem is solved to determine the amount of bandwidth $B(t)$ needed at any given time. Next we use this prescribed bandwidth at time t to formulate the "exact" Markovian loss model. Then at each time step numerically integrate the forward equations for this model and compute the transient blocking probabilities. Once the blocking probabilities are computed we compare them to their respective QoS bounds.

The numerical example consists of two heterogenous customer classes. Let customers of the first class arrival according to a Poisson process with mean rate $\lambda_1(t) = 30$, requesting 20 units of bandwidth and desiring no more then 4 percent blocking . Customers of second class arrive according to a nonhomogeneous Poisson process with mean rate $\lambda_2(t) = 40 + 10 \sin(2\pi t/80)$, requesting 5 units of bandwidth and desiring no more than 1 percent blocking.

For the numerical results presented, the planning horizon is 80 time units. It is assumed that the customer holding times are mutually independent and exponentially distributed with the mean of a single time unit.

The bandwidth function, $B(t)$, is a continuous function of time. In practice, a service provider changes the size of the network only at discrete times. The intervals on which the size of the network is held constant are called provisioning periods. The amount of bandwidth allocated over a provisioning period is the maximum of $B(t)$ over that provisioning interval. The provisioning periods can be made to be finer and finer. Thus as the provisioning period becomes infinitesimally small, the continuous provisioning solution is obtained.

The two period provisioning scenario is considered first. The top graph in Figure 11.7, is a plot of the transient blocking probabilities computed by numerically integrating the forward equations for the Markovian loss model with ghost states. The lower graph is a plot of the provisioning solution $B(t)$ which we use to compute the discrete approximation of $B(t)$ for exactly two provisioning periods. Notice at time 40 the apparent discontinuity in the blocking probabilities is reality a discontinuity of the *derivative* of the blocking probabilities, which are actually continuous functions of time. This phenomena is due to the generation of ghost states. At time 40, the amount of provisioned resources decreases instantaneously. This activates the non-preemptive service assumptions, thus blocking arrivals of new requests. Now compare the transient blocking probabilities to the QoS targets. It is seen that the transient blocking probabilities are in reasonable range of the targets. As the number of provisioning periods is increased, the transient blocking probabilities are closer to the QoS targets. In Figure 11.8, we consider the case of eight provisioning periods. The derivative discontinuities in the blocking probabilities are caused by the generation of ghost states. The reasoning follows from above. Finally, turning to the continuously provisioned system, the transient blocking probabilities approach the desired QoS requirement for each class.

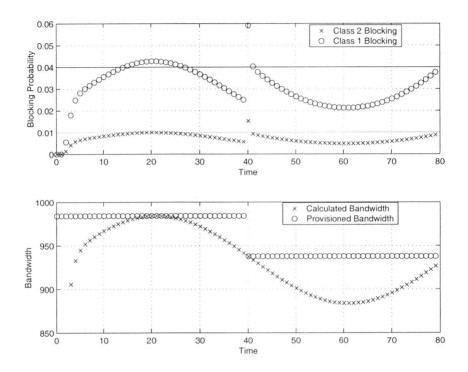

Figure 11.7.   Two period provisioning example.

4.   Summary

We have presented three canonical problems that arise from the Erlang loss model. These problems have a natural interpretation for a network service provider. The QoS problem is a classical problem that Erlang addressed in 1917. The pricing problem is the topic of another paper [4]. Much of this paper was dedicated to solving the provisioning problem. An asymptotic provisioning solution for a system offering multiple services was presented. A numerical example was also given in which there were two types of services and non-stationary demand for the services. It was observed that this provisioning methodology performs as desired. The provisioning solution is a result of an asymptotic scaling of the offered load. Therefore, we expect more desirable results as the demand for services increases. In the numerical example we assumed that the service time distributions were exponential. We should note that our provisioning solution is also valid for phase-type service distributions, where the mean offered load satisfies a system of n differential equations where n is the number of phases.

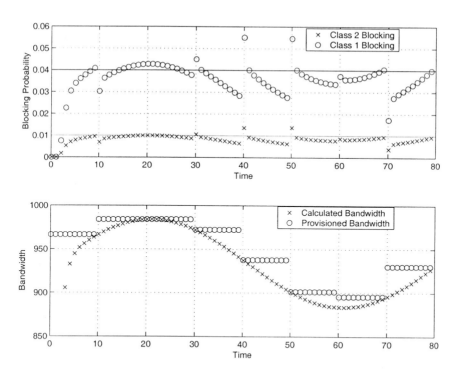

Figure 11.8. Eight period provisioning example.

The provisioning solution is a planning tool for a network service provider that is offering multiple differentiated services that each have unique QoS guarantees. The bandwidth function, $B(t)$, can be used as schedule for capacity management. Our methodology for computing the provisioned bandwidth schedule is lightweight and computationally inexpensive. This is because the function ψ can be simply computed from a lookup table. Therefore we can compute the provisioning schedule in realtime given forecasted demand for the services. The ability to compute the provisioning solution in realtime is a valuable property of our methodology.

References

[1] Courcoubetis, C.A. and Reiman, M.I. "Pricing in a Large Single Link Loss System," *Teletraffic Engineering in a Competitive World, P. Key and D. Smith (editors)*, Elsevier, pp. 737-746, 1999.

[2] Erlang, A. K. "Solutions of Some Problems in the Theory of Probabilities of Significance in Automatic Telephone Exchanges," *The Post Office Electrical Engineers' Journal; (from the 1917 article in Danish in Elektroteknikeren vol. 13)*, pp. 189–197, 1918.

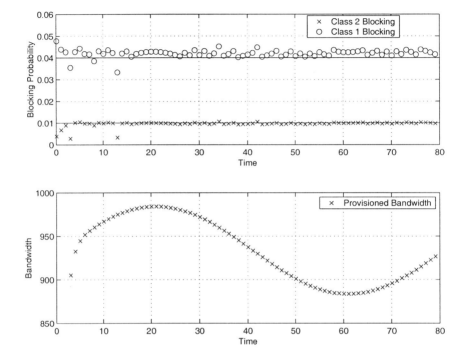

Figure 11.9.   Continuous provisioning example.

[3] Jennings, O. B., Mandelbaum A., Massey, W. A., and Whitt, W. "Server Staffing to Meet Time-Varying Demand," *Management Science*, pp. 1383–1394, 1996.

[4] Hampshire, R. C., Massey, W. A., and Wang, Q. "Dynamic Pricing for On-Demand Bandwidth Services," *Bell Laboratories Technical Report, 2002.*

[5] Jagerman, D. L. "Nonstationary Blocking in Telephone Traffic," *Bell System Technical Journal*, pp. 625–661, 1975.

[6] Jagerman, D. L. "Some Properties of the Erlang Loss Function," *The Bell System Technical Journal*, pp. 525–551, 1974.

[7] Kelly, F. P. "Reversibility and Stochastic Networks," John Wiley & Sons Ltd., 1979.

[8] Keon, N. and Anandalingam, G. "Real Time Pricing of Multiple Telecommunication Services Under Uncertain Demand," *Proceedings of the 7th International Conference on Telecommunication Systems, Modelling and Analysis*, pp. 28–47, 1999.

[9] Lanning, S., Massey, W. A., Rider, B. and Wang, Q. "Optimal Pricing in Queueing Systems with Quality of Service Constraints," *Proceedings of the 16th International Teletraffic Congress - ITC 16*, pp. 747–756, 1999.

[10] Massey, W. A. and Wallace, R. B. "An Asymptotic Optimal Design of the M/M/C/K Queue for Call Centers," submitted in 2002 to the *Selected Proceedings of the Council for African American Researchers in the Mathematical Sciences.*

[11] Massey, W. A. and Whitt, W. "An Analysis of the Modified Offered Load Approximation for the Nonstationary Erlang Loss Model," *Annals of Applied Probability*, pp. 1145–1160, 1994.

[12] Mitra, D. and Morrison, J. "Erlang Capacity and Uniform Approximations for Shared Unbuffered Resources," *IEEE/ACM Trans. Networking*, pp. 558-570, 1994.

[13] Reiman, M. I. "A Critically Loaded Multiclass Erlang Loss System," *Queueing Systems*, pp. 65–82, 1991.

Chapter 12

AUTONOMIC ADMISSION CONTROL FOR NETWORKED INFORMATION SERVERS

Giuseppe A. Paleologo

Mathematical Sciences Department, IBM T.J. Watson Research Center

PO BOX 218, Yorktown Heights, NY 10598

gappy@us.ibm.com

Nicholas Bambos

Department of Management Science and Engineering

Terman Engineering Center, Stanford University, CA 94305

bambos@stanford.edu

Abstract

While the issue of enabling performance guarantees on the Internet has been the subject of intense research in recent years, the problem of enabling QoS guarantees in edge servers has received relatively little attention. The need for QoS guarantees is already present in today's internet: while most backbones operate at a low level of utilization, web servers are often congested and are the main cause for the delay experienced by the end user. Here, we present a novel approach to admission control and resource allocation of sessions in edge servers. The model we adopt is quite general and its implementation does not depend on the type of application supported by the server (e.g., http or SSL). We model the system as a single server accessed by $N + 1$ users. N users have a lower bound on QoS, while one "super-user" aggregates the best-effort traffic to the server. The control rules admit a simple interpretation. Admitted classes "track" a target delay which is slightly smaller than their lower bound. The choice of a conservative target protects them from the performance degradation caused by the arrival of candidate classes into the system. On the other hand, candidate classes follow a "slow start" mechanism, similar to the update rule for TCP Reno. The intuitive rationale for this choice is similar to that of congestion-control algorithms: by increasing their priorities slowly, the candidate classes do not degrade the QoS of the admitted classes below their upper bounds. This resource allocation algorithm enjoys several attractive properties: it is *measurement-based*, since it only relies on the measurement of each class' delay during a busy cycle; it is *de-*

centralized, since each class updates its priority based on local information; and finally it is *closed-loop*, while most admission control schemes are open-loop. As a consequence, the algorithm does not require signaling to admit a new class.

Based on the above assumptions, we prove that the control scheme is asymptotically correct in the following sense: i) for small values of the constant ϵ and large values of a the average delay of the admitted classes is always less than their required bounds; ii) if the candidate classes are admissible, i.e., there exist a set of priorities for the server such that the average delay of both admitted and candidate classes are less than their upper bounds, then the candidate flows will be admitted.

Keywords: Admission Control, Autonomic Computing , Quality of Service, Queueing Systems

1.   Introduction

While the issue of enabling performance guarantees on the Internet has been the subject of intense research in recent years, the problem of enabling QoS guarantees in edge servers has received relatively little attention. The need for QoS guarantees is already present in today's Internet: while most backbones operate at a low level of utilization, web servers are often congested and are the main cause for the delay experienced by the end user. Of particular interest is the design and implementation of algorithms that enable service guarantees for multimedia applications. For this class of applications it is important to guarantee bounds on delay and/or loss rate; at the same time, audio and/or video streaming applications tax system resources and can easily lead to congestion. The issue arises whenever

- two or more users share the same server;

- each user requires lower bounds on one or more QoS metrics, which must be guaranteed during the time he accesses the shared resources; and

- the perceived QoS is influenced by the presence of other users and their required lower bounds.

In principle, it is possible to imagine a centralized "omnipotent resource manager" (or ORM)[1] that has the ability to:

1 receive the desired service requirements from the users and the current state of utilization from the server;

2 know the exact relationship between the amount of resources allocated to each user and the resulting QoS level, and decide whether adequate spare resource capacity exists to admit new users; and

3 allocate resources within the server based on the information gathered in the first two steps.

The time interval during which a user shares the server is termed *session*. The process by which users request resources, receive a response regarding the request of resources, and release the resources at the end of the session is called *signaling*, and corresponds to items 1 and 3 of our list. The process by which a new user is guaranteed admission is called *admission control* and corresponds to item 2 of our list. The time interval between the session initiation of a new user and the admission decision epoch is termed *set-up phase*.

Implementing an ORM is understandably difficult. Step 1 requires signaling from the users to the ORM. Step 2 is the admission control algorithm. The last step requires the implementation of a resource reservation mechanism. Of the functionalities outlined above, admission control is the most challenging. One possible approach is to model the server as a queueing system, and to model a user session as an arrival process of a certain type. On this basis, admission decision rules can be derived. We refer to this approach by the term *white box*. Several white-box analyses have been proposed for admission control in network elements (Choudhury, 1994; Courcoubetis, 1995; Elwalid, 1993; Gibbens, 1995; Gibbens, 1997). A drawback of the white box approach is that it is only successful in a few cases. In order to be analytically tractable, the models used to obtain the decision rule often abstract away some important features of the system under consideration, thus resulting in inaccurate decision rules. To alleviate the dependency on model assumptions, we propose a novel approach to admission control. Our approach employs dynamical measurements of QoS to capture the dependence between resource allocation and received service. In our framework, the measurement is performed by the end node, and is therefore termed an end-to-end measurement. Based on such measurements, the user requests a new resource allocation, by updating its priority value. Thus, we do not need to specify a model for the server, but rely instead only on measurements performed at the end-points. To capture the nature of the relationship between resource allocation and performance, we impose some monotonicity condition on this relationship.

Our approach is related to two strands of research. First is the Measurement-based admission control (MBAC), approach which has been proposed in the networking community (Gibbens, 1997; Gibbens, 1995; Grossglauser, 1999; Jamin, Danzig, Shenker and Zhang, 1997; Jamin, Shenker, and Danzig, 1997) and in the domain of web server admission control (Bruno, 1999; Kanodia, 2000; Li, 2000). In this framework, the admission decision is based on measurement of the load at the network element and/or of the load of individual users. The measurement-based approach has the advantage of reducing the decision complexity and of being robust to changes in assumptions on the traffic characteristics of users and to changes in the decision rules. A variation of this scheme delegates the measurement and admission decision to the users themselves. In the set-up phase, users measure their end-to-end quality of service by sending a train of probing packets and decide whether to start their session or not based on this information. Because of its user-based end-to-end nature, this class of admission control algorithms has been termed End-to-end Measurement-based Admission Control (EMBAC) (Bianchi, 2000; Elek, 2000; Kelly, 2000). A significant advantage of EMBAC schemes is that it shifts the burden of the decision from the network element to the user. Thus, there is no need for exchanging messages among resources accessed by a user, since the decision is not taken by the resource units. Our algorithm belongs to this class, since the decision is taken by the users and is based on end-to-end measurements of the quality of service.

A second line of research that is closely related to our proposal relates to admission control and link protection in wireless networks. Since wireless links can only support a finite number of radio channels, they face a problem: the quality of communication depends on the Signal-to-Interference ratio experienced by a call, which in turn depends on the transmitting power of other users. In a series of papers, Bambos *et al.*(Bambos, 1998; Bambos, 1995; Chen, 1994) formulate a power-based admission procedure for the admission of incoming calls in a wireless network. Their proposal is partially based on an earlier paper by Foschini and Miljanic (Foschini, 1993).

When analyzed in the light of the more recent literature on admission control, the scheme shows several desirable features. First, it is *end-to-end* and *measurement-based*, since every call measures its own QoS. Second, it does not require complex signaling because the admission decision is taken by the candidate user. Finally, it is *feedback-based*: the admission decision is taken after repeated measurements of the QoS of both candidate and admitted users, during which each user dynamically adjusts his transmission power. In other words, our proposal has some elements in common with the recent area of research termed *autonomic computing* (citeIBM2001). Each user probes the environment and adapts to changes based on local information; his actions are aimed at the protection and improvement of his perceived benefit.

2.   Algorithm Description

We consider a system in which a number of users access a remote server. The basic elements of the system are depicted in figure 12.1. The QoS metric of interest is the average delay. There are $N+1$ users. Users $1, \ldots, N$ correspond to multimedia sessions, while user 0 is a best-effort user. Multimedia users have associated priorities x_i, and have required upper bounds on delay equal to $D_i^{\max}$; the best-effort user is assigned priority $x_0 = 1$ and has no minimal QoS requirement. The server has capacity C and is shared among these users, and adopts a Generalized Processor Sharing (GPS) policy to schedule packets; i.e., for each pair i, j of backlogged users at time t, the service rates c_i, c_j of the

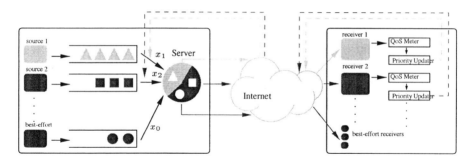

Figure 12.1. A processing systems shared by three users. x_i is the priority of user i.

two users satisfy the relationship $c_i/c_j = x_i/x_j$. The relative priority of user i is defined as $\phi_i = x_i/(\sum_{\ell=1}^{N} x_\ell + 1)$, and the capacity share allocated to user i is equal to $C\phi_i$. In our proposal, we define sampling intervals $[n\Delta, (n+1)\Delta)$. We see admission control as an explicit resource allocation scheme between users. The allocation of server capacity is based on the priority values chosen by the user. During each sampling interval, the end-node corresponding to user i collects measurements of packet delays and produces an estimate D_i of the average delay. The QoS metric is defined as $q_i = 1/(D_i + 1)$. Note that the QoS increases as the measured delay decreases. If the measurement period is sufficiently long, we can ignore errors in the measurement and consider D_i as a deterministic function of the priority ϕ_i. We also assume that D_i is a decreasing function of the server capacity allocated to user i or, equivalently, to the value of the relative priority ϕ_i. The priority value x_i is updated at the end of the sampling interval by the end-node, following a rule that constitutes the core of the resource allocation algorithm. The rule is decentralized, since it is based only on local information: the QoS estimate q_i, the minimal QoS requirement $v_i = 1/(D_i^{\max} + 1)$, and the user's admission state; i.e., whether it has been admitted or it still is in the set-up phase. We term a user in the set-up phase a *candidate user*. Conversely, *admitted users* have been guaranteed a QoS level equal or above some lower bound for the duration of the session. We denote the set of admitted and candidate users during interval n by $\mathcal{A}(n)$ and $\mathcal{C}(n)$ respectively. We use $\mathcal{U}$ to denote the set of all users.

We introduce the following parameters; $\epsilon > 0, \kappa > 0, x_{\text{floor}} > 0, n_{\max} \in \mathbb{Z}_+$. The priority updating rule is described below.

- **Candidate User.** User i begins the set-up phase at $t = 0$ with initial priority value $x_i(0) = x_{\text{floor}}$. At every epoch t_n, the measured QoS $q_i(n)$ is compared to $(1 - \epsilon)^{-1}v_i$. If $q_i(t_n) > (1 - \epsilon)^{-1}v_i$, then the session is admitted; i.e., $\mathcal{A}(n + 1) = \mathcal{A}(n) \cup \{i\}$ and $\mathcal{C}(n + 1) = \mathcal{C}(n) - \{i\}$.

Otherwise, the priority is increased according to the law

$$x_i(n+1) = x_i(n) + \kappa \epsilon x_i(n). \qquad (12.1)$$

If the number of sampling intervals since the beginning of the set-up phase exceeds $n_{\max}$, the user is refused admission and leaves the system.

- **Admitted User.** At the end of every interval, admitted user i uses the QoS estimate $q_i(\mathbf{x}(n))$ to update the priority according to the law

$$x_i(n+1) = x_i(n) + \kappa x_i(n) \left(1 - \frac{q_i(n)}{(1-\epsilon)^{-1}v_i} \right). \qquad (12.2)$$

- **Best-Effort user.** User 0 keeps a fixed priority $x_0 = 1$ for all $t > 0$.

The scheme has a rather intuitive interpretation. Candidate users probe the system and gradually increase their priorities based on their observations. The update rule for candidate users describes a "slow start" of priorities. The intuition behind this rule is the following: by increasing its priority, a candidate user increases its own QoS and degrades the QoS of admitted users. However, by keeping a constant rate of change $(x_i(n+1) - x_i(n))/x_i(n)$, it does not degrade their QoS excessively. The parameter ϵ is a measure of the aggressiveness of candidate users during the set-up phase. A candidate user is admitted when his sample QoS averaged over the set-up phase exceeds the minimal bound v_i inflated by the factor $(1-\epsilon)^{-1}$.

On the other side, admitted users follow a "sense and respond" policy. The update rule for admitted users also has a simple interpretation: each admitted user tracks the minimal QoS bound $(1-\epsilon)^{-1}v_i$. The quantity $((1-\epsilon)^{-1}-1)v_i$ could be interpreted as a "safety margin". It is such that the temporary service degradation due to the entrance of new candidate users does not take the QoS level of each attribute below v_i. In the limit of $\epsilon \downarrow 0$ the safety margin becomes $\epsilon v_i + o(\epsilon)$. Finally, the factor κ determines the rate of change of both updating rules, so that a smaller value of κ will cause candidate users to be less aggressive in seeking admission and admitted users to be less aggressive in responding to QoS fluctuations.   Figures 12.2, 12.3 illustrate the evolution of a system comprised of two users, each with QoS bound $v_i = 1$ and $\epsilon = 0.1$. At time 0, user 1 is admitted and user 2 begins its set-up phase In Figure 12.2 we show the trajectory of priorities. The level sets $\{\mathbf{x} : \mathbf{q}(\mathbf{x}) = \mathbf{v}\}, \{\mathbf{x} : \mathbf{q}(\mathbf{x}) = (1-\epsilon)^{-1}\mathbf{v}\}$ are also shown. We can observe how the QoS of user 1 never falls below its minimal bound, and how the system converges to a stable point $\mathbf{x}^*$ given by the solution of the system of equations $\mathbf{q}(\mathbf{x}^*) = (1-\epsilon)^{-1}\mathbf{v}$. In figure 12.3 we show the evolution of priorities in time. The candidate user follows an exponential increase rule, and the admitted user updates its priority in order to protect its QoS. The system converges quickly after the candidate users switches to the admitted state.

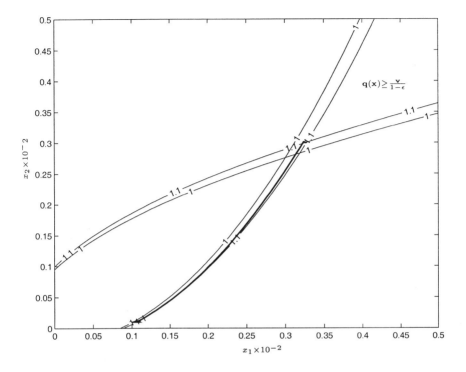

$$q(x) \geq \frac{v}{1-\epsilon}$$

Figure 12.2. Trajectory of priorities in the space of priorities.

The model has a direct counterpart in the problem of admission control in the wireless link. Consider a wireless communication system with a set of transmitter-receiver pairs (links) sharing the same channel. The transmitter at each node has an infinite queue of packet to send (Bambos, 1998). The probability of successful transmission is a monotone increasing function of the signal-to-interference ratio (SIR) of link i, defined as

$$q_i(\mathbf{x}) = \frac{G_{ii}x_i}{\sum\limits_{i \neq j} G_{ij}x_j + \eta_i}. \tag{12.3}$$

The parameter $G_{ij} > 0$ is the power gain from the j-th transmitter to the i-th receiver and x_i is the power of the i-th transmitter. The thermal noise at the i-th receiver is $\eta_i > 0$. For each link, there is a SIR threshold requirement v_i, reflecting a certain quality of service that the link needs to operate properly. Suppose that, at some epoch $t = 0$, the links in the subset of links $\mathcal{A}$ are admitted, i.e. $q_i \geq v_i$ for all $i \in \mathcal{A}$. If the remaining "candidate" links $\mathcal{C}$ seek admission, the problem faced by the admission control algorithm is to admit the links in $\mathcal{C}$ whenever there exists a vector of powers $\hat{\mathbf{x}}$ supporting the required

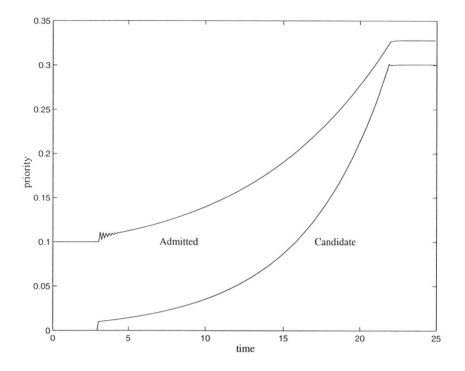

Figure 12.3.   Evolution of priorities in time.

QoS of all links; i.e., $q_i(\hat{\mathbf{x}}) \geq v_i$ for all $i \in \mathcal{U}$. In their original paper (Chen, 1994), Chen, Bambos and Pottie propose the following power updating rule for admitted and candidate links:

$$x_i(n+1) = (1+\epsilon)x_i(n) \qquad\qquad i \in \mathcal{C} \qquad\qquad (12.4)$$

$$x_i(n+1) = x_i(n)\frac{(1+\epsilon)v_i}{q_i(\mathbf{x}(n))} \qquad\qquad i \in \mathcal{A}. \qquad\qquad (12.5)$$

The above equations resemble the admission control rules we introduced. To make the comparison more precise, first consider Equation (12.2), and let $\kappa = 1$. By using the identity $1 - x = 1/x - 1 + o(x - 1)$, we have

$$x_i(n+1) = x_i(n) + x_i(n)\left(1 - \frac{q_i(\mathbf{x}(n))}{(1-\epsilon)^{-1}v_i}\right)$$

$$= x_i(n) + x_i(n)\left(\frac{(1-\epsilon)^{-1}v_i}{q_i(\mathbf{x}(n))} - 1\right) + o\left(\frac{q_i(\mathbf{x}(n))}{(1-\epsilon)^{-1}v_i} - 1\right)$$

$$= x_i(n)\frac{(1+\epsilon)v_i}{q_i(\mathbf{x}(n))} + x_i(n)\frac{v_i}{q_i(\mathbf{x}(n))}o(\epsilon) + o\left(\frac{q_i(\mathbf{x}(n))}{(1-\epsilon)^{-1}v_i} - 1\right).$$

As for Equation (12.1), it has the same form as in the proposal by Bambos *et al.* From this discussion, it is clear that the equations for wireless access control are a linearized version of Equations (12.1) and (12.2) in the limit $\epsilon \simeq 0$, and $q_i(\mathbf{x}) \simeq (1 - \epsilon)^{-1}v_i$.

3. Correctness of the Algorithm

For any resource allocation/admission control scheme there are two fundamental issues that need to be addressed. The first is the QoS protection of admitted users: the measured QoS level must be equal to or greater than the lower bound guaranteed to each admitted user during the session. The second one is the correctness of the admission decision: a candidate user must be admitted if and only if both its QoS and that of admitted users are protected.

To characterize the properties of the algorithm, we analyze the stability properties of the system of difference equations (12.1) and (12.2) in the case of "slow" dynamics, i.e., of $\kappa \simeq 0$. In this limit, the trajectory of the original system can be approximated by the solution of the following ODE system

$$\frac{dx_i}{dt} = \epsilon x_i \qquad\qquad i \in \mathcal{C} \qquad (12.6)$$

$$\frac{dx_i}{dt} = x_i \left(1 - \frac{q_i(\phi_i(\mathbf{x}))}{(1 - \epsilon)^{-1}v_i} \right) \qquad i \in \mathcal{A}. \qquad (12.7)$$

More precisely, let $\mathbf{x}^\kappa(n)$ be the solution of the original system, and let $\bar{\mathbf{x}}^\kappa : \mathbb{R} \to \mathbb{R}_+^N$ be the piece-wise linear function defined as

$$\bar{\mathbf{x}}^\kappa(t) = \mathbf{x}^\kappa(\lfloor t/\kappa \rfloor) + (\mathbf{x}^\kappa(\lfloor t/\kappa \rfloor + 1) - \mathbf{x}^\kappa(\lfloor t/\kappa \rfloor))(t/\kappa - \lfloor t/\kappa \rfloor).$$

In the limit $\kappa \downarrow 0$, we have $\bar{\mathbf{x}}^\kappa(t) \to \mathbf{x}(t)$ in the metric defined on continuous functions $d(\mathbf{x}(\cdot) - \bar{\mathbf{x}}^\kappa(\cdot)) = \int_0^\infty e^{-t}\|\mathbf{x}(t) - \bar{\mathbf{x}}^\kappa(t)\|dt$.

To prove the above properties we consider the following setting. Suppose that at time 0 the priorities of users $1, \ldots, N$ are $(x_1(0), \ldots, x_N(0))$. In most multimedia applications, sessions are long-lived with respect to the duration of the set-up phase. In the following, we make the simplifying assumption that sessions have infinite duration, and that the maximum allowed duration T of the set-up phase is infinite. We discuss the effect of relaxing these assumptions in section 5.

The first theorem shows that admitted users receive a QoS that is always greater than or equal to their minimal bounds for the entire duration of this session.

Theorem 1 (protection of admitted users) *For all $t \geq 0$, we have*

$$q_i(\phi_i(\mathbf{x}(t))) \geq v_i \qquad i \in \mathcal{A}(t).$$

Proof: We show that inequalities $q_i(\phi_i(\mathbf{x}(t))) \geq v_i$ hold for any admitted user i. Assume that, for some time t there is a nonempty subset S of admitted users $A(t)$ such that $q_i(\phi_i(\mathbf{x}(t))) = v_i$, if $i \in S$, and $q_j(\phi_j(\mathbf{x}(t))) > v_j$ for all remaining admitted users $j \in A - S$. We note that $\partial\phi_j/\partial x_k < 0$ when $j \neq i$, so that

$$
\frac{\partial\phi_i}{\partial x_j}x_j\left(1 - \frac{q_j(\mathbf{x})}{(1-\epsilon)^{-1}v_j}\right) > \frac{\partial\phi_i}{\partial x_j}x_j\left(1 - \frac{1}{(1-\epsilon)^{-1}}\right) \qquad \begin{matrix} i \in S, \\ j \in A(t) - S. \end{matrix}
$$

Furthermore we have

$$
\frac{\partial\phi_i}{\partial x_j}\epsilon x_j > \frac{\partial\phi_i}{\partial x_j}x_j\left(1 - \frac{1}{(1-\epsilon)^{-1}}\right).
$$

Then it follows that, if $i \in S$, we have

$$
\begin{aligned}
\frac{d\phi_i}{dt} &= \sum_{\ell \in \mathcal{U}} \frac{\partial\phi_i}{\partial x_\ell}\frac{dx_\ell}{dt} \\
&\geq \sum_{\ell \in A(t)} \frac{\partial\phi_i}{\partial x_\ell}x_\ell\left(1 - \frac{q_i}{(1-\epsilon)^{-1}v_i}\right) + \sum_{\ell \in C(t)} \frac{\partial\phi_i}{\partial x_\ell}\epsilon x_\ell \\
&= \sum_{\ell \in A(t)} \frac{\partial\phi_i}{\partial x_\ell}x_\ell\left(1 - \frac{1}{(1-\epsilon)^{-1}}\right) + \sum_{\ell \in C(t)} \frac{\partial\phi_i}{\partial x_\ell}x_\ell\left(1 - \frac{1}{(1-\epsilon)^{-1}}\right) \\
&= \epsilon\left(\sum_{\ell \in \mathcal{U}} x_\ell + 1\right)^{-2} \\
&> 0.
\end{aligned}
$$

Since the QoS metric $q_i(\phi_i)$ is an increasing function of the priority, it follows that the QoS is strictly increasing whenever $q_i(\phi_i) = v_i$, and therefore the inequality $q_i(\phi_i) < v_i$ can never hold. ∎

The above theorem has an intuitive interpretation. Whenever a user reaches the lower bound of QoS, the rate of increase $\dot{x}_i/x_i$ of the priority is equal to ϵ, which is sufficient to offset the possible negative effects on QoS caused by the action of candidate users. A result that is complementary to the protection of admitted users is presented in the next corollary.

Corollary 2 *For all $i \in A(t)$, $q_i(\phi_i) \leq (1-\epsilon)^{-1}v_i$ holds for the entire session duration.*

Proof: We show that for all admitted user i, the inequalities $q_i(\phi_i(\mathbf{x}(t))) \leq (1-\epsilon)^{-1}v_i$ hold. Assume that, for some time t, we have $q_i(\phi_i(\mathbf{x}(t))) = (1-\epsilon)^{-1}v_i$, and $q_j(\phi_j(\mathbf{x}(t))) < (1 - \epsilon)^{-1}v_j$ for all remaining admitted users $j \in \mathcal{A}(t)$. Then,

$$\frac{d\phi_i}{dt} = \sum_{j \in \mathcal{U}} \frac{\partial \phi_i}{\partial x_j} \frac{dx_j}{dt}$$

$$\leq \frac{\partial \phi_i}{\partial x_i} x_j \left(1 - \frac{q_i}{(1 - \epsilon)^{-1}v_i} \right) + \sum_{j \in \mathcal{C}(t)} \frac{\partial \phi_i}{\partial x_j} \epsilon x_j$$

$$< 0 .$$

The last inequality follows from $\partial \phi_i / \partial x_j < 0$ if $i \neq j$. ∎

We now show that the algorithm admits a new user whenever there are enough resources to support its minimal bounds on QoS. The following theorem states that, if there exists a vector of priorities such that all users in the system receive a QoS greater than or equal to their minimal bounds, then all the candidate users will be admitted.

Theorem 3 (admission of candidate users) *If there exists at least one vector of priorities* $\mathbf{x}$ *such that*

$$q_i(\phi_i(\mathbf{x})) \geq (1 - \epsilon)^{-1}v_i, \qquad i \in \mathcal{U} \tag{12.8}$$

with the strict inequality verified by at least one user, then all users are admissible.

Proof: By assumption, there is a vector $\mathbf{x}$ such that $\phi_i(\mathbf{x}) > q_i^{-1}(1 - \epsilon)^{-1}v_i$ for all $i \in \mathcal{U}$. If we define $w_i = q_i^{-1}((1 - \epsilon)^{-1}v_i)$, the set of inequalities (12.8) are equivalent to $A\mathbf{x} \geq \mathbf{w}$, with $A = (I - \mathbf{w}e^T)$, I the identity matrix and $e = (1, 1, \ldots, 1)^T$. By summing over each component and rearranging the terms we obtain $e^T\mathbf{w} < 1$. First we show that there exists a unique nonnegative solution to the linear system

$$A\mathbf{x} = \mathbf{w} . \tag{12.9}$$

To verify this, notice that A is a strictly diagonally dominant matrix, i.e., $|(A)_{ii}| > \sum_{j \neq i} |(A)_{ij}|$ (Berman, 1979); hence it is nonsingular, and Equation 12.9 has a unique solution. It is immediate to verify that the solution is given by the positive vector $\mathbf{x_w} = (1 - e^T\mathbf{w})^{-1}\mathbf{w}$.

Let $\mathbf{x_w}$ be the unique solution of Equation (12.9). Let

$$a = \max \left\{ \max_{\ell \in \mathcal{U}} \frac{x_{\mathbf{w},\ell}}{x_\ell(0)}, 1 \right\}$$

$$\mathbf{y} = a\mathbf{x_w} .$$

Notice that $q_i(\phi_i(a x_{\mathbf{v}})) \geq (1 - \epsilon)^{-1} v_i$. Define the set $S = \{\mathbf{x} : 0 \leq \mathbf{x} \leq \mathbf{y}\}$, and define

$$\tau = \epsilon^{-1} \min_{\ell \in \mathcal{C}} \log \left(\frac{y_\ell}{x_\ell(0)} \right)$$

$$i = \arg \min_{\ell \in \mathcal{C}} \log \left(\frac{y_\ell}{x_\ell(0)} \right).$$

First, we observe that the inequalities $x_\ell(t) \leq y_\ell, \ell \in \mathcal{C}, t \in [0, \tau)$ follow immediately from the definitions of $x_{\mathbf{v}, \ell}, \tau$ and from Equation (12.6). The inequalities $x_\ell(t) < y_\ell, \ell \in \mathcal{A}, t \in [0, \tau)$ also hold. To show this, assume by contradiction that this is not true, and define t^* be the first exit time of an admitted user from the set S, i.e. $t^* = \inf\{t \in [0, \tau) : x_\ell(t) \geq a x_{\mathbf{v}, \ell}, \ell \in \mathcal{A}\}$. Also let j be the admitted user such that $x_j(t^*) = y_j$. Based on the previous remark we have that

$$x_\ell(t^*) \leq y_\ell, \qquad\qquad \ell \in \mathcal{C}$$
$$x_\ell(t^*) \leq y_\ell, \qquad\qquad \ell \in \mathcal{A} - \{j\}.$$

The above inequalities imply that

$$\frac{x_j(t^*)}{\sum\limits_{\ell \in \mathcal{U}} x_\ell(t^*) + 1} > \frac{y_j}{\sum\limits_{\ell \in \mathcal{U}} y_\ell + 1} \geq q_j^{-1}((1 - \epsilon)^{-1} v_j)$$

and therefore $q_j(\mathbf{x}(t^*)) > (1 - \epsilon)^{-1} v_j$, which contradicts Corollary 2.

We want to show that, at time τ, the status of user i is admitted. Assume, by contradiction that user i is still candidate. We showed that in the interval $[0, \tau]$ the following inequalities hold:

$$x_\ell(t) \leq y_\ell, \qquad\qquad \ell \in \mathcal{C}$$
$$x_\ell(t) \leq y_\ell, \qquad\qquad \ell \in \mathcal{A}.$$

Choosing $t = \tau$, this implies that

$$\frac{x_i(\tau)}{\sum\limits_{\ell \in \mathcal{U}} x_\ell(\tau) + 1} > \frac{y_i}{\sum\limits_{\ell \in \mathcal{U}} y_\ell + 1} \geq q_i^{-1}((1 - \epsilon)^{-1} v_i)$$

and therefore $q_i(\mathbf{x}(\tau)) > (1 - \epsilon)^{-1} v_i$, which is inconsistent with the initial assumption that user i is candidate. It follows that user i must have been admitted at some time $\tau' \in [0, \tau)$. The reasoning can be repeated by induction, after updating the set of admitted and candidate users and setting τ' as the new time origin. ∎

The following result shows that, if a minimal allocation exists, the system converges to the "minimal allowed priorities" $\mathbf{x_w}$ *independently of the initial values of the priorities.*

Corollary 4 *If $A = \mathcal{U}$ and there exists a vector of priorities $\mathbf{x}$ such that*

$$q_i(\phi_i(\mathbf{x})) \geq (1 - \epsilon)^{-1} v_i$$

for all $i \in \mathcal{U}$, then $\mathbf{q}(\mathbf{x}(t)) \to \delta \mathbf{v}$ as $t \to \infty$.

Proof: Define $\mathbf{y}$, $\mathbf{w}$, S as in Theorem 3. The trajectory $\mathbf{x}(t)$ is contained in the compact set S, and the ODE system admits only one equilibrium point $\mathbf{x_w}$. LaSalle's Theorem (Khalil, 1996) implies that $\mathbf{q}(\mathbf{x}(t)) \to (1 - \epsilon)^{-1} \mathbf{v}$. ∎

4.   Convergence Rate

When a new user is admitted, say user N, it changes the equilibrium point of the system from $\mathbf{x_w}$ to a new point $\mathbf{x_{w'}}$. It is easy to verify by direct differentiation that $\mathbf{x_{w'}} \gg \mathbf{x_w}$. If the number of users is large, it is reasonable to assume that the admission of a new user does not significantly change the equilibrium point: the vector of priorities converges to the new equilibrium point starting in a neighborhood of it. If the attractor is hyperbolic (something that we will show below), the behavior of the dynamic system is well approximated by the linearized version of the same system. The study of the linearized system provides insights on the convergence rate of the algorithm to equilibrium.

Without loss of generality, assume that $\mathcal{U} = A$. The system of Equations (12.6, 12.7) can be linearized in $\mathbf{x_w}$. That is,

$$\frac{d}{dt}\mathbf{x} = DJ(\mathbf{x} - \mathbf{x_w}),$$

where D is a diagonal matrix defined by

$$(D)_{ii} = \frac{x_{\mathbf{w},i}}{(1 - \epsilon)^{-1} v_i} \frac{d}{d\phi_i} q_i(\phi_i) \Big|_{\phi_i = \phi_i(\mathbf{x_w})}$$

and J is defined as

$$(J)_{ij} = \frac{\partial \phi_i(\mathbf{x})}{\partial x_j} \Big|_{\mathbf{x} = \mathbf{x_w}}$$

By Liapunov's indirect method (Khalil, 1996), the point $\mathbf{x_w}$ is stable and hyperbolic if all the eigenvalues of DJ have negative real part.

We recall that a matrix A is a Z-matrix if it takes the form $A = qI - P$, where $P \geq 0$ and $q \in \mathbb{R}$. Furthermore, if the spectrum of P is less than q, then A

is termed an M-matrix. In the light of the above definitions, $\mathbf{x_w}$ is stable and hyperbolic if and only if $-DJ$ is an M-matrix.

We use the following Lemma, proved in (Berman, 1979; Th. 6.2.7).

Lemma 5 *Let A be a Z-Matrix. A is an M-matrix if and only if and there is a vector $\mathbf{x} \gg 0$ such that $A\mathbf{x} > 0$.*

Since $(J\mathbf{x})_i = \left(\sum_{\ell \in \mathcal{U}} x_\ell + 1 \right)^{-2} > 0$, the conditions of the Lemma 5 hold, so that J is an M-matrix. To establish the hyperbolicity of $\mathbf{x_{\delta v}}$ we need one last lemma.

Lemma 6 *If A is a non-singular M-matrix and B is a strictly positive diagonal matrix, then BA is a non-singular M-matrix.*

Proof: It suffices to show that $(BA)^T$ is an M-matrix. Since A^T is an M-matrix, according to Lemma 5 there is a vector $\mathbf{x} \gg 0$ such that $A^T\mathbf{x} > 0$. Define $\mathbf{y} = D^{-1}\mathbf{x}$. Then $(BA)^T\mathbf{y} = A^T B^{-1}\mathbf{x} > 0$. Using again lemma 5 in the reverse direction the result follows.   ∎

Based on the previous result, the system converges with exponential rate to the fixed point $\mathbf{x_w}$.

5.   Design Trade-offs

The properties of the admission control/resource allocation scheme that we have obtained are asymptotically valid in the limit $\kappa \downarrow 0$. Therefore, they serve as guiding principles in the implementation of the scheme itself, but cannot ensure that the scheme will be effective in any application without adapting the algorithm to each specific application. Therefore, we review the role of each parameter that figures in the application and discuss its effect on the convergence properties of the model. The parameters used in the algorithm are x_{floor}, Δ, $n_{\max}$, κ, and ϵ.

We recall that a new user sets the priority equal to x_{floor}. When arriving into the system, a candidate user reduces the aggregate server capacity available to other users by a factor equal to $(\sum_{\ell \in \mathcal{U}} x_\ell + 1)/(\sum_{\ell \in \mathcal{U}} x_\ell + x_{\text{floor}} + 1)$. As a result, the discontinuity in value of priorities might cause the set of feasible allocations to become empty, which in turn would cause a ramp-up of priorities and, eventually, the drop-off of all the users' sessions when priorities reach their upper bound. Therefore, a small value of x_{floor} is desirable, because it would reduce the shock due to a new arrival. Yet, there are drawbacks to choosing a small x_{floor}, because it prolongs the set-up phase. By reducing x_{floor} by a factor K, we add a time approximately equal to $\ln(K)/\epsilon$ to the set-up phase. Similarly, choosing a high value of $n_{\max}$ increases the likelihood of admission of the candidate user, but at the same time increases the duration of the set-up time.

	Advantages	Disadvantages
x_{floor}	shorter set-up	disrupts admitted users
$n_{\max}$	better chances of admission	longer set-up phase
κ	faster convergence	far from asymptotic regime
Δ	assumptions on noise not satisfied	faster convergence
ϵ	faster convergence	system admits fewer users

Table 12.1. Design trade-offs in the choice of the parameters. The advantages and disadvantages are relative to the case of large values for the parameters.

To assess the role of the sampling interval Δ and of the parameter κ, it is useful to consider the time scales of the limit process. If an event such as the admission of a candidate user occurs at time t in the ODE limit, it occurs approximately at the $\lfloor t/\kappa \rfloor$-th iteration in the original process with step size κ. In the "physical time" of the original process, the event occurs at time $\Delta \times T/\kappa$. Therefore, a smaller interval Δ seems desirable, since it reduces the set-up phase, and so does an increase in the step size κ. The basic disadvantage in reducing Δ is that the QoS measurement might become subject to noise. Also, we notice that we assumed in our treatment that the time needed to update the priorities is much smaller than the sampling interval. This is often the case when the priorities are updated via an out-of-band control mechanism, or if the interval between updates is equal to several round-trip times. If the two time scales become comparable, the effect of updating delays must be explicitly taken into account into the model.

The main objection to increasing κ is that the quality of the ODE approximation, and therefore the correctness of the algorithm, degrades with the increase in κ.

The parameter ϵ enjoys an intuitive interpretation as the parameter regulating the "soft start" of the candidate users and the "safety margin" of the admitted users. If we increase the value of ϵ, the duration of the set-up phase decreases approximately as $1/\epsilon$. Correspondingly, the safety margin increases as well, which results in higher QoS bounds for admitted flows. As a consequence, a smaller number of users might be admitted into the system.

These fundamental design trade-offs are summarized in Table 12.1, where we list the advantages to increasing each one of the parameters.

6. Conclusions and Future Research

We have presented an admission control and resource allocation scheme for QoS-sensitive applications. We articulated our framework based on a design principle: the system under consideration should allow the implementation of a *priority interface* between users and resources. The resource allocation at the server is determined only by the values of the priorities of the users accessing the element. In the proposal, neither do users have access to nor do they have control on the internal operations of the server. Such an interface has the advantage of allowing users to control heterogeneous network elements, as long as they can be controlled through priorities. Examples of such systems abound both in wireline and wireless networks.

We are interested in soft guarantees; i.e., the expected QoS received by a user is above his minimal requested bound for the session duration. The algorithm is measurement-based and end-to-end. With respect to the first property, users measure their QoS over a time interval. Moreover, measurements are taken on an end-to-end basis. The QoS metrics are observed not at the level of the individual network element, but along the whole route traversed by packets. Such measurements are usually easier to obtain than measurements taken at the level of the single network element. For example, information obtained from acknowledgement packets to estimate service delay and packet loss is currently used in congestion-control mechanisms such as TCP.

In order to prove properties on the correctness of our approach, we require only a weak assumption of the relationship between measured QoS q_i and the relative priority ϕ_i assigned to a generic user i; namely, that q_i be an increasing function of ϕ_i. This monotonicity assumption can be justified either by showing its validity within a specific model, or on a phenomenological basis; i.e., by validating it in the physical setting of interest.

We plan to extend this work in several directions. The first is methodological. In the past, stochastic approximation methods have been used in the queueing theory literature to optimize the performance of a queueing system with respect to some design parameter, such as the capacity of a server. In many applications, it would be useful to develop methods that use stochastic approximation not only for system design or capacity planning, but also to characterize the dynamic behavior of the QoS metrics of a queueing system, in the spirit of the ODE method of Ljung and Kushner (Kushner, 1997). These results can be very useful to show that the QoS degrades below a certain threshold for the users, or to prove that a specific control mechanism results in a measured QoS that exhibit properties such as "social optimality".

A second direction for research is in the area of applications. The algorithm we have proposed relies only on the existence of a priority interface and, indirectly, on the ability of the network elements to allocate resources to each user based on these priorities. This generality allows us to experiment with potential network settings. In particular, the issue of service guarantees in *heterogeneous* networks is of particular interest. These are networks comprised of servers, wireline, wireless networks. Implementing admission control algorithms that depend on domain-specific signaling or scheduling could be very challenging. In our proposal, all the network elements would be based on a priority-based scheduling algorithm. Although these algorithm differ in their of which GPS is an approximation and on the implementation of a priority interface between users and resources on the control plane.

Acknowledgments

The first author would like to thank Samer Takriti (IBM Research) for suggesting a streamlined proof of Theorem 3, and an anonymous referee for providing insightful comments.

Notes

1. This is an engineering counterpart of that mythical creature, the "benevolent dictator" concocted by microeconomists.

References

N. Bambos. Toward power-sensitive network architectures in wireless communications: concepts, issues, and design aspects. *IEEE Personal Communications*, 5(3):50–59, 1998.

N. Bambos, S.C. Chen, and G.J. Pottie. Radio link admission algorithms for wireless networks with power control and active link quality protection. In *Proceedings of IEEE INFOCOM 1995*, 1995.

A. Berman and R.J. Plemmons. *Nonnegative Matrices in the Mathematical Sciences*. Academic Press, 1979.

G. Bianchi, A. Capone, and C. Petrioli. Throughput analysis of end-to-end measurement-based admission control in ip. In *Proceeding of IEEE INFOCOM 2000*, Tel Aviv, 2000.

J. Bruno, J. Brustoloni, E. Gabber, B. Ozden, and A. Silberschatz. Retrofitting quality of service into a time-sharing operating system. In *Proceedings of the 1999 USENIX Annual Technical Conference*, 1999.

S.C Chen, N. Bambos, and G.J. Pottie. On distributed power control for radio networks. In *Proceedings of ICC/SUPERCOMM 1994*, 1994.

G.L. Choudhury, D.M. Lucantoni, and W. Whitt. On the effectiveness of effective bandwidths for admission control in ATM networks. In *ITC*, volume 14, pages 411–420, 1994.

C. Courcoubetis, G. Kesidis, A. Ridder, J. Walrand, and R.R. Weber. Admission control and routing in ATM networks using inferences from measured buffer occupancy. *IEEE Transactions on Communications*, 43(2-4):1778–1784, 1995.

V. Elek, G. Karlsson, and R. Ronngren. Admission control based on end-to-end measurements. In *Proceedings of IEEE INFOCOM 2000*, 2000.

A.I. Elwalid and D. Mitra. Effective bandwidth of general markovian traffic sources and admission control of high speed networks. *IEEE/ACM Transactions on Networking*, 1(3):329–343, 1993.

G.J. Foschini and Z. Miljanic. A simple distributed autonomous power control algorithm and its convergence. *IEEE Transactions on Vehicular Technology*, 42(4):641–646, 1993.

R.J. Gibbens, F.P. Kelly, and P.B. Key. A decision-theoretic approach to call admission control. *IEEE Journal on Selected Areas in Communications*, 13(6), 1995.

R.J. Gibbens and F.P. Kelly. Measurement-based connection admission control. In *15th International Teletraffic Congress Proceedings*, 1997.

M. Grossglauser and D. Tse. A framework for robust measurement-based admission control. *IEEE/ACM Transactions on Networking*, 7(3):293–309, 1999.

I.B.M. *Autonomic Computing: IBM's Perspective on the State of Information Technology.* available at http://www.research.ibm.com/autonomic/manifesto/.

S. Jamin, P. Danzig, S. Shenker, and L. Zhang. A measurement-based admission control algorithm for integrated services packet networks. *IEEE/ACM Transactions on Networking*, 5(1):56–70, 1997.

S. Jamin, S. Shenker, and P. Danzig. Comparison of measurement-based admission control algorithms for controlled-load service. In *Proceeding of IEEE INFOCOM '97*, 1997.

V. Kanodia and E.W.Knightly. Multi-class latency-bounded web services. In *Proceedings of IEEE/IFIP IWQoS 2000*, 2000.

F. P. Kelly, P. B. Key, and S. Zachary. Distributed admission control. *IEEE Journal on Selected Areas in Communications*, 18, 2000.

H.K. Khalil. *Nonlinear Systems*. Prentice-Hall, NJ, 1996.

H. J. Kushner and G. G. Yin. *Stochastic Approximation Algorithms and Applications*. Springer-Verlag, NY, 1997.

K. Li and S. Jamin. A measurement-based admission-controlled web server. In *Proceeding of IEEE INFOCOM 2000*, Tel Aviv, 2000.

Chapter 13

PAQM: PRO-ACTIVE QUEUE MANAGEMENT FOR INTERNET CONGESTION CONTROL

Seungwan Ryu
Department of Industrial Engineering
University at Buffalo (SUNY)
Buffalo, NY14260-2050
sryu@eng.buffalo.edu

Christopher Rump
Department of Industrial Engineering
University at Buffalo (SUNY)
Buffalo, NY14260-2050
crump@eng.buffalo.edu

Abstract   We argue that active queue management (AQM) based congestion control should be adaptive to dynamically changing traffic. We outline requirements for this adaptivity in what we call *proactive* queue management. We propose the Pro-Active Queue Management (PAQM) scheme, which can provide proactive congestion avoidance and control using an adaptive congestion indicator and control function for a wide range of traffic environments. PAQM stabilizes the queue length around a desired level while giving smooth and low packet loss rates independent of the traffic load. We introduce and analyze a feedback control model of TCP/AQM dynamics, and use this to build a discretized control implementation of the PAQM method. A simulation study with a wide range of realistic traffic conditions suggests that PAQM outperforms other AQM algorithms such as Random Early Detection (RED) (Floyd, 1993), Random Early Marking (REM) (Low, 1999) and Proportional-Integral (PI) controller (Hollot, 2001b).

Keywords: Congestion Control, Active Queue management (AQM), Random Early Detection (RED), Proactive AQM (PAQM), Feedback Control, Proportional-Integral-Derivative (PID) Control.

1.   Introduction

Active queue management (AQM) is a group of FIFO-based queue management mechanisms in a router to support end-to-end congestion control in the Internet. Two main functions are used in AQM: one is the congestion indicator (to detect congestion) and the other is the congestion control function (to avoid and control congestion). Until Random Early Detection (RED) (Floyd, 1993) was proposed by the Internet Engineering Task Force (IETF) for deployment (Braden, 1998), FIFO-based tail drop (TD) was the only AQM mechanism used in the network. The TD mechanism uses the instantaneous queue length as a congestion indicator, and controls congestion by dropping packets when the buffer becomes full. Although simple and easy to implement, TD has two well-known drawbacks, the lock-out and full queue phenomena (Braden, 1998).

One possible solution to overcome the drawbacks of the TD algorithm is to drop packets in the routers before the buffer becomes full so that a source can respond to congestion before buffers overflow. RED achieves this enhanced control by introducing probabilistic early packet dropping. Probabilistic packet dropping is employed in order to avoid a bias against bursty traffic and global synchronization. RED also enhanced the congestion indicator by introducing queue length averaging. In particular, RED uses an exponentially-weighted moving average (EWMA) queue length not only to detect incipient congestion but also to smooth the bursty incoming traffic and its resulting transient congestion.

Following RED, many AQM-based extensions such as SRED (Ott, 1999), BLUE (Feng, 1999a), Adaptive-RED (Feng, 1999b), REM (Low, 1999), etc., have been proposed. In order to control Internet traffic effectively and efficiently, most AQM proposals recommend using the (average) queue length as a congestion indicator. AQM algorithms try to avoid congestion, stabilize queue dynamics and maintain low end-to-end delay using a sophisticated packet drop function based on average queue lengths and other parameters in a router.

However, many AQM proposals have shown severe problems with the (average) queue length as a congestion indicator (Christiansen, 2001; Feng, 1997; Hollot, 2001b; May, 2000; Misra, 2000). More precisely, there exists a mismatch between the *macroscopic* (or long-term) design goals of using the average queue length and the *microscopic* (or short-term) behavior of the actual queue length (Feng, 1997; Hollot, 2001b; May, 2000; Misra, 2000).

Since, these algorithms only use the (average) buffer occupancy to measure the severity of congestion, the congestion detection and control is *reactive* to current or past congestion not *proactive* to incipient congestion. For example, the congestion detection method in RED can detect and respond to long-term traffic patterns using exponentially weighted average queue lengths. However, it is unable to detect incipient congestion caused by short-term traffic load changes. In this case, the implicit congestion notification fed back to end hosts by a packet drop may be the wrong control signal, and can possibly make the congestion situation worse. Moreover, the *insensitivity* of the congestion indicator to the changing traffic load may cause *unfair* packet dropping among connections.

As a result, AQM parameter configuration has been a main design issue since RED was first proposed in 1993. Each modified AQM proposal that followed has been designed for a particular traffic condition, not for realistic IP traffic nor a heterogeneous traffic environment. In addition, it has been reported that 90% of Internet traffic is TCP traffic, and $50 - 70\%$ of TCP traffic consists of short-lived web-like *mice* traffic (Christiansen, 2001) that did not exist in 1993. We conjecture that the parameter configuration problem arises mainly from the gap between the design goals of AQM and the characteristics of real IP traffic.

To address these problems, it is necessary for an AQM mechanism to have a more efficient congestion indicator and control function. To avoid or control congestion *proactively* before it becomes a problem, both the congestion indicator and control function of an AQM should be adaptive to changes in the traffic environment such as in the amount of traffic, the fluctuation of traffic load, the nature of traffic, etc.

In Section 2, we show the relationship between a congestion indicator and the input traffic load. We also give requirements for an AQM control to be adaptive to dynamically changing traffic environments. Then we propose the *Pro-Active Queue Management (PAQM)* mechanism, which can detect incipient congestion as well as control congestion effectively and proactively. The goals of PAQM are to control congestion proactively, to stabilize the queue length around a desired level and to give smooth and low packet loss rates to each flow.

To achieve these goals, an efficient congestion prediction and control capability is important. In section 3, we use a classical proportional-integral-derivative (PID) feedback control method in designing PAQM not only to have the anticipatory congestion detection and control capability but also to achieve a long-term control performance such as acceptable queue length behavior (or equivalently delay), acceptable packet loss rates or high link utilization.

In Section 4, we verify the performance of PAQM under various traffic environments and compare the performance to other AQM algorithms via simulation using the ns-2 simulator (NS-2 simulator). Section 5 provides a summary of our conclusions and suggests directions for future study.

2.   Pro-Active Queue Management (PAQM)

In this section, we first show the relationship between the input traffic load and the two main functions of AQM algorithms: the congestion indicator and the control function. Then we give requirements for an AQM control to be adaptive to dynamically changing traffic. Finally, we propose PAQM for adaptive congestion indication and control.

2.1   Adaptive congestion indicator and control function

Since each transmission control protocol (TCP) source controls its sending rate through window size[1] adjustment (Stevens, 1997; Alman, 1999), the aggregate input traffic load (the offered load), λ_t, is proportional to the total window size of all connections, W, i.e., $W \propto \lambda_t(R + Q_t/C)$, where R is the average propagation delay of all connections, Q_t/C is the queueing delay at a router, C is the output link capacity and Q_t is the current queue length. Because of limited traffic processing capacity at a router, e.g., finite buffer size and output link capacity, not all the offered traffic load λ_t is carried at a router. Thus the *carried traffic load*, λ_t, will be fraction of offered traffic load that is not dropped at a router, i.e., $\lambda_t = \lambda_t(1 - P_d)$, where, P_d is the packet drop probability. Hence,

$$W = \lambda_t(1 - P_d)(R + Q_t/C), \quad \text{and} \tag{13.1}$$

$$P_d = \begin{cases} 1 - \dfrac{W}{\lambda_t(R + Q_t/C)} & \text{, if } \lambda_t \geq C \\ 0 & \text{, otherwise.} \end{cases} \tag{13.2}$$

In a time-slotted model[2], the current queue size Q_t is a function of current input traffic load λ_t, i.e, $Q_t = (\lambda_t - C)\Delta t + Q_t$ 1, where Δt is the unit length of a time slot. However, the incipient congestion will be a function of the queue length of the next time slot, Q_{t+1}, not a function of Q_t. Therefore, to detect *incipient* congestion *proactively* not *current* congestion *reactively*, the packet drop probability, P_d, should be an increasing function of Q_{t+1} (or equivalently an increasing function of λ_{t+1}). Unfortunately, most AQM algorithms such as RED (Floyd, 1993), REM (Low, 1999), or PI-controller (Hollot, 2001b) use only the past traffic history such as Q_t (or the average queue length $\overline{Q}$) as a congestion indicator. As a result, these AQM algorithms are unable to detect

---

[1]Total number of TCP sessions (or IP packets) outstanding in the network.
[2]In this model, time is divided into small time slots. At the end of each time slot, the queue size, Q_t, and total amount of input traffic, λ_t, is calculated. For example, the simplest time-slotted model is a model that uses packet inter-arrival time as a unit time slot.

incipient congestion adaptively to the traffic load variations. We argue that it is necessary to have an accurate congestion measure, Q_{t+1}, and corresponding control function, $f(Q_{t+1})$, to detect and control congestion proactively.

2.2   Pro-Active Queue Management (PAQM)

We propose PAQM to overcome the reactive congestion control problems of existing AQM algorithms. PAQM can detect incipient congestion as well as current congestion using an adaptive congestion indicator and control function. The goals of PAQM are to control congestion proactively, to stabilize the queue length around a desired level and to give smooth and low packet loss rates to each flow.

For proactive congestion control, PAQM enhances the control function by introducing a predictive traffic measure for the adaptive congestion indication. First, a predicted queue length for the next time slot, $\hat{Q}_{t+1}$, is made based on the measured carried traffic loads of the current and previous time slot, λ_t and $\lambda_{t\ 1}$ (or equivalently Q_t and $Q_{t\ 1}$). More precisely, the current traffic change status, S_t, is obtained from the current queue length change, $\gamma_t = Q_t - Q_{t\ 1}$ via

$$S_t = \begin{cases} 1 & \text{, if } \gamma_t \geq 0 \\ -1 & \text{, otherwise.} \end{cases} \tag{13.3}$$

The tendency of the input traffic of the previous two time-slots, $S = S_t * S_{t\ 1}$, is used to predict the queue length change. If $S = 1$, then this indicates either a monotonic building or draining of queued traffic, in which case the tendency (or changing rate) is $\gamma_t/\gamma_{t\ 1}$ and the predicted amount of change in queued traffic is $\hat{\gamma}_{t+1} = \gamma_t(\gamma_t/\gamma_{t\ 1})$. If $S \neq 1$, then this indicates that the tendency of the input traffic has changed, in which case the predicted amount of change in queued traffic is obtained by linear extrapolating (Astrom, 1995) of the current change in queued traffic, i.e., $\hat{\gamma}_{t+1} = \Delta t(\gamma_t/\Delta t) = \gamma_t$. Thus,

$$\hat{\gamma}_{t+1} = \begin{cases} \gamma_t \dfrac{\gamma_t}{\gamma_{t\ 1}} & \text{, if } S = 1 \\ \gamma_t & \text{, otherwise.} \end{cases} \tag{13.4}$$

Then, a predicted queue length for the next time slot is given by $\hat{Q}_{t+1} = \hat{\gamma}_{t+1} + Q_t$.

To make the queue length agree with a desired level (and to maintain stable link delays as a result), a desired queue length, Q_{ref}, is introduced in PAQM. To ensure each flow has better performance, such as a non-oscillatory transmission rate, PAQM attempts to maintain smooth and low packet loss rates with an enhancement of the control function. To achieve these goals, two measures are obtained for both the current traffic (i.e., Q_t and $Q_{t\ 1}$) and the predicted traffic (i.e., $\hat{Q}_{t+1}$) by comparison with Q_{ref}. These measures represent the amount of surplus/slack traffic. First, Q_t and $Q_{t\ 1}$ are compared with Q_{ref}, and the proportional amount of the current surplus/slack traffic is obtained as

$$Q_{surp1} = \frac{[(Q_t + Q_{t\ 1})/2] - Q_{ref}}{Q_{ref}}. \tag{13.5}$$

Second, the predicted proportional amount of surplus/slack traffic[3], Q_{surp2}, is obtained using $\hat{Q}_{t+1}$ and Q_{ref} via

$$Q_{surp2} = \frac{\hat{Q}_{t+1} - Q_{ref}}{B - Q_{ref}} \tag{13.6}$$

where B is the buffer capacity.

When the current queue length exceeds the reference queue length, $Q_t > Q_{ref}$, the packet drop probability, P_d, is increased either by $\alpha * Q_{surp1}$ when $Q_{t\ 1}$ is greater than Q_{ref}, or by $\alpha * Q_{surp2}$ when $\hat{Q}_{t+1}$ is greater than Q_{ref}, where α is a small constant. On the other hand, when the current queue length is less than the reference queue length, $Q_t < Q_{ref}$, P_d is decreased either by $\alpha * Q_{surp1}$ when $Q_{t\ 1}$ is also less than Q_{ref}, or by $\alpha * Q_{surp2}$ when $\hat{Q}_{t+1}$ is less than Q_{ref}. In this way, PAQM enables the queue length to stay around the desired queue length (Q_{ref}) and the queueing delay to be stable, independent of traffic loads. A pseudo code of PAQM algorithm appears below.

```
if (Qt > Qref)
    if (Qt 1 > Qref)
        Qsurp1 = (((Qt + Qt 1)/2) - Qref)/Qref;
        pd := α * Qsurp1;
    else if (Q̂t+1 > Qref)
        Qsurp2 = (Q̂t+1 - Qref)/(B - Q)ref);
        pd := α * Qsurp2;
else
    if (Qt 1 < Qref)
        Qsurp1 = (((Qt + Qt 1)/2) - Qref)/Qref;
        pd := α * Qsurp1;
    else if Q̂t+1 < Qref
        Qsurp2 = (Q̂t+1 - Qref)/(B - Q)ref);
        pd := α * Qsurp2;
```

---

[3]The current amount of surplus/slack traffic, $[(Q_t + Q_{t\ 1})/2]\ Q_{ref}$, is normalized by Q_{ref} for better scaling of the discrete implementation of the PI control part. The amount of the predicted surplus or slack traffic, $\hat{Q}_{t+1}\ Q_{ref}$, is normalized by the surplus buffer capacity $B\ Q_{ref}$ for better scaling of the discrete implementation of the D control part. (See section 3.4)

3. Control theoretic design of an AQM algorithm

In this section we first introduce a feedback control modelling approach for TCP/AQM dynamics (Hollot, 2001b). For the implementation of a control-theoretic AQM model, we introduce a discretized approach for the TCP/AQM model. We then analyze RED and PI-controller in terms of feedback control. Finally, we propose a digital implementation of our PAQM controller.

3.1 Feedback control and TCP congestion control with AQM

TCP congestion control dynamics with an AQM scheme can be modelled as a feedback control system (Fig. 13.1). In this model, the feedback control system consists of: 1) a desired queue length at a router (i.e., *reference input*) denoted by Q_{ref}, 2) the queue length at a router as a plant variable (i.e., a *controlled variable*) denoted by Q, 3) a *plant* which represents a combination of subsystems such as TCP sources, routers and TCP receivers that send, process, and receive TCP packets respectively, 4) an *AQM controller* which controls the packet arrival rate to the router queue by generating a packet drop probability, p_d, as a control signal, 5) a *feedback signal* which is a sampled system output (i.e., queue length) used to obtain the error term, $Q_{ref} - Q$.

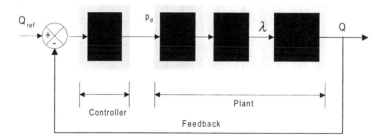

Figure 13.1. Feedback control modeling of TCP congestion control with an AQM algorithm

In (Misra, 2000), a system of nonlinear differential equations for TCP/AQM dynamics was developed using fluid flow analysis that ignores the TCP time-out mechanism. Then in (Hollot, 2001a), a linearized TCP/AQM dynamic model was developed and analyzed especially for TCP/RED dynamics in terms of (feedback) control theory. There, the forward-path transfer function of the plant, $P(s) = P_{TCP}(s) \cdot P_{queue}(s) \cdot e^{-sR_0}$, was given by

$$P(s) = \left(\frac{\frac{R_0 C^2}{2N^2}}{s + \frac{2N}{R_0^2 C}} \right) \cdot \left(\frac{\frac{N}{R_0}}{s + \frac{1}{R_0}} \right) \cdot e^{-sR_0} \qquad (13.7)$$

where N is a load factor (number of TCP connections), R_0 is a round trip time, C is the link capacity and e^{-sR_0} is the time delay.

3.2   The RED controller

Since the forward-path transfer function of TCP flows has two non-zero poles, it is a type 0 system (Kuo, 1995). Thus there always exists constant steady-state error for the step-function input. Since $\lim_{s \to 0} P(s) = [(R_0 C^3)/(4N^2)] =: K$, the steady-state error of the forward-path transfer function is $e_{ss} = R/(1 + K)$, where R is the reference input to eliminate this constant steady-state error.

RED attempts to eliminate the steady-state error by introducing the exponentially weighted moving average (EWMA) of queue lengths (or of the error terms[4] (Aweya, 2001a)) as an integral (I)-control to the forward-path transfer function. However, since RED introduces a range of reference input values, i.e., any queue length between two thresholds, min_{th} and max_{th}, rather than an unique reference input in I-control, the TCP/RED model shows oscillatory system dynamics. Moreover, a very small smoothing weight factor ($w_Q = 0.002$ or $1/512$) for the current queue length in the calculation of the EWMA queue length was recommended in (Floyd, 1993). This parameter setting creates an effect of large integral time in I-control, and may be accompanied by a large overshoot (Kuo, 1995). As a result, RED shows oscillatory queue length dynamics and gives poor performance under a wide range of traffic environments.

3.3   Proportional-Integral (PI) controller

If a unique reference input is introduced to an AQM controller, the steady-state error of the TCP dynamics with an AQM controller can be eliminated. Thus, the Proportional-Integral (PI)-controller with a constant desired queue length has been proposed in (Hollot, 2001b). The idea behind the PI-controller is to make the queue length agree with the desired queue length, Q_{ref}, by introducing an I-control to the AQM. Using the linearized TCP/AQM dynamics, the PI-controller has been proposed not only to improve responsiveness of the TCP/AQM dynamics but also to stabilize the router queue length around Q_{ref}. The latter can be achieved by means of integral (I)-control, while the former can be achieved by means of proportional (P)-control using the instantaneous queue length rather than using the EWMA queue length. The resulting PI-controller is capable of eliminating the steady-state error regardless of the load level. The discretized packet drop probability at time $t = kT$ (Hollot, 2001b)

---

[4]The filtering of the queue length is equivalent to the filtering (integration) of the error terms.

is

$$p(kT) = p((k-1)T) + a\delta_Q(kT) - b\delta_Q((k-1)T) \qquad (13.8)$$

where $f_s = 1/T$ is the sampling frequency, which is recommended to be $10 - 20$ times the link speed (Hollot, 2001b), a and b are constants and $\delta_Q = Q - Q_{ref}$ is a deviation of the queue length from the desired queue length, Q_{ref}. The recommended design rules (Hollot, 2001b) are

$$w_g = \frac{2N}{(R^+)^2 C}, \quad K_{PI} = w_g \left| \frac{(\frac{jw_g}{P_{queue}} + 1)}{\frac{(R+C)^3}{(2N)^2}} \right|, \qquad (13.9)$$

where w_g is the unity-gain crossover frequency and K_{PI} is a PI-control gain.

In the PI controller, the control signal from the controller, $u(t)$, is a differential equation

$$u(t) = K_P \left[e(t) + \frac{1}{T_I} \int_0^t e(\tau)d\tau \right], \qquad (13.10)$$

where $e(t) = Q_t - Q_{ref}$ is the error term, K_P is a proportional gain and T_I is the integral time. From (13.10) we can obtain a first-order difference equation for the digital implementation of the PI controller as

$$u(k) = K_P \left[e(k) + \frac{\Delta t}{T_I} \sum_{i=0}^{k} e(i) \right],$$

where $k = \lfloor t/\Delta t \rfloor$ is the number of discrete sampling times, and $u(i)$ and $e(i)$ represent the discretized control signal and the error term at time $t = i\Delta t$, respectively. Then, from the discretized velocity PI-control (Isemann, 1989), the discretized instantaneous control signal, $\Delta u(k) = u(k) - u(k-1)$, and the control signal at time k, $u(k)$, are

$$\Delta u(k) = K_P \left\{ [e(k) - e(k-1)] + \frac{\Delta t}{T_I} e(k-1) \right\},$$

$$u(k) = u(k-1) + K_P e(k) - K_P \left(1 - \frac{\Delta t}{T_I} \right) e(k-1). \quad (13.11)$$

In a digital implementation of the PI controller (Hollot, 2001b), each packet is dropped (or marked) with a probability updated in every fixed time interval T. From (13.11), the packet drop parameters in (13.8) are $a = K_P$ and $b = K_P(1 - \Delta t/T_I)$.

3.4 PAQM-controller

The goals of our PAQM-controller are to avoid and control congestion proactively by anticipating incipient congestion, to stabilize the queue length at a router around a desired queue length, Q_{ref}, and to provide acceptable quality of service (QoS) such as bounded (maximum) queueing delay, higher link utilization, etc., under a wide range of network traffic situations. The PAQM controller takes advantages of the anticipatory capability of derivative (D)-control for prediction and reduction of upcoming error as well as the capability of the PI control for elimination of steady state error. A simple block diagram of the PAQM-controller is shown in Figure 13.2.

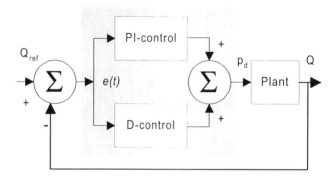

Figure 13.2.   A simple block diagram of the PAQM-controller as a PID-controller

For the digital implementation of PAQM-controller, the traffic history of two recent time slots is used for two reasons: 1) the dynamic changes of network traffic with time and 2) the recent observation of Poisson-like network traffic behavior under heavy traffic loads[5] (Cao, 2001a; Cao, 2001b). To stabilize the queue length to the desired level, Q_{ref}, a velocity PID controller (Isemann, 1989) is used in the discretized PAQM-controller. The rationale for using a velocity PID controller is that the velocity PID controller updates the control signal recursively by summing the current rate of change of the control signal, $\Delta u(k)$, and the previous control term, $u(k-1)$. Also, a velocity PID-controller can provide better control performance from its anticipatory control nature.

The first part of the PAQM controller is the *Proportional-Integral (PI)* control. The velocity control implementation of this PI-control is

$$u(k) = K_P \left[e(k) + \frac{\Delta t}{T_I} \sum_{i=k-2}^{k-1} e(i) \right].$$

Since T_I consists of two timeslots ($T_I = 2\Delta t$), the instantaneous PI-control signal, $\Delta u(k) = u(k) - u(k-1)$, is

$$\Delta u(k) = K_P \left\{ e(k) - \frac{1}{2} \left[e(k-1) + e(k-3) \right] \right\}.$$

Since $e(k-1) + e(k-3) = (Q_{k\;1} - Q_{ref}) + (Q_{k\;3} - Q_{ref}) = Q_{k\;1} + Q_{k\;3} - 2Q_{ref}$,

$$\Delta u(k) = K_P \left\{ e(k) - \left[\frac{Q_{k\;1} + Q_{k\;3}}{2} - Q_{ref} \right] \right\}. \tag{13.12}$$

Since the current queue length, Q_k, and at most two recent queue lengths, $Q_i, i = k-1, k-2$, can be used for the integration (or summation) of errors, (13.12) is modified to use at most two recent queue lengths rather than using $Q_{k\;3}$ for a discretized velocity PI control. In particular, if both Q_k and $Q_{k\;1}$ are greater than Q_{ref} (or less than Q_{ref}), the average surplus (or slack) amount of traffic is calculated using the *Trapezoidal-Integral rule* (Kuo, 1995). The packet drop probability p_d is adjusted proportional to the amount of surplus or slack traffic. In the case of surplus traffic, the packet drop probability becomes aggressive by increasing p_d proportional to the amount of surplus traffic. In the case of slack traffic, the packet drop probability becomes conservative by decreasing p_d proportional to the amount of slack traffic. The PI control equation is

$$p_d(k) = p_d(k-1) + \alpha \left[\frac{Q_k + Q_{k\;1}}{2} - Q_{ref} \right] \tag{13.13}$$

where α is a control gain. For better scaling of the discrete implementation of the PAQM, the current amount of surplus/slack traffic, $[(Q_t + Q_{t\;1})/2] - Q_{ref}$, is normalized by Q_{ref}. This value represents the fraction of the amount of current surplus/slack traffic to the desired queue level. Thus, the normalized PI control equation is

$$Q_{surpl} = \frac{[(Q_t + Q_{t\;1})/2] - Q_{ref}}{Q_{ref}} \tag{13.14}$$

The second part of the PAQM controller is the *Derivative (D)* control. In a discretized velocity D-control,

$$\begin{aligned}
\Delta u(k) &= \frac{K_P K_D}{\Delta t} \left[e(k) - 2e(k-1) + e(k-2) \right] \\
&= K_P K_D \left[\frac{e(k) - e(k-1)}{\Delta t} - \frac{e(k-1) - e(k-2)}{\Delta t} \right]
\end{aligned}$$

where K_P and K_D are a proportional gain and a derivative time, respectively. From the relation between a differential equation and a difference equation,

$$\frac{d^2 e(t)}{dt^2} \approx \frac{e(k) - 2e(k-1) + e(k-2)}{(\Delta t)^2}$$

and

$$\Delta u(k) \approx K_P K_D \left[\Delta t \frac{d^2}{dt^2} e(t) \right].$$

Then $\Delta t \frac{d^2}{dt^2} e(t)$ represents the predicted amount of an acceleration of changes on $e(t)$ in time Δt ahead, i.e., $e(t + \Delta t) = e(t) + K_P K_D [\Delta t \frac{d^2}{dt^2} e(t)]$. Then the tendency (acceleration) of the input traffic is obtained from the discretized implementation of a velocity D-control using traffic history. K_D is the unit length of a timeslot, i.e., $K_D = \Delta t$. Hence,

$$\begin{aligned}
\Delta u(k) &= K_P K_D \left[\frac{e(k) - 2e(k-1) + e(k-2)}{\Delta t} \right] \\
&= K_P [Q_k - 2Q_{k\ 1} + Q_{k\ 2}]
\end{aligned} \tag{13.15}$$

Since the tendency of the change on $e(t)$ is $\gamma_k / \gamma_{k\ 1}$ in (13.4), the predicted error for the next time slot, $\Delta t \frac{d^2}{dt^2} e(t)$, and the incipient congestion indicator, i.e., the predicted queue length for the next time slot, $\hat{Q}_{k+1}$, can also be obtained practically for both cases of $S = 1$ and $S \neq 1$ using (13.4). If $S = 1$,

$$\begin{aligned}
\Delta t \frac{d^2}{dt^2} e(t) \approx \Delta u(k) &= \frac{e(k) - 2e(k-1) + e(k-2)}{\Delta t} \\
&= \frac{Q_k - 2Q_{k\ 1} + Q_{k\ 2}}{\Delta t} = \left(\gamma_k \frac{\gamma_k}{\gamma_{k\ 1}} \right) \frac{1}{\Delta t}
\end{aligned}$$

If $S \neq 1$, the predicted error for the next time slot in the PAQM controller is the same as the linear extrapolation method (Astrom, 1995).

With the above two cases of the velocity D-control implementation, the PAQM controller is able to give a more accurate estimate of the predicted error and generate a more accurate control signal for the next time slot. The predicted queue length for the next time slot is $\hat{Q}_{k+1} = \hat{\gamma}_{k+1} + Q_k$ and the corresponding predicted error is $\hat{e}(k+1) = \hat{Q}_{k+1} - Q_{ref}$. Then the D-control equation is

$$p_d(k) = p_d(k-1) + \alpha [\hat{Q}_{k+1} - Q_{ref}]$$

where α is a control gain. For better scaling of the discrete implementation of PAQM, the predicted amount of surplus or slack traffic in the next time slot, $\hat{e}(k+1) = \hat{Q}_{k+1} - Q_{ref}$, is normalized by the surplus buffer capacity, $B - Q_{ref}$. Since the normalization factor, $B - Q_{ref}$, represents the buffer capacity for absorbing the transient surplus bursty traffic without losses, the normalized value represents the fraction of the amount of surplus/slack traffic to the surplus buffer capacity. The normalized D-control equation is

$$p_d(k) = p_d(k-1) + \alpha \left[\frac{\hat{Q}_{k+1} - Q_{ref}}{B - Q_{ref}} \right] \qquad (13.16)$$

4.   Simulation study

In this section, we compare the performance of the PAQM algorithm with other AQM algorithms such as RED (Floyd, 1993), REM (Low, 1999) and PI controller (Hollot, 2001b) under packet drop mode. This comparison is done via simulation over a wide range of traffic conditions using the ns-2 simulator (NS-2 simulator).

4.1   Simulation setup

We use a simple bottleneck network topology as shown in Figure 13.3. The network consists of two routers, nc0 and nc1, with 9 TCP/Reno sources and 9 logically connected destinations. These 9 pairs of sources and destinations are connected to nc0 and nc1 respectively. All TCP connections are connected to the routers, nc0 and nc1, with link speeds of 30Mbps. The propagation delay between TCP source i (srci) and nc0 as well as between nc1 and destination i (desti) is $5i$ ms, $i = 1, \ldots, 9$. The bottleneck link between nc0 and nc1 is assumed to have a link speed of 10Mbps and a propagation delay of 10ms. Thus, the logically connected source and destination pairs are connected with round-trip propagation delays ranging from 40ms to 200ms. All sources and destinations are assumed to use TD queue management with sufficient buffer capacity. The buffer at the bottleneck link uses an AQM algorithm and has capacity of 300 packets, which is twice the bandwidth-delay product (BDP)[6].

We consider two types of traffic flows: *elephants* (long-lived FTP flows) and *mice* (short-lived flows). There are n FTP *elephant* flows connected to each TCP source. Also, there are a total number of 50 short-lived *mice* flows are at the sources with 1 second of average life time. Each packet is assumed to have an average size of 1000 bytes. With this simulation environment we examine the performance of PAQM, and compare with other AQM algorithms such as RED (Floyd, 1993), REM (Low, 1999) and PI controller (Hollot, 2001b).

In RED, recommended parameter values (RED webpage) are used. In REM, we use the parameter values recommended in (Low, 2000). In PI controller, we use the parameters a, b, w_g and T obtained from using the recommended de-

---

[6]Since the average propagation delay is $120ms$, BDP ($120ms$ $10Mbps$) is 150 packets.

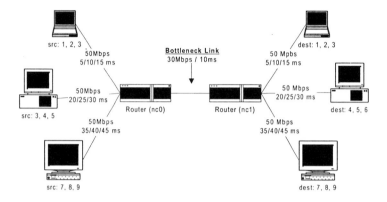

Figure 13.3.   Simulation network topology

sign rule (13.9). From the simulation setup, we set N and R^+ to 90 and 280ms in (13.9), respectively, so that $w_g = 1.8367$ and $f_s = 1/T = 10 * w_g/(2\pi) = 2.9232\text{Hz}$ follow from the recommended design rule[7]. Then, from (13.11), $a = K_P = 1.441 * 10^{-3}$ and $b = K_P(1 - \Delta t/T_I) \approx 1.441 * 10^{-3}$. In PAQM, α is set to $B * 10^{-5} = 0.003$. For the digital implementation of REM, the PI controller and PAQM, the sampling frequency (f_s) is set to 10Hz ($= 35 * w_g/(2\pi)$) rather than 2.9232Hz ($10 * w_g/(2\pi)$) for better digital implementation[8]. Hence, the unit length of a time-slot (T) is the a half of the minimum RTT value ($\min RTT/2 = 100\text{ms}$[9], i.e., 10Hz). Because RED updates control parameters at every packet arrival, it is implemented approximately with the link speed. A summary of the parameter settings of each AQM algorithm is shown in Table 13.1.

We study three different traffic scenarios to examine the performance and the adaptability of PAQM and other AQM algorithms to various traffic situations.

---

[7]We set these parameters under assumptions that the traffic load is at a medium level and the desired queue length, Q_{ref}, is 200 packets. Specifically, $N = 90$ represents the initial number of FTP flows and $R^+ = 280ms$ is sum of the average propagation delay ($120ms$) and the desired queueing delay ($160ms$). Also f_s is assumed to be 10 times $w_g/(2\pi)$ in (Hollot, 2001b).

[8]More frequent sampling gives better digital approximation of a continuous time control system, and it is recommended that the sampling frequency should be more than 20 times the natural frequency (Franklin, 1998), here we use 10Hz.

[9]If we set $Q_{ref} = 200$, then the mean queueing delay is 160ms. Since RTT is sum of queueing delay and the propagation delay, minimum RTT is 200ms.

AQM algorithms	parameters
RED	$w_Q = 0.002, max_p = 0.1, max_{th} = 200, min_{th} = 70$
REM	$\alpha = 0.1, \gamma = 0.01, \phi = 1.001, Q_{eb} = 200$
PI-controller	$a = 1.441 \quad 10^{-3}, b = 1.441 \quad 10^{-3}, Q_{ref} = 200$
PAQM	$\alpha = 0.003, Q_{ref} = 200$

Table 13.1.   A summary of parameter setting of each AQM algorithms

4.2   Simulation I: Bursty FTP traffic

In this experiment, we study the response of the AQM algorithms to a sudden change of traffic load in the presence of long-lived persistent FTP flows only. Each source generates $n = 20$ FTP flows. The simulation begins with 5 sources generating $5n = 100$ FTP flows. To study the impact of sudden increase/decrease of the traffic load on the performance of AQM algorithms, 4 more sources are added creating 80 additional FTP flows in the time interval $[50.0, 100.0]$ seconds. Thus, the maximum number of FTP flows is $9n = 180$ in the time interval $[50.0, 100.0]$.

Figure 13.4 shows the queue length dynamics of the PAQM, REM, RED and PI controller algorithms. The queue length of PAQM shows stable dynamics around the desired queue length, $Q_{ref} = 200$ packets, impervious to the traffic load change. The queue length with REM returns to a low level shortly after the traffic load change to reach the philosophy of REM, i.e., *match rate, clear buffer*. The queue length with RED stays around $max_{th} = 200$ packets. Thus, RED behaves like tail-drop (TD) with a buffer capacity max_{th} in time $[50.0, 100.0]$ as pointed out in (Ott, 1999). The queue length dynamics under the PI controller fluctuate severely with time because PI controller is very sensitive to the queue length sampling frequency[10].

Figure 13.5 shows the packet loss probabilities of the AQM algorithms. PAQM shows smooth and low packet loss probabilities over time with slightly more packet dropping in the peak time period $[50.0, 100.0]$. PAQM increases and decreases the packet loss probability slightly and adaptively according to the traffic load change. Also, by allowing the queue length to stay around Q_{ref} with acceptable deviation (Fig. 13.4), PAQM prevents unnecessary and/or consecutive packet drops. REM shows quite stable but higher and slightly increasing packet loss probabilities than PAQM. The RED shows packet loss probabilities that are extremely sensitive to the traffic load changes. Hence, packet

---

[10] If we set the sampling frequency 5   10 times higher than recommended value in (Hollot, 2001b), $T = $ 10ms for example, then the PI controller shows quite stable queue length dynamics. However, this increased sampling frequency increases the computational overhead.

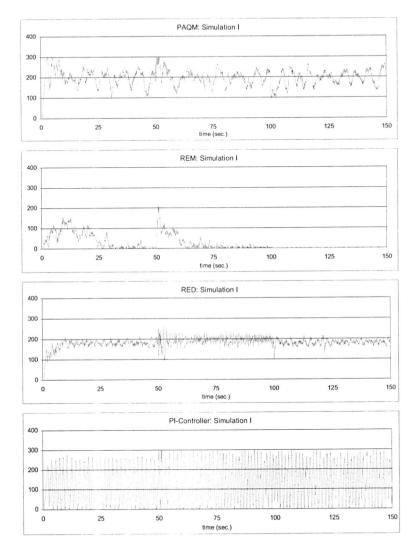

Figure 13.4. Queue lengths of AQM algorithms under traffics only with FTP flows and load level changes: PAQM, REM, RED, and PI controller.

loss probabilities of RED in the time interval [50.0, 100.0] are much higher and bursty than with PAQM or REM. The packet loss probability with PI controller fluctuates severely over time.

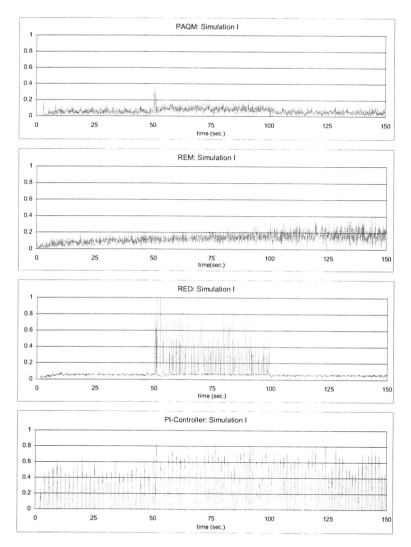

Figure 13.5. Packet loss probabilities of AQM algorithms: PAQM, REM, RED, and PI controller.

In general, high and bursty packet loss involves many packet losses at about the same time. If these packets belong to different flows, these flows experience losses at about the same time. They then may experience global synchronization as a result. On the other hand, if these packets belong to bursty sources, there exists bias against bursty sources. These biases against bursty sources and the global synchronization can be eliminated effectively by achieving stable and low packet loss probabilities over time.

Figure 13.6 shows frequencies of the packet loss probabilities for the AQM algorithms at the sampled times in the time interval $[50.0, 100.0]$. Most packet loss probabilities for PAQM and REM are distributed below 0.2 and 0.3 respectively. Thus, PAQM and REM can effectively remove bias against bursty sources by maintaining smooth and low packet loss probability. In contrast, RED and PI-controller show nonzero frequencies of packet loss probabilities above 0.3. This means that PI-controller and RED show high and bursty (i.e., multiple) packet losses, and thus these algorithms can cause bias against bursty sources and/or global synchronization.

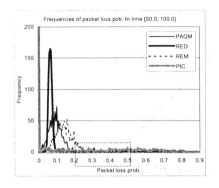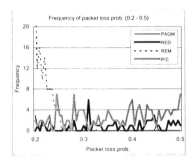

Figure 13.6.   Histogram of frequencies of packet loss probabilities of AQM algorithms.

Figure 13.7 shows the packet loss probability and link utilization of each AQM algorithm under different traffic load levels n, with n ranging from 5 to 40. (Recall that Figures 13.4, 13.5, and 13.6 were for the case $n = 20$.) PAQM shows significantly lower packet loss probabilities than the other AQM algorithms for all traffic load levels. Consequently, the link utilization with PAQM is higher than with REM and PI controller, and nearly the same as RED for all traffic load levels.

4.3   Simulation II: Bursty FTP traffic with mice flows

In this experiment, the impact of the traffic load increase/decrease from simulation I on the performance of an AQM algorithms is examined with a different traffic mix consisting of a number of FTP elephant and mice flows. The simulation scenario is the same as simulation I except that 50 additional mice flows are added throughout the simulation run.

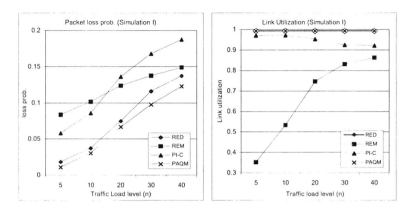

Figure 13.7. Packet loss probabilities and link utilization of AQM algorithms under several different load levels

Figure 13.8 shows the queue length dynamics of the AQM algorithms in simulation II. The queue length of PAQM shows stable dynamics around $Q_{ref} = 200$ packets, independent of the traffic load change. The queue length of REM returns to a low level after the traffic load change. However, the length of the time to return to a low level is much longer than in simulation I because of additional mice flows. The queue length of RED shows similar dynamics to simulation I with larger deviation because of the additional mice flows. The queue length dynamics of PI controller fluctuate severely, similar to simulation I.

Figure 13.9 shows the packet loss probabilities of the AQM algorithms in simulation II. PAQM and REM show packet loss dynamics similar to simulation I but at slightly higher levels. With mice flows, RED shows packet loss probabilities that now fluctuate throughout the entire simulation experiment. The packet loss probability with PI controller fluctuates severely over time as before.

Figure 13.10 shows the packet loss probability and link utilization of each AQM algorithm under different traffic load levels n in simulation II. As in simulation I, PAQM shows lower packet loss probabilities than the other AQM algorithms for all traffic load levels. The link utilization with PAQM is higher than with REM and PI controller, and is almost the same as RED for all traffic load levels.

4.4 Simulation III: increasing traffic scenario

In this experiment, the adaptability of AQM algorithms to increasing traffic load levels with time is examined. The simulation starts with light traffic load consisting of 1 source spawning 20 ($n = 20$) FTP and 5.6 mice flows. Then,

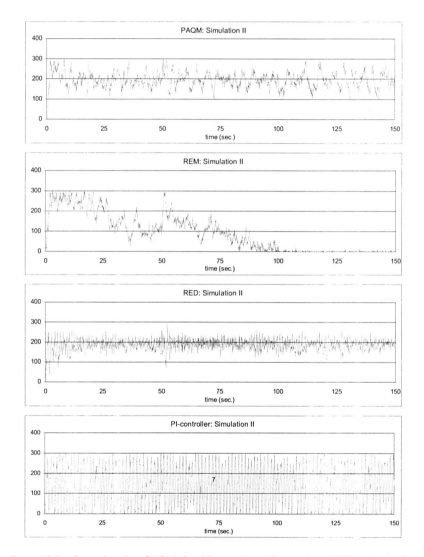

Figure 13.8.   Queue lengths of AQM algorithms under traffic consists of FTP and mice flows and load level changes: PAQM, REM, RED, and PI controller.

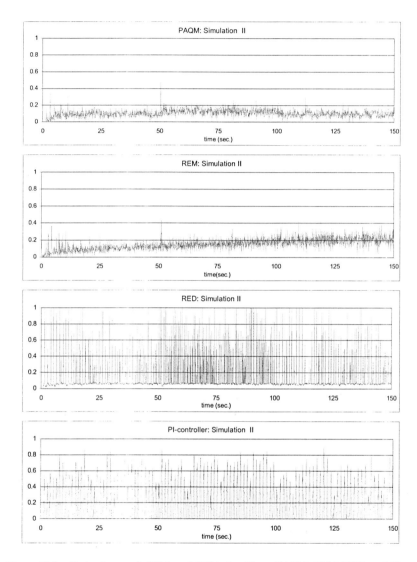

Figure 13.9. Packet loss probabilities of AQM algorithms: PAQM, REM, RED, and PI controller.

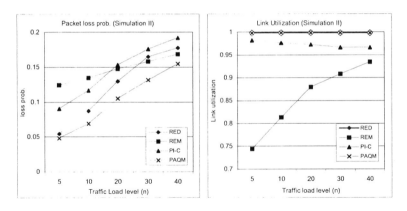

Figure 13.10. Packet loss probabilities and link utilization of AQM algorithms under several different load levels

every 10 seconds an additional source of 20 FTP and 5.6 mice flows is added until time 100.0. Thus, at time 100.0 there will be 9 sources with 230 flows (180 FTP and 50 mice).

Figure 13.11 shows the queue length dynamics of the AQM algorithms in simulation III. The queue length of PAQM shows stable dynamics around the desired queue length, $Q_{ref} = 200$, impervious to the increasing traffic loads with time. The queue length with REM returns to a low level shortly after the traffic load subsides (i.e., after 100.0 seconds). The queue length with RED increases as traffic load increases in time $[0.0, 50.0]$. Thereafter, RED behaves like tail-drop (TD) with a buffer capacity max_{th}. The queue length dynamics under the PI controller fluctuate severely with time, similar to simulations I and II.

Figure 13.12 shows the packet loss probabilities of the AQM algorithms in simulation III. PAQM shows smooth, low and initially increasing packet loss probabilities as the traffic load increases with time. REM shows quite stable but continually increasing packet loss probabilities, higher than PAQM. Since the packet loss probability with RED is extremely sensitive to the traffic load change, packet loss probabilities of RED in the time interval $[50.0, 150.0]$ are much higher than with PAQM or REM. The packet loss probability with PI controller fluctuates severely with time.

Figure 13.13 shows the packet loss probability and link utilization of each AQM algorithm under different traffic load levels n. PAQM shows lower packet loss probabilities than the other AQM algorithms for all traffic load levels. The link utilization with PAQM is higher than with REM and PI controller, and almost the same to that with RED for all traffic load levels.

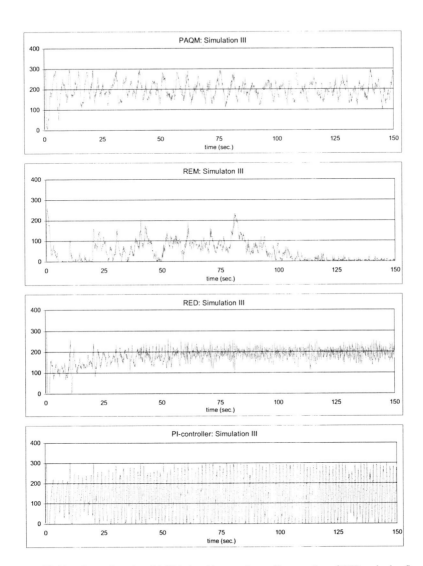

Figure 13.11. Queue lengths of AQM algorithms under traffics consists of FTP and mice flows with increasing loads: PAQM, REM, RED, and PI controller.

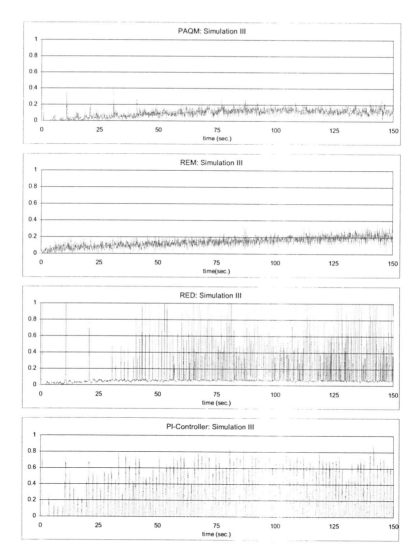

Figure 13.12.   Packet loss probabilities of AQM algorithms: PAQM, REM, RED, and PI controller.

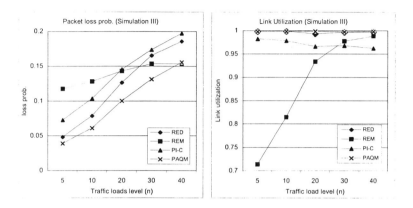

Figure 13.13. Packet loss probabilities and link utilization of AQM algorithms under several different load levels

4.5 Summary of simulation studies

Through simulation study we examine the performance of PAQM algorithm and compare it with other AQM algorithms. REM shows stable packet loss probability in all traffic scenarios. However, the queue length dynamics were very sensitive to the traffic load change, and took a long time to reach the philosophy of REM, i.e., *match rate, clear buffer.* Also REM shows significantly lower link utilization than other AQM algorithms. RED shows TD-like queue management under medium or higher traffic loads as pointed out in (Ott, 1999) with severe oscillation of packet drop probabilities. Also, RED shows severe fluctuation in packet drop probabilities with different traffic mix and/or traffic loads. The PI controller shows severe fluctuation in both queue length dynamics and the packet loss probabilities for all three traffic scenarios.

PAQM shows robust and anticipatory congestion control, independent of the traffic mix, traffic load changes and different traffic load levels. In addition, PAQM shows lower packet loss probability and higher link utilization than other AQM algorithms under various traffic load levels. Thus, PAQM can prevent unnecessary and/or consecutive packet drops, which may cause performance degradation of sources. In summary, PAQM outperforms other AQM algorithms in terms of the queue length dynamics, the packet loss probability and link utilization.

5. Conclusions

It is necessary for an AQM-based congestion control algorithms to control congestion adaptively to a wide range of traffic loads in order to provide acceptable quality of service (QoS) such as bounded stable delay and low packet loss rates. We have outlined requirements for an AQM to avoid and/or control congestion adaptively to dynamically changing traffic loads. These requirements include an ability to detect and control congestion *proactively* based on incipient congestion, not *reactively* based on the current congestion.

We designed an adaptive and proactive AQM algorithm, called *PAQM*, using a classical Proportional-Integral-Derivative (PID) feedback control approach. On the one hand, with the introduction of a derivative (D) control, PAQM can achieve short-term system performance such as fast response and proactive control to the changing traffic load using anticipatory traffic prediction and control. On the other hand, with the introduction of a proportional-integral (PI) control, PAQM also can achieve long-term performance such as the elimination of steady-state error by introducing a desired queue length (Q_{ref}) as a reference input to maintain the mean queue length around.

As a result, PAQM shows robust and adaptive congestion control performance under various traffic situations. In particular, PAQM shows stable queue length dynamics around a desired level with low and smooth packet loss rates independent of the traffic loads and the traffic mix situations. Through simulation we show that PAQM outperforms other AQM algorithms such as RED, REM and the PI controller algorithm in terms of queue length dynamics, the packet loss probability and link utilization.

In terms of practical implementation, PAQM has comparably little computational overhead. In RED, EWMA queue length and the packet drop probability are calculated at every packet arrival while maintaining several parameters such as w_Q, min_{th}, max_{th}, max_p, etc. In REM, EWMA queue length, EWMA packet arrival rate and the packet drop probability are calculated at every packet arrival while maintaining parameters such as α, γ, ϕ, Q_{eb}, etc. In contrast, PAQM and PI-controller can be easily implemented with less sampling frequency (5Hz in this study) compared to the link speed (i.e., 1250Hz) implementation of RED while maintaining fewer parameters than RED and REM. Therefore, the computational complexity and overhead at a router can be reduced significantly using PAQM.

There are several issues for further study. First, to examine the impact of the queue length sampling frequency (or equivalently the length of the time-slot value, $T (= \Delta t)$) on the performance of PAQM, we hope to find a relationship between the optimal T value and the offered traffic load. We are working also to find the optimal control gain, α, and the stability margin of PAQM control through control-theoretic modelling and analysis. Further, we are examining the performance of PAQM in terms of per-flow (or user-centric) performance measures such as per-flow goodput, fairness and per-flow response time. Finally, we will examine the impact of Explicit Congestion Notification (ECN) (Ramakrishnan, 1999) marking on the performance of PAQM.

References

Alman, M., V. Paxson and W. Stevens, "TCP congestion control," *IETF RFC2581*, April 1999.

Astrom, K., and T. Hagglund, *PID Controllers: Theory, Design, and Tuning*, Instrument Society of America, Second edition, 1995.

Athuraliya, S., and S. H. Low, "Optimization flow control, II: Implementation," *submitted for publication*, May 2000.

Aweya, J., M. Ouellette, and D. Y. Montuno, "A Control Theoretic approach to Active Queue Management," *Computer Networks*, 36(2-3), pp. 203-235, 2001.

Aweya, J., M. Ouellette, D. Y. Montuno, and A. Chapman, "A Load Adaptive mechanism for Buffer Management," *Computer Networks*, 36(5-6), pp. 709-728, 2001.

Braden, B., J. Crowcroft, B. Davie, S. Deering, D. Estrin, S. Floyd, V. Jacobson, G. Minshall, C. Partridge, L. Peterson, K. Ramakrishnan, S. Shenker, J. Wroclawski and L. Zhang, "Recommendations on Queue Management and Congestion Avoidance in the Internet," *IETF RFC2309*, April 1998.

Cao, J., W. S. Cleveland, D. Lin, and D. X. Sun, "Internet traffic tends to Poisson and Independence as the load Increases," *Bell Labs Tech. Report*, Bell labs, 2001.

Cao, J., W. S. Cleveland, D. Lin, and D. X. Sun, "On the Nonstationarity of Internet traffic," *Proc. of ACM SIGMETRICS2001*, pp. 101-112, 2001.

Christiansen, M., K. Jaffey, D. Ott, and D. Smith, "Tuning RED for web traffic," *IEEE/ACM Trans. Networking*, 9(3), pp. 249-264, June 2001.

Feng, W., D. Kandlur, D. Saha, and K. Shin, "Techniques for eliminating packet loss in congested TCP/IP networks," *Technical Report CSE-TR-349-97*, University of Michigan, 1997.

Feng, W., D. Kandlur, D. Saha, and K. Shin, "Blue: a new class of active queue management algorithms," *Technical Report CSE-TR-387-99*, University of Michigan, 1999.

Feng, W., D. Kandlur, D. Saha, and K. Shin, "A Self-configuring RED gateway," *Proceedings of INFOCOM'99*, 1999.

Floyd, S., V. Jacobson, "Random Early Detection gateways for congestion avoidance," *IEEE/ACM Trans. Networking*, 1(4), pp. 269–271, 1993.

Floyd, S., R. Gummadi, and S. Shenker, "Adaptive RED: An algorithm for Increasing the robustness of RED's active queue management," *submitted for publication*, 2001.

Floyd, S., "RED webpage," http://www.aciri.org/floyd/red.html.

Franklin, G., J. Powell, and M. Workman, *Digital Control of Dynamic Systems*, Addison-Wesley, Third edition, 1998.

Hollot, C. V., V. Misra, D. Towsley, and W. Gong, "A Control theoretic analysis of RED," *Proceedings of INFOCOM'2001*, 2001.

Hollot, C. V., V. Misra, D. Towsley, and W. Gong, "On designing improved controllers for AQM routers supporting TCP flows," *Proceedings of INFOCOM'2001*, 2001.

Isermann, R., *Digital Control Systems Volumn I: Fundamentals, Deterministic Control*, Springer-Verlag, Second Revised version, 1989.

Kuo, B. C., *Automatic Control Systems*, John Wiley & Sons, Inc., Seventh edition, 1995.

Low, S. H., D. Lapsley, "Random Early Marking: an optimization approach to Internet congestion control," *Proceedings of IEEE ICON'99*, 1999, Brisbane, Australia.

May, M., C. Diot, B. Lyles, and J. Bolot, "Influence of active queue parameters on aggregate traffic performance," *Technical Report $n^0$3995*, INRIA, Sophia Antipolis, France, 2000.

McCanne, S., and S. Floyd, "UCB/LBNL/VINT Network Simulator - ns (version 2)," http://www.isi.edu/nsnam/ns/, 1996.

Misra, V., W. Gong, and D. Towsley, "Fluid-based analysis of a network of AQM routers supporting TCP flows with an application to RED," *Proceedings of ACM SIGCOMM2000*, 2000.

Ott, T. J., T. V. Lakshman, and L. Wong, "SRED: Stabilized RED," *Proceedings of IEEE IN-FOCOM'99*, 1999.

Ramakrishnan, K., and S. Floyd, "A proposal to add explicit congestion notification (ECN) to IP," *IETF RFC2481*, January 1999.

Stevens, W., "TCP Slow-Start, Congestion Avoidance, Fast Retransmit, and Fast Recovery algorithms," *IETF RFC2001*, January 1997.

Chapter 14

A FRAMEWORK FOR DYNAMIC ROUTING AND FEEDBACK REGULATION OF PACKET-SWITCHED NETWORKS

Yi-Ju Chao

InterDigital Communications Corporation

yi-ju.chao@interdigital.com

Blaise Morton

Morton Consulting Corporation

blaisemorton@msn.com

Abstract   This paper presents a new modeling, analysis, and design methodology for the control of traffic in packet-switched networks. The basic framework is developed in terms of chains, making use of the boundary and coboundary operators of algebraic topology. All steady-state deterministic and stochastic (e.g. Jackson network) routing solutions are parameterized, and the acyclic solutions are characterized. A load-balancing scheme using coboundary feedback and dynamic inversion is described.

Keywords: Dynamic routing, Dynamic inversion, Jackson networks, Coboundary feedback, Algebraic topology, Graph theory, Optimal control, Network performance, Network steady state.

1.   Introduction

This paper presents a new modeling, analysis and design methodology for the control of traffic in packet-switched networks. This methodology focuses on achievable network performance in a global sense (for example, best management of an Autonomous System). It is assumed the network topology is perfectly known, and it is also assumed that the input rates of flows from entry nodes to exit nodes can be reasonably well predicted, estimated or measured as part of the control approach. Our method is to provide routing tables (either static or dynamic) for the routers to determine to which node messages are forwarded based on their destination node and routing tables.

The primary motivation for this research is the development of a system of analytical methods for design of packet-switched networks of general topology that meet specified performance requirements/goals. The analytical approach follows these stages.

1 The network topology is characterized in the language of graph theory (e.g., tree, 0-chain, 1-chain)[15], [10]. By this means the set of steady-state routing solutions is parameterized by the space of cycles of the network.

2 A particular steady-state solution is selected, based on performance requirements. This solution is found by optimizing a cost function of the steady-state link fluxes and node queue lengths over the space of steady-state routing solutions. It is used to generate a stationary routing algorithm for the stochastic queueing system.

3 To compensate for high-frequency fluctuations of message inputs, the routing tables are modified by use of state feedback (e.g. queue length measurements). This state feedback introduces a dynamic component to effect load-balancing among the nodes of the network.

The above topics have been addressed by researchers in the past, but we have not seen a general methodology that brings all these issues together the way we do here.

For example, Jackson in the early paper [12] formulated Markovian networks where queues on nodes and steady-state flows on links are characterized. The Jackson model can be viewed as an approximation of large, packet-switched networks. Jackson's queueing network was developed in a framework using double indices of nodes, where the first index indicates the source node of a message and the second index indicates the target node for the single movement of a message.

Different types of routing schemes of packet-switched networks can be found in [2], but none of them really connects queueing and routing together as we do here. Another popular approach is to apply operations research concepts from *multi-commodity flow* problems to routing problems of circuit-switched or virtual circuit-switched types of networks. Here we cite F. P. Kelly's and R. J. Gibbens's series of studies [13], [8] and [9] on dynamic routing. They formulate network models on the path space and use estimates of blocking probabilities in a scheme for implementing admission control policies.

We distinguish our formulation from these previous works by our introduction of algebraic topology in order to provide a global, analytic representation of routing solutions that accounts for the dynamics of queuing at nodes and fluxes on links.

Our approach of separation of control into two stages - low-bandwidth steady-state policies and high-bandwidth fluctuation regulation - is not a new concept. Previous researchers have studied steady-state policies for routing problems by considering fluid limits (first-order statistics) of large-scale networks, then they have used queue-length feedback in schemes to reduce workload (in which workload is a function of queuing) [17], [18]. What we bring is a systematic, analytical way to deal with static/dynamic routing in networks having general topology.

When considering load-balancing in a network of general topology, one analytic problem is how to produce a routing solution that will achieve the load-balancing objective. In Section 6 we show a constructive theorem/algorithm of algebraic topology for converting desired queue-length adjustments at nodes (in order to achieve load-balancing) into an adjustment of routing solution on links. This technique is called coboundary feedback control. The study of *Load-balancing* by itself is an interesting topic. The reader is referred to [11] for performance of load-balancing principles and [1] for an allocation strategy for a type of network. For load-balancing algorithms in various problems the reader is referred to [3], [7], [16] and [23].

In Section 7, as an example application of our framework, we show one way to compute dynamic corrective feedback commands for node fluxes using a technique called dynamic inversion, which is an established method for aerospace control [5], [6] and [19]. The purpose of the dynamic inversion method in this context is to load-balance queues among network nodes and keep operating near a desired steady state. There are many ways to load-balance according to different objectives. The reason we chose dynamic inversion is its simplicity, more sophisticated methods can be applied using the same framework. In our discussion in Section 7 we illustrate a basic control concept/principle – a control parameter is selected to trade peak performance (greedy algorithm) for robustness.

One feature of our control methodology is the ability to provide analytical tools that quantify the relations between key system/control parameters and performance measures. Specifically, we present

1 A framework for modeling the global packet flow through the network. This framework provides an analytical formulation of network fluxes and queues on networks of general topology.

2 The link between deterministic and stochastic steady-state solutions. Especially, we study the connection of our algebraic framework to Jackson networks and explain how to parameterize the probability density function for the associated stochastic Jackson networks.

3 A coboundary-feedback methodology for rigorous implementation of load-balancing schemes, and an example of a simple load-balancing scheme based on dynamic inversion. Load-balancing techniques for packet-switched networks of general topology are represented in the language of algebraic topology.

In comparison with the state-of-the-art Transmission Control Protocol / Internet Protocol (TCP/IP) or virtual-circuit type of protocols (e.g. Asynchronous Transfer Mode (ATM)), we also see many differences. One key feature of our control methodology is the form of the routing solution. In general, we make use of multi-path routings, rather than Open Shortest Path First (OSPF) routing for TCP/IP [21] [14] or pre-configured virtual-circuit switches. Secondly, the objective of our control methodology is requirement-oriented rather than best effort. The requirements are achieved by optimization of a cost function to pick a global steady-state operating point, and to use queueing feedback control to drive the network state toward the desired equilibrium. One advantage of our method is to provide analytical tractability, which is important for design and planning of high-performance reliable networks. By contrast, it is difficult to analyze expected performance of networks controlled by TCP, and it is particularly hard to predict QoS. We also distinguish our control methodology from virtual-circuit switched type of routing (e.g. ATM) because we allow dynamic routing of flows through the network, to achieve load-balancing for efficient utilization of network resources.

Our control methodology is implemented in a two-step approach:

1 periodically select the best quasi-steady-state solution to compute routing tables in a low-bandwidth outer-loop feedback

2 use higher bandwidth inner-loop feedback, making small adjustments to the steady-state routing tables, to prevent congestion due to high-frequency variations in input traffic.

The most obvious way to implement the outer-loop control is functionally centralized, but it could be implemented distributed at each node of the network. For this first step we envison a type of protocol similar to the Routing Information Protocol (RIP) or the Interior Gateway Routing Protocol (IGRP) [21], [14], exchanging control information between nodes periodically to achieve the design objective. In the second step the implementation of the inner-loop control may be functionally distributed to accommodate high bandwidth control loops. In this case distributed algorithms are to be studied for achieving the objective. Or, if transport delays due to geographical distance are not too large compared with inner-loop bandwidth, the inner-loop control may be functionally centralized. In consequence, there might be high bandwidth allocated to the control plane to achieve the high frequency control loops.

The paper is organized as follows. First, in Sections 2 and 3 we develop the notation needed for deterministic modeling of packet flow through the network. In these sections we present the parametrization of steady-state solutions and the characterization of acyclic solutions. In Section 4 we introduce the corresponding notation for stochastic Jackson networks and parameterize the density functions for all steady-state solutions. In Section 5 we discuss in general terms how optimization of steady-state performance can be approached using our framework. Then, in Section 6, we introduce the notion of coboundary feedback as a systematic approach to load balancing. Using coboundary feedback we can reduce the effects of flow variation, relieving sporadic congestion, while keeping the global flow close to the desired (optimally designed) steady-state operating point. To show how coboundary feedback might be used in practice, we use dynamic inversion to demonstrate one concept in Section 7. Section 8 provides numerical examples illustrating the methodology. Section 9 is a summary of the mathematical methods and techniques used in this paper.

2.   Notation

We consider a topological graph G with N nodes (routers) and M links interconnecting them. We assume that the first R nodes are boundary routers, through which all messages enter and leave the network. The remaining $N - R$ nodes represent core-network nodes.

Our description of networks will be developed using standard graph-theoretic concepts [15], [10]. Let the N nodes be labelled $a(i)$ for $i = 1, ..., N$. Nodes $a(i)$ for $i = 1, ..., N$ are connected by links $b(j)$ for $j = 1, ..., M$. We do not allow links $(a(i), a(i))$ leading from a node $a(i)$ to itself, so all the links are of the form $b(j) = (a(j_1), a(j_2))$ with $j_1 \neq j_2$.

We will distinguish between $(a(j_1), a(j_2))$ and $(a(j_2), a(j_1))$; the distinction is a matter of orientation. Messages can flow in either direction through any link. The choice of orientation can be changed at will, to suit whatever problem is being studied, but a standard default is that the link $b(j) = (a(j_1), a(j_2))$ is *directed positively* if and only if $j_1 < j_2$. To represent message flow from $a(j_2)$ to $a(j_1)$ on link $(a(j_1), a(j_2))$ with $j_1 < j_2$, we use a negative coefficient whose magnitude represents the amount of flow.

The flows of networks are described in the following graph theoretic language. Let C_0 denote the set of zero-chains, defined to be the set of all summations (14.1)

$$C_0 = \{\sum_{i=1}^{N} f(i)a(i) | f(i) \in \mathbf{R}\} \qquad (14.1)$$

where the coefficients $f(i)$ lie in the set of a real numbers $\mathbf{R}$. Let C_1 denote the set of 1-chains, defined to be the set of all summations (14.2)

$$C_1 = \{\sum_{n<m}^{N} g(n,m)(a(n),a(m))|g(n,m) \in \mathbf{R}\} \qquad (14.2)$$

where the coefficients $g(n,m)$ lie in the set of real numbers $\mathbf{R}$. Notice that in (14.2) the summation is over the $\frac{N(N-1)}{2}$ terms for which $n < m$. An important defining condition for C_1 is that the coefficient $g(n,m)$ must be zero when $a(n)$ and $a(m)$ are not connected by links. For oriented models we identify $(a(n),a(m)) = -(a(m),a(n))$.

There are two important linear operators between the spaces C_0 and C_1. The *boundary* operator $\partial : C_1 \to C_0$ and the *coboundary* operator $\delta : C_0 \to C_1$ are defined by (14.3) (14.4).

$$\partial(\sum_{i<j}^{N} g(i,j)(a(i),a(j))) = \sum_{i<j}^{N} g(i,j)(a(j) - a(i)) \qquad (14.3)$$

and

$$\delta(\sum_{i=1}^{N} f(i)a(i)) = \sum_{a(j)\in N(a(i))}^{N} f(i)(a(j),a(i)), \qquad (14.4)$$

where $N(a(i)) = \{a(j)|a(j) \text{ is a neighbor node of } a(i)\}$. Neighbor nodes of $a(i)$ are those nodes $a(j)$ that share a link with the node $a(i)$.

The *degree* operator $deg : C_0 \to \mathbf{R}$ is defined:

$$deg(\sum_{i=1}^{N} f(i)a(i)) = \sum_{i=1}^{N} f(i). \qquad (14.5)$$

The *cycles* of the network are characterized as follows. Define the set of cycles $Z \subset C_1$ to be the subset of C_1 mapped to zero by the boundary operator (14.3)

$$Z = ker(\partial : C_1 \to C_0) = \{c \in C_1 : \partial(c) = 0\} \qquad (14.6)$$

There is a natural way to map paths through the network into 1-chains. Consider a path $p = [a(j_1), b(1), a(j_2), b(2), ..., b(t-1), a(j_t)]$ where $a(j_1)$ is the starting node, $b(1)$ is the directed link connecting $a(j_1)$ to the second node $a(j_2)$, $b(2)$ connects $a(j_2)$ to $a(j_3)$, etc., and $b(t-1)$ is the final link leading to $a(j_t)$. Associate with this path p the 1-chain $\phi(p) = \sum_{i=1}^{t} b(i)$. Note that the boundary of $\phi(p)$ is $a(t) - a(1)$, the zero-chain representing the difference between the source and the destination. This mapping from paths to 1-chains is not invertible, as may be seen by considering a closed figure-eight path.

A network with no cycle ($Z = 0$) is called a *tree*. For tree networks there is only one direct (without backing up) route for messages between any two nodes, and the routing problem is trivial. In a network with one or more cycles it becomes possible to find multiple direct routes, and the routing problem becomes interesting.

We restrict attention to *connected* networks, i.e. networks for which there is a path connecting any pair of points. Two operators: *inclusion* $i : Z \to C_1$ and $[\times \sum a(n)] : \mathbf{R} \to C_0$ are defined.

$$i(z) = z \quad \forall z \in Z. \tag{14.7}$$

and

$$[\times \sum a(n)](f) = \sum_{n=1}^{N} fa(n) \quad \forall f \in \mathbf{R}. \tag{14.8}$$

We introduce a definition for a sequence of mappings $(g_i : \Omega_{i-1} \to \Omega_i)$ for $i = 1, \cdots$

$$\cdots \Omega_{i-1} \overset{g_i}{\to} \Omega_i \overset{g_{i+1}}{\to} \Omega_{i+1} \overset{g_{i+2}}{\to} \Omega_{i+2} \cdots \tag{14.9}$$

Definition 1 *A sequence of linear operators is called "exact" if and only if "image of g_i = kernel of g_{i+1}" in Ω_i.*

Consider a connected network. From algebraic topology there is a standard result that the sequences of operators (14.10) and (14.11) are exact:

$$0 \to Z \overset{i}{\to} C_1 \overset{\partial}{\to} C_0 \overset{deg}{\to} \mathbf{R} \to 0 \tag{14.10}$$

and

$$0 \to \mathbf{R} \overset{[\times \sum a(i)]}{\to} C_0 \overset{\delta}{\to} C_1 \to C_1/\delta(C_0) \to 0 \tag{14.11}$$

We refer the reader to [22] for a proof of these standard results.

As a consequence of (14.10) we can compute

$$dim(Z) = dim(C_1) - dim(C_0) + 1 = N - M + 1 \tag{14.12}$$

and from (14.11) we find

$$dim(\delta(C_0)) = dim(C_0) - 1 = M - 1 \tag{14.13}$$

so in fact

$$dim(Z) + dim(\delta(C_0)) = N = dim(C_1) \tag{14.14}$$

Equation (14.12) is known as Euler's formula for the dimension of the space of cycles in a graph.

Next, we introduce inner products $<,>_0$ on C_0 and $<,>_1$ on C_1 by definitions (14.15), (14.16)

$$< a_i, a_j >_0 = \begin{cases} 1 & \text{if } i = j \\ 0 & otherwise \end{cases} \tag{14.15}$$

and

$$< (a_i, a_j), (a_k, a_l) >_1 = \begin{cases} 1 & \text{if } i = k, j = l, \text{ for } i < j, k < l \\ 0 & otherwise \end{cases} \tag{14.16}$$

and extending linearly. That is, for

$$F = \sum_{n=1}^{N} f(n)a(n) \in C_0$$

and

$$G = \sum_{n=1}^{N} g(n)a(n) \in C_0$$

we have

$$< F, G >_0 = \sum_{n=1}^{N} f(n)g(n). \tag{14.17}$$

and for

$$H = \sum_{n<m}^{M} h(n,m)(a(n), a(m)) \in C_1$$

and

$$K = \sum_{n<m}^{N} k(n,m)(a(n), a(m)) \in C_1,$$

we have

$$< H, K >_1 = \sum_{n<m}^{N} h(n,m)k(n,m). \tag{14.18}$$

For $F = \sum_{n=1}^{N} f(n)a(n) \in C_0$, we define the C_0-norm

$$\|F\|_{C_0} = < F, F >_0^{1/2} = \left[\sum_{n=1}^{N} f(n)^2 \right]^{1/2}. \tag{14.19}$$

For $H = \sum_{n<m=1}^{N} h(n,m)(a(n), a(m)) \in C_1$, we define the C_1-norm

$$\|H\|_{C_1} = < H, H >_1^{1/2} = \left[\sum_{n,m=1}^{N} h(n,m)^2 \right]^{1/2}. \tag{14.20}$$

We say that two subsets A, B of C_0 are orthogonal if and only if $< a, b >_0 = 0$ for $a \in A$ and $b \in B$ (similarly for any two subsets of C_1).

One fundamental result from graph theory is that C_1 can be written as the orthogonal direct sum $C_1 = Z \oplus \delta(C_0)$. This means that Z and $\delta(C_0)$ are orthogonal and together span C_1. We end this section with a proof of this important result.

Lemma 1 *For all $f \in C_0$, $g \in C_1$ we have*

$$< g, \delta f >_1 \;\; = \;\; < \partial g, f >_0 \qquad (14.21)$$

Proof: By linearity it suffices to verify the equation in the special case where $f = a(i)$ and $g = (a(j), a(k))$. But this is easy because both sides are zero if i, j, k are different, both sides are 1 if $i = k$, and both sides are -1 if $i = j$. Q.E.D.

From the lemma we readily have the theorem.

Theorem 1 $C_1 = Z \oplus \delta(C_0)$

Proof: If g in C_1 satisfies $\partial g = 0$ then for any $f \in C_0$ we have

$$< g, \delta(f) >_1 \;\; = \;\; < \partial g, f >_0 \;\; = \;\; < 0, f >_0 \;\; = \;\; 0 \qquad (14.22)$$

so Z and $\delta(C_0)$ are orthogonal. But we also know the inner-product $< \;, \;>_1$ is positive definite, so the intersection of Z and $\delta(C_0)$ is zero. By equation (14.14) we know the dimensions of these two spaces are complementary, so $C_1 = Z \oplus \delta(C_0)$.

3. Deterministic Network Models

We consider discrete-time network models with fixed reference time interval 1. Let C_0^R and C_1^R denote the R-dimensional vector spaces of zero-chains and 1-chains respectively. As previously discussed, R is the number of boundary (input/output) nodes, and N is the total number of nodes. We introduce the following notation in C_0^R. The network exogenous input rate $U(s)$ from time $s - 1$ to time s is denoted

$$U[s] = \sum_{n=1}^{N} (U_n^1[s], \cdots, U_n^R[s]) a(n) \in C_0^R,$$

where $U_n^r[s]$ is the rate of the number of messages entering the network at node $a(n)$ with destination the boundary node $a(r)$.

The queue $Q(s)$ at time s is denoted

$$Q[s] = \sum_{n=1}^{N} (Q_n^1[s], \cdots, Q_n^R[s]) a(n) \in C_0^R,$$

where $Q_n^r[s]$ is the number of messages in the queue at node $a(n)$ with destination node $a(r)$.

The network state $X(s)$ at time s is denoted

$$X[s] = \sum_{n=1}^{N} (X_n^1[s], \cdots, X_n^R[s]) a(n) \in C_0^R,$$

where $X_n^r[s]$ is the number of messages at node $a(n)$ (in the queue or in the processor) with destination node $a(r)$.

The output rate $Y(s)$ from the network from time $s - 1$ to time s is denoted

$$Y[s] = \sum_{i=1}^{N} (Y_n^1[s], \cdots, Y_n^R[s]) a(n) \in C_0^R,$$

where $Y_n^r[s]$ is the rate of the number of messages leaving the network at node $a(n)$ with the destination node $a(r)$ (only $Y_r^r[s]$ has non-zero values).

Similarly, the internal network flux (or link flux) $T(s)$, which is defined as the rate of the number of messages flowing on links from time $s - 1$ to time s, is denoted by an R-dimensional vector $T(s) \in C_1^R$

$$T[s] = \sum_{n<m=1}^{N} (T_1(n, m)[s], \cdots, T_R(n, m)[s])(a(n), a(m)) \in C_1^R$$

for which $T_r(n, m)$ is the rate of the number of messages flowing through link $(a(n), a(m))$ (between nodes $a(n)$ and $a(m)$) with destination node $a(r)$. Our sign convention is such that, because $n < m$, if $T_r(n, m)$ is positive then the flow is from $a(n)$ to $a(m)$, while if $T_r(n, m)$ is negative then the flow is the same magnitude but in the other direction.

To make the most efficient use of notation, we assume that messages of any given type flow only one direction between any two connected nodes during any timestep. Because of this assumption we can determine from $T(s)$ exactly how many messages travel over each link (and exactly how many flow into/out of each node) during a single timestep. This assumption represents a constraint on the set of routing solutions we can generate. It seems reasonable enough, because it is inefficient to route messages headed for a single destination back and forth between a pair of connected nodes.

The operators ∂, δ, deg, etc. we defined earlier on C_0 and C_1 can be extended naturally to C_0^R and C_1^R by acting term-by-term on the vector components. For example, $deg(U)$ is the real $R - vector$ whose r^{th} component is the total input rate of messages entering the network with destination node a(r). The norms are extended in the natural way as well, for example: $\| T \|_1^2 = \sum_{r=1}^{R} \| T_r \|_1^2$. Also, in the following when we multiply (divide) elements of C_0 and C_1 by a real R-vector we mean component-by-component multiplication (division).

It is easy to verify that the conservation of messages flowing through the network is expressed by what we call the fundamental dynamic equation, which is represented in C_0^R by

$$X[t_2] = X[t_1] + \int_{t_1}^{t_2} U[s] - Y[s] + \partial(T[s])ds. \qquad (14.23)$$

for $0 \le t_1 < t_2$.

In the case of steady states, for all s we have $U[s] \equiv U, Y[s] \equiv Y, T[s] \equiv T$. In addition, the vector X drops out of the fundamental equations (14.23), leaving

$$0 = U - Y + \partial(T) \in C_0^R. \qquad (14.24)$$

For jump processes (e.g. Possion Processes), equation (14.23) is true for any sample path, but this equation by itself does not provide much information for control of the network. In Section 4 we consider Jackson networks (see [20] for details) with Markovian routing rates (or intensities) on links T, exogenous Poisson input rates U and output rates Y. We will also prove in Theorem 4 that for the steady-state stochastic case equation (14.24) is also true.

Our method for determining the desired steady-state routing policy is based on analysis of the set of solutions T of (14.24) given U and Y. The set of all possible steady-state routing solutions for a given network is easily characterized in the following two theorems.

Theorem 2 *Let U, Y be any nonnegative vectors of steady-state input rate and output rate for the network. Then there is a steady-state routing solution T to the fundamental equation (14.24) if and only if $deg(Y - U) = 0$.*

Proof. By exactness of the sequence (14.10) we know there is an element $T_0 \in C_1^R$ satisfying $\partial(T) = Y - U$ if and only if $deg(Y - U) = 0$. Q.E.D.

As a matter of terminology, we call any $T \in C_1^R$ for which $\partial(T) = Y - U$ a *virtual routing solution* for the steady-state network problem with input U and output Y. When the virtual solution T satisfies the routing constraints (such as bounded link capacities) we call it a solution for the routing problem.

Theorem 3 *Suppose $deg(Y - U) = 0$, and let T_0 be a virtual solution. Then the set of all virtual solutions is of the form $T(C) = T_0 + \sum_{j=1}^{L} C_j z_j$ where $L = M - N + 1$ is the dimension of the space Z of cycles, z_j is a basis of Z, and C is an $R \times L$ real matrix whose j^{th} column is C_j.*

Proof. By exactness of the sequence (14.10) we know the kernel of the mapping ∂ is the subspace Z of C_1. Q.E.D.

Theorem 3 shows that for $L > 0$ there is an infinite set of virtual routing solutions $T(C)$ whenever a single solution T can be found. As we shall see, nonuniqueness of solutions is a necessary (in fact, desirable) consequence of cycles in the network, but many of the solutions can be seen to be impractical. For example, there are solutions in which messages are routed around a closed path once, many times or even forever. We want to eliminate those solutions that have embedded message loops of this type. We call those steady-state solutions without message loops *acyclic*.

It is easy to characterize acyclic (virtual) solutions. We will do it two ways: algebraically and geometrically.

The algebraic characterization is as follows. Let T_0 be a virtual solution, consider the set of all virtual solutions $T(C) = T_0 + \sum_{j=1}^{L} C_j z_j$. Then T_0 is acyclic if and only if there is no C for which every coefficient $T_r(m, n)(C)$ has magnitude less than or equal to $|T_r(m, n)(0)|$, with strict inequality for at least one coefficient. Though this characterization is abstract, it will be used in Section 6 to prove that a constructive algorithm generates acyclic solutions.

The geometric characterization is as follows. Let T be a virtual solution, and for each r consider the component $T_r \in C_1$. Pick a new orientation of G so that the direction of those links on which T_r is negative are reversed. Then the virtual solution T is acyclic if and only if, for all r, the new orientation generates a partial ordering of the subgraph G_1 of G consisting of those links for which the coefficients of T_r are nonzero.

One good feature of this partial ordering is that a particular message will never return to a node once it has passed through it. Each message will continue to flow downstream until it reaches its ultimate destination. Of course, the downstream direction will be different for different destination nodes, so this notion of downstream direction depends on destination node and is not an absolute attribute of the overall network.

In the context of practical network-routing problems, the partial ordering eliminates the possibility that a packet is trapped in the network. Trapped packets cause an increase of network loads in addition to the effective loss of the packet in question, so it is good to prevent them.

4.   Topological Formulation of Jackson Networks

The topological formulation of packet-switched networks can be applied to Jackson stochastic networks. We still assume N nodes and R types of messages. The r-th type of message is defined as those with destination node $a(r)$. We consider Jackson networks in which multiple types of messages move between the nodes according to independent Markovian routing rates (intensities) and their service rates depending on the states of the nodes.

We use the same notation as section 3 to represent the Poisson arrival intensities from outside, routing intensities between nodes, and the intensities of messages departing from the network.

Let

$$X_t = \sum_{n=1}^{N} [X_n^1(t), \cdots, X_n^R(t)] a(n) \in C_0^R(\mathbf{Z}^+ \cup \{0\})$$

where $\mathbf{Z}^+ \cup \{0\}$ is the set of nonnegative integers, be a stochastic process that represents the number of messages at the nodes in the network with single-message movement, in which $X_n^r(t) \in \mathbf{Z}^+ \cup \{0\}$ represents the number of r-type messages at node $a(n)$ at time t. Let x denote the coordinates of the state space in which X_t takes values.

We say a network is open if there are exogenous inputs and outputs. Let U be the Poisson intensities of exogenous inputs,

$$U = \sum_{n=1}^{N} (U_n^1, \cdots, U_n^R) a(n) \in C_0^R(\mathbf{R}^+ \cup \{0\})$$

in which U_n^r is the intensity of Poisson arrivals for the r-type messages at node $a(n)$.

We assume that whenever the network is in state x, the time to the next movement of a single r-type message from node $a(j)$ to node $a(k)$ is exponentially distributed. The assumption of exponential times to movements is satisfied under the following conditions.

1 Whenever the network is in state x, the time to the next departure of the r-th type of messages from node j is exponentially distributed with rate $\Phi_j(x_j^r)$.

2 Each departure of a r-type message from j is routed to node k with probability $P_{jk,r}$, independent of everything else. Notice that $\sum_k P_{jk,r} = 1$.

All $P_{jk,r}$ are nonnegative with $P_{jj,r} = 0$, and $\Phi_j(x_j^r)$ is positive except that $\Phi_j(x_j^r) = 0$ if $x_j^r = 0$. The time to the next movement of a single r-type message from node $a(j)$ to node $a(k)$ is exponential with rate $P_{jk,r}\Phi_j(x_j^r)$. Under the above assumptions, the system is called a Jackson Network of multiple types of messages. For open networks we denote $P_{0k,r}$ as the probability that messages of type r from outside of the network arrive at the node $a(k)$. We also denote $P_{k0,r}$ as the probability that messages of type r leave the network at node $a(k)$.

Jackson networks have been studied in numerous papers in the literature. The reader is referred to [20] for related studies or to [4] for a thorough survey. One advantage of Jackson networks is that, given a set of Markovian routing probabilities $P_{jk,r}$ among nodes, there are closed forms for the invariant measures of network steady states. The invariant measures are fully characterized by the exponentially distributed service rate $\Phi_j(x_j^r)$ and solutions $w_{j,r}, j \in N$

(if they exist) of the following *routing balance equations or traffic equations*

$$w_{j,r} = \sum_{k \leq N} w_{k,r} P_{kj,r}, \quad j = 0, 1, \cdots, N \qquad (14.25)$$

with $w_{0,r} = \sum_{n=1}^{N} U_n^r, \forall r$.

We now develop the connection between the algebraic topological formulation and the *routing balance equations or traffic equations*. We denote

$$P = (P_{nm,r})_{0 \leq n,m \leq N; 1 \leq r \leq R}$$

and

$$W = (w_{n,r})_{0 \leq n \leq N; 1 \leq r \leq R}.$$

Notice that for each r the indices for P are $0 \leq n, m \leq N$ and we do not require $n \leq m$.

Given a pair (P, W), we readily establish a mapping from (P, W) to (T, U, Y) as follows. Although T is defined in oriented C_1^R with $n < m$, the above mapping is well-defined (recall we identify $(a(n), a(m)) = -(a(m), a(n))$).

$$T_r(n, m) = P_{nm,r} w_{n,r} - P_{mn,r} w_{m,r} \quad \forall n < m,$$

$$U_r(n) = P_{0n,r} w_{0,r}$$

and

$$Y_r(n) = P_{n0,r} w_{n,r}.$$

Notice that in the above the mapping from (P, W) to (T, U, Y) is not unique. The non-uniqueness can be seen by considering on a link $(a(j_1), a(j_2))$ with $P_{j_1 j_2} = (b - c)$, for some real numbers b, c such that $0 < b - c < 1$ from node $a(j_1)$ to $a(j_2)$ will produce the same T as $P_{j_1 j_2} = b$ from node $a(j_1)$ to $a(j_2)$ and $P_{j_2 j_1} = c$ from node $a(j_2)$ to $a(j_1)$. However, if we restrict the set of (P, W) with $P_{jk} P_{kj} = 0, \forall j, k$, then the uniqueness can be achieved.

Conversely, we define the mapping from (T, U, Y) to (P, W). For any $T \in C_1^R$ we define, for $1 \leq n, m \leq N$,

$$\theta = (\theta_r(n, m))_{1 \leq n,m \leq N; 1 \leq r \leq R}$$

where, for $1 \leq n, m \leq N$,

$$\begin{cases} \theta_r(n, m) = T_r(n, m) & \text{if } T_r(n, m) \geq 0 \\ \theta_r(m, n) = -T_r(n, m) & \text{if } T_r(n, m) < 0 \\ \theta_r(m, n) = 0 & otherwise \end{cases}$$

The above formulas are just to map directed fluxes to the magnitude of fluxes between nodes. We now can define P by

$$P_{nm,r} = \begin{cases} 0, & \text{for } \sum_m \theta_r(n, m) = 0 \\ \frac{\theta_r(n,m)}{\sum_m \theta_r(n,m)} & otherwise \end{cases} \qquad (14.26)$$

and

$$P_{0n,r} = U_r(n)/\sum_n U_r(n), \tag{14.27}$$

$$P_{n0,r} = Y_r(n)/\sum_n Y_r(n). \tag{14.28}$$

We also can define W by

$$w_{0,r} = \sum_n U_r(n),$$

and

$$w_{j,r} = \sum_m \theta_r(j,m) \quad \forall j \neq 0.$$

In summary, there is a bijection

$$(U,Y,T) \leftrightarrow \{(P,W) : P_{jk}P_{kj} = 0 \quad \forall k,j\}.$$

Moreover, there is an algebraic equivalence between the *routing balance equations or traffic equations* (14.25) and the fundamental equation (14.24), as stated in the following theorem.

Theorem 4 *The fundamental equation*

$$U - Y + \partial(T) = 0 \in C_0^R$$

and the routing balance equation

$$w_{j,r} = \sum_{k \leq N} w_{k,r} P_{kj,r}, \quad \forall j = 1, \cdots, N,$$

for $P_{jk}P_{kj} = 0, \forall j, k$, are equivalent algebraically.

Proof. The algebraic equivalence follows the bijection between (P,W) and (T,U,Y). Q.E.D.

Theorem 2 proves that there exists a steady-state virtual routing solution $T \in C_1^R$ of the fundamental equation if and only if $deg(Y - U) = 0$. There is an equivalent theorem for Jackson networks, its form provides a parametrization of the set of solutions of the routing balance equations.

Theorem 5 *Suppose we are given a set of data W and $P_0 = (P_{j0,r})$. Then the set of solutions (P,W) to the routing balance equations (14.24) for which the following pair of equations are satisfied:*

$$w_{0,r} = \sum_{j=1}^N P_{j0,r} w_{j,r} \quad \forall r \tag{14.29}$$

$$P_{jk}P_{kj} = 0 \qquad\qquad (14.30)$$

is parametrized by the set of real $R \times L$ matrices C as in Theorem 3.2.

Proof. Since (14.29) is equivalent to $deg(U) = deg(Y)$, existence of a solution of (14.25) is a simple result of theorem 2 and theorem 4. Moreover, the parametrization of (P, W) is a result of theorem 3 and theorem 2. Q.E.D.

The above theorems show a bijection between the set

$$\{(U, Y, T) : U - Y + \partial(T) = 0, deg(U) = deg(Y)\}$$

and the set of *virtual* solutions (P, W) of (14.25) contained in

$$\{(P, W) : w_{0,r} = \sum_{j=1}^{N} P_{j0,r}w_{j,r}, P_{jk}P_{kj} = 0 \quad \forall k, j\}.$$

The condition $P_{jk}P_{kj} = 0$ is reasonable since it is not desirable to have a steady-state routing strategy that sends packets of the same type back and forth over the same link.

What we have shown is the following: for given Poisson exogenous arrival rates and weights W at the nodes, the set of compatible Markovian routing rates P with $P_{jk}P_{kj} = 0$ on the graph G is parametrized by the space of cycles. When the graph is not a tree, a particular solution P is not unique. Generally speaking, it is desirable to have non-uniqueness because it gives more flexibility in designing routing solutions.

Moreover, as shown in [20], for a given set of exogenous Poisson arrival rates, the stationary distributions of Jackson processes on the graph G can be written as an explicit formula in terms of $\Phi_j(x_j^r)$ and W. Accordingly, our Theorem 5 also shows that the set of Markovian routing rates to achieve the same stationary distributions of queueing at nodes is parametrized by C.

5.   Selecting a Nominal Steady-State Solution

The nominal steady-state solution is obtained by optimizing the expected value of a cost function defined on the network link fluxes T, state vector X and B, which is the assumed value of the input intensity vector U (see Figure 14.1). The optimization is taken over the set of matrices C which parametrize the steady-state routing solutions $T(C)$ as in Theorem 3. In the simplest scenario, B is merely a specified parameter, independent of C, though the situation becomes more complicated when admission control is necessary. In this paper we do not address the role played by admission control, so B is just a parameter independent of C. The stochastic process X does depend on T, however, and therefore depends implicitly on C as well.

The general form of cost function, assuming no admission control, we consider here is given by

$$H(T(C), X(T(C))), \quad \text{where} \quad H : C_1^R \times C_0^R \to R^+$$

is a function of link fluxes and node states. H depends parametrically on the assumed input intensities B and the service rates Φ. The desired C is found by optimizing the expected value of H over $\{C : T(C) \text{ is acyclic}\}$.

Note that this general form of cost function can be used to represent many of the performance metrics commonly used: waiting time, average queueing length, and throughput, for example. A simple example showing expected waiting time as a function of C is shown in example 2 in Section 8.

Figure 14.1. Steady-State Outer-Loop Network Model.

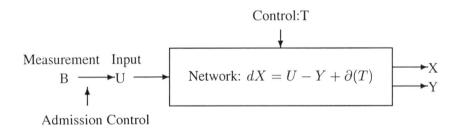

6. Coboundary Feedback

Section 5 provides a quasi-steady-state-control methodology for the routing problem. Real network inputs are not stationary, and routing solutions based on quasi-steady-state models will experience periods of degraded performance because of congestion. To improve performance we adopt a two-step approach:

1 periodically select the best quasi-steady-state solution, as already discussed, to compute routing tables in a low-bandwidth outer-loop feedback

2 use higher bandwidth inner-loop feedback, making small adjustments to the steady-state routing tables, to prevent congestion due to high-frequency variations in input traffic rates.

In those cases where the actual throughput is close to the assumed value $deg(U)$, this two-step approach alone might be adequate for good performance. If

$deg(U)$ is too large for extended periods of time it might become necessary to supplement this two-step approach with admission control.

To compute the higher-bandwidth, corrective feedback signal we will make use of the coboundary map. The basic theorem behind our approach is:

Theorem 6 *Let $B \subset C_0$ be the kernel of $deg : C_0 \to \mathbf{R}$. There is an invertible map $A : B \to B$ such that $\partial \circ \delta \circ A = Identity : B \to B$*

Proof: By the exactness of (14.11) we know that $\delta : B \to C_1$ is injective. But we also know that $\delta(B)$ is orthogonal to $Z = kernel(\partial)$, so $\partial \circ \delta : B \to C_0$ is also injective. Finally, by the exactness of (14.10) we know that $\partial(C_1) \subset B$, so the composition $\partial \circ \delta : B \to B$ is invertible. Put $A = (\partial \circ \delta)^{-1}$. Q.E.D

As a first application of this theorem we show how to construct an acyclic virtual solution to the steady-state problem. We state this construction as a lemma.

Lemma 2 *For the steady-state routing problem, suppose U and Y satisfy the necessary condition $deg(Y - U) = 0$. Let A be the mapping in the previous theorem. Then $T = \delta(A(Y - U))$ is an acyclic virtual solution.*

Proof: By the construction of A we know that $\partial(T) = Y - U$, so T is a virtual solution. To show T is also acyclic we verify that T satisfies the algebraic condition. By construction we know that T is orthogonal to Z (because $T \in \delta(C_0)$), hence for any $z \in Z$ we know that

$$\| T + z \|_1^2 = \| T \|_1^2 + \| z \|_1^2 \geq \| T \|_1^2 \qquad (14.31)$$

so it is not possible to reduce any of the magnitudes of the coefficients of T while leaving the other magnitudes unchanged. Q.E.D.

In the proof of this lemma we implicitly used a fact that makes it possible to compute the composition $\delta \circ A : B \to C_1$ without computing A. For any $y \in C_0$ satisfying $deg(y) = 0$ the computational algorithm is:

1 Find any $p \in C_1$ such that $\partial(p) = y$

2 Project p onto $\pi(p)$ in the orthogonal complement of Z in C_1

3 Then $\delta(A(y)) = \pi(p)$

When L (the number of cycles) is small, the orthogonal projection π is the identity minus a low-rank matrix (rank $= L$), and the above algorithm is much easier than computing $\delta \circ A$ directly.

As an interesting aside, the message flow arising from the image of the coboundary map (for each component T_r of T) is analogous to the electrical current flow through a resistor network in the topology of G (a different flow for each r, depending on sources). This relation is not essential to our approach so we do not develop it here.

For the rest of this section we turn our attention to load balancing. Depending on the objective, there are many ways to use coboundary feedback to balance the load among nodes. Here we describe one approach in detail. The first example in Section 8 shows how the approach can work in practice.

Suppose messages are flowing through the network according to the selected steady-state T, and it turns out that the queue $Q(i)$ at node $a(i)$ is longer than expected. Also, suppose there is another node $a(j)$ where the queue $Q(j)$ is shorter than expected. Ideally, we would like to move messages directly from the queue at $a(i)$ to the queue at $a(j)$, but there is no mechanism to do that. Instead, we use feedback control to reroute (temporarily) messages in such a way that $a(i)$ is likely to get shorter and $a(j)$ is likely to get longer. To accomplish this:

1 Pick some desired rate of decrease $F(i)$ of the queue $Q(i)$, and some tolerable rate of increase $F(j)$ of the queue $F(j)$ such that $deg(F(j) - F(i)) = 0$.

2 Put $\Delta T = \delta(A(F(j) - F(i)))$, as in Lemma 2.

3 Generate new routing probabilities $P_{ij,k}$ based on $T + \Delta T$.

The resulting flow will have the average property that, in comparison with the original flow associated with T, fewer messages are routed to node a(i) and more are routed to node a(j). The service rates at these two nodes are not changed, so $Q(i)$ will have a better chance of growing shorter while $Q(j)$ will be more likely to grow longer. This change in routing policy is only temporary, it will be reassessed frequently, and it will be discontinued when the queue lengths are closer to their expected sizes. In this way the likelihood of serious congestion is reduced.

In general, for any desired adjusted flow-rate $F \in C_0^R$ satisfying $deg(F) = 0$, we can construct the correction $\Delta T = \delta \circ A(F)$ so that $\partial(T + \Delta T) = Y - U + F$.

By picking F to be nonzero only on the core nodes, the net flux between boundary nodes remains unchanged while the traffic is rerouted through the core network. In the deterministic model, queues will diminish at nodes where the coefficients of F are negative, and queues will grow at nodes where the coefficients of F are positive. In the stochastic case, the probability that part of network is congested is lower.

The main problem with this approach is: it may turn out that the new routing solution $T + \Delta T$ generated in the above procedure is not implementable. For example, the new solution will invariably try to send extra messages out of the overcrowded node, and that extra flux might violate the link capacity or node processing rate. In that case, the only possible solution is to add a cycle C to $T + \Delta T$ (cyclic adjustment) in such a way as to cancel the unrealizable portion of the perturbed solution. When cyclic adjustment of the coboundary feedback is realizable there are often many ways to do it – the first case in Section 8 gives one example. In general there might not be any way to find a cyclic adjustment that satisfies all constraints, in that case a different F must be chosen. This issue requires further attention, we leave the matter for a later paper.

In summary, this section shows a method to achieve load balancing by designing a new virtual routing solution $T + \Delta T$ using queueing feedback at nodes. The first step of the approach is to pick a nodal flux correction F, satisfying $deg(F) = 0$, that represents the desired transfer of messages from long queues to short queues. Then the coboundary feedback is $\Delta T = \delta \circ A(F)$, which might require cyclic correction by C so that the final solution $T + \Delta T + C$ is realizable. As a result, the expected value of the load balancing correction should be the specified F. In the next section we show one method of picking F by "Dynamic Inversion".

7.   Dynamic Inversion

In designing an inner-loop feedback, there are many strategies for choosing the desired change in nodal flux F. Without taking into account the detailed constraints of the network topology or the specific form of the cost function it is not possible to talk about optimal inner-loop solutions. In order to illustrate the approach without too much extra work we choose an approach to inner-loop control called dynamic inversion.

The idea of dynamic inversion is to pick a desired dynamic equation for driving system state errors to zero, based on the nominal model and real-time state measurements, and then compute the appropriate feedback signal to realize that equation. There are many dynamic equations that might work. To illustrate the approach we pick something simple.

Define $Backlog = deg(X)$, so $Backlog$ is the vector whose r^{th} component $Backlog^r$ is the number of messages of type r in the network. When $Backlog$ is too big we engage admission control until it passes below a preset limit. When $Backlog$ is equal to its expected value, we want a control law that drives the queue lengths to their expected values. When $Backlog$ is smaller than expected we want to keep $Backlog$ small and at the same time take preventative action against congestion. One feedback strategy that might realize these goals is as follows: use the measured quantities X and $Backlog$, and let $E(X)$ and $E(Backlog)$ be the expected values of X and $Backlog$ from the selected outer-loop control. Assume each component of $E(Backlog)$ is greater than zero. Then

1 Pick a desired time-constant τ for driving errors to zero

2 Put $\rho = Backlog/E(Backlog)$ (element-by-element division)

3 Put $F = (\rho * E(X) - X)/\tau$ to be the desired change in nodal flux

The motivation behind this F is explained in the following four features. First,

$$deg(F) = (\rho * E(Backlog) - Backlog)/\tau = 0 \qquad (14.32)$$

so F is a legitimate candidate for coboundary feedback. Second, when $Backlog$ is at its expected value, F is negative at nodes where the load is heavier than expected and positive at nodes where the load is lighter than expected, so F has the right signs for a corrective flux. Third, the corrective flux is inversely proportional to the time-constant τ (note that the dynamic equation implied by this feedback law is a first-order lag with time constant τ). Choice of τ represents a standard control trade: if τ is too big the feedback does nothing until errors are huge, if τ is too small then the feedback signals might become too large and lead to undesired oscillations in the control signals. And fourth, when $Backlog$ is different from expectations, the formula will tend to rebalance the flows on a prorated basis, which might or might not be a good thing to do.

As in other engineering applications, one needs to look at the objectives, the environment (in this case, traffic properties) and the system hardware to decide on an appropriate feedback law. For example, one variation of the above proposed method may be to weight by the service rates of each node while computing F and still maintain $deg(F) = 0$. We hope that the control law shown here illustrates the general concept well enough so that those who want to use a different control law will see how to apply the methodology.

8. Examples

We use two numerical examples to show how to use the methodology. In the first example we illustrate the application of the algebraic topological language to a network represented by the graph in Figure 14.2. In the graph there are four nodes $a(1), a(2), a(3)$ and $a(4)$ ($N = 4$) and five directed links ($M = 5$) connecting the four nodes. There are 2 ($M - N + 1 = 2$) independent cycles.

Consider input rates $1/2$ at node $a(1)$ and $1/2$ at node $a(4)$, denoted by $U = 1/2a(1) + 1/2a(4) \in C_0$, and output rate 1 at node $a(3)$, denoted by $Y = a(3) \in C_0$. Notice that the message type depends only on its target node, so in this example there is only one type of message and all the states are scalars (they are vectors of dimension R when there are R types of message). It can be seen that

$$deg(Y - U) = deg(Y) - deg(U) = 1 - 1/2 - 1/2 = 0,$$

therefore there exits a steady-state routing solution to (14.24).

Figure 14.2.   A Network Model.

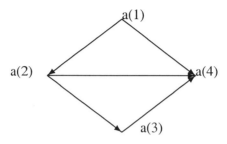

For a small example like this it is easy to write down a routing solution by inspection:

$$T_0 = 1/2(a(1), a(2)) + 1/2(a(2), a(3)) - 1/2(a(3), a(4)) \in C_1.$$

One can easily check that T_0 is a steady-state routing solution to equation (14.24):

$$\partial T_0 = 1/2a(2) - 1/2a(1) + 1/2a(3) - 1/2a(2)$$
$$-1/2a(4) + 1/2a(3) = Y - U.$$

The set of all steady-state routing solutions T is parametrized

$$T(r, s) = T_0 + rZ_1 + sZ_2$$

$$= (1/2 + r)(a(1), a(2)) + (1/2 + s)(a(2), a(3)) + (r - s)(a(2), a(4))$$
$$-r(a(1), a(4)) + (s - 1/2)(a(3), a(4)).$$

The special subset of acyclic solutions is given by r and s that satisfy the conditions: $-1/2 \le s \le 1/2$ and either

1 $-1/2 \le r \le 0$, or

2 $0 \le r \le s$

We now construct $A : B \in C_0 \to B \in C_0$, where $B = ker(deg)$, such that $\partial \circ \delta \circ A = $ identity $: B \to B$ (as in theorem 6). We have by definition:

$$\delta(a(1)) = (a(2), a(1)) + (a(4), a(1))$$

$$\delta(a(2)) = (a(1), a(2)) + (a(4), a(2)) + (a(3), a(2))$$

$$\delta(a(3)) = (a(2), a(3)) + (a(4), a(3))$$

$$\delta(a(4)) = (a(1), a(4)) + (a(2), a(4)) + (a(3), a(4)).$$

Pick a basis of B: since B is the kernel of deg, the dimension of B is the number of nodes minus 1.

$$b_1 = a(1) - a(2)$$

$$b_2 = a(2) - a(3)$$

$$b_3 = a(3) - a(4).$$

We have

$$\delta(b_1) = 2(a(2), a(1)) + (a(4), a(1)) - (a(4), a(2)) - (a(3), a(2))$$

$$\delta(b_2) = (a(1), a(2)) + 2(a(3), a(2)) + (a(4), a(2)) - (a(4), a(3))$$

$$\delta(b_3) = (a(2), a(3)) - (a(1), a(4)) - (a(2), a(4)) + 2(a(4), a(3))$$

Therefore, we also have

$$\partial\delta(b_1) = 3a(1) - 4a(2) + a(3) = 3b_1 - b_2$$

$$\partial\delta(b_2) = -a(1) + 4a(2) - 3a(3) = -b_1 + 3b_2$$

$$\partial\delta(b_3) = a(1) + 3a(3) - 4a(4) = b_1 + b_2 + 4b_3.$$

From the above, we have

$$A^{-1} = \begin{bmatrix} 3 & -1 & 0 \\ -1 & 3 & 0 \\ 1 & 1 & 4 \end{bmatrix},$$

where the n-th row is the coefficients of $\partial\delta(b_n)$ and the n-th column is the coefficient of b_n. We thus have the linear operator $A : B \mapsto B$ defined by

$$A = \begin{bmatrix} 3/8 & 1/8 & 0 \\ 1/8 & 3/8 & 0 \\ -1/8 & -1/8 & 1/4 \end{bmatrix},$$

where the operator is defined on the basis $[b_1, b_2, b_3]$ of B, satisfying

$$A(b_1) = 3/8 b_1 + 1/8 b_2,$$

$$A(b_2) = 1/8 b_1 + 3/8 b_2,$$

$$A(b_3) = -1/8 b_1 - 1/8 b_2 + 1/4 b_3.$$

One can easily check that

$$\partial\delta A(b_i) = b_i \; \forall i = 1, 2, 3.$$

Having prepared the algebraic topological formulation of the network, we now consider the control methodology. Let's assume the nominal steady-state routing solution (of the outer-loop control) is

$$T_0 = 1/2(a(1), a(2)) + 1/2(a(2), a(3)) - 1/2(a(3), a(4)),$$

which is the shortest-path routing where messages arriving at node $a(1)$ are directed on the path from $a(1)$, to $a(2)$, and then to $a(3)$, and messages arriving at node $a(4)$ are directed to node $a(3)$ on link $(a(4), a(3))$ directly.

We now consider the inner-loop control. We want to consider the special case where we have an excess of messages in the queue at $a(2)$, while a deficit is found in $a(4)$. To simplify the computations, assume $E(X_2) = 1 = E(X_4)$. Ignore queues at $a(1)$ and $a(3)$, so that $\rho = (X_2 + X_4)/2$ and the desired queue-length correction flux is $F = K(X, \tau) * (a(4) - a(2))$ where $K(X, \tau) = (X_2 - X_4)/(2 * \tau)$. Now we have the coboundary feedback equation

$$\Delta T = \delta \circ A(F) = K(X, \tau) * [(a(2), a(1))/4 + (a(2), a(4))/2 +$$

$$(a(2), a(3))/4 + (a(1), a(4))/4 + (a(3), a(4))/4]$$

It is easy to verify that the flow $T_0 + \Delta T$ for sufficiently large τ does indeed have the properties we asked for. Note in particular that more messages flow to $a(4)$ and fewer flow to $a(2)$ when $X_2 - X_4$ is positive, and that the corrective flux reduces in magnitude as $X_2 - X_4$ goes to zero until the steady-state solution is resumed when load balancing has been achieved.

A possible problem with this solution is that the flow from $a(2)$ to $a(3)$ is now supposed to be $1/2 + K(X, \tau)/4$ and that might not be possible (see the discussion at the end of Section 6). In that case, we can add the cyclic adjustment $C_1 = K(X, \tau) * [(a(3), a(2)) + (a(2), a(4)) + (a(4), a(3))]/4$, so that

$$T_0 + \Delta T + C_1 = (a(1), a(2)) * (1/2 - K(X, \tau)/4) + (a(1), a(4)) * K(X, \tau)/4 +$$

$$3 * (a(2), a(4)) * K(X, \tau)/4 + (a(4), a(3))/2 + (a(2), a(3))/2$$

In this case, $3/4$ of the load-balancing flow is sent directly from $a(2)$ to $a(4)$, and the other $1/4$ is a redirection of the flow originating at $a(1)$. In case this situation is not acceptable for some reason, another cycle C_2 can be added so that all of the load-balancing is done by re-directing part of the flow originating at node $a(1)$. Different solutions may be preferred depending on other features of the network, but it is clear that the set of all load-balancing solutions of this type is parameterized by the set of cycles.

In our second example we see how selection of the steady-state routing solution can affect a meaningful cost function. This example will help illustrate the concepts discussed in Section 5.

Consider the nominal steady-state solution of Figure 14.3, where we assume Poisson input rate

$$U = \lambda a(1)$$

and each message is addressed to node $a(5)$, thus in steady state

$$Y = -\lambda a(5).$$

We also assume Poisson routing rates between nodes. Each node has one server with exponentially distributed service rate 10. In steady state, each node can be approximated by an M/M/1 queue with arrival rates depending on routing rates. The family of acyclic routing solutions T satisfying

$$\partial(T) + U - Y = \partial(T) + \lambda a(1) - \lambda a(5) = 0$$

is parametrized by the variable p as follows

$$T = p\lambda(a(1), a(2)) + p\lambda(a(2), a(4)) + p\lambda(a(4), a(5))$$

$$+(1 - p)\lambda(a(1), a(3)) + (1 - p)\lambda(a(3), a(5)),$$

for some $p \in [0, 1]$.

We compare three nominal steady-state routing solutions – the shortest path, the minimax, and the coboundary methods. In the shortest-path method the number of hops from the source node to the target node is minimized. Its routing solution is, with $p = 0$,

$$T = \lambda(a(1), a(3)) + \lambda(a(3), a(5)).$$

In the minimax method the maximum of all the link flow is minimized. Its routing solution is, with $p = 1/2$,

$$T = 1/2\lambda(a(1), a(2)) + 1/2\lambda(a(2), a(4)) + 1/2\lambda(a(4), a(5))$$

$$+1/2\lambda(a(1), a(3)) + 1/2\lambda(a(3), a(5)).$$

We include the coboundary solution $p = 2/5$ to compare what happens when the flows are selected to mimic the current-flux in an electric circuit with current source at $a(1)$, sink at $a(5)$ and unit resistors at the nodes. If we cared about minimizing the sum of squares of link fluxes over the network then this coboundary flow would be a good thing to minimize. That cost function does not arise naturally for communication networks, however, so this case is included only to show what happens for a different value of the parameter p. The coboundary solution $p = 2/5$ is:

$$T = 2/5\lambda(a(1), a(2)) + 2/5\lambda(a(2), a(4)) + 2/5\lambda(a(4), a(5))$$

$$+3/5\lambda(a(1), a(3)) + 3/5\lambda(a(3), a(5)).$$

Figure 14.3. An example of the nominal steady-state solution.

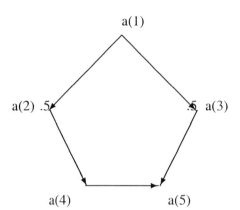

Table 14.1. Waiting Time Comparison

λ	Shortest path	Minimax	Coboundary
Formula	$1/(10 - \lambda)$	$3/(20 - \lambda)$	$3/(50 - 3\lambda) + 4/(50 - 2\lambda)$
1	0.1111	0.1584	0.1471
6	0.2500	0.2143	0.1990
15	∞	0.6000	0.8000

We now compare the average waiting time of a message of the three methods in Table 14.1. When the system is heavily loaded, the waiting time of the shortest path is significantly higher than the others. The waiting time for Minimax and Coboundary are not significantly different. When the system in lightly loaded, the coboundary method is slightly better than the minimax, while the system load increases, the minimax is slightly better than the coboundary. Different assumptions about the environment may lead to different choices of nominal steady-state solutions. These three cases illustrate how the performance of the nominal steady-state solutions may depend on the expected traffic environment and on the parameter p.

9. Summary

We presented a new approach to modeling, analysis and design for control of traffic in packet-switched networks.

Our approach combines deterministic network theory, in which link capacities are the dominant network limitation, with queueing theory, in which service rates at nodes are the dominant network limitation. Our approach relies heavily on analytic techniques from two areas of mathematics.

The first set of mathematical tools used to develop the methodology is taken from algebraic topology. Vectors of zero-chains represent the network state (numbers of messages of each type at each node), and vectors of one-chains represent the message transfer rates (rates at which messages of each type are sent over each link). The standard boundary and coboundary operators between zero-chains and one-chains are introduced, along with their exact sequences. A deterministic, discrete-time model is then presented, along with necessary and sufficient conditions for the existence of solutions for the steady-state routing problem. The full set of solutions to the steady-state routing problem is parametrized by a matrix C of size $R \times L$, where R is the number of target nodes and L is the dimension of the space of cycles of the graph G representing the network. We characterize the special set of solutions which do not contain message loops so that we can make sure our steady-state solutions are message-loop free (acyclic). This special set is represented by a compact subset of matrices C.

The second set of mathematical tools comes from stochastic Jackson network models in queueing theory. The traffic model B now represents the Poisson intensities of messages entering the network. We show that solutions T to the deterministic steady-state problem give rise to stationary distributions for an (open) Jackson network. From T we show how to compute the routing probabilities $(P_{ij,k})$ = probability that a message of type k at node $a(i)$ will be sent to neighboring node $a(j)$ and the stationary distributions of the network state X_i^k = number of messages of type k at node $a(i)$ for the stochastic network.

Our control methodology is composed of a low-bandwidth outer-loop feedback method to achieve expected steady states, and a high-bandwidth inner-loop feedback method to prevent congestion due to high-frequency variations in traffic rates.

In this way we solve the global steady-state routing problem by optimizing the expected value of a function $H(T(C), X(T(C))$ where H is any objective function of the steady-state link fluxes $T(C)$ and the number of messages of each type at each node $X(T(C))$. This optimization is taken over the compact subset of C for which $T(C)$ has no message loops (acyclic), so the probability of closed message loops in the stationary stochastic model is zero. In a real network the choice of optimal C would be updated periodically to reflect changes in the quasi-steady-state flow via feedback in the outer-loop (low bandwidth) part of the control.

Because real network traffic rates fluctuate significantly from mean rates, congestion is a continual problem. If the congestion spreads throughout the network, admission control is the only reliable cure. For those cases where the congestion is local and can be resolved by rerouting traffic, however, we introduce a high-bandwidth inner-loop control, which tunes the routing probabilities in (near) real time, helping to bring overcrowded queues back below the upper bounds associated with steady-state expectations. In this way we achieve load-balancing. This inner-loop control is computed by applying the coboundary operator to measured state errors (differences between expected steady state and observed numbers X_i^r of messages) at the nodes. Cyclic adjustment is applied as needed to accommodate practical system constraints.

The use of inner-loop coboundary control complements the use of outer-loop cycle control in a natural mathematical way, because the set of one-chains of G is exactly the orthogonal sum of the cycles of G and coboundaries of G.

References

[1] Alanyali, M., Hajek, B. Analysis of simple algorithms for dynamic load balancing. Mathematics of Operations Research 1997; Vol. 22, No. 4.

[2] Bertsekas, D., Gallager, R., *Data Networks*, Second Edition. Prentice Hall, 1992.

[3] Chiu, G. M., Raghavendra, C. S., Ng., S.M. Resource allocation with load balancing consideration in distributed computing systems. Proceedings of IEEE Infocom 1989; 89:758-765.

[4] Disney, R. L., Konig, D. Queueing networks: a survey of their random processes. SIAM Review 1985; Vol.27, No.3.

[5] Elgersma, M. Control of nonlinear systems using partial dynamic inversion. Ph. D. Thesis in Electrical Engineering, University of Minnesota, 1988.

[6] Enns, D. M., Bugajski, Hendrick, R., Stein, G. Dynamic inversion: an evolving methodology for flight control design. International Journal of Control 1994; 59:71-91.

[7] Ganger, G. R., Worthington, B. L., Hou, R. Y., Patt., Y. N. Disk subsystem load balancing: disk stripping vs. conventional data placement. Proceedings of 26th Hawaii International Conference on System Science 1993; 1:40-49.

[8] Gibbens, R. J., Kelly, F. P. Dynamic routing in fully connected networks. IMA J. Math. Contr. Inform. 1990; 7:77-111.

[9] Gibbens, R. J., Kelly, F. P., Key, P. B. Dynamic alternative routing modeling and behaviour. Proceedings of the 12th Int. Teletraffic Congress 1988; 3.4A-3.

[10] Gondran, M., Minoux, M., *Graphs and Algorithms*. Wiley, 1984.

[11] Hajek, B. Balanced loads in infinite networks. The Annals of Applied Probability 1996; Vol. 6, No. 1:48-75.

[12] Jackson, J. R. Networks of waiting lines. Operations Res.; 5:518-552.

[13] Kelly, F. P. Loss networks. The Annals of Applied Probability 1995; Vol.1, 3:1189 - 1198.

[14] Lammle T., *CCNA Cisco Certified Network Associate*, 2nd Ed.. Sybex, 2000.

[15] Lefschetz, *Topology*. Second Edition. Chelsea publishing, 1956.

[16] Liu, H. T., Silvester, J. An approximation performance model for load-dependent interactive queues with application to load balancing in distributed systems. Proceedings of IEEE Infocom 1988; 88:956-965.

[17] Meyn, S. P. Feedback regulation for sequencing and routing in multiclass queueing networks. SIAM J. Control and Optimization 2000.

[18] Meyn, S. P. Sequencing and routing in multiclass networks part II: workload relaxation. SIAM J. Control and Optimization 2000.

[19] Morton, B., Enns, D. M., Zhang, B. Stability of dynamic inversion control laws applied to nonlinear aircraft pitch-axis models. International Journal of Control 1996; 63:1-25.

[20] Serfozo, R., *Introduction to Stochastic Networks*. New York: Springer-Verlag, 1999.

[21] Shaughnessy, T., *CISCO A Beginner's Guide*. McGraw Hill, 2000.

[22] Tutte, W., *Graph Theory*. Cambridge University Press, 2001.

[23] Willebeck-LeMair, M. H., Reeves, A. P. Strategies for dynamic load balancing on highly parallel computers. IEEE Transactions Parallel Distrib. Systems 1993; 9:979-993.

Chapter 15

DELAY-CONSTRAINED MULTI-RING CONSTRUCTION FOR ORDERED MULTIPOINT-TO-MULTIPOINT COMMUNICATIONS *

Yassine Boujelben
INRS-EMT, Place Bonaventure
800, de la Gauchetière O. Suite 6900
Montréal, QC, H5A 1K6

André Girard
INRS-EMT, Place Bonaventure
800, de la Gauchetière O. Suite 6900
Montréal, QC, H5A 1K6

Jean-Charles Gregoire
INRS-EMT, Place Bonaventure
800, de la Gauchetière O. Suite 6900
Montréal, QC, H5A 1K6

Abstract   We describe a hierarchical topology for connecting users in large scale, Internet-based multipoint-to-multipoint applications. The multicast group is partitioned into *sub-groups*. Users who need to quickly transmit a lot of information to each other are gathered in the same sub-group which is connected by a *sub-ring*. All sub-rings are interconnected by a *backbone ring*. This two-level topology forms a *multi-ring*. We formulate an optimization problem to determine the topology that maximizes the bandwidth on the backbone, subject to delay constraints. We propose a heuristic to solve this problem and we show by simulation the good

---

*The completion of this research was made possible thanks to Bell Canada's support through its Bell University Laboratories R&D program.

performance of our approximations. We show also that our heuristic is very promising in terms of computing time and backbone stability.

Keywords: Network design, multipoint-to-multipoint applications, multi-ring, delay bounds, Lagrangean decomposition.

1. Introduction

Many multimedia distributed applications such as audio and video conferencing, collaborative environments, multi-player games and distributed interactive simulation need efficient multipoint transmission and require quality of service (QoS) guarantees to run correctly. IP multicast, described in RFC 1112 [6], was considered the best candidate to support these new applications. In the last decade, many attempts have been made to identify efficient and large scale IP multicast routing mechanisms and a reliable multicast transport service. However, many issues such as group management, multicast address allocation, session management, support for heterogeneous receivers, reliability and security still limit the commercial deployment of IP Multicast [7, 10].

Support for QoS, scalability and group management are among the most demanding requirements that IP multicast must support. Many QoS criteria depend on application characteristics. For example, real-time interactive applications require bounded delay, video-based applications require large bandwidth, applications based on fairness like games or electronic auctions involve synchronized play-out and ordering and so on. In addition, IP multicast introduces another difficulty to the QoS routing problem since different members of the same multicast group may require different QoS delivery levels.

Scalability is required by the actual huge size of the Internet which connects millions of users. Any Internet based application must have sufficient capabilities to group a large number of users. Naturally, taking into account scalability concerns while solving QoS problems is a very hard task.

Finally, group management is a very important challenge for IP multicast. The current service model does not consider receiver authorization, transmission authorization and group creation which will affect the security of the applications. Certainly, this prevents the use of multicast services in business networks which represent a very important market segment.

This large number of problems inherent to IP multicast has led some researchers not to believe any more in Deering's original architecture [6] and to start looking for an alternative. The idea is motivated by the possibility for end systems to implement multicast services on top of IP unicast. Consequently, end systems will form the nodes of an *overlay* structure in which each *edge* corresponds to an IP layer unicast *path* [5]. In the remainder of this work, we will distinguish between the overlay level and the IP level which we will some-

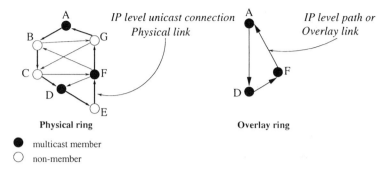

Figure 15.1. Physical and overlay rings

time call the physical level since it describes the real topology of the network. Therefore, links in the IP level are called *physical* links. The main advantage of the overlay approach to multicast is that it does not require implementation of multicast capabilities in routers, which is supposed to accelerate the deployment of multicast. However, QoS functionality cannot be provided by end systems alone and thus has to be supported at the IP layer. Moreover, an overlay structure incurs some redundant traffic on physical links which limits its application domain to small sized and sparse groups.

IP multicast improves performance in the network layer but it suffers from lack of manageability. On the other hand, overlay approaches cannot perform as well as IP multicast but are simpler to manage. To benefit from both techniques, we propose a new approach for connecting and managing multicast groups. This approach is based on connecting all members of a multicast group on one or many rings depending on the application. Our choice of ring topology is motivated by the following arguments:

■ It is possible to implement multicast services on a ring on top of IP unicast. In fact, as we can see on figure 15.1, we distinguish between

    – A *physical ring* in which each link is a unicast connection between two nodes which can be members or non-members of the multicast group; e.g., group members A and D are connected via non-member nodes B and C.

    – An *overlay ring* connecting only group members with *paths*, each path is a chain of unicast connections between two neighboring group members and corresponds to an *overlay link*.

■ A ring is a *closed* topology. This means that messages originated by a source on the ring will return back to that source which then removes them from the ring. This feature can be used to implement efficient member authentication, source authorization and reliability procedures.

- A ring is an *ordered* topology. This means that every node has to know only its predecessor and its successor. This feature allows easy implementation of message ordering procedures which are very important for interactive and fairness based applications.

- A ring is a *linear* topology, so its throughput is limited by the minimum bandwidth over all arcs and buffer overflow can be avoided.

- Since every node on the ring has exactly one successor, there is no need to duplicate messages in routers. Moreover, there is no route computing to perform. The router copies messages it is interested in and then forwards them on its ring output interface.

- A comparative study between ring and tree embedding undertaken by Bladi and Ofek [2] shows that tree embedding is not always the best strategy in terms of end-to-end delay bound, overall bandwidth allocated to the multicast group and the signaling overhead for sharing of the resources allocated to the group. The advantages of ring embedding are clearer for dynamic and adaptive group multicast.

However, there are also several drawbacks to a ring topology:

- Rings may require as many as 25% more links than a tree topology [12].

- End-to-end delay is proportional to ring size.

- A failure on one link or one node affects the entire ring. However, it is possible to duplicate output and input interfaces in clockwise and counterclockwise directions. We will not consider reliability problems in this study.

- Adding a new member requires *opening* the ring. The same problem occurs when a member wants to leave the group. Moreover, since the ring is a linear topology, it is not throughput scalable. That means that adding a new node may decrease the throughput if the links used to connect it to the ring have lower bandwidth.

The objective of this work is to propose solutions to some of these problems. We will be particularly interested in solving the end-to-end delay problem in order to improve the scalability of multicast applications. We propose a hierarchical topology in which the multicast group is partitioned into *sub-groups*, each one of them connected by a *sub-ring*. All sub-rings are interconnected by a *backbone ring*. This two-level topology is called a *multi-ring*. In the remainder of this paper, we will be interested in the modeling of a delay-constrained multi-ring problem with respect to some practical constraints such as on-line connection of dynamic multicast groups, bandwidth efficiency and scalability.

In the next section, we discuss the opportunities offered by an overlay multiring for multicast services. In section 3, we formulate the optimization problem for the delay-constrained multi-ring construction problem. In section 4, we propose a solution method based on a Lagrangean relaxation. In section 5, we present some numerical results. Finally, in section 6, we summarize our conclusions and discuss future work.

2. Delay-bounded ring construction problem

2.1 Characterization of multicast multimedia applications

Most real-time multimedia distributed applications are delay-sensitive. This is why the most common performance metric used in communication networks is related to delay. Unfortunately, end-to-end delay in a ring topology is linear versus the ring size which causes scalability problems. In order to solve this problem, we assume that for a given group partition we can propose a hierarchical multicast structure which minimizes end-to-end delays and improves scalability. Our solution is based on the following observations:

- In real life, a many-to-many application is more likely to be a set of few-to-few applications due to social interaction issues [7] or to the application itself.

- Receivers in large scale interactive applications are not, in general, interested in the same information at the same time [9, 11] or they require different levels of QoS. For example, in figure 15.2 we have 12 cars on a racing circuit in a multi-player game. We suppose that each user controls one car. As we can see, user c_2 will be more interested in information about user c_1 than c_9. Moreover, c_2 cannot tolerate delayed information from c_1 because otherwise the race will not have any sense. The interesting points are that first, users c_1 and c_2 may be very far away of each other in the network while c_2 and c_9 may be close, and second, the amount of traffic to be transmitted from c_1 to c_2 is much higher than that from c_1 to c_9.

Based on this, we can partition the multicast group according to receiver interests or QoS requirements. In figure 15.2, we have partitioned the racing circuit arbitrarily into 6 overlapping sub-circuits which corresponds to 6 overlapping multicast *sub-groups*. In this example, users are continuously moving from one sub-group to another and the multicast group is very dynamic which involves very frequent topology rearrangements. We will discuss in subsection 2.3 several constraints related to dynamic groups but we will not consider maintenance issues in this work. We assume that the multicast group is static in the long-term and we will be interested in the problem of constructing an initial topology, a problem which is common to both static and dynamic applications.

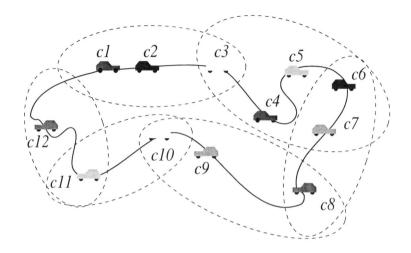

Figure 15.2. A racing circuit

We hope that the solution to this problem will lead to a simple and efficient rearrangement heuristic which is the subject of ongoing research.

In the remainder of this work, we will consider the racing game example for illustrative purpose. However, we find many other short-term static applications such as virtual distributed battle games where the battlefield may be partitioned into many battle areas, each with its own armies. In this example, preserving causal ordering among related messages is very important. Indeed, action (e.g. shell firing) must be observed before its effect (target destruction). Virtual tournaments (e.g. Chess tournament) are also examples of short-term static applications.

In this work, we will not deal with partition techniques. We suppose that we have already built the sub-groups according to QoS requirements. Given this partition, we can proceed to construct the overlay and then the physical topologies.

2.2   Overlay multi-ring construction

A *multi-ring* is obtained from a ring network by appending sub-rings to edges of the ring and, recursively, to edges of sub-rings [1]. This procedure is known as the augmentation of ring networks which is intended to decrease the ring's diameter. In order to construct an overlay multi-ring from a given partition of a multicast group we make the following definition:

Definition 1

Let g^k and g^l be two sub-groups of a multicast group G and n any node in G. If $n \in g^k$ and $n \in g^l$ then g^k and g^l are said to be adjacent.

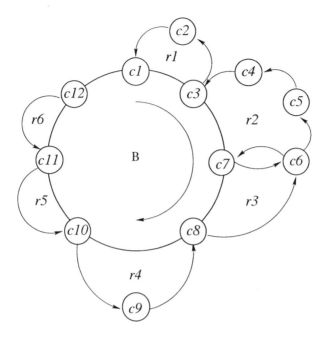

Figure 15.3. The overlay multi-ring of the racing circuit

If we model a sub-group with a node and the adjacency relation with an arc, the resulting graph must be connected. Otherwise, we have sub-groups which are independent from the others and can be viewed as different multicast groups. We connect all these nodes in a common ring called the *backbone ring*. Every sub-group must have two different nodes on the backbone in order to ensure interconnection survivability. The sub-rings will be then constructed separately. The choice of backbone nodes and its number is important and has a significant effect on the multi-ring stability. Stability is measured according to the capacity of the backbone ring to connect sub-rings without being rearranged. Many practical constraints would be considered in this choice which is the object for an ongoing work. For the example of figure 15.2, we obtain the multi-ring of figure 15.3. Note that c_6 and c_7 belong to 2 sub-groups and show up on 2 sub-rings r_2 and r_3.

2.3   Physical multi-ring construction problem

Given the overlay multi-ring of figure 15.3, the physical multi-ring is constructed so that end-to-end delays are maintained within given bounds. This problem is a set of interdependent constrained traveling salesman problems. Since the traveling salesman problem is shown to be NP-hard, our problem will be much more complex due to delay and topology coupling constraints.

Although we will propose later an efficient heuristic to solve this problem, it will be very expensive in terms of computing time to solve the overall problem whenever a change in group membership occurs. Furthermore, real-time multicast applications cannot tolerate frequent large topological changes as packets are constantly in flight within the multi-ring. For these reasons, we will not deal with multi-ring maintenance issues but try to prevent frequent updates by choosing appropriate multi-ring construction policies.

According to this framework, we believe that the objective function should be chosen so that the backbone ring remains stable as long as possible when the sub-rings change; if the topology of one sub-ring changes, the number of neighboring sub-groups affected must be as small as possible. Clearly, it is difficult to express formally an objective function which describes exactly these criteria. However, we propose to maximize the backbone ring throughput. We shall study later with numerical computation how close we are to the expected objective which is defined in terms of performance perceived by the customer. The ring throughput is the maximum flow that can be sent on the ring. It corresponds to the minimum bandwidth over all links on the ring. When the traffic load on a sub-ring increases due to new sub-group memberships, the traffic on the backbone will increase consequently because there is at least one link in common and the new members will generate traffic to other sub-groups. If the backbone ring throughput does not support the extra traffic load, the backbone ring must be rearranged which affects the overall topology. So, when we maximize the backbone ring throughput the need for global rearrangement will decrease and the multi-ring will be more stable. A global rearrangement may also be necessary when the delay bound on one sub-ring is reached and its critical link is the one which interconnects the sub-ring with the backbone. Maximizing the backbone throughput will make this situation less likely to occur.

The main advantage of this objective is its simplicity. Its drawback however, which is also related to the ring topology, is that the only value that determines the objective function is the value of the smallest link bandwidth. Other link bandwidths do not affect the optimal solution value. In practice, this choice is not so constraining since the backbone nodes have, in general, the highest capacities and we can find many network configuration procedures to eliminate low bandwidth links from the backbone.

3.   Physical network model

3.1   Problem description

The physical network is a connected, directed, asymmetric graph $G = (V, E)$ where the vertex set V contains N network nodes and the edge set E represents the unidirectional communication links between the nodes. Each node is identified by a unique IP address, so we suppose that a bijective relation exists between a node in the overlay network and a node in the physical network. Each communication link $(i, j) \in E$ has a capacity C_{ij} in packets per second which may be different from C_{ji}.

We are interested in constructing a multi-ring for a multipoint-to-multipoint communication defined by the multicast group G. This group is partitioned into a set of K sub-groups $\{g^1, g^2, \ldots, g^K\}$. We can choose the common nodes between sub-groups to form the backbone group g^B. However, any other method can be applied.

We introduce two sets of binary variables:

- x_{ij}^B: indicates whether or not arc (i, j) is included in the backbone ring;

- x_{ij}^k: indicates whether or not arc (i, j) is included in the kth sub-ring.

Note that the x_{ij}^k variables depend on the configuration of the backbone, i.e., the x_{ij}^B variables. In fact, let the multi-ring given in figure 15.4 be a physical topology of the overlay multi-ring given in figure 15.3. Sub-group g^1 contains nodes 1, 2 and 3. However, to construct sub-ring r^1, we must consider one of these two possible sub-groups, $\{1, 10, 7, 8, 3, 2\}$ or $\{3, 11, 12, 1, 2\}$, in order to reduce the number of physical links used by the multi-ring and take advantage of the unicast connections already set up. Recall that our proposed overlay approach consists of implementing application-level multicast connections on top of IP-level unicast connections. If the first sub-group alternative is chosen, we must consider the constraints $x_{1,10}^1 = x_{10,7}^1 = x_{7,8}^1 = x_{8,3}^1 = 1$ when solving the first sub-ring construction problem.

We suppose that each sub-group g^k generates two kinds of traffic:

1. a high quality traffic of A^k packet/s which is transmitted between the members of the same sub-group;

2. a low quality traffic of $A^{k,B}$ packet/s which is transmitted on the backbone to the other sub-groups. We do not consider the adjacency of sub-groups to define this traffic so all sub-groups will receive the same traffic from the backbone. For example, in the multi-ring of figure 15.3 the members of sub-ring r_2 and those of sub-ring r_4 will receive the same traffic $A^{1,B}$ from sub-ring r_1.

This approach alleviates the traffic load on the backbone without disturbing the application since the neighboring nodes still continue to receive a high quality traffic on the sub-rings. Thus, it should be possible to connect more nodes on the backbone while providing adequate QoS to the applications.

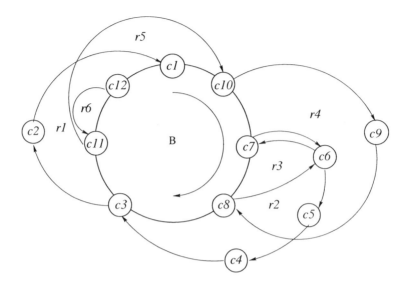

Figure 15.4.   The physical multi-ring

Let a_{ij} be the traffic flow in packet/s on arc (i, j). Then a_{ij} is given by the following expression:

$$a_{ij}(\mathbf{x}_{ij}) = \sum_{k=1}^{K} \left(A^{k,B} x_{ij}^B + A^k x_{ij}^k \right), \tag{15.1}$$

where $\mathbf{x}_{ij} = [x_{ij}^B, x_{ij}^1, \dots, x_{ij}^k, \dots, x_{ij}^K]$ is the decision vector.

The average delay per packet (queuing time) on each arc (i, j) is a function of the flow a_{ij} and the capacity C_{ij}. We assume that $D_{ij}\left(a_{ij}(\mathbf{x}_{ij}), C_{ij}\right)$ is a given nonlinear non decreasing function of the traffic a_{ij} on the link which gives the delay on arc (i, j) and presents a barrier at C_{ij}. We assume also that the total delay on a ring is additive by arc.

We are given $K + 1$ delay bounds:

- Δ^B for the backbone ring;

- Δ^k for each subsidiary sub-ring r^k.

From the discussion above, we expect that $\Delta^k \ll \Delta^B$.

3.2   Mathematical formulation

The mathematical formulation of the delay-bounded multi-ring construction problem **P1** is given by

$$\max_{\mathbf{x}} \min_{(i,j)|x_{ij}^B=1} C_{ij} \tag{15.2}$$

$$\sum_{i,j=1}^{N} D_{ij}\left(a_{ij}(\mathbf{x}_{ij}), C_{ij}\right) x_{ij}^{B} \;\le\; \Delta^{B} \tag{15.3}$$

$$\sum_{i,j=1}^{N} D_{ij}\left(a_{ij}(\mathbf{x}_{ij}), C_{ij}\right) x_{ij}^{k} \;\le\; \Delta^{k} \tag{15.4}$$

$$x_{ij}^{k} \;\ge\; \sum_{(p,q)} \delta_{pq}^{k}\, \mathcal{I}_{ij}(p,q,B) \tag{15.5}$$

$$\sum_{i\in g^{B}} x_{ij}^{B} = 1 \quad \text{and} \quad \sum_{i\in g^{B}} x_{ji}^{B} = 1 \;\; \forall j \in g^{B} \tag{15.6}$$

$$\sum_{i\in g^{k}} x_{ij}^{k} = 1 \quad \text{and} \quad \sum_{i\in g^{k}} x_{ji}^{k} = 1 \;\; \forall j \in g^{k} \tag{15.7}$$

$$\sum_{i,j\in S} x_{ij}^{B} \le |S| - 1 \quad \forall \quad S \subset g^{B} \text{ and } 2 \le |S| \le |g^{B}| - 1 \tag{15.8}$$

$$\sum_{i,j\in S} x_{ij}^{k} \le |S| - 1 \quad \forall \quad S \subset g^{k} \text{ and } 2 \le |S| \le |g^{k}| - 1 \tag{15.9}$$

$$x_{ij}^{B} \text{ and } x_{ij}^{k} \;\in\; \{0,1\}. \tag{15.10}$$

The objective function (15.2) maximizes the backbone ring throughput. The constraints (15.3) and (15.4) are for delay bounds. In constraint (15.5), which ensures that the final topology is a multi-ring, we have introduced two indicator functions:

$$\delta_{pq}^{k} = \begin{cases} 1 & \text{if nodes } p, q \in g^{k} \quad \forall k \in \{1,2,\ldots,K\}, \\ 0 & \text{otherwise,} \end{cases} \tag{15.11}$$

and

$$\mathcal{I}_{ij}(p,q,B) = \begin{cases} 1 & \text{if arc } (i,j)|x_{ij}^{B} = 1 \text{ is in physical path } (p,q) \\ & \text{on the backbone ring,} \\ 0 & \text{otherwise,} \end{cases} \tag{15.12}$$

Note that we cannot determine the value of indicator function $\mathcal{I}_{ij}(p,q,B)$ unless we know the backbone ring configuration. We will see later how we can overcome this hard constraint. Constraints 15.6 and 15.7 ensure that for each node there are only one incoming and one outgoing links, so the topology is linear. Constraints 15.8 and 15.9 are known as *Subtour Elimination Constraints*. They prevent from closing the cycle unless all nodes are included in the ring.

The MAX-MIN operator in the objective function is not suitable to establish optimality conditions for this problem. So, we introduce a new variable $\theta = \min_{(i,j)|x_{ij}^{B}=1} C_{ij}$ which is the backbone ring throughput and we add the following constraints to problem **P1**

$$\theta \le C_{ij} \quad \forall (i,j)|x_{ij}^{B} = 1 \tag{15.13}$$

Note that this constraint is not defined for arcs (i, j) such that $x_{ij}^B = 0$. In order to make the θ variable independent from decision variables $\mathbf{x}$, we assume that we know an upper bound $\bar{\theta}$ of the maximum ring throughput on the network. For example, we can put $\bar{\theta}$ equals to the maximum bandwidth of the network. The new constraint is replaced with

$$\theta \leq C_{ij}x_{ij}^B + (1 - x_{ij}^B)\bar{\theta} \quad \forall(i, j), \tag{15.14}$$

which can be written also as

$$\bar{\theta} - \theta \geq (\bar{\theta} - C_{ij})x_{ij}^B \quad \forall(i, j). \tag{15.15}$$

Define $\theta' = \bar{\theta} - \theta$ and $C'_{ij} = \bar{\theta} - C_{ij}$. We obtain finally the following constraint

$$\theta' \geq C'_{ij}x_{ij}^B \quad \forall(i, j), \tag{15.16}$$

and the objective function will be expressed as

$$\min \theta' - \bar{\theta}. \tag{15.17}$$

The delay constraints (15.3) and (15.4) tie all variables of the problem via the flow parameter a_{ij}. The problem becomes very hard to solve since there is no obvious decomposition of the coupled ring construction subproblems. Therefore, we expand problem **P1** with another set of independent decision variables f_{ij} representing the total traffic on link (i, j) and we add new constraints (15.18) to reflect the fact that these variables are linked to the original $\mathbf{x}$ variables

$$f_{ij} \geq \sum_{k=1}^{K} \left(A^{k,B}x_{ij}^B + A^k x_{ij}^k\right). \tag{15.18}$$

Normally, Eq. (15.18)should be equality constraints. Writing them as inequality constraints does not change the optimal solution for the following reasons: they do not appear in the objective and if Eq. (15.21)is a strict inequality, Eqs. (15.22) and (15.23) will be satisfied because the delay functions $D_{ij}(.)$ are increasing in f_{ij}. Introducing these new variables will allow us to decompose the problem into independent flow allocation problems on each link as we will see later.

  These constraints guarantee that the flow which can be routed on each arc is greater than the traffic generated by all sub-groups that use this link. Note that the optimality of problem **P1** does not depend on the value of flows and this is why we have formulated the conservation constraints as inequalities which is sufficient to verify the feasibility conditions of the solution of the new problem **P2** and then the equivalence of the two problems. Problem **P2** is formulated as follows

$$\min_{\mathbf{x},\mathbf{f},\theta'} \theta' \tag{15.19}$$

$$\theta' \geq C'_{ij} x^B_{ij} \quad (\mu_{ij}) \tag{15.20}$$

$$f_{ij} \geq \sum_{k=1}^{K} \left(A^{k,B} x^B_{ij} + A^k x^k_{ij} \right) \quad (\lambda_{ij}) \tag{15.21}$$

$$\sum_{i,j=1}^{N} D_{ij} \left(f_{ij}, C_{ij} \right) x^B_{ij} \leq \Delta^B \tag{15.22}$$

$$\sum_{i,j=1}^{N} D_{ij} \left(f_{ij}, C_{ij} \right) x^k_{ij} \leq \Delta^k \tag{15.23}$$

$$x^k_{ij} \geq \sum_{(p,q)} \delta^k_{pq} \mathcal{I}_{ij}(p,q,B) \tag{15.24}$$

$$\sum_{i \in g^B} x^B_{ij} = 1 \quad \text{and} \quad \sum_{i \in g^B} x^B_{ji} = 1 \; \forall j \in g^B \tag{15.25}$$

$$\sum_{i \in g^k} x^k_{ij} = 1 \quad \text{and} \quad \sum_{i \in g^k} x^k_{ji} = 1 \; \forall j \in g^k \tag{15.26}$$

$$\sum_{i,j \in S} x^B_{ij} \leq |S| - 1 \quad \forall \quad S \subset g^B \text{ and } 2 \leq |S| \leq |g^B| - 1 \tag{15.27}$$

$$\sum_{i,j \in S} x^k_{ij} \leq |S| - 1 \quad \forall \quad S \subset g^k \text{ and } 2 \leq |S| \leq |g^k| - 1 \tag{15.28}$$

$$x^B_{ij} \text{ and } x^k_{ij} \in \{0,1\}. \tag{15.29}$$

4. Dual problem formulation and solution

4.1 Lagrangean relaxation

The basic approach to the solution procedure is Lagrangean relaxation. We dualize constraints (15.20) and (15.21) into the objective with two associated non-negative Lagrange multiplier vectors μ and λ, respectively. The resulting Lagrangean is given by

$$\mathcal{L}(\theta', \mathbf{x}, \mathbf{f}, \mu, \lambda) = \theta' - \bar{\theta} - \sum_{i,j=1}^{N} \mu_{ij} \left[\theta' - C'_{ij} x^B_{ij} \right] - \tag{15.30}$$

$$\sum_{i,j=1}^{N} \lambda_{ij} \left[f_{ij} - \sum_{k=1}^{K} \left(A^{k,B} x^B_{ij} + A^k x^k_{ij} \right) \right]$$

$$\mathcal{L}(\theta', \mathbf{x}, \mathbf{f}, \boldsymbol{\mu}, \boldsymbol{\lambda}) + \bar{\theta} = (1 - \sum_{i,j=1}^{N} \mu_{ij})\theta' + \sum_{i,j=1}^{N} \left[\mu_{ij} C'_{ij} + \lambda_{ij} A^B \right] x_{ij}^B +$$

$$\sum_{k=1}^{K} A^k \sum_{i,j=1}^{N} \lambda_{ij} x_{ij}^k + \sum_{i,j=1}^{N} -\lambda_{ij} f_{ij} \qquad (15.31)$$

where $A^B = \sum_{k=1}^{K} A^{k,B}$ is the traffic on the backbone ring. In order to have bounded dual function, we add a redundant constraint

$$0 \le \theta' \le \bar{\theta} - \underline{\theta}, \qquad (15.32)$$

where $\underline{\theta}$ is a lower bound for θ. A possible value for $\underline{\theta}$ is equal to the minimum link bandwidth in the network. We can put $\underline{\theta}$ equals to zero but if we make the variation $\bar{\theta} - \underline{\theta}$ tighter we obtain smoother dual function.

The dual function is given by

$$w(\boldsymbol{\mu}, \boldsymbol{\lambda}) = \min_{\theta', \mathbf{x}, \mathbf{f}} \mathcal{L}(\theta', \mathbf{x}, \mathbf{f}, \boldsymbol{\mu}, \boldsymbol{\lambda})$$

$$= w_1(\boldsymbol{\mu}) + w_2(\boldsymbol{\lambda}) + \sum_{k=1}^{K} w_3^k(\boldsymbol{\lambda}) + w_4(\boldsymbol{\lambda})$$

where the partial dual functions are given by

1 The backbone ring throughput subproblem

$$w_1(\boldsymbol{\mu}) = \min_{\theta'}(1 - \sum_{i,j=1}^{N} \mu_{ij})\theta' \qquad (15.33)$$

$$0 \le \theta' \le \bar{\theta} - \underline{\theta}.$$

2 The backbone ring construction subproblem

$$w_2(\boldsymbol{\lambda}) = \min_{\mathbf{x}^B} \sum_{i,j=1}^{N} \left[\mu_{ij} C'_{ij} + \lambda_{ij} A^B \right] x_{ij}^B \qquad (15.34)$$

$$\sum_{i \in g^B} x_{ij}^B = 1$$

$$\sum_{i \in g^B} x_{ji}^B = 1$$

$$\sum_{i,j \in S} x_{ij}^B \le |S| - 1 \quad \forall S \subset g^B \text{ and } 2 \le |S| \le |g^B| - 1$$

$$x_{ij}^B \in \{0, 1\}.$$

3 The K sub-ring construction subproblems for a given backbone configuration

$$w_3^k(\lambda) = \min_{\mathbf{x}^k} \sum_{i,j=1}^{N} \lambda_{ij} A^k x_{ij}^k \qquad (15.35)$$

$$x_{ij}^k \geq \sum_{(p,q)} \delta_{pq}^k \mathcal{I}_{ij}(p,q,B)$$

$$\sum_{i \in g^k} x_{ij}^k = 1$$

$$\sum_{i \in g^k} x_{ji}^k = 1$$

$$\sum_{i,j \in S} x_{ij}^k \leq |S| - 1 \quad \forall S \subset g^k \text{ and } 2 \leq |S| \leq |g^k| - 1$$

$$x_{ij}^k \in \{0,1\}.$$

4 The flow allocation subproblem

$$w_4(\lambda) = \min_{\mathbf{x},\mathbf{f}} \sum_{i,j=1}^{N} -\lambda_{ij} f_{ij} \qquad (15.36)$$

$$\sum_{i,j=1}^{N} D_{ij}(f_{ij}, C_{ij}) x_{ij}^B \leq \Delta^B \quad (u)$$

$$\sum_{i,j=1}^{N} D_{ij}(f_{ij}, C_{ij}) x_{ij}^k \leq \Delta^k \quad (v^k)$$

$$f_{ij} \geq 0 \quad (w_{ij}).$$

Note that the non-negativity constraints in subproblem (15.36) are redundant because of constraint (15.21). The solution to subproblem (15.33) is straightforward: if $\sum_{i,j=1}^{N} \mu_{ij} \geq 1$, $\theta' = \bar{\theta} - \underline{\theta}$; otherwise, $\theta' = 0$. The backbone ring construction subproblem (15.34) is an unconstrained traveling salesman problem (TSP) and can be solved using one of the existing efficient algorithms which give an exact solution to the Asymmetric TSP. To solve the K sub-ring construction subproblems (15.35), we need the optimal solution for the backbone ring construction subproblem (15.34). Similarly, to solve the flow allocation subproblem (15.36) we need the optimal solution for the multi-ring construction subproblems (15.34) and (15.35). Because of the coupling between the subproblems, we need to solve all of them to optimality at the same time in order to have the exact value of the dual function. This is as difficult as solving the original problem and we want to take advantage of the problem structure to

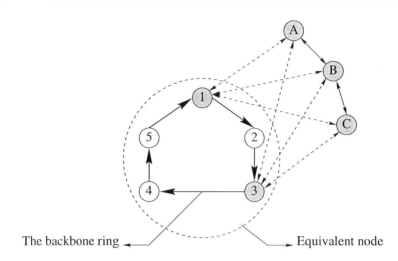

Figure 15.5. An equivalent node example

solve each problem independently, based on the solution of the other problems, leading to an iterative procedure for the solution of the subproblems.

We will propose in the next section a solution procedure for the multi-ring construction subproblems (15.34) and (15.35) after which we discuss some solution methods for the flow allocation subproblem (15.36).

4.2   The multi-ring design subproblems

Rather than using the formal expression (15.5) which may complicate the solution of subproblem (15.35), we propose the following sequential procedure:

Backbone construction: Construct the backbone ring by solving subproblem (15.34). We use a sequential, lowest-first, branch and bound algorithm based on the Assignment Problem relaxation and a subtour elimination branching scheme [4, 3]. This algorithm gives an exact solution of a large scale, asymmetric traveling salesman problem. Therefore, we obtain an optimal solution $\mathbf{x}^B$ for the backbone ring.

Equivalent node: In order to construct a sub-ring, the backbone is viewed as an *equivalent node*, N_B, which belongs to all sub-groups. There are two ways to connect this node to the other nodes depending on the orientation of the path connecting the nodes of a sub-group on the backbone. For example, in figure 15.5, the optimal backbone ring is given by the following sequence of nodes $\{1, 2, 3, 4, 5\}$ and we have to construct a sub-ring connecting the sub-group $g = \{1, 3, A, B, C\}$. There are two possible paths to connect nodes 1 and 3: the first one is (1,2,3) in which node 2

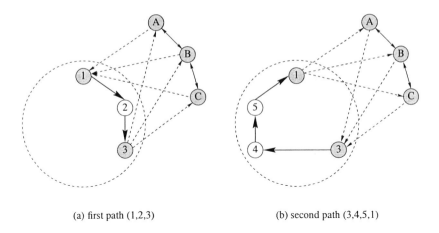

(a) first path (1,2,3)   (b) second path (3,4,5,1)

Figure 15.6.   The two possibilities of the sub-ring connection

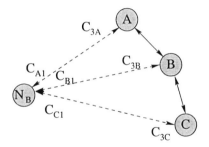

Figure 15.7.   The capacitated equivalent network

must be added to the sub-group and the second is (3,4,5,1) in which nodes
4 and 5 must be added to the sub-group. We select the orientation that has
the smallest number of hop. This is not necessarily optimal with respect
to our objective function but we expect that in most cases, this is the best
choice and a simple hop counting metric. If the first path is chosen, then
only the arcs shown in figure 6(a) should be considered. Otherwise, the
opposite orientations are considered as shown in figure 6(b). A simple
hop counting metric d can be used to determine the shortest path to be
considered. Therefore, we obtain the following rule for any path (p, q)

$$\text{if} \quad d(p, q) \leq d(q, p) \quad \Rightarrow \quad p \to q$$
$$\text{if} \quad d(p, q) > d(q, p) \quad \Rightarrow \quad q \to p.$$

In the example of figure 15.5, the orientation $1 \to 3$ will be chosen.

Sub-ring construction: Subproblem (15.35) can then be solved in order to construct the kth sub-ring connecting the kth sub-group augmented by the equivalent node N_B. In the example of figure 15.5, the sub-ring is constructed on the capacitated equivalent network of figure 15.7 where only the capacities of the arcs connecting the equivalent node to the other nodes of the sub-groups are shown.

We have proposed a simple sequential procedure to solve subproblems (15.34) and (15.35). It gives an optimal solution to the multi-ring construction problem without considering the delay constraints. Due to the decomposition, these constraints will be handled separately in subproblem (15.36).

4.3   The flow allocation subproblem

For subproblem (15.36), given the decision vectors $\mathbf{x}^B$ and $\mathbf{x}^k$ obtained from subproblems (15.34) and (15.35), we derive the first order optimality equations in order to establish some flow allocation rules. The Lagrangean of this problem is given by

$$
\begin{aligned}
&\mathcal{L}^f(\mathbf{f}, u, \mathbf{v}, \mathbf{w}) \\
&= \sum_{i,j=1}^{N} -\lambda_{ij} f_{ij} + \sum_{i,j=1}^{N} u\left(D_{ij}(f_{ij}, C_{ij})x_{ij}^B - \Delta^B\right) + \\
&\quad \sum_{k=1}^{K} v^k\left(\sum_{i,j=1}^{N} D_{ij}(f_{ij}, C_{ij})x_{ij}^k - \Delta^k\right) - \sum_{i,j=1}^{N} w_{ij} f_{ij} \\
&= \sum_{i,j=1}^{N}\left[-\lambda_{ij} f_{ij} + \left(u x_{ij}^B + \sum_{k=1}^{K} v^k x_{ij}^k\right) D_{ij}(f_{ij}, C_{ij}) - w_{ij} f_{ij}\right] - \\
&\quad u\Delta^B - \sum_{k=1}^{K} v^k \Delta^k,
\end{aligned}
\tag{15.37}
$$

where u and v^k are non-negative Lagrange multipliers associated respectively with the delay bound constraints for the backbone ring and the K sub-rings, and $\{w_{ij}\}$ are non-negative Lagrange multipliers associated with the non-negativity constraints.

This subproblem is then arc-separable. We thus compute the gradient of $\mathcal{L}^f(\mathbf{f}, u, \mathbf{v}, \mathbf{w})$ relative to the flow variables f_{ij} and obtain the first order optimality condition for arc (i,j)

$$
\frac{\partial \mathcal{L}^f}{\partial f_{ij}} = -\lambda_{ij} - w_{ij} + \left(u x_{ij}^B + \sum_{k=1}^{K} v^k x_{ij}^k\right) \frac{\partial D_{ij}(f_{ij}, C_{ij})}{\partial f_{ij}}
$$

$$= -\lambda_{ij} - w_{ij} + \Phi_{ij}\frac{\partial D_{ij}(f_{ij}, C_{ij})}{\partial f_{ij}} = 0$$

where

$$\Phi_{ij} = ux_{ij}^B + \sum_{k=1}^{K} v^k x_{ij}^k \tag{15.38}$$

is a multiplier for arc (i, j) which belongs to the multi-ring. The first order optimality condition will be expressed as

$$\lambda_{ij} + w_{ij} = \Phi_{ij}\frac{\partial D_{ij}(f_{ij}, C_{ij})}{\partial f_{ij}}. \tag{15.39}$$

If we model the arcs as $M/M/1$ queues, then the weighted average delay on arc (i, j) is given by

$$D_{ij}(f_{ij}, C_{ij}) = \frac{f_{ij}}{C_{ij} - f_{ij}}. \tag{15.40}$$

In that case, the first order optimality condition becomes

$$(\lambda_{ij} + w_{ij})(C_{ij} - f_{ij})^2 = \Phi_{ij}C_{ij} \tag{15.41}$$

and we have the following cases:

1 If $\lambda_{ij} > 0$ then the optimal flow is given by

$$f_{ij} = Cij - \sqrt{\frac{\Phi_{ij}C_{ij}}{\lambda_{ij}}}. \tag{15.42}$$

Note that we have considered by complementary conditions that $w_{ij} = 0$.

2 If $\lambda_{ij} = 0$ then

- if $\Phi_{ij} = 0$ then we can affect whatever nonzero value of flow to f_{ij}. We choose $f_{ij} = a_{ij}$, which is the request on arc (i, j), if $a_{ij} < C_{ij}$; otherwise $f_{ij} = C_{ij}$.

- if $\Phi_{ij} > 0$ then we have necessarily $f_{ij} = 0$ and $w_{ij} = \dfrac{\Phi_{ij}}{C_{ij}}$.

An exact solution of this subproblem can then be obtained with a subgradient method.

We propose also an approximative method in order to speed up the subgradient method. Assume that we have an active delay constraint $l \in \{B, 1, \ldots, K\}$

$$\sum_{i,j=1}^{N} \frac{f_{ij}}{C_{ij} - f_{ij}}x_{ij}^l = \Delta^l. \tag{15.43}$$

We solve this equation separately for each arc (i, j) with a delay bound equals to $\delta^l/|g^l|$ where $|g^l|$ is the cardinality of the group g^l. We obtain the value of the flow on each arc (i, j) in sub-ring r^l

$$f_{ij}^l = C_{ij} \frac{\delta^l}{|g^l| + \delta^l}. \tag{15.44}$$

We repeat this procedure for all $l \in \{B, 1, \ldots, K\}$. Finally, the value of the feasible flow f_{ij} is given by

$$f_{ij} = \min_{l \in \{B, 1, \ldots, K\}} f_{ij}^l. \tag{15.45}$$

We call this approximative method the mean delay bound approach **(MDB)** for the flow allocation subproblem. We propose also a second way to partition delay bound which we call the weighted delay bound approach **(WDB)**. In this approach the delay bound on each arc is equal to $\Delta^l a_{ij}/\sum_{(i,j)} a_{ij}x_{ij}^l$.

From these approximations, we get a new description of f_{ij} which can be viewed as the maximum flow that can be allocated on each arc without violating the delay constraints. We then use the approximative result of (15.45) instead of solving the nonlinear program (15.36) and apply a subgradient method to optimize the dual problem.

5.   Numerical Examples

To validate our method, the multi-ring of figure 15.3 is again considered. We assume that we have a complete capacitated directed graph of 12 nodes with the following parameters: $\underline{\theta} = 10$, $\bar{\theta} = 84$, $C_{max} = 153$ packet/sec. We assume that we have a uniform packet size. The delay bounds are computed so that the flow on each arc do not exceed $8/9$ of the capacity. So, by a simple computing we obtain $\Delta^l = 8|g^l|$.

Our first objective is to compare different solutions to the flow allocation subproblem obtained with the three proposed approaches to the flow allocation subproblems: the exact solution given by a subgradient method, which we call **(SGM)**, the **(MDB)** and **(WDB)** approaches. In each case, we compute the backbone throughput versus the traffic load on the multi-ring. In each simulation, we display the multi-ring using a publicly available graphing package, called Dot [8]. For the following low demand vector $[A^B = 10, A^1 = 5, A^2 = 5, A^3 = 5, A^4 = 5, A^5 = 5, A^6 = 5]$ we obtain the multi-ring shown in figure 15.8. In this figure, the circle nodes correspond to the backbone nodes and the triangle nodes correspond to the sub-ring nodes. The solid black lines are the backbone links and they are labelled with the pair: capacity-demand. The throughput of the backbone is equal to the upper bound of the maximum throughput, $\bar{\theta} = 84$, so the solution is optimal. We call arc $(10,1)$ the cutting arc of the backbone since it corresponds to the minimum bandwidth.

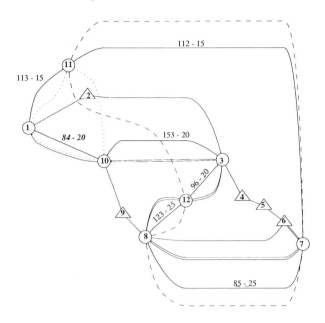

Figure 15.8.   The multi-ring for a demand vector A=[10,5,5,5,5,5,5]

Now, we compute the solution for the three mentioned approaches versus the traffic demand variation A^B on the backbone, A^1 on sub-ring r^1 which contains the cutting arc and A^2 on sub-ring r^2 which does not contain the cutting arc. The results are shown respectively in figures 15.9, 15.10 and 15.11. In figure 15.9, the performance of **MDB** approach is very close to the exact solution. The performance of **WDB** is less good because when we increase the load on all arcs of the backbone it is more efficient to partition the delay bound with equal proportions on all arcs. When we increase the traffic load on the sub-ring r^1 the two approaches have almost the same performance in terms of traffic load as shown in figure 15.10. However, the solution given by **MDB** is closer to the exact solution than that obtained by **WDB**. For the two approximative approaches, almost 85% of the traffic load obtained with the exact solution is reached. In figure 15.11, when we increase traffic load on sub-ring r^2, the solution of **MDB** is even closer to the exact solution than that obtained by **WDB**. However, **WDB** is more efficient in terms of maximum traffic load, it performs as well as the exact solution. Note that when the cutting arc is not in the sub-ring, the feasible traffic load on this sub-ring may exceed the maximum throughput of the backbone which is a very advantageous feature for the multi-ring connection strategy.

The second experiment that we have made consists of measuring the execution time of **WDB** and **MDB** approaches versus **SGM**. The results reported

Table 15.1.   Computing time in seconds

A^1	10	20	25	50	55	56	60	66
(SGM)	4.1	4.1	4.8	20.5	80.8	98.3	88.7	330.2
(MDB)	0.1	0.1	0.1	0.1	0.7	2.5	-	-
(WDB)	0.1	0.1	0.1	0.1	0.1	0.1	-	-

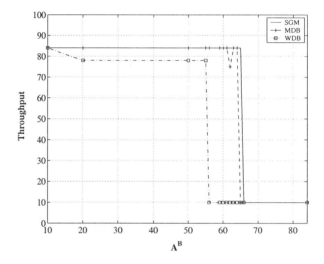

Figure 15.9.   Throughput versus A^B

in Table 15.1 show that the time execution ratio between the exact and the approximative approach is up to 100 in some cases.

The final experiment is related to stability. We have measured how often the topology is changed when the traffic load on the backbone and sub-ring r^1 increases. We report the results on figures 15.12 and 15.13 which show the number of topology changes versus the traffic load. The procedure to plot these figures is quite simple: when a change occurs we increase the number of topology changes by 1; otherwise it is kept unchanged. We note that the topology is stable when the traffic load is low. However, when the traffic load increases, the topology is no more stable because the number of feasible solutions becomes small. This is well illustrated on plots relative to the exact approach **(SGM)**. For approximative approaches, stability is less sensitive to the traffic load because the flow allocation in these cases is less granular. Consequently, choosing to maximize the backbone ring throughput is supported by these results.

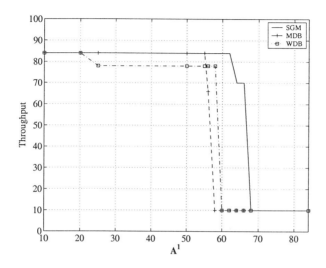

Figure 15.10. Throughput versus A^1

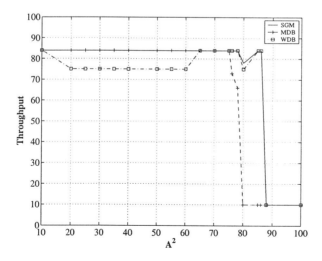

Figure 15.11. Throughput versus A^2

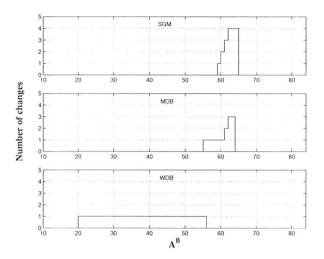

Figure 15.12.   Topology changes versus A^B

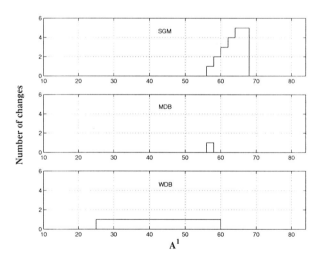

Figure 15.13.   Topology changes versus A^1

6. Conclusion

We have proposed in this paper a new technique to connect nodes in a multipoint-to-multipoint communication networks. This technique is based on a two-level hierarchical multi-ring topology implemented as an overlay on top of the IP unicast layer. It solves many problems inherent to multipoint applications such as scalability, ordering, end-to-end delays and implementation issues. We have established a mathematical formulation for the corresponding design problem and we have proposed an efficient heuristic to solve this NP-hard problem. Numerical simulations have shown the good performance of our approximative approaches in terms of traffic load and the gap from optimality. Our heuristic is also very promising in terms of computing time and backbone stability. We will study in future work its feasibility for real-time applications.

References

[1] W. Aiello, S. N. Bhatt, F. R.K. Chung, A. L. Rosenberg, and R. K. Sitaraman. Augmented ring networks. *IEEE trans. on Parallel and Distributed Systems*, 12(6):598–609, June 2001.

[2] M. Bladi and Y. Ofek. Ring versus tree embedding for real-time group multicast. In *Proc. IEEE INFOCOM'99*, pages 1099–1106, 1999.

[3] G. Carpaneto, M. Dell'Amico, and P. Toth. Algorithm 750: CDT: A Subroutine for the exact solution of large-scale, Asymmetric Travelling Salesman Problems. *ACM Transactions on Mathematical Software*, 21(4):410–415, December 1995.

[4] G. Carpaneto, M. Dell'Amico, and P. Toth. Exact solution of large-scale, Asymmetric Travelling Salesman Problems. *ACM Transactions on Mathematical Software*, 21(4):394–409, December 1995.

[5] Y. Chu, S. G. Rao, and H. Zhang. A case for end system multicast. In *Proceedings of ACM SIGMETRICS, Santa Clara,CA*, pages 1–12, June 2000.

[6] S. Deering. Host extensions for IP multicasting. *RFC 1112*, August 1989.

[7] C. Diot, B. Levine, B. Lyles, H. Kassem, and D. Balsiefen. Deployment issues for the IP multicast service and architecture. *IEEE Network*, January 2000.

[8] E. Koutsofios and S. C. North. Drawing graphs with *dot*. Technical report, August 1993.

[9] B. N. Levine, J. Crowcroft, C. Diot, J.J. Garcia-Luna-Aceves, and J. F. Kurose. Consideration of receiver interest for IP multicast delivery. In *Proc. IEEE INFOCOM'2000*, pages 470–479, April 2000.

[10] B. Quinn and K. Almeroth. IP Multicast applications: Challenges and solutions. *RFC 3170*, September 2001.

[11] T. Wong, R. H. Katz, and S. McCanne. An evaluation on using preference clustering in large-scale multicast applications. In *Proc. IEEE INFOCOM'2000*, pages 451–460, April 2000.

[12] B. Yener, S. Chen, and O. Günlük. Optimal packing of group multicastings. In *Proc. IEEE INFOCOM'98, San Francisco, CA*, April 1998.

Chapter 16

EFFICIENT BANDWIDTH IN MULTIMEDIA DISTRIBUTION NETWORKS WITH GUARANTEED QUALITY OF SERVICE

Joakim Kalvenes
Edwin L. Cox School of Business
Southern Methodist University, U.S.A.

Neil Keon
Edwin L. Cox School of Business
Southern Methodist University, U.S.A.

Abstract   In spite of predictions to the contrary, video on demand service has yet to become a significant channel for distribution of audiovisual entertainment to consumers' homes. The main reason for the delay in development in this market can be attributed to a lack of cost-efficient distribution channels for this type of transmissions. In this work, we examine the quality of service requirements for delivery of video on demand services and develop a new measure of bandwidth requirements for this type of network transmissions. A limited simulation experiment is performed with which we derive the overlay bandwidth requirements for a single movie stream viewed simultaneously by multiple consumers with randomly distributed starting times. We conclude that video on demand service can be offered at reasonable quality of service with relatively modest overlay network transmission capacity requirements.

Keywords: Video on demand, efficient bandwidth, quality of service, multimedia distribution

1.   Introduction

The popular press contains many references to the potential for video on demand, bandwidth auctions and bandwidth trading. There is already a number of entrants (e.g., Arbinet, Bandex and Enron) into the latter two of these hoped-for markets, although the combined valuation of these companies/divisions is disappointing. Video on demand, on the other hand, has yet to be offered to consumers other than in small-scale market trials. This work considers the bandwidth requirements for true video on demand delivery using overlay network services.[1]

We define video on demand as an audiovisual service delivered in real time to the consumer's home over a communication link. The consumer has access to features similar to those available on a video cassette recorder or a digital video disk player, including play, near-instant fast-forward, rewind, replay, etc., at the consumer's discretion. Video on demand is, thus, fundamentally different from pay per view service which is a scheduled broadcast available to those who pay to decode the transmission. We assume that consumers are willing to pay for video on demand service if the transmission is of sufficient quality. We define quality of service as the combination of a guaranteed maximum packet loss rate and a maximum end to end delay in delivery of packets from the video server to the consumer's television set, so as to provide the above mentioned video cassette recorder or digital video disk player features.

In our model, we assume that there is an on-line video content provider who seeks to deliver video on demand services to a number of consumers. In order to do so, the content provider needs a reliable communication link to the consumer's home. Much research has been conducted to provide more reliable service on the Internet. Two main approaches exist. In one stream of research, Kelly et al., 1998 and Edell et al., 1999 proposed usage-based charges to control user behavior through the creation of multiple service classes and, thereby, induce users to behave fairly and efficiently. Similarly, Mackie-Mason and Varian, 1995 proposed a pricing scheme for prioritizing packets at network nodes. While these methods certainly improve quality of service for the prioritized traffic, they do not provide any quality of service guarantee even for single packets, and the expected end to end quality of service of a stream of packets remains an open issue. In fact, if data packets are routed over the Internet or any other type of best effort network, then the end to end delay can never be guaranteed, even if such mechanisms as packet priorities are introduced.[2]

Instead of using the Internet for video packet transport, we propose distribution of video on demand over a private overlay network. On such a network, quality of service guarantees are offered through content provider acquisition of the bandwidth required for a transmission (Jordan and Jiang, 1996; Low

---

[1] Bandwidth is currently available as a metered (pay for the utilized bit rate for the duration of the transmission) service from, e.g., Level3. The bandwidth customer pays a monthly fee for access to a common carrier's facility, but the transmission cost is entirely variable and service is not contingent upon a service contract with long duration.

[2] Although it is possible to do path reservations to guarantee end to end delay, such methods do not scale well and the overhead traffic becomes excessive.

and Varaiya, 1993). In its simplest form, reservations are made for network resources based on posted prices (Cocchi et al., 1993; Korilis and Lazar, 1995; Masuda and Whang, 1999). Through self-selection, customers would segment into different priority classes based on willingness to pay for network resources. For instance, the network provider could offer multiple paths between two network nodes and price them differently. Few customers would select the most expensive path and, consequently, the highest-priced path would have the shortest expected end to end delay. In an attempt to solve the service provider's pricing problem, Wang et al., 1996 formulated the pricing decision as a constrained optimal control problem and proposed a three-stage solution procedure. Unfortunately, the solution procedure proves to be computationally intractable. In conclusion, although pervasive, the Internet does not provide a network with guaranteed quality of service delivery of data and, thus, it is not suitable for video on demand delivery.

On the other hand, the existing infrastructure with which the consumer connects to the Internet provides a sufficient platform for video on demand delivery from the consumer's Internet service provider. In order for the content provider to deliver guaranteed quality service to the consumer, it is necessary to establish an alternative communication link to the Internet between the content provider and the consumer's Internet service provider. This can be accomplished with the use of an overlay network (Birman, 2001) provided by a third party on an as-needed basis. On an overlay network, quality of service guarantees can be offered simply by allocating sufficient resources to specific sessions. In order to do so, de Veciana et al., 1995 combined the conventional practice of fixed offered prices with the alternative approach of allowing users to share resources so as to realize multiplexing gains. As an alternative approach, Keon and Anandalingam, provide a method for solving for the optimal prices by service class for a private network with call admission, where each service class may have unique quality of service guarantees and all connections within a service class are multiplexed. In other words, this provides a framework by which the overlay network provider may determine the prices charged for overlay bandwidth.

To summarize, in order to provide video on demand service to consumers, the content provider will use an overlay network for video transmission. The service provider will purchase the necessary overlay bandwidth in real time from a third-party network operator. The overlay bandwidth purchases will ensure delivery of video packets to the consumer's network access point at a sufficient quality of service level. From this point, the video packets are transported over the consumer's Internet access line (such as DSL or cable modem) to the consumer's home. Although the Internet is not suitable for real-time transportation of video packets, it can still be used for other parts of the process, including search for movies, transaction processing, and promotional efforts, thus creating a seamless integrated user interface. Consequently, a system that integrates transaction processing over the Internet with overlay network delivery of video packets may prove more attractive than a system that relies on overlay bandwidth (i.e., a private network) alone.

2.   Quality of Service in Video on Demand Provisioning

In video on demand, consumers receive a continuous stream of packets that combined make up the content of the transmission. The packets arrive in the order in which they will be consumed. For instance, a packet could be a frame or part of a frame of video and 30 such frames are displayed in sequence every second. If a packet disappears in transmission, the consumer's video display program will interpolate its content from previous frames and proceed without the missing frame. Similarly, since the video packets have to be displayed in order, packets that are delayed for a long time (i.e., so long that they cannot be used without interruption of the video screening) will be treated as lost and discarded upon eventual arrival. Finally, if a packet contains errors, it may also have to be discarded. Thus, three factors contribute to the quality of service of a video on demand distribution system. If only a small number of packets are lost, delayed or in error, the displayed video quality will be high.

When providing video on demand service over a network, traffic consisting of video packets intended for different consumers is generated at the edge of the network by a video on demand server. Server configuration has been studied recently by Zamora et al., 2000 and Wong and Chan, 2001. We assume that the video on demand server has been configured so that video service is possible. The traffic generated at the network edge is, then, routed over the network to reach a local distribution point (which we call the Internet service provider's facility) from where the packets are delivered over the access line to each consumer's home. Demand for video services is assumed to be a random process over which the content provider has no control in the short term. Additionally, consumers may choose to stop and resume the transmission stream at any point during a session. Thus, the arrival of video packets at the network edge router can be characterized as a random process.

The term effective bandwidth as used in this work is the minimal amount of bandwidth required to satisfy some maximum packet loss requirement given the number of connections, n, the buffer size, x, and a maximum loss requirement, e (see Perros and Elsayed, 1996 for a review). The instantaneous effective bandwidth can be expressed as

$$b_{\text{effective}} = f(n, x, e). \tag{16.1}$$

At the edge node, there is buffer space to guard against packet overflow resulting in lost packets. The smaller the buffer size, the higher the probability that packets will be lost at the edge node. On the other hand, the larger the

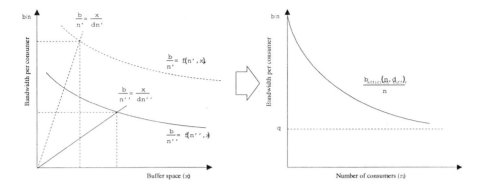

Figure 16.1. Efficient bandwidth for simultaneous consumption.

buffer at the edge node, the longer the maximum delay will be since the maximum delay at the edge node is equal to the maximum queue length divided by the buffer drain rate. The buffer drain rate is equivalent to the nominal bandwidth (transmission rate) of the network. The relationship between bandwidth, b, maximum possible buffer delay, d_{buffer}, and buffer size, x, is given by the equation

$$d_{\text{buffer}} = \frac{x}{b}. \tag{16.2}$$

The end to end delay from the content provider to the consumer is the sum of the queueing delay at the edge node, the packet loading time at the edge node, the propagation time over the transmission lines (which is negligible), the packet loading time onto the access line at the Internet service provider's facility, and any additional delays incurred between the content provider and the Internet service provider. The delay from the Internet service provider to the consumer depends on the Internet access mode available to the consumer. The bandwidth on this line is denoted by b_{local}.

Suppose that the maximum end to end delay that is tolerable to consumers for video on demand service is $\hat{d}$. Let u be the standard packet length for video on demand distribution. The maximum delay requirement on an overlay network is defined as

$$\hat{d} \geq \left[\frac{u}{b_{\text{local}}} + \frac{u}{f(n, x, e)} + \frac{x}{f(n, x, e)} \right]. \tag{16.3}$$

The first term in Equation (16.3) represents the packet loading time on the access network portion, while the second and third terms represent the packet loading time and the maximum queueing time, respectively, on the overlay network.

Table 16.1.   Resource requirements for North American video standards.

Video Quality	Coding Format	Bandwidth (Kbps)	Frames per Second	Resolution (pixels)
VHS	MPEG-1	512 – 1,500	30	352 by 240
DVD	MPEG-2	1,500 – 6,000	30	704 by 480

Consider any instant at which n is fixed and assume that bandwidth is the costly resource. We define the *efficient bandwidth*, $b_{\text{efficient}}$, as the minimum amount of bandwidth on the overlay network that guarantees packet loss rate and maximum queueing delay at the edge node, i.e., the solution to the problem

$$\min \quad b_{\text{effective}} \tag{16.4}$$

subject to (16.1), (16.2) and (16.3). In this solution, d_{buffer} is chosen so that $d_{\text{buffer}} = \hat{d} - u/d_{\text{local}} - u/b_{\text{efficient}}(n, d_{\text{buffer}})$, i.e., (16.3) holds with equality.

The efficient bandwidth locus $b_{\text{efficient}} = g(n, d_{\text{buffer}})$ can be generated by solving (16.4) for a range of simultaneous sessions, n. A stylized representation of the resulting curve is depicted in Figure 16.1. For a given packet loss rate, buffer size, traffic requirement per user and maximum delay, the efficient bandwidth function is increasing in n at a marginally decreasing rate. As n goes to infinity, the efficient bandwidth per user goes from above to the average demand per consumer. The decrease in the marginal requirement per user of efficient bandwidth is reflective of the multiplexing gains from aggregating stochastic demand from a large number of independent traffic sources.

Since the cost of buffer space is virtually zero, the content provider will choose to use as much buffer space as possible while meeting the maximum queueing delay constraint so as to minimize the necessary bandwidth while meeting the packet loss probability. Thus, x can be considered a parameter as soon as the content provider has solved this technical problem of system configuration.

Note that if $u/b_{\text{local}} > \hat{d}$, then video on demand cannot be delivered at the required quality of service level. In such a case, the consumer must give up picture resolution to still meet the delay and packet loss probability requirements. Typical video characteristics and associated bandwidth requirements for video on demand service are illustrated in Table 16.1.

3.   Dimensioning by Simulation

We have defined effective bandwidth for a given buffer size and packet loss probability (due to buffer overflow) previously. For the numerical example, we will set the loss probability to zero by assigning the buffer capacity to the maximum observed buffer occupancy in a buffer of infinite length.

We begin by defining a trace of a given video which we wish to offer over a given number of simultaneous connections, n. The trace, given by a set of variables, s_t, gives the bits in each individual frame of the video, i.e., s_1 is the size in bits of the frame that will be transmitted at time 1 and so on. The total length of the video is T frames. For the 'Star Wars' video trace used in the simulations (Rose, 1995), the resolution is 384 by 288 pixels (VHS quality) encoded with 24 frames per second. The segment used has 40,000 frames with an average size of 9.3Kbits and a peak size of 125Kbits.

With n users, randomly offset in their starting times the aggregated traffic is given by

$$S_t = \sum_{i=1}^{n} x_{t+T} \cdot U_i, \qquad (16.5)$$

where T is the number of frames in the trace, U_i are i.i.d Uniform [0,1] random variables and $x = [s, s]$ is a vector with dimension $2T$, which allows us to define any arbitrary addition of n simultaneous connections that could be played in an endless loop.

We wish to model real-time video on demand, with full playback and fast-forward capability available. Therefore, we take the conservative approach of assuming a simulation clock with ticks of one frame time. That is, for a video encoded at 24 frames per second, the simulation clock advances every 1/24 seconds. One clock cycle is required to deposit a frame of any size in the buffer, i.e., a frame is only available for transmission in the period after it is deposited in the buffer used to aggregate and smooth the traffic of all connections. Buffer contents at the end of period t, denoted by b_t, is given by the previous buffer contents less the portion of the buffer served during one clock cycle and increased by the size of the next frame to be transmitted. We have

$$b_t = \begin{cases} b_{t-1} - nc + S_{t+1} & \text{if } b_{t-1} > nc; \\ S_{t+1}, & \text{otherwise.} \end{cases} \qquad (16.6)$$

In other words, during period t, frame $t + 1$ must be loaded for each of the connections and each frame t is transmitted (transmission capacity permitting). The buffer contents at the beginning of time t (i.e., b_{t-1} which is the reported buffer contents at the end of time $t - 1$) must have included the frame s_t as b_t includes the frame s_{t+1}. Please note that, given an observation of the aggregate trace S_t for n connections, we perform the above calculations in an endless loop where $T + 1$ is reassigned to be equal to t_1.

After a period of time, the endless loop as described above will reach a steady state, so that the same cycle of buffer contents will repeat endlessly. Therefore, in steady state, a single pass through the entire set S_t for $t = 1, ..., T$ is sufficient

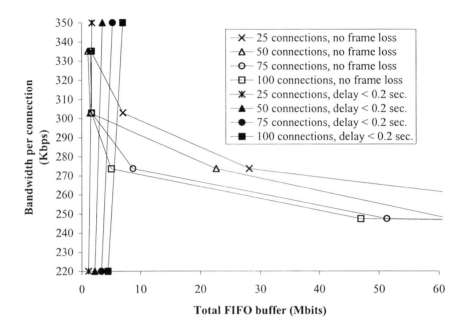

Figure 16.2.   Numerical calculation of efficient bandwidth for Star Wars trace.

to determine the maximum buffer contents, $\hat{b}_i$ of simulation run i, i.e.,

$$\hat{b}_i = \max_t \{b_t\}. \tag{16.7}$$

We can repeat the runs to arrive at a worst case value, $\bar{b}$, for the maximum buffer content, with confidence increasing in the number of simulation runs,

$$\bar{b} = \max_i \{b_i\}. \tag{16.8}$$

The worst observed steady state buffer content is always the worst case, so it is not necessary to model the transient effects of the temporal shifts in the trace caused by fast-forwarding. Rewinding actually lessens the load on the video server since that function could be offered with local storage at the user end.

Maximum delay in the buffer is then a special case of the familiar expression

$$d_{\text{buffer}} = \frac{\bar{b}}{nc}. \tag{16.9}$$

Using simulations as just described we generated the following curves for various values of n and c, with the resulting value $\bar{b}$ shown on the horizontal axis

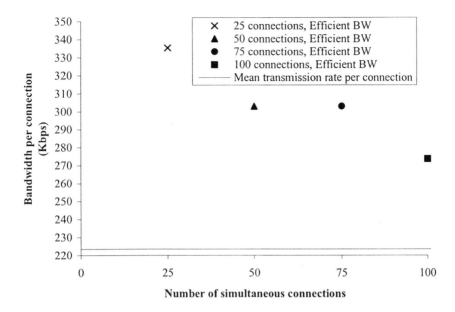

Figure 16.3.   Numerical efficient bandwidth locus for Star Wars trace.

in Figure 16.2 for the 100 simulation runs performed. This plot corresponds to the theoretical representation in Figure 16.1. We observe that for a maximum delay of 200 ms, 100 users require a total buffer allocation of 5Mbit (or 625KB), and a bandwidth per connection of 273 Kbps, for a total 27.3Mbps. Please note, however, that limiting the simulation runs to 100 traces implies that we may have missed some rare events that would demand additional resources in order to meet the delay and loss requirements. Therefore, the presented graph serves as an illustration rather than a solid empirical validation of the theoretical model.

In addition to the curves, we have superimposed the linear delay function, $c = \bar{b}/nd$ for various values of d. The locus of the intersections provides the provisioning plots for given delay bounds displayed in Figure 16.3. Thus, the points in this figure represent valid resource allocations that would ensure that is no loss in transmission at a delay bound of 200 ms. The points are determined for each demand level (number of connections) by selecting the point on the curve in Figure 16.2 labeled no frame loss, that relates transmission rate to maximum buffer occupancy, that satisfies both the delay and loss constraints. Note that bandwidth requirements are decreasing in the number of connections, as expected.

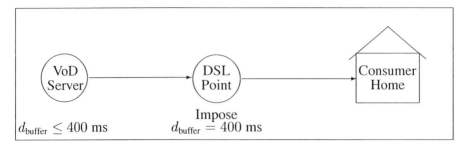

Figure 16.4.   Architecture for video on demand service with guaranteed quality of service.

Consider the video on demand provisioning architecture displayed in Figure 16.4. We have calculated the buffer requirement for the video on demand server and the communication link from this server to the DSL connection point. To complete the configuration, we need to find the buffer requirement at the DSL connection point and the bandwidth requirement on the DSL line. Unfortunately, smoothing of the video stream in the video server buffer destroys the stochastic properties of the original video stream, making it difficult to assess the requirements for the DSL portion of the connection. However, if all incoming video packets are held at the DSL connection point until they are delayed by the maximum delay requirement for the overlay network, the original traffic stream can be regenerated. The same method of analysis can now be performed for an imaginary video server at the DSL connection point with only one video customer in the system. There is no point in holding the video packets at the DSL connection point once they have arrived here, so the calculation of the requirements for the DSL portion of the connection represents a worst-case scenario.

Table 16.2 displays the buffer and bandwidth requirements for a single user for the given video stream. Suppose the overlay network from the video on demand service provider to a neighborhood DSL service point with 100 customers has been provisioned so that the maximum delay is 400 ms. In order to guarantee an end to end maximum delay of $\hat{d}$, we must have sufficient bandwidth available on the DSL transmission line for each customer so that the sum of delay on the overlay network and on the DSL line satisfies the end to end delay requirement of $\hat{d}$. If, for instance, $\hat{d} = 500$ ms, then DSL line capacity of 1,261 Kbps is sufficient to offer VHS resolution video on demand service that satisfies customer quality of service requirements. For such a DSL connection, the DSL connection point must have a buffer of 125Kbits (15Kbytes).

Table 16.2. Resource requirements for a single connection over a DSL line.

DSL Line Speed (Kbps)	Maximum Buffer Occupancy (Kbits)	Maximum Buffer Delay (sec)
2,996	125	0.042
2,245	125	0.056
1,683	125	0.074
1,261	125	0.099
945	125	0.132
708	944	0.332
531	4,332	8.160
398	8,050	20.230
298	15,058	50.492
224	∞	∞

4. Summary and Conclusions

In this report, we propose an architecture for video on demand service with quality of service guarantees. To capture the essential elements of bandwidth provisioning with quality of service guarantees for both packet loss probability and end to end delay, we introduce the concept of efficient bandwidth. In contrast to previous approaches to providing bandwidth with quality of service guarantees, our method exploits multiplexing gains in transmission while simultaneously guaranteeing both a maximum packet loss probability and a maximum end to end packet delay.

A limited simulation study suggests that video on demand service can be offered to consumers with reasonable resources at a quality that is within acceptable range. Of particular interest is that, if quality of service requirements are met with a high probability (99.999% of the time), multiplexing gains are achieved already for a modest number of simultaneous connections. Further study with a broader range of video streams is required to validate the results of this preliminary report.

References

Birman, K. P. (2001). Technology challenges for virtual overlay networks. *IEEE Transactions on Systems, Man and Cybernetics: Part A*, 31(4):319–323.

Cocchi, R., Shenker, S., Estrin, D., and Zhang, L. (1993). Pricing in computer networks: motivation, formulation, and example. *IEEE/ACM Transactions on Networking*, 1(6):614–627.

de Veciana, G., Kesidis, G., and Walrand, J. (1995). Resource management in wide-area atm networks using effective bandwidths. *IEEE Journal on Selected Areas in Communications*, 13(6):1081–1089.

Edell, R. J., McKeown, N., and Varaiya, P. P. (1999). Billing users and pricing for tcp. *IEEE Journal on Selected Areas in Communications*, 13(7):1162–1175.

Jordan, S. and Jiang, H. (1996). A pricing model for high speed networks with guaranteed quality of service. *IEEE InfoCom*, (March):888–895.

Kelly, F. P., Maullo, A. K., and Tan, D. K. H. (1998). Rate control in communication networks: Shadow prices, proportional fairness and stability. *Journal of the Operational Research Society*, 49:237–252.

Keon, N. and Anandalingam, G. Optimal pricing for multiple services in telecommunications networks offering quality of service guarantees. Forthcoming in *IEEE/ACM Transactions on Networking*.

Korilis, Y. A. and Lazar, A. A. (1995). On the existence of equilibria in noncooperative optimal flow control. *Journal of the ACM*, 42:584–613.

Low, S. H. and Varaiya, P. P. (1993). A new approach to service provisioning in atm networks. *IEEE/ACM Transactions on Networking*, 1(5):547–553.

Mackie-Mason, J. K. and Varian, H. (1995). Pricing the internet. *IEEE Journal on Selected Areas in Communications*, 13(7):1141–1149.

Masuda, Y. and Whang, S. (1999). Dynamic pricing for network service: Equilibrium and stability. *Management Science*, 45(6):857–869.

Perros, H. G. and Elsayed, K. M. (1996). Call admission control schemes: a review. *IEEE Communications Magazine*, 34(11):82–91.

Rose, O. (1995). Statistical properties of mpeg video traffic and their impact on traffic modeling in atm systems. In *Proceedings of the 20th Annual Conference on Local Computer Networks*, pages 397–406.

Wang, Q., Peha, J. M., and Sirbu, M. A. (1996). The design of an optimal pricing scheme for atm integrated services networks. *Journal of Electronic Publishing*, 2(1).

Wong, E. W. M. and Chan, S. C. H. (2001). Performance modeling of video-on-demand systems in broadband networks. *IEEE Transactions on Circuits and Systems for Video Technology*, 11(7):848–859.

Zamora, J., Jacobs, S., Eleftheriadis, A., Chang, S.-F., and Anstassiou, D. (2000). A practical methodology for guaranteeing quality of service for video-on-demand. *IEEE Transactions on Circuits and Systems for Video Technology*, 10(1):166–178.